GENDER, PSYCHOLOGY, AND JUSTICE

PSYCHOLOGY AND CRIME

General Editors: Brian Bornstein, University of Nebraska, and
Monica Miller, University of Nevada, Reno

Gender, Psychology, and Justice

The Mental Health of Women and
Girls in the Legal System

Edited by Corinne C. Datchi and Julie R. Ancis

NEW YORK UNIVERSITY PRESS
New York

NEW YORK UNIVERSITY PRESS
New York
www.nyupress.org

References to Internet websites (URLs) were accurate at the time of writing. Neither the author nor New York University Press is responsible for URLs that may have expired or changed since the manuscript was prepared.

ISBN: 978-1-4798-1985-0 (hardback)
ISBN: 978-1-4798-8584-8 (paperback)

For Library of Congress Cataloging-in-Publication data, please contact the Library of Congress.

New York University Press books are printed on acid-free paper, and their binding materials are chosen for strength and durability. We strive to use environmentally responsible suppliers and materials to the greatest extent possible in publishing our books.

Manufactured in the United States of America

10 9 8 7 6 5 4 3 2 1

Also available as an ebook

CONTENTS

ACKNOWLEDGMENTS

Gender, Psychology, and Justice is the product of collaborative efforts and a friendship that began five years ago when we, Corinne and Julie, served on the Executive Board of the Section for the Advancement of Women of the American Psychological Association's Society for Counseling Psychology. It seemed natural to work together on a project that reflected our commitment to social justice and advocacy as expressed through our research, training, and clinical practice with diverse women and girls. We shared a common interest in gender and multicultural issues and were actively engaged in research and practice in various areas of the legal system. During our respective terms as chairs of the Section for the Advancement of Women, we created initiatives related to women and girls in the justice system. We believed it was critical to more broadly call attention to the experiences of women and girls in the justice system. Because this population is often invisible to a broader public, including mental health professionals, the importance of offering not only information but also specific recommendations that addressed women's and girls' unique concerns seemed crucial. This book developed from our many conversations and the enthusiasm and receptiveness of the authors who contributed to this volume.

With the support of Jennifer Hammer, our editor at NYU Press, we have increased the book's capacity to raise awareness and guide a wide audience. I, Corinne, was also fortunate to receive support from Seton Hall University to focus on my responsibilities as editor. We also thank Donjae Catanzariti, a counseling psychology doctoral student at Seton Hall University, for helping us prepare the manuscript for submission.

The stories of girls and women throughout the book speak to the need for significant justice reform. We thank the courageous and resilient women who expressed their stories and the authors and advocates who engage in this work. This work requires courage and an open heart, and we acknowledge all who have demonstrated both.

Introduction

Gender, Psychology, and Justice

CORINNE C. DATCHI AND JULIE R. ANCIS

If one really wishes to know how justice is administered in a country, one does not question the policemen, the lawyers, the judges, or the protected members of the middle class. One goes to the unprotected—those, precisely, who need the law's protection most!—and listens to their testimony.
—James Baldwin, 1985

Gender structures social interactions in ways that frequently place girls and women at a disadvantage in many justice systems across the world (United Nations Office on Drugs and Crime 2008). More specifically, gender-related norms, assumptions, stereotypes, and biases often influence women's and girls' initial and repeated contact with justice officials as well as their vulnerability and victimization in legal settings. Together with racial, class, sexual, and other structural inequalities, they shape the way diverse women and girls experience justice decisions and interventions; they also determine the unique outcomes of their interactions with legal and mental health practitioners.

The American Psychological Association Guidelines for Psychological Practice with Girls and Women (APA 2007) define gender as a multilevel phenomenon: Intrapersonally, gender refers to the cognitive schemas, beliefs, and attitudes that guide individuals' expression of their social identities in relational contexts. It also refers to the process whereby individuals engage in presentations of self that deviate or conform to gender norms and expectations (Butler 1999, 2004). At a macro-systemic level, gender is a societal structure that determines individuals' social status and their access to resources, power, and privileges (Ayman and Korabik 2010).

The criminological literature has made visible the gendered nature of the criminal justice system. Feminist criminologists and legal scholars have well documented how gender restricts girls' and women's access to equitable justice through mechanisms that are evident, tacit, or hidden. They have demonstrated that gender influences the justice system's responses to female offending and victimization (Belknap 2015; Silvestri and Crowther-Dowey 2008; Sprott, Zimring, and Doob 2009; Wykes and Welsh 2009). They have also identified the pathways that lead to girls' and women's involvement with the criminal justice system, as well as the unique challenges girls and women encounter as a result of sexual and physical violence, mental health problems, unmet health-care needs, substance dependence, family responsibilities, and discrimination in employment and education (Belknap 2015; Davies 2011; Morash 2005; Van Gundy and Baumann-Grau 2013).

Feminist criminologists and legal scholars have identified the conditions that explain the unprecedented increase in women's and girls' arrests and incarceration since the 1970s. These numbers have continued to rise at rates that surpass those of boys and men (Mauer 2013; Minton and Zeng 2015), although the majority of female offenders commit nonviolent crimes that do not represent a risk for public safety (e.g., stealing, running away, violating court orders). Changes in policies—rather than changes in behaviors—explain why increasingly more women and girls are caught up in the net of the criminal justice system (Sprott, Franklin, and Doob 2009; The Sentencing Project 2007). These include the creation of new offenses and sentencing guidelines that have exposed women and girls with a history of victimization and substance abuse to a greater level of justice interventions (Kerig and Ford 2014; Travis, Western, and Redburn 2014). For example, at the peak of the war on drugs, the percentage of women sentenced to prison for drug-related, nonviolent crimes increased by more than 800 percent from 1986 to 1999 (American Civil Liberties Union 2005). The new drug policies of the 1980s and 1990s resulted in women's criminalization and incarceration for possession, personal use, and street-level sale of illicit substances. Although women's role in the drug trade was minor compared to that of men, they were subjected to the same mandatory-minimum sentencing laws.

The justice practices of the past forty years have been largely based on conceptual principles and assumptions—including personal theories about men and women—more than scientific evidence about what works to prevent crime (Travis, Western, and Redburn 2014). Among these conceptual principles is the emphasis on gender neutrality and equality in criminal justice, or the beliefs that the same laws are appropriate for both men and women and that men and women should be treated equally or similarly for the same crimes, when in fact, the application of criminal laws has often relied on gender bias and knowledge derived from the study of male offending (Belknap 2015; King and Foley 2014). Examples of this include mandatory and dual arrest laws in cases of domestic violence, whereby women victims of abuse are arrested and sometimes prosecuted (see chapter 2, Walker and Conte), or situations when sex-trafficked women are treated by judicial officials as consenting agents (see chapter 3, Bryant-Davis, Adams, and Gray).

Similar processes and approaches exist in the area of family court with a presumption in some jurisdictions and states that shared custody, or the equal involvement of a biological mother and father in parenting, is most beneficial, with limited attention to factors such as the psychological significance of attachment to primary figures or the presence of abuse (Bryan 2006; see also chapter 1, Ancis). This is the case even in the most extreme situations, such as family violence. For example, women are often punished by family courts for violating "friendly parent" assumptions (i.e., the premise that each parent should provide the opportunity for the other to have a loving and open relationship with the opposite parent) when reporting abuse during divorce and custody disputes (Dragiewicz 2010).

Since the 1970s, feminist scholars have investigated the processes that perpetuate gender discrimination and double standards in legal settings. In the criminal and juvenile justice system, they have highlighted paternalistic attitudes and practices that contribute to the differential treatment of male and female offenders. The term "chivalry" has been used to describe the view that women and girls are childlike and delicate, and the belief that justice officials have the responsibility to remove women and girls from risky situations (Javdani, Sadeh, and Verona 2011). In the courtroom, these beliefs have translated into greater leniency towards women and girls, provided their behaviors and crimes were congruent with gender norms and roles (Rodriguez, Curry, and Lee 2006). They have also resulted in the use of incarceration as a protective measure against further abuse and as a mechanism to regulate women's and girls' conduct and sexuality (Javdani et al. 2011). Double standards for parenting are also evident in family court where noninvolved fathers are awarded custody while mothers who have been primary caretakers have to painstakingly prove parental fitness (Dragiewicz 2010).

The disregard for women's experiences, combined with gender stereotypes, often contributes to biased and unjust outcomes, as well as the perpetuation of myths that influence court decisions (Danforth and Welling 1996). For example, negative perceptions in family court of female litigants as spiteful make women vulnerable to legal decisions based on faulty and unsubstantiated beliefs about parental alienation, and increase the risk that they will lose custody of their children.

Race and economic status further complicate the issue of gender discrimination in different arenas of the justice system. Social scientists have called attention to the overrepresentation of poor African American women and girls behind bars in the United States (Carson 2014; Mauer 2013; Saada Saar et al. 2015). They have also linked changes in the racial composition of female correctional populations to the emergence of a new definition of the female offender as a "real" criminal, angry and aggressive, rather than a vulnerable woman with rehabilitation needs (McCorkel 2013). These findings underscore the importance of examining the experience of justice-involved women and girls through the lens of multiple categories of analysis, including gender, race, class, and sexuality.

With the exception of research in some areas such as domestic violence, which is defined as a gender-related crime, psychologists have been mostly absent from discussions about women and girls in the justice system. In particular, they have not fully engaged in systematic and comprehensive research that evaluates the psychosocial outcomes of justice practices for women and girls; nor have they made a substantial contribution to the development and implementation of problem-solving justice, therapeutic jurisprudence, and gender-informed programming for diverse justice-involved populations. In some instances, mental health professionals—including psychologists—have perpetuated mythology about girls and women through unsubstantiated and nonscientific theories and practices, influenced by gender-biased assumptions, such as the notion of a "masochistic personality" in the case of abused women or "parental alienation syndrome" in the case of allegations of child abuse.

While knowledge about justice-involved women and girls is expanding—in particular knowledge of the pathways that lead them to crime—including exposure to abuse and poverty, substance dependence, and mental illness—only a small number of specialized programs and services address their unique health-care needs and the challenges they encounter in securing employment, safe and affordable housing, childcare, and transportation (Ney, Ramirez, and Van Dieten 2012). Criminologist Barbara Owen and her social work colleagues, Barbara Bloom and Stephanie Covington, have proposed evidence-based principles to advance gender responsiveness in criminal justice practices, and identified key components of programming for women and girls: awareness and knowledge of gender differences in social positioning and privilege; emphasis on safety, self-worth, connectedness, and relationships; and a comprehensive and integrative approach to women's and girls' social, emotional, and psychological concerns. A handful of interventions for justice-involved women have been developed and tested, and they are now listed in the National Registry of Evidence-Based Programs and Practices: Beyond Trauma, Helping Women Recover, Seeking Safety, and Forever Free. Yet very few interventions target the specific risk factors that lead to girls' involvement with the justice system (Office of Juvenile Justice and Delinquency Prevention 2010).

The dissemination and availability of gender-specific programs in diverse legal settings and their implementation and effectiveness with culturally and socially diverse women warrant greater attention. So does the translation of reliable and valid psychological research into evidence-based legal practices. Therapeutic jurisprudence (TJ), first introduced in 1987, provides an interdisciplinary framework for the use of psychological science to improve justice, minimize bias, and maximize the positive effects of legal decisions and interventions (Freckelton 2008). TJ is a field of inquiry that focuses on the administration of the law and its impact on individual and collective well-being (Hora, Schma, and Rosenthal 1999; Wexler 2011; Winick 1997). It draws attention to the therapeutic and antitherapeutic outcomes of legal rules and procedures as well as the roles and behaviors of justice officials. TJ represents a psychologically oriented and empirical approach to the application of the law with a view toward positive behavior change and rehabilitation, autonomy, and choice, rather than punishment and incapacitation (Wexler 2011). It calls for the use of social science, its theories and methods, to study the legal system (Freckelton 2008), and offers guiding principles for problem-solving justice or the use of the law to address chronic social and public health concerns such as substance abuse and family violence (Winick 1997; Redlich and Han 2014). In sum, therapeutic jurisprudence highlights the relation between the law and the welfare of individuals and communities, raises important questions about the impact of legal practices on physical and mental health, and identifies goals and scientific methods for justice reforms that will benefit those who "need the law's protection most" (Baldwin 1985, 527).

About Gender, Psychology, and Justice

This book contributes to the field of therapeutic jurisprudence by offering a careful examination of women's and girls' experiences in multiple arenas of the U.S. justice system, from their initial contact with law enforcement to their interaction with prosecutors, judges, and other court officials. The book answers questions about the therapeutic and nontherapeutic impact of legal rules and procedures on women and girls, with special attention to the theories and/or assumptions that have informed the responses of the justice system to the biopsychosocial needs of women and girls, and the use of research—or lack thereof—in legal decision making and interventions. The authors highlight the structural barriers that limit women's and girls' access to health care, housing, and employment, and that increase their risk for justice-system involvement. They discuss how the narrow focus on individual-level factors in justice procedures and programming and the corresponding disregard for external conditions may push women and girls further into the justice system, isolate them from their families and communities, and make it more difficult for them to achieve an independent lifestyle. The authors also provide recommendations for advancing evidence-based practice in justice settings, for translating psychological evidence and guidelines into legal procedures, and for increasing gender sensitivity and responsiveness in the training of justice and mental health professionals.

To understand the unique concerns of diverse women and girls, it is essential to study how systems of social privilege and inequality influence women's and girls' experiences of the law. The authors in this book use the concept of intersectionality as a frame of analysis (Crenshaw 2005) to make visible the interlocking processes by which race, gender, class, and other social structures determine the distribution of social resources and power and the social location of diverse women and girls in the U.S. justice system (Barak, Leighton, and Cotton 2014). They attend to the intersection of women's and girls' multiple social identities in their discussion of the therapeutic and antitherapeutic application of the law, and in their recommendations for culturally and gender-sensitive practice with justice-involved women and girls. For example, in chapter 3, Thema Bryant-Davis, Tyonna Adams, and Anthea Gray explain how gender and poverty are linked to a punitive approach to criminal justice that further disempowers and harms victims of sex trafficking: Gender stereotypes shape the perception that women and girls are consenting individuals who engage in commercial sex acts, and poverty reduces their ability to defend themselves against prosecution and sentencing. Ironically, traffickers and consumers who have access to economic, social, and political resources are better equipped to avoid criminalization and involvement in the justice system. Likewise, chapter 5 and chapter 6 describe how poverty, race, and gender intersect in ways that increase women's and girls' risk for incarceration, through the perpetuation of structural disparities in health care, transportation, housing, or employment, and through the paternalistic and tacit administration of the law as a means to regulate girls' conformity to prevailing gender norms.

The authors take a primarily qualitative approach to understanding women's and girls' lived experiences in relation to their social, cultural, and political environments. Qualitative research provides an opportunity to study previously unexplored topics (Morrow 2007). It developed from the need to investigate complex and dynamic relations between interacting elements of psychological phenomena, to study individual actions in their natural environments in order to increase the ecological validity of findings, and to define the nature, patterns, and meanings of human behaviors in real-world contexts (Camic, Rhodes, and Yardley 2003; Creswell 2013; Marecek 2003). Qualitative naturalistic research emphasizes descriptive language rather than quantification to represent and explain human behaviors in specific situations, and employs unique strategies to establish the truthfulness or credibility of the findings, such as negative case selection and peer debriefing, selected in consonance with the study's epistemological framework (Cho and Trent 2006; Dennis 2013; Gergen and Gergen 2003; Lub 2015).

Women's and girls' stories collected during the author's research and clinical activities provide rich descriptions of the administration of the law and its impact on diverse female participants in the U.S. justice system. They constitute a preferred source of information for the analysis of complex social, interactional, and intrapersonal phenomena, and occupy a central position in the book's discussions of intersectionality and therapeutic jurisprudence. The authors listen to the testimonies of women and girls and consider the meanings they attribute to their interactions with justice officials, with special attention to their perceptions of legal rules and procedures. While examining current scientific evidence about legal interventions, the authors concurrently honor the perspectives and voices of diverse women and girls to determine what empirical knowledge is missing or at odds with women's and girls' stories. For example, in chapter 4, Corinne Datchi highlights the co-existence of two narratives in drug treatment courts: a dominant and explicit narrative based on the findings of quantitative studies that show drug court is an effective strategy against addiction and crime, and a covert, subdued narrative that emerges from women's testimonies and that suggests specific drug court interventions may have antitherapeutic effects on their mental health.

The authors examine external conditions that make women's and girls' social identities (e.g., gender, race, class) more or less salient in justice settings, and demonstrate why these conditions must be considered in order to determine the meanings of women's and girls' actions and to select appropriate legal and psychological interventions. Chapters 7 and 8 situate the "delinquent" behaviors of lesbian, transgender, and gender-nonconforming girls in the context of family rejection and violence to explain how running away and physical aggression may constitute girls' way of coping with adverse circumstances. Chapters 8 and 9 highlight how changes in the criminal justice system have resulted in the increased use of detention to control girls' and women's nonviolent, drug-related behaviors. Lastly, chapter 10 highlights the salience of race in the treatment of undocumented Mexican immigrants by U.S. Border Patrol agents: Racial marking overshadows immigrants' gendered identity, and is a mechanism that contributes to the dehumanization of Mexican immigrants and that supports the use of excessive force against both men and women.

This volume focuses on the subjective experiences of women and girls, with the intention of offering new perspectives on what works and does not work in the U.S. justice system. The primarily qualitative approach of the book, combined with attention to existing quantitative research, makes it possible to identify core psychological and structural processes that help explain variations in outcomes and provide insight into the therapeutic mechanisms linked to greater gender sensitivity in the administration of the law. It serves not to identify the causes of women's and girls' behaviors but to explain the meanings of these behaviors in specific legal settings and to illuminate the conditions that shape women's and girls' responses, including mental health outcomes, to legal interventions. In addition, the focus of the book on women's and girls' stories responds to the challenge of conducting gender-sensitive quantitative research in settings where women and girls represent a small—yet growing—percentage of the population and where their specific circumstances are often buried within statistics that capture the characteristics of the male majority (Immarigeon 2011).

The Chapters

This book is composed of two parts. Part 1 focuses on multiple arenas of the justice system, ranging from less restrictive community-based settings (e.g., family courts and drug treatment courts) to juvenile detention centers and correctional facilities. Specifically, chapters in part 1 highlight the theories, rules, and assumptions that underlie justice practices in those settings and consider how legal interventions match the concerns women and girls express in research and clinical interviews. The chapters also examine how the intersections of race, gender, class, and sexual orientation determine the responses of justice officials and their interactions with diverse women and girls. Part 2 highlights common themes in the experiences of specific populations: transwomen; lesbian, bisexual, questioning, gender-nonconforming, and transgender girls; poor women; and undocumented Mexican women. The chapters examine the circumstances that lead to female populations' contact with the justice system, the unique needs and legal status of particular groups of women and girls in diverse legal settings, as well as the biopsychosocial outcomes that result from women's and girls' interactions with justice officials. The chapters in both part 1 and part 2 conclude with recommendations for improving the integration of psychological principles and guidelines into justice practices, and explain how women and girls would benefit from this integration.

Part I: Women and Girls in Various Justice Settings

In chapter 1, Julie R. Ancis describes women litigants' experiences in family court. She outlines the ways in which power and control during marriage or partnership may be perpetuated in the legal arena during divorce and custody disputes. Although many authors have explored the various disadvantages that abuse survivors face when encountering the legal system and strategies used to disadvantage one party (Bryan 2006; Goodman and Epstein 2011; Winner 1996), discussion of power and control tactics frequently used in divorce and custody proceedings by abusive ex-partners, and often upheld by the legal system, is very limited. The author uses research based on in-depth interviews with diverse women engaged in divorce and custody disputes to examine gender biases in courtroom procedures and judicial decision making about child support, custody, and visitation.

In chapter 2, Lenore E. A. Walker and Carlye B. Conte examine how recent justice reforms have created barriers to seeking legal protection for victims of intimate partner violence. Specifically, they discuss women's experiences of mandatory and dual arrest laws originally designed to enhance the effectiveness of criminal justice interventions in incidents of domestic battering. They highlight how gender biases complicate the application of these laws, and how this has led to the criminalization of women's strategies for coping with interpersonal violence and trauma. They also describe how the judicial processes in which battered women get entangled often disregard the specific needs of victims and result in decreased safety. Race and immigration intersect with gender in ways that shape the unique circumstances of battered women. "Women, Do-

mestic Violence, and the Criminal Justice System" emphasizes the complexity of intimate partner violence and the need for a contextualized
approach to justice interventions. The chapter concludes with the description of an evidence-based and trauma-informed program designed
to empower battered women in the criminal justice system.

Similarly, chapter 3 calls attention to the criminalization and prosecution of human trafficking victims in the United States. The authors,
Thema Bryant-Davis, Tyonna Adams, and Anthea Gray, link sexist beliefs to disparities in the legal processing of sex traffickers and their victims; they explain how gender norms and roles support the view that
sex-trafficked women and girls are consenting agents of the sex trade,
who willingly exchange sex for money, although sex trafficking, by definition, involves the use of coercion. Victims of sex trafficking are forced
to enter and remain in the sex industry at a young age; and while in the
sex trade, they become adults who live in fear, under the control of traffickers. The authors also examine how race and poverty put victims at a
disadvantage in the justice system, limiting their access to information
and resources that are necessary for protecting themselves against unfair,
and even abusive, treatment by traffickers and justice officials. Gender-
related myths about sex trafficking limit justice officials' awareness and
understanding of the violence, exploitation, and trauma sex-trafficked
women and girls experience. The effects of trauma on the mental and
physical health of victims are exacerbated when sex-trafficked women
and girls come into contact with the justice system, are treated as criminals, and are offered little protection from their traffickers and abusers.
To conclude, the authors argue for a multilevel approach to the social
problem of sex trafficking and the development of treatment programs
for victims.

In chapter 4, Corinne C. Datchi focuses on women's experiences in
adult drug treatment courts. Drug treatment courts offer community-
based correctional alternatives to incarceration for nonviolent felons
who engage in criminal activities to sustain their drug use. They use
a variety of methods—including urinalysis, breathalyzers, and jail—to
monitor drug offenders' adherence to a sober, prosocial lifestyle, and
enforce their compliance with drug treatment. The scope of the courts'
surveillance power extends to the addicts' home, place of employment,
treatment provider, and recovery community. The chapter examines

women's perception of how a drug court defines and addresses their addictions through a system of reward and punishment. It brings to light the medical and psychological theories that operate within drug court and inform the drug court team's understanding of addiction and deviance, in particular, the idea that addiction is a disease beyond the control of the individual. These theories promote a universal view of addiction and the addict that conceals human differences and makes it difficult to consider the context of gender and race in legal decisions and practices.

In chapter 5, Elizabeth A. Lilliott, Elise M. Trott, Nicole C. Kellett, Amy E. Green, and Cathleen E. Willging examine the social processes that lead to women's return to prison in poor and underserved rural areas of the United States: The privatization of health-care services, the paucity of community-based resources and postrelease assistance with treatment, employment, and housing, the neoliberal policies that emphasize individual responsibility and ignore the impact of social disadvantages, and gender and racial stereotypes are factors that make prisons an inevitable "choice" for women with a criminal history. Imprisonment offers the promise of shelter, food, health care, and human bonding, while reentry is associated with deprivation and social marginalization. For women prisoners, returning to small rural communities presents enormous challenges. The success of their release from the criminal justice system depends on their ability to meet the conditions of their discharge, to break away from antisocial kin and peer networks, to secure employment, and/or to remain sober. This chapter explains that achieving those tasks is not a matter of individual will and choice, but an issue that requires structural change and greater availability and access to comprehensive treatment programs.

In chapter 6, Kendra R. Brewster and Kathleen M. Cumiskey share the insight they gained from their participation in a tutoring program for teenage girls in a detention facility. They argue that the girls' experience of incarceration was characterized by ambivalence and contradictions: On the one hand, the girls found safety in the juvenile justice facility and gained access to basic resources such as food, shelter, and health care. However, their relationships with the staff reproduced some of the abusive dynamics the girls experienced at home. The authors discuss how the use of punitive and harsh discipline, threats, and yelling to manage the behaviors of girls behind bars could intensify conduct problems and lead to girls' further involvement in the juvenile justice system through transfers to more secure facilities. They also suggest that mental health and educational services for girls in juvenile facilities offer a space where girls can care for and be cared for by others and develop healthy models of relating; where they can have a voice; and where they can redefine their identity, not as delinquent teens but as girls with strengths and career aspirations. However, psychological and educational programs may also have unintended consequences: They help at-risk girls build a bond with the juvenile justice staff and the facility rather than the home they will return to upon their release. The authors argue that it is important to consider how programming within juvenile justice facilities may facilitate ongoing contact with the girls' communities and relatives, and prepare the former as well as the latter for the girls' reentry. Strengthening girls' connection with their communities and families, addressing the dynamics of abuse that lead girls into the juvenile justice system, and helping girls build vocational skills and gain access to essential resources are processes that may help prevent girls' further involvement in the criminal justice system.

Part II: Specific Populations of Justice-Involved Women and Girls

In chapter 7, Alexis Forbes and Kevin L. Nadal describe the gender-based violence transwomen are exposed to both inside and outside the criminal justice system, including hate crimes, mistreatment by police officers, and physical and sexual assault during detention. They highlight the criminalization of gender nonconformity through profiling and unlawful arrests, the violation of transwomen's rights to safety, and the barriers to legal protection from social, physical, and emotional harm. Verbal humiliation, threats, destruction of property, and denial of gender-affirming medical and mental health care are some of the discriminatory practices that transwomen experience in the criminal justice system. These are forms of abuse that increase transwomen's social marginalization and vulnerability, and prevent them from gaining access to justice. The authors also discuss how legal measures such as administrative or solitary confinement, designed to protect transwomen during detention, have produced adverse consequences, in particular increased psychological stress and limited access to social interactions and prison programming. To increase fairness in legal interventions, the authors encourage the use of existing gender-affirming treatment guidelines. They also note the need for social advocacy and systemic change and for the creation of inclusive environments at the level of families, communities, and institutions.

Chapter 8 expands the discussion on non-gender-conforming and nonheteronormative populations in the justice system. The authors, Angela Irvine, Aisha Canfield, and Jessica Roa, point out the invisibility of lesbian, bisexual, questioning, gender-nonconforming, and transgender (LBQ/GNCT) girls in the juvenile justice system. In particular, they note that questions about youth's sexual orientation are absent from risks and needs assessment, although scientific evidence has established a link among youth's LBQ/GNCT identity, family and school conflict, homelessness, and involvement in the juvenile justice system. The authors discuss the harmful consequences that result from the oversight of youth's sexual orientation and gender identity, including reliance on stereotypes and biases, harsh punishment of gender-nonconforming behaviors, reproduction of abuse, and the lack of adequate and scientifically based programming for LBQ/GNCT girls.

In chapter 9, Erica G. Rojas, Laura Smith, and Randolph M. Scott-McLaughlin II call attention to the link between poverty and women's entanglement with the criminal justice system. Overwhelmingly, incarcerated women are poor women of color with low levels of education and limited opportunities for employment. They come from disenfranchised neighborhoods where tough-on-crime policies have resulted in the exponential growth of correctional female populations and have exacerbated social disadvantage. Without the financial resources necessary for effective legal representation, poor women of color experience harsher punishment compared to White middle-class women, for nonviolent crimes that represent survival strategies. This chapter uses an intersectional lens to highlight the interconnectedness of socio-structural processes and show how classism and patriarchy operate simultaneously and conjointly to create barriers that limit women's ability to move out of poverty and correctional supervision. In particular, the authors discuss the laws and policies that bar justice-involved women from public assistance, keep them in situations of economic deprivation, and reduce their ability to resist entanglement with the criminal justice system. They also highlight women's mental health needs and their difficulties in accessing adequate medical care inside and outside of the criminal justice system.

Chapter 10 adds to the discussion of social, political, and legal factors that contribute to the criminalization of poverty. Anna Ochoa O'Leary examines the link among the U.S. Border Patrol's mistreatment of undocumented Mexican immigrants, the criminalization of illegal immigration, and the racial biases that dehumanize Mexicans and give license to deny due process rights. Border-crossing narratives suggest that both men and women are equally exposed to acts of violence by Border Patrol agents during arrest and detention. These include threats, verbal degradation, and sexual and physical abuse. To some extent, the dehumanization of undocumented immigrants conceals gender differences. This chapter also highlights the dearth of studies on undocumented immigration, border-crossing violence, and its impact on women's mental health. This may be due to the transient nature of immigrant populations and the lack of transnational research partnerships on both sides of the U.S.-Mexico border. Given the traumatic nature of women's immigration experiences, it is crucial to identify and understand the unique psychological outcomes Mexican women suffer during migration, arrest, and detention, and to evaluate the resources that are available to them in specific familial, social, cultural, and legal contexts.

The volume concludes with a chapter that examines how the psychology of men may support the promotion of gender-sensitive practices in the U.S. justice system. Jonathan Schwartz and Jennifer Bahrman provide an overview of the discipline, its theories, and research on gender-role conflict and gender-role strain. They discuss how these two concepts can expand our understanding of the social processes that criminalize women involved in the sex trade, willingly or through coercion. They explain how men's beliefs about how they should be, feel, think, and act determine their attitudes towards women (e.g., the extent to which they objectify and devalue women who sell sex), their acceptance of prostitution, and their participation as consumers of sexual services. The authors also highlight how gender norms render male consumers invisible and therefore immune to legal processing. The authors argue that it is critical to use the principles of the psychology of men to bring into focus men's roles and responsibilities in the victimization of women through prostitution and sex trafficking. They also discuss the need for prevention programming that targets male consumers of illegal sexual services and is based on empirical knowledge produced by studies in the field of the psychology of men.

Conclusion

This book offers an interdisciplinary discussion of how gender, race, national origin, sexual orientation, and class influence justice practices and their effects on diverse women's and girls' social and psychological well-being. It attempts to foreground the tacit rules and implicit theories that underlie legal decisions and interventions; it also evaluates the use, or nonuse, of scientific evidence in various justice settings with diverse female populations. The aim is to increase awareness of women's and girls' concerns, to identify knowledge gaps and research needs, and to provide directions for translating existing scientific findings into gender- and culturally sensitive practices. Increased awareness and knowledge is a first and necessary step towards justice, equal opportunity, and fairness for all. However, it is not enough. Systemic change requires that we use this empirical knowledge to formulate new guiding principles for the therapeutic administration of the law.

REFERENCES

American Civil Liberties Union. 2005. "Caught in the Net: The Impact of Drug Policies on Women and Families," https://www.aclu.org.

American Psychological Association. 2007. "Guidelines for Psychological Practice with Girls and Women." *American Psychologist* 62 (9): 949–79. doi: 10.1037/0003-066X.62.9.949.

Ayman, Roya, and Karen Korabik. 2010. "Leadership: Why Gender and Culture Matter." *American Psychologist* 65 (3): 157–70.

Baldwin, James. 1985. *The Price of the Ticket: Collected Non-Fiction, 1948–1985.* New York: St Martin's.

Barak, Gregg, Paul Leighton, and Allison Cotton. 2014. *Class, Race, Gender, and Crime: The Social Realities of Justice in America.* Blue Ridge Summit, PA: Rowman and Littlefield.

Belknap, Joanne. 2015. *The Invisible Woman: Gender, Crime, and Justice,* 4th ed. Stamford, CT: Cengage Learning.

Bryan, Penelope. 2006. *Constructive Divorce: Procedural Justice and Sociolegal Reform.* Washington, DC: American Psychological Association. doi: 10.1037/11300-000.

Butler, Judith. 2004. *Undoing Gender.* New York: Routledge.

Butler, Judith. 1999. *Gender Trouble: Feminism and the Subversion of Identity.* New York: Routledge.

Camic, Paul M., Jean E. Rhodes, and Lucy Yardley. 2003. "Naming the Stars: Integrating Qualitative Methods into Psychological Research." In *Qualitative Research in Psychology: Expanding Perspectives in Methodology and Design.* Edited by Paul M. Camic, Jean E. Rhodes, and Lucy Yardley, 3–15. Washington, DC: American Psychological Association.

Carson, Ann E. 2014. "Prisoners in 2013." Bureau of Justice Statistics, http://www.bjs.gov.

Cho, Jeasik, and Allen Trent. 2006. "Validity in Qualitative Research Revisited." *Qualitative Research* 6 (3): 319–40. doi: 10.1177/1468794106065006.

Crenshaw, Kimberle. 2005. "Mapping the Margins: Intersectionality, Identity Politics, and Violence against Women of Color (1994)." In *Violence against Women: Classic Papers.* Edited by Raquel Kennedy Bergen, Jeffrey L. Edleson, and Claire M. Renzetti, 282–313. Auckland, New Zealand: Pearson Education New Zealand.

Creswell, John W. 2013. *Qualitative Inquiry and Research Design: Choosing among Five Approaches.* Thousand Oaks, CA: Sage.

Danforth, Gay, and Bobbie Welling. 1996. "Achieving Equal Justice for Women and Men in the California Courts: Final Report." Judicial Council of California Advisory Committee on Gender Bias in the Courts, http://www.courtinfo.ca.gov.

Davies, Pamela. 2011. *Gender, Crime, and Victimisation.* London: Sage.

Dennis, Barbara. 2013. "'Validity Crisis' in Qualitative Research: Still? Movement toward a Unified Approach." In *Qualitative Research: A Reader in Philosophy, Core Concepts, and Practice.* Edited by Barbara Dennis, Lucinda Carspecken, and Phil Francis Carspecken, 3–37. New York: Peter Lang.

Dragiewicz, Molly. 2010. "Gender Bias in the Courts: Implications for Battered Mothers and Their Children." In *Domestic Violence, Abuse, and Child Custody.* Edited by Mo T. Hannah and Barry Goldstein, 5-1–5-19. Kingston, NJ: Civic Research Institute.

Freckelton, Ian. 2008. "Therapeutic Jurisprudence Misunderstood and Misrepresented: The Prices and Risks of Influence." *Thomas Jefferson Law Review* 30: 575–95.

Gergen, Mary M., and Kenneth J. Gergen. 2003. "Qualitative Inquiry: Tensions and Transformations." In *The Landscape of Qualitative Research: Theories and Issues,* 2nd ed. Edited by Norman K. Denzin and Yvonna S. Lincoln, 575–610. Thousand Oaks, CA: Sage.

Goodman, Lisa A., and Deborah Epstein. 2011. "The Justice System Response to Domestic Violence." In *Violence against Women and Children: Navigating Solutions.* Edited by Mary P. Koss, Jacquelyn W. White, and Alan E. Kazdin, 215–35. Washington, DC: American Psychological Association.

Hora, Peggy Fulton, William G. Schma, and John T. A. Rosenthal. 1999. "Therapeutic Jurisprudence and the Drug Treatment Court Movement: Revolutionizing the Criminal Justice System's Response to Drug Abuse and Crime in America." *Notre Dame Law Review* 74: 439–537.

Immarigeon, Russ. 2011. "Women and Girls in the Criminal Justice System: Policy Issues and Practice Strategies." Civic Research Institute, http://www.civicresearchinstitute.com.

Javdani, S., N. Sadeh, and E. Verona. 2011. "Gendered Social Forces: A Review of the Impact of Institutionalized Factors on Women and Girls' Criminal Justice Trajectories." *Psychology, Public Policy, and Law,* 17 (2), 161–211. doi: 10.1037/a0021957.

Kerig, Patricia K., and Julian D. Ford. 2014. "Trauma among Girls in the Juvenile Justice System." National Child Traumatic Stress Network, http://www.nctsn.org.

King, Erica, and Julian E. Foley. 2014. "Gender-Responsive Policy Development in Corrections: What We Know and Roadmap for Change," https://s3.amazonaws.com.

Lub, Vasco. 2015. "Validity in Qualitative Evaluation: Linking Purposes, Paradigms, and Perspectives." *International Journal of Qualitative Methods* 14 (5): 1–8. doi: 10.1177/1609406915621406.

Marecek, Jeanne. 2003. "Dancing through Minefields: Toward a Qualitative Stance in Psychology." In *Qualitative Research in Psychology: Expanding Perspectives in Methodology and Design.* Edited by Paul M. Camic, Jean E. Rhodes, and Lucy Yardley, 49–69. Washington, DC: American Psychological Association.

Mauer, Marc. 2013. "The Changing Racial Dynamics of Women's Incarceration." The Sentencing Project, http://sentencingproject.org.

McCorkel, Jill A. 2013. *Breaking Women: Gender, Race, and the New Politics of Imprisonment.* New York: NYU Press.

Minton, Todd D., and Zhen Zeng. 2015. "Jail Inmates at Midyear 2014," http://www.bjs.gov.

Morash, Merry. 2005. *Understanding Gender, Crime, and Justice.* Thousand Oaks, CA: Sage.

Morrow, Susan L. 2007. "Qualitative Research in Counseling Psychology: Conceptual Foundations." *Counseling Psychologist* 35 (2): 209–35.

Ney, Becki, Rachelle Ramirez, and Marilyn Van Dieten. 2012. "Ten Truths That Matter When Working with Justice-Involved Women," http://cjinvolvedwomen.org.

Office of Juvenile Justice and Delinquency Prevention. 2010. "Girls' Delinquency," http://www.ojjdp.gov.

Redlich, Allison D., and Woojae Han. 2014. "Examining the Links between Therapeutic Jurisprudence and Mental Health Court Completion." *Law and Human Behavior* 38 (2): 109–18. doi: 10.1037/lhb0000041.

Rodriguez, S. Fernando, Theodore R. Curry, and Gang Lee. 2006. "Gender Differences in Criminal Sentencing: Do Effects Vary across Violent, Property, and Drug Offenses?" *Social Science Quarterly* 87 (2): 318–33.

Saada Saar, Malika, Rebecca Epstein, Lindsay Rosenthal, and Yasmin Vafa. 2015. "The Sexual Abuse-to-Prison Pipeline: The Girls' Story," http://rights4girls.org.

Sentencing Project. 2007. "Women in the Criminal Justice System: Briefing Sheets," http://www.sentencingproject.org.

Silvestri, Marisa, and Chris Crowther-Dowey. 2008. *Gender and Crime.* Los Angeles: Sage.

Sprott, Jane B., Franklin E. Zimring, and Anthony N. Doob. 2009. *Justice for Girls? Stability and Change in the Youth Justice Systems of the United States and Canada.* Chicago: University of Chicago Press.

Thoennes, Nancy, and Patricia Tjaden. 1990. "The Extent, Nature, and Validity of Sexual Abuse Allegations in Custody/Visitations Disputes." *Child Abuse and Neglect* 14: 151–63.

Travis, Jeremy, Bruce Western, and Steve Redburn, eds. 2014. *The Growth of Incarceration in the United States: Exploring Causes and Consequences.* Washington, DC: National Academies Press.

United Nations Office on Drugs and Crime. 2008. "Handbook for Prison Managers and Policy Makers on Women and Imprisonment." United Nations Office on Drugs and Crime, https://www.unodc.org.

Van Gundy, Alana, and Amy Baumann-Grau. 2013. *Women, Incarceration, and Human Rights Violations: Feminist Criminology and Corrections.* Farnham, UK: Ashgate.

Wexler, David B. 2011. "From Theory to Practice and Back Again in Therapeutic Jurisprudence: Now Comes the Hard Part." *Monash University Law Review* 37 (1): 33–42.

Winick, Bruce J. 1997. "The Jurisprudence of Therapeutic Jurisprudence." *Psychology, Public Policy, and Law* 3 (1): 184–206.

Winner, Karen. 1996. *Divorced from Justice: The Abuse of Women and Children by Divorce Lawyers and Judges.* New York: HarperCollins.

Wykes, Maggie, and Kirsty Welsh. 2009. *Violence, Gender, and Justice.* Los Angeles: Sage.

PART I

Women and Girls in Various Justice Settings

1

Women and Family Court

Abuse and Contested Custody

JULIE R. ANCIS

I expected the judge to listen to all sides of the case. This
was my opportunity to have my side heard and understood.
Finally, a place where professionals who deal with this kind
of thing would hear me out and make decisions in the best
interest of my children and family. I couldn't be more wrong.
—Mother in contested custody case, 2012

Most contested custody cases are eventually settled out of court, but a
subset are essentially prolonged battles. These are the approximately
5 percent of custody cases that the courts view as high-conflict cases.
Abusive ex-spouses often use family court litigation to continue to
control and harass their former partner (Ancis 2012, 2015; Jaffe et al.
2008). Similarly, a Department of Justice study found that high rates of
domestic violence exist in families referred for child custody evaluations
(Saunders, Faller, and Tolman 2011). It is estimated that 90 percent of
contested custody cases involve abusive fathers (Hannah and Goldstein
2010).

Understanding the sociocultural context of women's experiences in
family court, especially those who are subject to abusive ex-partners
and -husbands, is essential to comprehending the ways in which gender intersects with other identities to impact women and children's
legal status and well-being. Effective and sensitive approaches in such
cases require a level of education and training that most mental health
professionals and justice officials do not receive. Consequently, ineffective and sometimes harmful decisions and interventions are implemented, resulting in secondary and tertiary trauma for women and

children. While all states have statutes requiring that the child's best interests be considered in custody and visitation decisions, a lack of understanding and bias with regard to abuse and related dynamics prevent the implementation of practices that are truly in the best interests of children and families. This chapter includes qualitative data from several studies of women who have engaged in divorce and custody proceedings. Quotations are used to illustrate themes and salient issues that arose in in-depth, semistructured, and open-ended interviews with women litigants (see Ancis and Watson 2016; Watson and Ancis 2013).

Intimate Partner Violence and Family Court

Women who decide to leave an abuser frequently do so in order to protect their children from the deleterious effects of an abusive environment (Bryan 2006). When leaving an abusive relationship, women often seek justice and protection from the legal system. Specifically, women who are married to abusive partners may seek a divorce and, if they are mothers, custody of their children. Often, however, the tactics of power and control experienced in relationships with abusers may continue to manifest during the dissolution of the relationship and pervade legal proceedings (American Psychological Association [APA] 1996; Neilson 2004; Pagelow 1993; Stahly 1999). The legal system quickly becomes another avenue and arena through which her abuser may perpetrate abuse (Taylor, Stoilkov, and Greco 2008).

Although the legal definition of abuse differs according to jurisdiction, intimate partner violence (IPV) is generally defined as behavioral patterns intended to assert or gain power and control over another (Shipway 2004). Broadly defined, IPV is not limited to physical assault, and may also encompass sexual, emotional, and economic abuse. Emotional abuse is commonly perpetuated by those with particular personality characteristics, which often include a disregard for and a violation of the rights of others, manipulativeness, deceitfulness, and a lack of remorse. Women who leave abusive relationships and are subsequently involved in prolonged and contested custody cases frequently describe ex-partners as possessing such qualities and related behaviors, behaviors that are then manifest in divorce and custody proceedings and beyond

(Ancis 2012). Custody proceedings are fertile ground for the continuation of abusive maneuvers and tactics.

Moreover, many women perceive such adversarial tactics on the part of abusive and controlling exes as motivated by spite and vindictiveness, or as punishment for their leaving the relationship (Watson and Ancis 2013).

> He just really wants to punish me and keep me out of her [daughter's] life. And he was able to use the court to continue abusing me and to get power over me again. . . . This is about revenge; he wants to punish me to get back at me, and the best way for him to do that is to take what was most important to me away. And not only that, even though he's done it, he's still not happy. He still wants control over me. It's like he hasn't let go of me. Not that he loves me and wants to be married to me, but he's very invested in being able to abuse me. (Lea, age 42, White woman)

There exist a number of ways in which abuse dynamics may continue during legal proceedings and beyond. Former husbands/partners may prolong the case through unnecessary emergency hearings, fail to supply appropriate documents, thereby leading to delays and repeated requests, and seek an increase or decrease in child support (depending upon who was the recipient). Women also describe intimidation and/or harassment tactics such as receiving hateful emails from ex-partners (Bryan 2006; Watson and Ancis 2013).

One common tactic abusers use in family court may include seeking full custody even when they were relatively absent or uninvolved as a parent (Araji and Bosek 2010; Bancroft and Silverman 2002; Watson and Ancis 2013). This tactic is often effective, as women are less likely to report abuse to authorities for fear of losing their children (Kaser-Boyd 2004). Many tactics, such as prolonging the case and pursuing full custody, are perceived as attempts to get the mothers to acquiesce and agree to unfavorable terms, especially financial terms. Custodial challenges pursued by abusive partners may be motivated by financial gain so that the economically disadvantaged and abused wife will be required to pay child support (Gender Bias Study of the Court System in Massachusetts [Gender Bias Study] 1990; Stahly 1999). Abusive former husbands/partners who are granted full custody often attempt to limit mothers' visitation.

Bias in Family Court

A number of studies have demonstrated that relative to men, women are largely disadvantaged during divorce and custody disputes (Bemiller 2008; Heim et al. 2002; Johnson, Saccuzzo, and Koen 2005; Kernic et al. 2005; Neustein and Lesher 2005; Stahly et al. 2004). Several major studies (e.g., see Araji and Bosek 2010; Dragiewicz 2010; Saunders et al. 2011; Voices of Women Organizing Project [VOW] 2008) have described the particular gender bias and injustice that abuse survivors encounter within divorce and custody disputes. The legal system's response to domestic violence and abuse has historically been poor (Muraskin 2012), leaving victims without sufficient protection. Family courts have been described as "badly in need of oversight and repair" (VOW 2008, 5) as they have become places in which protective mothers experience secondary trauma.

Studies related to domestic violence and contested custody cases in a number of states (e.g., Alaska [2006], Pennsylvania [2003], Arizona [2003], Massachusetts [2002], and California [2002]; see Araji and Bosek 2010) consistently demonstrate that within family courts, women's credibility in terms of abuse allegations was frequently questioned; evidence of abuse was disregarded, minimized, or ignored (e.g., attorneys neglected to mention abuse during cases); and women were not allowed to speak, be heard in court, or discuss domestic violence or child abuse. Women also encountered double standards for parenting (e.g., noninvolved fathers were frequently awarded custody while mothers who had been primary caretakers had to painstakingly prove parental fitness); and women were often punished for violating "friendly parent" assumptions (i.e., the premise that each parent should provide the opportunity for the other to have a loving and open relationship with the opposite parent) when reporting abuse during divorce and custody disputes (Dragiewicz 2010). As a result, decisions were made that placed children in danger (e.g., unsupervised visitation with abusive ex-partners was granted).

These findings are consistent with the pervasive biases and erroneous assumptions held by court personnel. These include beliefs that women are prone to make false allegations of abuse in custody disputes and that women tend to be emotionally unstable. Despite scientific evidence that supports their claims, women who assert allegations of child or spousal abuse are often viewed by court personnel as angry, vindictive, and overly emotional (Danforth and Welling 1996).

In fact, research suggests that fathers are more likely than mothers to make false accusations of child abuse in divorce and custody cases (21 percent versus 1.3 percent) (Bala and Schuman 2000); that childhood abuse claims are not more common in divorce and custody disputes than in other cases (Brown et al. 2000); and that childhood sexual abuse allegations in custody disputes are rare (less than 2 percent) (Thoennes and Tjaden 1990).

The Important Role of Custody Evaluators and Guardians ad Litem

Custody evaluators, also known as guardians ad litem (GALs), or special masters in some states, often play a central role in the divorce and custody disputes. They are responsible for conducting assessments, evaluations, and recommendations related to custody and visitation. Judges routinely rely upon GALs and custody evaluators to make recommendations in the "best interests" of the child(ren) (Bryan 2006). No standard definition of best interest exists. Thus, a uniform operationalization of this construct by researchers as well as practitioners is lacking (Krauss and Sales 2001). Nonetheless, all states, the District of Columbia, American Somoa, Guam, the Northern Moravia Islands, Puerto Rico, and the U.S. Virgin Islands have statutes requesting that the child's best interest be considered in custody and placement decisions (Child Welfare Information Gateway 2013).

The parameters of the role of GALs are not always clear, which has led to some frustration and confusion on the part of attorneys and litigants. Similarly, statutes or codes regarding the best interests of the child vary from state to state, permitting custody decision makers wide discretion (Hall, Pulver, and Cooley 1996). Qualifications, education, and training requirements differ from state to state. While most states require some sort of training, this training remains relatively limited, ranging from several hours to a couple of days (Ancis 2015).

Due to bias and a lack of training and education, it is not uncommon for custody evaluators to draw faulty conclusions when conducting evaluations/assessments. Evidence regarding the child's well-being, including academic and social adjustment, is ignored. In some cases, important information such as that related to the child's age or attachment to the mother is not considered.

A major issue that emerges in assessments and evaluations involves a lack of understanding or consideration of abuse. In some cases, the father's abuse is not taken into consideration or mentioned in GAL reports, and joint custody is recommended or custody is given to the abuser (Ancis 2012; Saunders et al. 2011).

Custody evaluators' negative stereotypes about women and myths about abuse in the context of divorce and custody disputes often contribute to biased and unjust outcomes in family court. Custody evaluators who believe that mothers' allegations of domestic violence (DV) are false also tend to possess other related beliefs, such as that DV survivors alienate children from the other parent; that DV is not an important factor in making custody decisions; and that DV survivors falsely allege child abuse (Saunders et al. 2011). Beliefs in patriarchal norms (i.e., women have reached equality with men) and social dominance (i.e., social hierarchies are good) are related to beliefs that alleged DV victims make false allegations and alienate their children, and that fathers do not falsely allege abuse (Saunders et al. 2011).

Moreover, custody evaluators who believe that DV allegations by mothers are false also tend to believe that children are hurt when survivors are reluctant to coparent (Saunders et al. 2011). Women who attempt to limit or block their exes' repeated harassing behavior may be seen as discouraging communication for the sake of the child. Thus, the whole context of abuse is discounted and the protective parent is blamed.

Evaluator hypotheses about the causes and consequences of DV relate to custody beliefs. Custody evaluators who consider a husband's coercive-controlling behavior are more likely to view DV as the cause of a mother's psychological symptoms. They are also more likely to believe that DV is important in custody decisions, that mothers do not make false allegations, and that victims do not alienate the children (Saunders et al. 2011).

The limitations of GALs' training have been criticized (Ducote 2002), as competent assessments of children and families typically require years of study in areas such as family dynamics, child development, testing, interviewing, diagnostics, and case conceptualization. Moreover, an understanding of cultural diversity and the way issues of race, ethnicity, gender, socioeconomic status, and sexual orientation intersect with family dynamics is crucial to sound assessment (Ancis 2004; Ancis and Jongsma 2007). In addition, issues of child abuse, personality disorders, physical disability, and substance abuse have a potentially profound impact on family systems. The limited training and experience in these areas may lead to suspect decision making (Bryan 2006; Greenberg and Shuman 2007).

Women who have been subject to lengthy custody disputes with custody evaluators describe how GALs' conclusions do not fit with their assessments or do not take into account relevant research (Ancis and Watson 2016).

> I mean it's like . . . she would state something in her report that favored me entirely, and the end result was like, um, oh but we're gonna give it to her father. It's like what?! (Rita, age 43, White mother who lost custody of her children)

Psychological Theories and Assumptions That Have Informed Justice Officials and Mental Health Practitioners

Many theories and assumptions about women in general, abused women, domestic violence (DV), and the needs of children have informed the responses of the justice system and mental health professionals. Unfortunately, some of these assumptions and theories are unfounded, unsubstantiated, and harmful (Neustein and Lesher 2005).

Most importantly, women's responses to abuse and violence are often misunderstood and misinterpreted. The tendency to minimize abuse within the court system, despite the above findings, serves to facilitate and encourage power and control tactics perpetuated by former partners. The particular personality characteristics of abusive former spouses and partners and the impact of abuse on women often lead the aggressor to be perceived as calm, cool, level-headed, logical, and believable, and the victim to be perceived as unbelievable, unstable, and overly emotional. Traumatic symptoms experienced and manifested in response to abuse may be viewed by court personnel (e.g., judges, attorneys, psychologists, GALs) as evidence that women are unstable and ineffectual parents, thereby resulting in custody being awarded to abusive spouses, some of whom are skilled at portraying themselves as virtuous and, ironically, as victims (Stahly 1999). Similarly, discrediting tactics tend to feed into preexisting gender biases that judges may possess (Harrison 2008; Winner 1996).

In fact, research has suggested that psychological profiles of abused women tend to demonstrate elevated scores on the Depression, Psychopathic Deviate, Paranoia, and Schizophrenia subscales of the Minnesota Multiphasic Personality Inventory–2 (Erickson 2006; Kahn, Welch, and Zillmer 1993; Rhodes 1992). Once they have established safety, however, their scores on these subscales return to those associated with general norms (Kaser-Boyd 2004).

Characterizations of protective parents as "vindictive," "hysterical," "paranoid," "manipulative," and the trash-can diagnosis of "borderline" perpetuate a belief that women should not be believed or have their concerns considered as valid. Such characterizations and pseudoscientific terminology are used to deflect or deny concerns about abuse and neglect. Expert evaluations in family court often refer to protective mothers as unstable, "paranoid-delusional," narcissistic, and histrionic (Neustein and Lesher 2005). Such characterizations are used to rationalize a loss of custody and even visitation (Neustein and Lesher 2005). Protective parents are portrayed as fabricating and likely to continue to "undermine" children's relationship with the father.

Mediation interventions, use of the "friendly parent" standard, and the demand for cooperation between biological parents are not only ineffective but potentially harmful. Instead of understanding that protective mothers have valid concerns about children's safety, women are sent the message to "get over it," ignore or deny their concerns, and encourage a friendly relationship between the children and their father no matter the circumstances.

A particularly harmful diagnosis that has been used to trump allegations of abuse is Parental Alienation Syndrome. Parental Alienation Syndrome has been generally defined as a child's denigration of a parent without justification. The creation of Parental Alienation Syndrome, otherwise known as "PAS," is partly the result of two major trends: (1)

a backlash against sexual-abuse survivors who disclosed the abuse and (2) an increase in the divorce rate in North America when both parents and child custody assessors became more likely to notice signs of child abuse (Caplan 2004). In recent years, use of the term "PAS" has been extended to include cases of all types in which a child refuses to visit the noncustodial parent, whether or not the child's objections entail abuse allegations.

Richard Gardner (1985, 1987), the creator of the concept and term, argued that the majority of children in child custody litigation suffered from the so-called disorder of Parental Alienation Syndrome. His focus was almost exclusively on mothers turning a child against the father, allegedly in order to obtain or retain custody of the child. According to Gardner, "evidence" of PAS includes a parent who refuses to force the children to visit their father (even when an abuse allegation is still being investigated) or a mother's and/or child's hesitancy to be interviewed in the presence of the father, the latter being alleged to result from manipulation by the mother. Children's inability or unwillingness to provide details of abuse is also used as evidence of PAS, even though that inability or unwillingness could actually be related to trauma reactions or fear of retaliation by the abuser, possibilities not acknowledged by Gardner. Gardner claimed that many reports of child sexual abuse in the context of divorce cases were false allegations, a belief unsubstantiated by research (Meier 2009).

Gardner's (1998b) questionable ethics and clinical judgment are reflected in the following: (1) he recommends joint interviews with an accused father and child in which the father directly confronts and "cross-examines" (242) the child about the allegation, and (2) he interprets a child's overt expression of fear of possible retaliation by the father as evidence of the child's embarrassment about lying rather than as possibly a valid fear of a truth-telling child whose father is abusive.

Despite the fact that PAS has been discredited by the American Psychological Association (APA), the National Council on Juvenile and Family Court Judges (NCJFCJ), and every major legal and psychological body as unscientific, the construct continues to be utilized in court so that the accuser's sanity and parenting ability are questioned, and the rights of the "alienated" parent become the focus of the case, rather than the needs of the child (Caplan 2004). Sometimes the PAS construct is used under a different label, such as "Malicious Mother Syndrome" (MMS) (Turkat 1997), "parental alienation," or just "alienation" (Goldstein 2016).

APA's authoritative "Report on Violence in the Family" pointedly criticizes the misuse of PAS in domestic violence cases and unequivocally finds that there is no scientific evidence of such a "syndrome." In 1996, the APA Task Force on Violence and the Family published a widely disseminated and relied-upon report titled "Violence and the Family." It is based on a comprehensive review of the literature and research on violence in the family. The report states, among other things,

> When children reject their abusive fathers, it is common for the batterer and others to blame the mother for alienating the children. They often do not understand the legitimate fears of the child. Although there are no data to support the phenomenon called parental alienation syndrome, in which mothers are blamed for interfering with their children's attachment to their fathers, the term is still used by some evaluators and courts to discount children's fears in hostile and psychologically abusive situations. (40)

Because of the PAS tactic, abused children have been placed in the hands of their abusers. According to the Leadership Council, each year, over fifty-eight thousand children are ordered into unsupervised contact with physically or sexually abusive parents following divorce in the United States. It has been reported that the PAS strategy was used in a large number of these cases. Women who speak up about a father's abusive behavior and are not viewed as promoting a positive relationship between a child and the father risk such a scenario (Hannah and Goldstein 2010). Courts fail to recognize valid complaints about domestic violence and sexual abuse as a result of discredited theories such as PAS and related practices. As a result, alleged abusers are given custody of the children, and protective mothers are limited to supervised visitation or no visitation (Goldstein 2016; Saunders et al. 2011).

> She did find him [i.e. the father] in contempt on four counts and found him to be abusive in front of the child, and that he was a poor role model, and a bunch of other things, and that he was stalking, harassing, and

abusing me. And she stopped the visitation because there was an open child abuse investigation. And that child abuse investigation was for a head injury, and they did have findings of abuse, which has been completely swept under the table where they said that his explanation of the head injury was not plausible. And they said there were findings of abuse. So we have findings of abuse, and they're still threatening with parental alienation. (Sue, age 47, White mother)

Other unsubstantiated and unscientific theories that women have brainwashed or used their children to spite their exes, gain attention, or project their sexual frustrations have been promulgated in family court. This includes accusing protective mothers of psychosis or paranoid delusions in the area of sexual abuse even when there is no history of such diagnosis or no indication that such a diagnosis exists in otherwise high-functioning women (Neustein and Lesher 2005). Invoking mental illness when a protective parent makes abuse allegations and then punishing her by taking away custody and/or visitation is unique to family court. A mental illness diagnosis indicates that her beliefs about sexual abuse are directly correlated with actions designed to prevent a relationship between the children and father, no matter the results of an assessment of abuse. That is, she has no control over her actions, as she is mentally ill. The effects of such diagnosis are devastating.

Specific Social and Psychological Concerns

The social and psychological costs of divorces and custody disputes, particularly with an abusive ex, are profound. A study of women's psychosocial experiences, during and after divorce custody disputes, revealed a range of psychological reactions (Ancis, Neelerambam, and Watson 2009). Emotional disempowerment was prevalent during the dispute. Depression, lack of hope, feeling a loss of control, frustration, and constant anxiety were common reactions. Increased vigilance was also common. This included the sense that one's life was being examined under a microscope. Women described having to be very careful about their behavior, their words, and their interactions with others, including their own children. This reaction was common even among women who had been on the receiving end of infidelity and abuse. Women tended to feel that those making important decisions held them to a higher standard. Attorneys emphasized that their behavior had to be "lily white," which was further confirmed by their experiences with custody evaluators and psychological and courtroom experiences.

The stress associated with potentially losing custody of one's children often left women questioning themselves and in a constant state of anxiety. Self-blame was prevalent among abused women, particularly when dealing with a system that denied or questioned whether the abuse actually occurred, as well as downplayed the psychosocial significance of such abuse. Those who lost custody were emotionally devastated.

> When I lost the custody after that emergency hearing I just felt like, it's hard to even put into words what I felt like, but it was like she died. I was so, it was just beyond horrible. And I remember that night I went into her room and I was laying in her bed in her room and just feeling like my life was forever changed, and my daughter has been taken away from me and given to this horrible, abusive man and I can't even protect her anymore. . . . I just wanted to die. The pain was just beyond anything; it was so horrible. And I feel like, I mean it's probably horrible to lose custody anyway, but the fact that I was so in fear for her life and her mental well-being because she was with this man that I had tried to protect her from and I couldn't. (Rachel, age 42, White woman)

Mounting attorney and legal fees served as a constant source of stress. Limited finances prevented women from taking a more offensive position or even defending themselves adequately. Difficulties with work were also prevalent. Decreased work performance was related to fatigue, loss of concentration, and time and energy spent in legal matters.

Custody disputes were particularly stressful, as participants had assumed the majority of the parenting responsibilities. Many described their exes' pursuit of custody as a form of retaliation for the participant initiating the divorce, or as a financial bargaining tactic. Furthermore, divorcing women's low self-esteem and psychological trauma made them more vulnerable to their husbands' and attorneys' attempts to influence them and thus more likely to accept unsatisfying or grossly inequitable offers, perhaps in an effort to avoid being revictimized, a result also described by Bryan (2006).

For many women, the conclusion of the process felt liberating. While some women described relief that the legal dispute was over, those who lost custody reported continued pain and distress. Participants described increased feelings of depression, low self-esteem, self-doubt, and distrust of others. Some described anger and difficulty coming to terms with the outcome of the proceedings.

Women described a lack of trust and disrupted interpersonal relationships after the process, as well as the inability of others to understand their experience. Participants, especially those who lost custody of their children after being the primary caretaker for many years, described changes in their relationship with their children. This extended into relationships with individuals in the community that were previously based on family events and activities. They described the loss associated with fractured ties with their community.

> My relationships really waned because you don't really have a lot of free time, and then when you're in the thick of it, you don't really feel like talking about it because you've talked about it until you're blue in the face with your attorney, you've had to write it down, you've had to think about it, you're confronting it on a daily basis; and so you just want the world to kind of go away. (Trina, age 43, White woman)

For many participants, the legal dispute left them in financial straits. The financial debt made it difficult, if not impossible, to pursue future legal issues as needed. Some found it difficult to maintain financial security and experienced guilt because of an inability to afford certain things for their children.

Physical difficulties both during and after dispute included a general deterioration in health and irregular eating habits and sleep patterns. The women also described changes in their weight as a result of stress and as a protective measure.

Gender and Multiculturally Sensitive Strategies

This chapter outlined the ways in which abusers perpetuate the dynamics of power and control in family court; the pervasive gender bias in family court; and the use of unscientific psychological theories and assumptions about women, particularly as pertains to survivors of domestic violence or those who allege sexual abuse. The chapter also described the role of GALs and other custody evaluators and the psychological and behavioral effects for women in prolonged custody cases.

Below are recommendations for mental health professionals and court professionals who often are called upon to assess, evaluate, counsel, consult, or provide expert testimony in such cases.

Recommendation #1: Avoid cookie-cutter approaches.

Family court recommendations often rely on formulaic, cookie-cutter approaches to custody and visitation schedules. Some jurisdictions have guidelines and suggestions for custody determinations and visitation schedules, or parenting plan guidelines, that are ostensibly based on research but that are arbitrary. Even when research on children is presented, the suggested parenting and scheduling options are not necessarily empirically based or directly linked to empirical research. For example, while a three–five-year-old may be able to tolerate longer periods of separation from attachment figures than a two-year-old, how this may translate to alternate weekends and one evening a week for a noncustodial parent is unclear. The degree to which the context or particular circumstances (e.g., abuse, violence, neglect, or who the primary caretaker has been) are factored into the plan is often left to the discretion of the custody evaluator and, finally, the judge. So, an infant whose primary caretaker has always been the mother, for example, may now be shuffled back and forth on a regular basis, thereby disrupting the attachment bond between the child and his/her primary caretaker.

At base is the need to truly consider the best interests of the children, as is the supposed standard in many jurisdictions. The APA Guidelines for Child Custody Evaluations in Family Law Proceedings (2010) indicate that psychologists strive to base any recommendations on the psychological best interests of the child. Issues such as who is the primary caretaker, to whom is the child most psychologically attached, what will be the impact of separating the child from his or her primary attachment figure, and what are the short- and long-term psychological and physical costs of granting access or custody to an abuser are essential to consider. Such questions put the child's well-being first.

Recommendation #2: Be cautious about pathologizing.

There is a tendency in family court to psychologize and pathologize survivors of abuse and mothers of survivors rather than to identify perpetrators and hold them accountable. PAS, for example, shifts attention away from the potentially dangerous behavior of the parent seeking custody to that of the custodial parent. The person who may be attempting to protect the child is instead presumed to be lying and emotionally poisoning the child. A mother's normal and valid responses to custody disputes, especially when there is abuse, is often taken as further evidence of her instability, vindictiveness, and hysteria. Legitimate and valid reactions to stress and trauma, such as abuse and custody disputes with abusive ex-partners/husbands, particularly when one is the primary caretaker, are often seen as proof of women's instability and are used to rationalize a change in custody. Moreover, court personnel are unduly persuaded by manipulative former spouses (Gender Bias Study 1990; Meier 2009; Winner 1996).

Mental health professionals and justice officials need to educate themselves about the dynamics of violence and its potential impact on a protective parent's emotional and behavioral response so as to not unduly pathologize women. Most women in divorce and custody cases do not falsely claim abuse. Rather, abuse is often the impetus for divorce. Women who are still married when disclosure of child sexual abuse occurs are often advised by protective services to take the child, leave the abuser, and file for divorce. So, often, disclosure of abuse leads to divorce, not the reverse.

Recommendation #3: Understand the research on women, domestic violence, child abuse, and impact on children.

The relationship between childhood sexual abuse and a host of symptoms in children, including posttraumatic stress disorder, behavior problems, and poor self-esteem, has been established (see Kendall-Tackett, Williams, and Finkelhor 1993). Moreover, childhood emotional abuse and neglect predict emotional and physical distress as well as lifetime exposure to trauma in adult women (Spertus et al. 2003).

Despite the fact that research also demonstrates a relationship between witnessing adult domestic violence and a host of behavioral, emotional, and cognitive-functioning problems among children (Edleson 1999), family courts often minimize the harmful impact of children's witnessing violence in the home (Hannah and Goldsten 2010). In fact, judgments about custody and visitation have ignored the impact of domestic violence on custody decisions or have minimized the effects of abuse (Araji and Bosek 2010; Hannah and Goldstein 2010).

Mental health professionals and justice officials must be educated about abuse, violence, and its impact on parenting. Batterers often increase their use and threats of violence during and following custody actions (Hart 1998). So, contrary to a common misperception among courts, parents' separation does not end the violence. Moreover, mental health professionals and courts must understand the immediate ill effects on children of witnessing domestic violence, as well as the long-term effects. Courts must be careful that friendly-parent provisions or other best-interest factors not be given greater consideration over domestic violence as a factor in custody decisions (Hornsby 2010). The National Council of Juvenile and Family Court Judges (NCFJCJ 1994) and the American Bar Association (1994) have both recommended placing abuse of one parent against another over other best-interest factors in contested custody cases. If this recommendation is followed, joint or sole custody would be denied to a person with a history of DV.

Recommendation #4: Understand the limits of evaluations.

Child sexual abuse may take a long time to uncover. In the majority of cases, there are no overt signs. Fondling and inappropriate touch do not reveal themselves in obvious ways. Moreover, children are often threatened not to disclose abuse. Abusers may keep children silent by saying things like, "Don't tell mommy about this. She will get mad at you. You won't get to see me anymore if you tell, and I will be mad at you." "I love you; we have a special relationship that others would not understand." The manipulations of abusers teach children to associate abuse with love and affection. Threats are also invoked, such as "I will send your dog away if you tell anyone." Denial and disassociation are common among abused children, which can result in a range of unpredictable reactions

(Corwin et al. 1987). Fear, self-blame, and difficulty talking about the abuse are some of the reasons why victims do not disclose.

Understanding child development and related cognitive levels of children is essential for those interviewing or counseling children. Unfortunately, those with limited to no training in child development who interview children may misinterpret the child's expressions. Children's concrete thinking or lack of ability to think abstractly impacts responses, as does their sense of time.

In cases of alleged child abuse, it is important to order a comprehensive evaluation by a competent professional specializing in child sexual abuse. Interviewers must be able to understand the ways in which children's developmental stage, as well as the context and process of forensic interviews, influence whether and how children disclose abusive experiences (Fivush and Shukat 1995; Lamb, Sternberg, and Esplin 1995; Walker 1993). Careful analysis and attention to scientific rigor is needed. A one-time, fifteen-minute assessment, which is often all that overburdened, underresourced court systems can manage, does not suffice. Moreover, each situation needs to be judged on a case-by-case basis.

Recommendation #5: Be aware of cognitive bias and consider alternative explanations.

Research on heuristics and cognitive bias offers insight into the types of mistakes and misinterpretations that custody evaluators may make. For example, confirmatory bias may occur when an evaluator develops a hypothesis early in his or her process, finds data to support it, confirms the hypothesis, and then stops testing it against new or different data that might undermine the hypothesis or effect a change of mind.

It is important that evaluators remain open-minded about the possibility of multiple explanations for events. For example, in many custody disputes, it is assumed that a child who is estranged from one parent was unduly influenced by the other parent. However, children may have valid and significant reasons to be fearful or angry (NCFCJ 1994). That is, they may be reacting to a violent, neglectful, or abusive parent (Kelly and Johnston 2001).

Faller (1998) has written that PAS fails to take into account alternative explanations for the child's and the mother's behavior, including the veracity of allegations and the mother having made an honest mistake. For example, a parent who refuses to force the children to visit their father (even when an abuse allegation is still being investigated) or does not "cooperate" with a court-ordered assessment is assumed to be involved in PAS rather than possibly perceiving accurately or even reasonably believing that the father or assessor may be biased against her child. Continual testing and checking one's assumptions and remaining aware of potential biases are of primary importance to informed and ethical decision-making practice.

Recommendation #6: Do not rely solely on expert opinion.

Although expert testimony is often useful, decision makers need to do their homework rather than rely uncritically on experts' views. This is particularly true in fields such as psychology and psychiatry, where even experts have a wide range of differing views, and professionals sometimes offer opinions beyond their expertise. An overreliance on experts who offer options that overstep the boundaries of their knowledge and competence and do so with the impression that their views are empirically validated is dangerous. Moreover, experts who rely on outdated and unfounded theories and assumptions are all too common. Their reliance on attorneys and courts for referrals and evaluations often creates a type of dual relationship that limits or interferes with objectivity.

Interestingly, while the majority of judges and attorneys prefer psychologists to social workers as custody evaluators (Bow and Quinnell 2001), social workers are more likely to believe that DV is an important factor when making custody-visitation decisions and that victims do not make false allegations, alienate children, or hurt them when they resist coparenting (Saunders et al. 2011).

Coupled with the limited training, another problem is that there is no accepted body of standards and guidelines or uniform model of practice that all GALs must follow (Ducote 2002). Practice guidelines developed by the Association of Family and Conciliation Courts (AFCC 1994) and the American Psychological Association's (APA) Guidelines for Custody Evaluations in Divorce Proceedings, formulated for psychologists, are "aspirational" in nature and not mandatory. As a result, many authors have criticized the methodology and usefulness of custody evaluations (Melton et al. 1997; O'Donohue and Bradley 2006).

Training in DV and the dynamics of abuse should be mandatory for all custody evaluators, court professionals, and GALs. This training must go beyond the superficial and include education about the power and control tactics that abusers engage in before, during, and after divorce and/or custody disputes. Other information should include the psychological, emotional, and behavioral impact of abuse on survivors and children, including survivors' staying with or returning to the abuser for a variety of reasons such as fear of losing one's children.

Recommendation #7: Promote reform.

Despite reports and articles documenting horrible abuse against child victims of domestic violence, significant reform in custody courts is lacking. Bartlow (2016) and her students interviewed judges and court administrators to explore court reform practices after the deaths of children by abusive fathers. Although the judges interviewed demonstrated substantial knowledge about domestic violence, no reforms were created as they assumed that the tragedy in their community was an exception. Inadequate training and the myth that women often make false allegations compound this belief.

Reforms would include mandatory judicial training in every state on the dynamics of abuse. Judges with little to no experience, understanding, or training are required to respond to domestic violence cases. Some states have specialized courts that handle domestic violence cases, making it more likely that court professionals will recognize patterns within and between cases (Bartlow and Goldstein 2016). Multidisciplinary teams such as those of mental health professionals and child and domestic violence experts are also warranted. Making the health and safety of women and children a priority would help to reduce negative practices that adversely impact their lives.

Conclusion

The chapter has outlined the sociocultural context of women's experiences in family court, particularly those who have experienced abuse by ex-partners or -husbands. Power and control dynamics experienced in the course of the partnership often continue to manifest during family court proceedings. A lack of understanding of abuse, coupled with myths and unsubstantiated theories, on the part of mental health professionals and judicial officials results in women's disadvantage in family court. GALs and other custody evaluators often lack training and education in domestic abuse, leading to faulty conclusions and recommendations regarding custody and visitation. Moreover, reform in the custody court system that takes into account scientific research on domestic violence is needed. Empirically informed strategies are needed to minimize the pathologizing of abuse survivors and avoid cookie-cutter approaches to family court decisions.

REFERENCES

American Bar Association. 1994. "The Impact of Domestic Violence on Children." Center on Children and the Law. A Report to the President of the American Bar Association, http://library.niwap.org.

American Psychological Association (APA). 2010. "Guidelines for Custody Evaluations in Family Law Proceedings." *American Psychologist* 65 (9): 863–67. doi: 10.1037/a0021250.

American Psychological Association (APA). 1996. "Report on Violence in the Family." APA Presidential Task Force on Violence and the Family. Washington, DC: American Psychological Association.

Ancis, Julie. 2015. "Abuse, Gender, and Family Court." Paper presented at meeting of the American Psychological Association, Toronto, CA.

Ancis, Julie. 2012. "Abuse and Its Perpetuation within Family Court: Implications for Psychologists." Paper presented at meeting of the American Psychological Association, Orlando, FL.

Ancis, Julie, ed. 2004. *Culturally Responsive Interventions: Innovative Approaches to Working with Diverse Populations.* New York: Brunner-Routledge.

Ancis, Julie, and Arthur Jongsma. 2007. *The Complete Women's Psychotherapy Treatment Planner.* Hoboken, NJ: Wiley.

Ancis, Julie, Kiranmayi Neelerambam, and Laurel Watson. 2009. "Psychosocial Impact of Divorce and Custody Disputes: Clinical Implications." Poster presented at meeting of the American Psychological Association, Toronto, Canada.

Ancis, Julie, and Laurel B. Watson. 2016. "Women's Experiences with and Perceptions of Guardians ad Litem in Divorce and Custody Disputes." In *Domestic Violence, Abuse, and Child Custody*, vol. 2. Edited by Mo T. Hannah and Barry Goldstein, 8-1-8-18. Kingston, NJ: Civic Research Institute.

Araji, Sharon K., and Rebecca L. Bosek. 2010. "Domestic Violence, Contested Child Custody, and the Courts: Findings from Five Studies." In *Domestic Violence, Abuse, and Child Custody*. Edited by Mo T. Hannah and Barry Goldstein, 6-1-6-32. Kingston, NJ: Civic Research Institute.

Arizona Coalition against Domestic Violence. 2003. "Battered Mothers' Testimony Project: A Human Rights Approach to Child Custody and Domestic Violence," http://www.thelizlibrary.org.

Association of Family and Conciliation Courts. 1994. "AFCC Model Standards of Practice for Child Custody Evaluation." *Family Court Review* 32: 504–13.

Bala, Nicholas, and John Schuman. 2000. "Allegations of Sexual Abuse When Parents Have Separated." *Canadian Family Law Quarterly* 17: 191–241.

Bancroft, Lundy, and Jay Silverman. 2002. *The Batterer as Parent: Addressing the Impact of Domestic Violence on Family Dynamics.* Thousand Oaks, CA: Sage.

Bartlow, Dianne R. 2016. "Judicial Response to Court-Assisted Child Murders." In *Domestic Violence, Abuse, and Child Custody*, vol. 2. Edited by Mo T. Hannah and Barry Goldstein, 12-2-12-43. Kingston, NJ: Civic Research Institute.

Bartlow, Dianne R., and Barry Goldstein. 2016. "Childproofing Custody Courts: What Can Be Learned from Child Murders Related to Custody Cases." In *Domestic Violence, Abuse, and Child Custody*, vol. 2. Edited by Mo T. Hannah and Barry Goldstein, 13-2-13-25. Kingston, NJ: Civic Research Institute.

Bemiller, Michelle. 2008. "When Battered Mothers Lose Custody: A Qualitative Study of Abuse at Home and in the Courts." *Journal of Child Custody* 5: 228–55.

Bow, James, and Francella Quinnell. 2001. "Psychologists' Current Practices and Procedures in Child Custody Evaluations: Five Years after APA Guidelines." *Professional Psychology: Research and Practice* 32: 261–68.

Brown, Thea, Margarita Frederico, Lesley Hewitt, and Rosemary Sheehan. 2000. "Revealing the Existence of Child Abuse in the Context of Marital Breakdown and Custody and Access Disputes." *Child Abuse and Neglect* 24 (6): 849–85.

Bryan, Penelope. 2006. *Constructive Divorce: Procedural Justice and Sociolegal Reform.* Washington, DC: American Psychological Association. doi: 10.1037/11300-000.

Caplan, Paula. 2004. "What Is It That's Being Called 'Parental Alienation Syndrome'?" In *Bias in Psychiatric Diagnosis*. Edited by Paula J. Caplan and Lisa Cosgrove, 61–67. Lanham, MD: Rowman and Littlefield.

Child Welfare Information Gateway. 2013. "Determining the Best Interests of the Child." Washington, DC: U.S. Department of Health and Human Services, Children's Bureau. https://www.childwelfare.gov.

Corwin, David L., Lucy Berliner, Gail Goodman, Jean Goodwin, and Sue White. 1987. "Child Sexual Abuse and Custody Disputes: No Easy Answers." *Journal of Interpersonal Violence* 2 (1): 91–105.

Danforth, Gay, and Bobbie Welling, eds. 1996. *Achieving Equal Justice for Women and Men in the California Courts: Final Report.* Judicial Council of California Advisory Committee on Gender Bias in the Courts, http://www.courts.ca.gov

Dragiewicz, Molly. 2010. "Gender Bias in the Courts: Implications for Battered Mothers and Their Children." In *Domestic Violence, Abuse, and Child Custody*. Edited by Mo T. Hannah and Barry Goldstein, 5-1-5-19. Kingston, NJ: Civic Research Institute.

Ducote, Richard. 2002. "Guardians ad Litem in Private Custody Litigation: The Case for Abolition." *Loyola Journal of Public Interest Law,* 106–39. Available at http://www.stopfamilyviolence.org (accessed January 29, 2010).

Edleson, Jeffrey L. 1999. "Children's Witnessing of Adult Domestic Violence." *Journal of Interpersonal Violence* 14 (8): 839–70.

Erickson, Nancy S. 2006. "Use of the MMPI-2 in Child Custody Evaluations involving Battered Women: What Does Psychological Research Tell Us? *Family Law Quarterly* 39 (1): 87–108.

Faller, Kathleen C. 1998. "The Parental Alienation Syndrome: What Is It and What Data Support It?" *Child Maltreatment* 3 (2): 100–115.

Fivush, Robyn, and Jennifer R. Shukat. 1995. "Content, Consistency, and Coherence of Early Autobiographical Recall." In *Memory and Testimony in the Child Witness.* Edited by Maria S. Zaragoza , John R. Graham, Gordon C. N. Hall, Richard Hirschman, and Yossef S. Ben-Porath, 5–23. London: Sage.

Gardner, Richard. 1998a. "Family Therapy of the Moderate Type of Parental Alienation." *American Journal of Family Therapy* 27: 195–212.

Gardner, Richard. 1998b. *The Parental Alienation Syndrome,* 2nd ed. Creskill, NJ: Creative Therapeutics.

Gardner, Richard. 1987. *The Parental Alienation Syndrome and the Differentiation between False and Genuine Sex Abuse.* Creskill, NJ: Creative Therapeutics.

Gardner, Richard. 1985. "Recent Trends in Divorce and Custody Litigation." *Academy Forum* 29 (2): 3–7.

Gender Bias Study of the Court System in Massachusetts (Gender Bias Study). 1990. *New England Law Review* 24: 745–52.

Goldstein, B. 2016. "Extreme Custody Decisions That Put Mothers and Their Children at Risk." In *Domestic Violence, Abuse, and Child Custody,* vol. 2. Edited by Mo T. Hannah and Barry Goldstein, 4-1–4-18. Kingston, NJ: Civic Research Institute.

Greenberg, Stuart, and Daniel W. Shuman. 2007. "When Worlds Collide: Therapeutic and Forensic Roles." *Professional Psychology: Research and Practice* 38 (2): 129–32.

Hall, Alex S., Chad A. Pulver, and Mary J. Cooley. 1996. "Psychology of Best Interest Standard: Fifty State Statutes and Their Theoretical Antecedents." *American Journal of Family Therapy* 24 (2): 171–80.

Hannah, Mo, and Barry Goldstein, eds. 2010. *Domestic Violence, Abuse, and Child Custody,* vol. 2. Kingston, NJ: Civic Research Institute.

Harrison, Christine. 2008. "Implacably Hostile or Appropriately Protective? Women Managing Child Conflict in the Context of Domestic Violence." *Violence against Women* 14 (4): 381–405. doi: 10.1177/1077801208314833.

Hart, Barbra J. 1998. "Safety and Accountability: The Underpinnings of a Just Justice System." Pennsylvania Coalition Against Domestic Violence. http://www.mincava.umn.edu.

Heim, Sheila, Helen Grieco, Sue Di Paola, and Rachel Allen. 2002. "California National Organization for Women: Family Court Report." http://website.canow.org.

Hornsby, Thomas. 2010. "Do Judges Adequately Address the Causes and Impact of Violence in Children's Lives in Deciding Contested Child Custody Cases?" In *Domestic Violence, Abuse, and Child Custody.* Edited by Mo T. Hannah and Barry Goldstein, 7-1–7-32. Kingston, NJ: Civic Research Institute.

Jaffe, Peter G., J. R. Johnston, C. V. Crooks, and N. Bala. 2008. "Custody Disputes involving Allegations of Domestic Violence: Toward a Differentiated Approach to Parenting Plans." *Family Court Review* 46: 500–522.

Johnson, Nancy E., Dennis P. Saccuzzo, and Wendy J. Koen. 2005. "Child Custody Mediation in Cases of Domestic Violence: Empirical Evidence of a Failure to Protect." *Violence against Women* 11: 1022–53.

Kahn, Fariah, Toni Welch, and Eric A. Zillmer. 1993. "MMPI-2 Profiles of Battered Women in Transition." *Journal of Personality Assessment* 60: 100–111.

Kaser-Boyd, Nancy. 2004. "Battered Woman's Syndrome: Clinical Features, Evaluation, and Expert Testimony." In *Sexualized Violence against Women and Children: A Psychology and Law Perspective.* Edited by B. J. Cling, 41–70. New York: Guilford.

Kelly, Joan B., and Janet R. Johnston. 2001. "The Alienated Child: A Reformulation of Parental Alienation Syndrome." *Family Court Review* 39 (3): 249–67.

Kendall-Tackett, Kathleen A., Linda M. Williams, and David Finkelhor. 1993. "Impact of Sexual Abuse on Children: A Review and Synthesis of Recent Empirical Studies." *Psychological Bulletin* 113 (1): 164–80.

Kernic, Mary A., Daphne J. Monary-Ernsdorff, Jennifer K. Koepsell, and Victoria L. Holt. 2005. "Children in the Crossfire: Child Custody Determinations among Couples with a History of Intimate Partner Violence." *Violence against Women* 11: 991–1021.

Krauss, Daniel A., and Bruce D. Sales. 2001. "The Child Custody Standard: What Do Twenty Years of Research Tell Us?" In *Handbook of Youth and Justice.* Edited by Susan O. White, 411–35. New York: Springer.

Lamb, Michael E., Kathleen J. Sternberg, and Philip W. Esplin. 1995. "Making Children into Competent Witnesses: Reactions to the Amicus Brief *In re Michaels.*" *Psychology, Public Policy, and Law* 1: 438–49.

Meier, Joan S. 2009. "A Historical Perspective on Parental Alienation Syndrome and Parental Alienation." *Journal of Child Custody* 6: 232–57.

Melton, Gary B., John Petrila, Norman G. Poythress, and Christopher Slobogin. 1997. *Psychological Evaluations for the Court,* 2nd ed. New York: Guilford.

Muraskin, Roslyn. 2012. *Women and Justice: It's a Crime.* Upper Saddle River, NJ: Prentice Hall.

National Council of Juvenile and Family Court Judges. 1994. *Model Code on Domestic and Family Violence.* Reno, NV: Author.

Neilson, Linda C. 2004. "Assessing Mutual Partner-Abuse Claims in Child Custody and Access Claims." *Family Court Review* 42 (3): 411–38. doi: 0.1177/153124450404200304.

Neustein, Amy, and Michael Lesher. 2005. *From Madness to Mutiny: Why Mothers Are Running from the Family Courts—and What Can Be Done about It*. Lebanon, NH: Northeastern University.

O'Donohue, William, and April R. Bradley. 2006. "Conceptual and Empirical Issues in Child Custody Evaluations." *Clinical Psychology* 6: 310–22. doi: 10.1093/clipsy.6.3.310.

Pagelow, Mildred. 1993. "Justice for Victims of Spouse Abuse in Divorce and Child Custody Cases." *Violence and Victims* 8: 69–83.

Price, Heather L., Kim P. Roberts, and Andrea Collins. 2013. "The Quality of Children's Allegations of Abuse in Investigative Interviews Containing Practice Narratives." *Journal of Applied Research in Memory and Cognition* 2 (1): 1–6.

Rhodes, Nancy R. 1992. "Comparison of MMPI Psychopathic Deviate Scores of Battered and Nonbattered Women." *Journal of Family Violence* 7 (4): 297–307.

Saunders, Daniel G., Kathleen Faller, and Richard M. Tolman. 2011. "Child Custody Evaluators' Beliefs about Domestic Abuse Allegations: Their Relationship to Evaluator Demographics, Background, Domestic Violence Knowledge, and Custody-Visitation Recommendations." Report submitted to the National Institute of Justice, U.S. Department of Justice. https://www.ncjrs.gov.

Shipway, Lyn. 2004. *Domestic Violence: A Handbook for Health Professionals*. New York: Taylor and Francis.

Spertus, Illyse, Rachel Yehuda, Cheryl M. Wong, Sarah Halligan, and Stephanie V. Seremetis. 2003. "Childhood Emotional Abuse and Neglect as Predictors of Psychological and Physical Symptoms in Women Presenting to a Primary Care Practice." *Child Abuse and Neglect* 27 (11): 1247–58.

Stahly, Geraldine B. 1999. "Women with Children in Violent Relationships: The Choice of Leaving May Bring the Consequence of Custody Change." *Journal of Aggression, Maltreatment, and Trauma* 2: 239–51.

Stahly, Geraldine. B., Linda Krajewski, Bianca Loya, Kiranjeet Uppal, Grace German, Wesley Farris, N. Hilson, and Jenna Valentine. 2004. "Protective Mothers in Child Custody Disputes: A Study of Judicial Abuse." In *Disorder in the Courts: Mothers and Their Allies Take on the Family Law System (A Collection of Essays)*. Edited by Helen Grieco, R. Allen, and J. Friedlin, 46–50. California National Organization for Women.

Taylor, David, Maria V. Stoilkov, and Daniel J. Greco. 2008. "Ex Parte Domestic Violence Orders of Protection: How Easing Access to Judicial Process Has Eased the Possibility for Abuse of the Process." *Kansas Journal of Law and Public Policy* 18: 83–133.

Thoennes, Nancy, and Patricia G. Tjaden. 1990. "The Extent, Nature, and Validity of Sexual Abuse Allegations in Custody/Visitation Disputes." *Child Abuse and Neglect* 14: 151–63.

Turkat, Ira D. 1997. "Management of Visitation Interference." *Judges' Journal* 36 (2): 17–21.

Voices of Women Organizing Project. 2008. "Executive Summary." In *Justice Denied: How Family Courts in NYC Endanger Battered Women and Children*. Battered Women's Resource Center. http://www.leadershipcouncil.org.

Walker, Anne G. 1993. "Questioning Young Children in Court: A Linguistic Case Study." *Law and Human Behavior* 17: 59–81.

Watson, Laurel B., and Julie R. Ancis. 2013. "Power and Control in the Legal System: From Partnership to Divorce and Custody." *Violence against Women* 19 (2): 166–86. doi: 10.1177/1077801213478027.

Winner, Karen. 1996. *Divorced from Justice: The Abuse of Women and Children by Divorce Lawyers and Judges*. New York: HarperCollins.

2

Women, Domestic Violence, and the Criminal Justice System

Traumatic Pathways

LENORE E. A. WALKER AND CARLYE B. CONTE

We met Wanda, a thirty-six-year-old woman, awaiting trial in jail and accused of battery on a law enforcement officer. Her attorney had asked us to evaluate her, as she had no recollection of assaulting the officer. Prior to her arrest, Wendy had received a letter from the parole board saying that the man who had attacked and killed her fiancé and kidnapped and attempted to kill her was about to be released from prison. Wanda, who had been substance free for several years, was so upset that she began drinking again as a way to calm herself and take away the pain that she was experiencing. The night of her arrest, she had been driving erratically and was stopped by the police. Apparently, Wanda resisted arrest, which is why she was charged and held in jail. While in jail, she attended a group that we ran for victims of domestic violence and other forms of trauma. During these groups, she realized that it was necessary to address not only her most recent traumatic experience but also the domestic violence and the physical and sexual abuse she experienced during childhood and in an earlier marriage. As a survivor of multiple traumatic experiences, Wanda needed trauma-specific treatment, not punishment for battery on a police officer or purely substance abuse treatment for her DUI. She had previously participated in psychotherapy and alcohol and other drug treatment; however, neither intervention dealt specifically with her trauma. She knew that being a victim of an attempted homicide and seeing her fiancé killed was definitely shocking; it was so distressing that it overshadowed the abuse she had experienced during childhood and with her former husband. When she learned that the attacker was about to be released from prison after serving his time, she became so upset that she began drinking to calm down her fears and anxiety. When stopped by the police for driving under the influence, she panicked and probably began experiencing dissociative symptoms as she thought the police officer was her attacker who had come back to kidnap and kill her. Not until she began trauma-specific treatment in jail was she able to both identify and start to heal from both the domestic violence and the other traumas she had experienced. Rather than going to trial and possibly receiving a prison sentence, Wanda was referred to a mental health court where the judge deferred her prosecution and sent her to a halfway house to receive trauma-specific treatment.

While women in the criminal justice system differ in demographic characteristics—race, ethnicity, socioeconomic status, and educational level—like Wanda, most share a history of physical, sexual, and emotional abuse (Green et al. 2005; Lynch et al. 2012). Additionally, posttraumatic stress disorder (PTSD), substance abuse, and other forms of mental illness are prevalent among justice-involved women who have experienced various forms of gender-based violence (James and Glaze 2006; Harlow 1999; DeHart et al. 2014). The intersection of economic disadvantage, untreated mental illness, self-medication, including substance abuse, childhood maltreatment, domestic violence, and trauma accounts for women's elevated risk of entering the justice system not only as victims but also as offenders (Bloom, Owen, and Covington 2004; Walker 2009).

This chapter will describe the pathways that lead to battered women's involvement in multiple arenas of the justice system and the compounded burden they experience as a result of their interaction with family, juvenile, civil, and criminal courts. Throughout this chapter, the literature on domestic violence will be reviewed and interspersed with personal research and clinical experience from working with battered women in a variety of contexts over the years. The legal framework of domestic violence will be analyzed through a discussion of social and legal reforms, feminist activism, and the passage of laws such as the Violence Against Women Act (VAWA). A historical and intersectional lens will be used to examine criminal justice responses to domestic violence and to highlight the benefits and consequences of justice reforms, such as mandatory arrest and no-drop policies, in the lives of diverse battered women. Lastly, this chapter will discuss the need for interventions that are gender-responsive and culturally sensitive. In particular, a feminist and trauma-informed therapeutic model will be proposed, based on the theoretical principles of survivor therapy. This survivor-focused, trauma-informed therapy model is supported by extensive and ongoing research that demonstrates its effectiveness in promoting healing, empowerment, and psychological well-being in the lives of battered women.

Domestic Violence, Intimate Partner Violence, and Gender Violence: Definitions and Prevalence

Definitions of domestic violence, intimate partner violence, and gender violence vary across disciplines, and these terms are often used interchangeably. "Gender violence" refers to all forms of violence against women, including sexual assault, rape, child sexual abuse, sexual exploitation by people in power or authority, sexual harassment in schools or workplaces, and human trafficking (United Nations 1993). "Domestic violence" or "intimate partner violence" is defined as physical, sexual, and/or psychological abuse that is committed by a former or current intimate partner (Centers for Disease Control 2014). Domestic violence can take many forms, but the underlying motivation is the same—power, control, and domination over the victim.[1]

Although both males and females can be victims and perpetrators of domestic violence, research has shown that the majority of domestic violence victims are female, and the majority of offenders are male (Truman and Morgan 2014). This pattern holds true across all time periods and all forms of domestic violence (Tjaden and Thoennes 2000). Data collected from the National Violence Against Women Survey (NVAW) indicated that there are approximately 4.8 million acts of physical and sexual assault committed against women by an intimate partner each year in the United States (Tjaden and Thoennes 2000). Although this translates to approximately one in four women who experience intimate partner violence at some point in their lifetime, it is likely that the true rate of violence against women goes vastly underreported. For example, approximately one-fifth of sexual assaults and one-fourth of all physical assaults are actually reported to the police (Tjaden and Thoennes 2000). Of the domestic violence incidents that are reported, around one-fifth involve the use of weapons, which significantly increases the risk for fatality (Truman and Morgan 2014). The rate of homicide related to domestic violence occurs at twice the rate for females as it does for males, with women making up 70 percent of victims killed by an intimate partner (Catalano et al. 2009).

Research using the Battered Woman Syndrome Questionnaire (BWSQ), an instrument used to collect data on battered women for the last thirty years (Walker 1984, 2006, 2009), has shown that acute battering incidents followed a temporal course. The findings of cross-national studies have supported the development of the cycle theory of domestic violence (Walker 1979), which describes interpersonal aggression as cyclical and fluctuating in intensity over time. Typical battering relationships begin with a period of courtship, and behaviors do not become abusive until the woman has made a commitment to the man in the form of living together or getting married. The abuse starts out slowly, and the first phase of the violence cycle is characterized by the building of tension and the use of tactics aimed at domination and control. Stress, pressure, and conflict escalate such that women feel trapped, hopeless, and afraid of the danger lying ahead. The tension continues to rise until the male partner explodes with anger. It is at this time that battering incidents and physical injuries occur, and that the police are called. Following the battering incident is a period of loving contrition during which the batterer may feel remorse, apologize, and assure that the abuse will never happen again. Alternatively, the abuser may blame the victim for his behavior, and promise that the violence will not reoccur if she does not do whatever it was that caused his acts of aggression. A batterer may also respond by showering his victim with love and affection, thus reminding her of the man he was during the courtship period.

The following quotation from one of our clients illustrates how batterers' behaviors work to keep their female partners hopeful and willing to stay in the relationship: "If it was all bad I would have left much sooner. I just kept holding on to that 5 percent of the time when he acted like he loved me. That false hope is what kept me in the relationship for so long." In psychological terms, our client described the process of intermittent reinforcement batterers use to maintain power and control over victims. There are also other reasons why women may stay in abusive relationships. These include the victim's emotional and economic dependency on the abuser, and her fear that he will follow through on his threats to harm her children or family. In addition, terminating the relationship does not usually stop the abuse. Batterers are likely to use the courts to continue their harassment and psychological abuse, especially if there are young children involved. (See Julie Ancis, chapter 1 in this book).

Mental and Physical Health Outcomes of Domestic Violence: A Trauma-Informed Perspective

Domestic violence is a form of complex trauma that produces psychological and physical distress (Walker 2002). Medical concerns include chronic illness such as cancer and diabetes, sexually transmitted diseases, gynecological and reproductive health problems, motility disability, irritable bowel syndrome, chronic fatigue syndrome, fibromyalgia, chronic pain, neurological complaints, dizziness, memory disturbances, and difficulty with concentration (Coker et al. 2002 Dillon et al. 2013; World Health Organization 2005). More than half of all domestic violence incidents result in some form of physical harm, and in the majority of cases, women do not seek medical treatment. Injuries include facial fractures, dental problems, broken bones, and neurological, internal, and soft tissue damage (Campbell and Boyd 2003; Dillon et al. 2013). Physical assaults can also lead to death, directly or indirectly, from cerebral vascular incidents, cardiac problems, and anoxia.

Trauma is also linked to hopelessness, dependency, and substance use. Battered women are fifteen times more likely than other women to use alcohol and nine times more likely to abuse other drugs (Gilfus 1993; Shipway 2004; Stark and Flitcraft 1996). Together with defense mechanisms (i.e., denial, minimization, rationalization), the use of substances is a strategy to cope with pain, anxiety, and other mental health problems, such as depression and trauma symptomatology, that result not from underlying mental disorders but from exposure to prolonged and relentless abuse (Platt, Barton, and Freyd 2009; Walker 2002). Studies have shown that posttraumatic stress disorder (PTSD) is an outcome of domestic violence, with rates ranging from 31 percent to 84 percent for battered women compared to 3.4 percent for the general population (Golding 1999; Jones, Hughes, and Unterstaller 2001). Anxiety presents in the form of generalized fear, apprehension, and worry. Social isolation, anhedonia, fatigue, appetite disturbances, difficulty concentrating, sadness, hopelessness, and feelings of worthlessness are common depressive symptoms (Nathanson et al. 2012; Walker 2009). Women who experience domestic violence are also more likely to endorse suicidal ideation and make suicidal gestures or attempts (Dillon et al. 2013; World Health Organization 2005).

"Battered Woman's Syndrome" (BWS), a subcategory of PTSD, is the term used to describe the constellation of symptoms that victims experience as a result of domestic violence (Walker 2006): (1) intrusive recollection of the traumatic events; (2) hyperarousal and high levels of anxiety; (3) avoidance behavior and emotional numbing (e.g., minimization, dissociation, depression); (4) disrupted interpersonal relationships; (5) body image distortions and somatic complaints; and (6) issues with sexual intimacy. The definition of BWS now includes a new group of symptoms that are equivalent to the negative alterations in cognition and mood of the PTSD diagnosis in the DSM-5. BWS has been used to understand victims' perceptions of themselves, their relationships, and their abuser. For example, the belief that the abuser is omnipresent and omniscient is characteristic of women with BWS. Catherine, a forty-year-old woman who was on trial for the murder of her abusive spouse, explained to the jury that at the time of the events she was terrified of her partner because he had put a loaded gun to her head and threatened to shoot her before passing out from too much drinking. He lay down on the bed, put the gun on the night table, and ordered her to lie next to him. Certain that he was going to kill her, she grabbed the gun and shot him. She did not think the bullet would incapacitate him, so she took a knife and stabbed his dead body repeatedly. BWS explains why Catherine believed her abusive husband could still harm her even after she had shot him dead.

Psychological abuse, like physical abuse, produces significant harm to victims' cognitive, emotional, and behavioral functioning. It involves the use of methods to isolate the victim, to induce debilitating exhaustion, to monopolize perceptions, to degrade and humiliate, to control the mind, and occasionally to induce hope that the abuse will end (Amnesty International 1975). We have worked with many women who described the long-lasting and damaging effects of abusive tactics such as threats, bullying, name calling, administration of drugs, and use of force. Compared to acts of physical violence (e.g., pushing, shoving, hitting, punching, kicking, hair pulling), psychological abuse and coercive control "erode a woman's self-esteem, self-confidence, and self-respect" (Williamson 2010) and produce feelings of helplessness that make it more difficult for women to leave an abusive relationship.

Barriers to Legal and Psychological Help: An Intersectional Perspective

At the domestic violence shelter where we provide trauma-specific psychotherapy services, diverse women participate in weekly group meetings designed to help them overcome the effects of past abuse and trauma. Their stories indicate how the intersection of gender, race, ethnicity, religion, and socioeconomic status makes their experience of intimate partner violence unique rather than universal. Leah, an African American woman, said it took a long time to disclose the abuse. She explained that she was ashamed to tell her family, and afraid that she would not be taken seriously if she contacted the criminal justice system because her spouse was Caucasian. Nadia was a German woman who had immigrated to the United States and married a Latino man. She reported that her husband's family told her the use of violence was "normal" in their culture, and it was her "duty" to be submissive. Nadia had no relatives in the United States; her husband's family was her only source of social support. She feared that if she disclosed the abuse she would lose custody of her children and be deported. Growing up, Ming, an Asian woman who spoke little English, had learned to be subservient. She believed that it was her responsibility as a wife to endure the violence inflicted upon her by her husband. She spent many years in the United States unaware of the support services available to victims of domestic violence.

The intersection of race, class, gender, religion, sexual orientation, and immigration status creates barriers that prevent many women from coming forward with allegations of abuse (Bograd 1999; Kasturirangan, Krishnan, and Riger 2004). Perpetrators of domestic violence may instill feelings of insecurity in their victims by emphasizing the importance of cultural values and by providing constant reminders that punishment, including hostility from the criminal justice system and ostracism from the community of origin, is more severe for members of ethnic, racial, religious, and sexual minorities (Brown 2012). The barriers to seeking legal and social help also develop from individuals' commitment to cultural norms and values. For example, a Latina woman may feel bound to cultural values such as *familismo* (family loyalty, solidarity, and cohesion), *machismo* (masculine ideals of superiority, strength, duty, honor, and respect) and *marianismo* (feminine ideals of subservience, submissiveness, nurturance, and purity) (Edelson, Hokoda, and Ramos-Lira 2007; Vidales 2010).

Alternatively, barriers may stem from the fear that pressing charges will validate existing stereotypes and bring shame to the community, or from collective distrust of the police and the courts (Anderson and Aviles 2006). For example, African American women may be reluctant to become involved with a criminal justice system that has participated in the reproduction of racism and failed to protect black communities (Goodman and Epstein 2008). Nikki's story below also shows that poverty and geographic location restrict women's ability to leave abusive relationships and survive on their own (Kasturirangan, Krishnan, and Riger 2004).

In group therapy, Nikki, a young single mother, spoke about the economic and physical barriers she faced during her marriage, after she moved out to a rural area with her husband and small children. Instead of things getting better, as he had promised, their relationship—and the abuse—got progressively worse. Nikki and her children were now geographically isolated and miles away from the nearest neighbor. Nikki's abuser quickly befriended members of their small community, making it impossible for Nikki to turn to others, including the local police, for help and protection. Nikki's abuser would often leave her and the children for days on end, with no access to transportation, a phone, money, or even food.

Religion and spirituality represent a source of both resiliency and vulnerability (Potter 2007). Some battered women turn to members of their religious community for assistance, whereas others hide the abuse due to lack of support in the congregation or because of conflict with religious beliefs (Barnett 2001). In group therapy, Paula, a Christian woman, stated that divorce was against her religion. She feared ostracism if she disclosed the abuse she was experiencing in her marriage. A member of her church whom she had approached about the issue discouraged her from leaving her husband and from filing for divorce, instead recommending that Paula attend religious counseling services with her spouse.

Immigrant women face help-seeking barriers that make them particularly vulnerable to gender-based violence (Erez and Hartley 2003): racism, stigma, fear of deportation and separation from their children, and lack of familiarity with the legal and social system of a foreign country (Kasturirangan, Krishnan, and Riger 2004). In most cases, immigrant women in abusive relationships live far away from extended family members. They are socially isolated, may not speak English, and thus may not be able to reach out to others for support. In addition, services may not be available in their native language. They experience stressors associated with resettlement and acculturation, including difficulty with employment, which compels them to rely on their spouse economically and psychologically. Cultural norms may also dictate how they respond to domestic violence. Others in their cultural community may encourage them to hide the abuse and resolve interpersonal conflict without legal interventions (Erez and Hartley 2003).

Maria, a Haitian woman, married a Haitian preacher who promised he would help her apply for a green card. The abuse started and Maria's husband withheld important information about her application for immigration status. The abuse escalated, and Maria became so terrified that she chose to leave the relationship and face the risk of deportation. Her husband contacted immigration services, and Maria was arrested and sent to a detention center. Fortunately, she was able to contact an attorney and used the Violence Against Women Act (VAWA) to petition for legal status. With the help of a psychologist who testified on her behalf, she successfully obtained a divorce and U.S. citizenship.

Unlike Maria, however, many immigrant women struggle to understand and navigate the intricacies of the U.S. legal system. They are unaware of the legal mechanisms they can use against abusive partners who threaten to report them to Immigration and Customs Enforcement (ICE), to withdraw immigration petitions, and to have them deported and lose custody of their children (Erez, Adelman, and Gregory 2009). These threats are a form of coercive control that forces immigrant women to suffer in silence and to comply with the demands of the abuser (Erez, Adelman, and Gregory 2009).

Homophobia and gender stereotyping intensify the harm victims experience in abusive same-sex relationships (Mallicoat 2012). The view that lesbian, gay, bisexual, transgender, or queer (LGBTQ) individuals are "unnatural, deviant, a threat to the status quo of existing gender relations in families and societies" (Hassouneh and Glass 2008, 311) makes it difficult to detect abuse in same-sex relationships. It also supports restricted access to social and legal support for sexual and gender-nonconforming minorities. A qualitative study of female same-sex intimate partner violence (FSSIPV) (Hassouneh and Glass 2008) highlighted the difficulty of identifying domestic violence in same-sex relationships based on a heteronormative view of violence. It also found that gender stereotypes—in particular the belief that women are inherently nonviolent—shapes our perceptions of female same-sex violence as less serious than heterosexual violence. Victims of FSSIPV may not call the police because they are worried their abusive partners will manipulate the responding officers into thinking they are the victim and not the aggressor. The police often use gender stereotypes to determine who the offender is: Their decision is based on their perception of the partners' emotionality, passivity, size, strength, and masculine presentation (Breci 2014; Hardesty et al. 2011).

How Battered Women Come in Contact with the Legal System

As providers of mental health services in a domestic violence shelter, we have worked with many battered women who were involved in various legal settings simultaneously, including civil, family, dependency, and criminal courts. These women attended the weekly support group we facilitated and talked about the stress they experienced as a result of continued contact with their abuser in multiple arenas of the justice system. For example, Sarah, a young mother, described the emotional, psychological, physical, and economic costs of participating in criminal proceedings against her abusive spouse, who had been arrested and who was facing deportation on criminal grounds because he was not a U.S. citizen. Sarah explained that her abuser's family attended every hearing and pleaded with her to not testify against him. They also were petitioning for custody of her one-year-old son, claiming that Sarah was an "unfit mother." In addition, Sarah was in the process of filing for divorce, and could not afford an attorney. In our support group, she discussed the difficulty of navigating the civil court system on her own.

Prior to her court appearances, Sarah felt extremely anxious, and had trouble sleeping and eating. Seeing her abuser on the stand elicited trauma symptoms such as flashbacks. Following her court appearances, she became severely depressed and had trouble getting out of bed. She described the extensive arrangements that were necessary for her to appear in court: taking time off work, arranging childcare for her one-year-old son, and finding transportation to the courthouse. She described her legal experience as "never-ending," and despite the strength it took for her to continue with the proceedings, she stated that she felt "disempowered and weak" every time she left the courtroom. At times Sarah would be so distressed that she was unable to attend a hearing. And even when she did go to court, she often could not understand what the judge was asking her. Sarah told her therapist that the judge and her lawyer were frustrated with her and that she was facing contempt charges.

Sarah's story illustrates the complexity of battered women's interactions with the justice system, beginning with the arrest of the perpetrator and continuing with the woman's participation in criminal proceedings as a witness against the domestic violence offender (Hartley 2003). Concurrently, women may come in contact with civil or family courts when they file for divorce or a civil order of protection (Heise 2011) and in cases of child custody and visitation (Saunders, Faller, and Tolman 2011). They may also be charged with failure to protect their child(ren) and therefore have to fight against the termination of their parental rights in dependency courts (Lemon 1999). In the criminal justice system, battered women who have retaliated against their abuser in response to prolonged and severe abuse may face criminal charges for domestic violence or even homicide. They may also become involved in criminal proceedings as codefendants if they participated in criminal activities with their abusive partner (Welle and Falkin 2000). Abuse and trauma increase the likelihood that they will falsely assume responsibility for a crime they did not commit for fear of reprisal, or because they wish to protect the abuser (Grabner et al. 2014; Conte, Grabner, and Walker 2015). For example, Carmen falsely confessed to abusing her three-year-old child, Julio, and told the police what her batterer asked her to say because she was afraid of further harm. She covered up for the perpetrator, believing the police would establish that it was he and not she who had killed her child. However, both Carmen and the batterer were charged with homicide.

Battered women who commit crimes under the coercive influence of an abusive partner become entrapped in what has been called a "romantic codefendant" relationship that makes them vulnerable to both personal and legal punishment, as they are "dually policed" by both the abuser and law enforcement personnel (Welle and Falkin 2000). Their restricted access to economic resources and their financial dependence on the abuser are key factors that account for their continued participation in criminal activities, including drug offenses and prostitution (Gilfus 2002; Mallicoat and Ireland 2014; Richie 1996). In most cases, it is the abusive partner who introduces the victim to drugs and provides her with substances that will feed and maintain her addiction and dependence on the batterer (Bennet 1998) before coercing her into prostitution to support the substance use (Farley 2003). Lynch and colleagues (2012) found that women with domestic violence histories were nearly four times as likely to engage in commercial sex work and twice as likely to engage in drug crimes compared to other incarcerated women. Drug use and prostitution represent battered women's efforts to survive their abuse; however, because they are also defined as criminal offenses, they increase battered women's risk of being further involved in the criminal justice system (Chesney-Lind and Pasko 2013).

The Legal Framework of Domestic Violence: Justice Responses and Unintended Consequences

Historically, men's violence towards their spouse was socially sanctioned, and women's access to legal protection severely restricted (Edwards 1996; Schechter 1982), making them vulnerable to various forms of domestic abuse (World Health Organization 2009; California Council on Gender 2013). Feminist activism in the United States has helped to reframe domestic violence as a social and public concern, rather than a private issue (Mallicoat 2012). In the 1980s, the Battered Women's Movement raised public awareness of gender-based violence and was critical in bringing about social, legal, and political reforms (Schechter 1982; Walker 2006). Battered women's shelters were created to provide refuge and protect both women and their children from further violence (Walker 2002). Until the 1970s, intimate partner abuse was not perceived as a criminal matter, and in the absence of significant injury, legal intervention was not deemed necessary (Erez 2002). To address police inaction on calls of domestic violence, mandatory arrest, pro-arrest, and preferred arrest laws were adopted (American Bar Association 2010; Han 2003; Hirschel et al. 2007; Sherman and Berk 1984). Mandatory arrest laws were intended to ensure that police would systematically respond to domestic violence calls (Miller and Meloy 2006), while preferred and pro-arrest laws allowed greater police discretion (Hirschel et al. 2007). In 1994, a year after the United Nations (1993) declared violence against women a human rights violation, Congress passed the Violence Against Women Act (VAWA) to "remedy the legacy of laws and social norms that serve to justify violence against women" (U.S. Department of Justice 2011). The reauthorization of VAWA in 2000 and again in 2005 strengthened the provisions of the original act, offering battered women increased protections and access to resources (U.S. Department of Justice 2011).

The social and legal reforms of the 1970s, 1980s, and 1990s have resulted in the criminalization of domestic violence and the development of new justice practices that have been criticized for being counterproductive and unduly traumatizing to victims (Hoyle and Sanders 2000). The legal system has been described as "biased, unsupportive, and underfunded," and personnel are often not trained to identify how domestic violence intersects with other forms of oppression and inequality (Barnett 2000; Hart 1996; Huisman, Martinez, and Wilson 2005). The system is fraught with many barriers that can make battered women feel unprotected and that can lower their motivation to engage in legal proceedings. When survivors pursue legal action, they often experience victim blaming, confusion, and conflict in ways that reduce their ability to seek help. In addition, the lack of support they receive from the justice system can delay or even prevent their healing from abuse and trauma.

Mandatory arrest laws, in particular, have produced adverse consequences for victims of domestic violence (Miller and Meloy 2006). Dual arrest is a probability when the police have difficulty differentiating between the perpetrator and the victim. One study showed that dual arrest occurs in approximately 2 percent of all domestic violence incidents and that the dual arrest rate is nearly twice as high when domestic violence arrests are mandated rather than preferred or discretionary (Hirschel et al. 2007).

Battered women who fight back in self-defense may also be wrongfully identified as the primary aggressor and arrested. The following story provides an example. Casey was a young mother with three children under the age of six. She was living in a low-rent apartment, barely making enough money to pay for daycare. She had left her children's father, Victor, but the latter kept harassing her, coming to the apartment to see the children—or so he said. He would show up unannounced, cause trouble, and use physical violence; yet, no one intervened, including Casey's landlord and neighbors and the security personnel of the community where she lived, until Casey, for the first time, tried to defend herself. The security guards heard both Casey and Victor scream, and called the police. When the police arrived, Casey appeared agitated and upset. The police determined that Casey had inflicted intentional physical harm on Victor, rather than that she tried to protect herself. Both Casey and Victor were arrested and taken to the police station, and the children placed under the custody of child protective services. Casey pleaded guilty after the judge told her she would go home and get her children back if she did so. Although there was strong evidence that this was a self-defense case, Casey decided not to contest her charges in order to protect her children. Casey now had a criminal record that prevented her from applying for a license to work as a nurse practitioner. In addition, she was mandated to attend a batterer's intervention program.

Like Casey, battered women who are misidentified as the primary aggressor or dually arrested for domestic violence face criminal charges. If they plead guilty to avoid additional time in jail and to return home to their children, they may be required to participate in batterer intervention programs that are often inappropriate, unwarranted, and designed for male abusers (Walker and Shapiro 2003). Once they are labeled as violent offenders, they lose access to protection services and victim assistance (Miller and Meloy 2006) and encounter increased stigmatization and marginalization (Moe 2007). Criminalizing a nonoffending woman who has experienced abuse not only invalidates her status as a survivor and reduces the likelihood that she will seek help from the criminal justice system but also exacerbates her trauma symptoms, in particular feelings of guilt, shame, powerlessness, and vulnerability.

No-drop policies are another form of legal intervention with unintended negative outcomes for the victims of domestic violence. They mandate the prosecution of individuals arrested for battering, whether or not the victim has agreed to press charges. They are designed to reduce attrition in domestic violence cases when victims choose not to participate in criminal prosecution (Corsilles 1994). However, these policies also define victims as noncooperative and draw attention to victims' disposition rather than the systemic barriers that account for their reluctance to engage in legal proceedings (Erez and Belknap 1998).

Legal interventions based on mandatory arrest laws and no-drop policies are intended to promote victim safety; however, they disempower survivors of domestic violence by taking away their ability to make choices (Goodman and Epstein 2008; Mallicoat 2012). They may also increase their vulnerability if, despite the need for legal protection, battered women do not call the police for fear that they will be forced to take legal action against the abuser (Novisky and Peralta 2015). When battered women participate in legal proceedings, they experience other forms of disempowerment, such as the reduction of criminal charges that minimize the severity of the crime and the harm caused to the victim (Hart 1996; Hartley 2003). Interactions between battered women and justice officials, such as prosecutors and judges, often reproduce the dynamics of abusive relationships by challenging women's self-sufficiency and personal control (Hart 1996; Hartley 2003). Battered women who testify against their abusers in court come upon legal restrictions that prevent them from describing the full extent of the abuse (Hartley 2003). They are also the target of victim-blaming tactics—such as questioning a woman on the stand as to why she would stay with an abuser or calling into question her mental health to undermine her credibility (Hart 1996; Barnett 2000).

Multiculturally and Gender-Responsive Strategies for Criminal Justice Interventions

The way survivors of domestic violence experience legal interventions can have a long-lasting impact on their psychological well-being (Barnett 2000). Therapeutic jurisprudence (TJ), which combines legal and psychological principles, provides a framework for maximizing the therapeutic effects of justice programs for victims of domestic violence (Cattaneo and Goodman 2010; Wren 2010). A TJ approach to domestic violence emphasizes access to services to help litigants solve their problems and minimize their continued involvement with the legal system. For example, domestic violence courts, which operate on the principles of therapeutic jurisprudence, ensure the safety and psychological well-being of women and their children while holding DV offenders accountable for their actions. Referral to treatment rather than incarceration is often recommended; however, if DV offenders do not comply, their case is sent back to regular court, or probation is revoked and prison time is ordered. The TJ approach to domestic violence also encourages cultural competence and survivor empowerment when working with diverse women at all stages of the judicial process. This includes culturally appropriate interactions between survivors and justice officials and the promotion of an active and empowering role for survivors during legal proceedings (Erez and Hartley 2003). In sum, the principles of therapeutic jurisprudence support the creation of conditions that make women feel safer when they come forward and seek legal assistance and thus promote positive social and psychological outcomes by taking women's plight seriously and by fostering their sense of power and control over the legal proceedings (Cattaneo and Goodman 2010).

Addressing the needs of diverse battered women prior to their involvement with the criminal justice system is ideal, yet not always realistic. As indicated throughout the chapter, many suffer in silence and come in contact with the criminal justice system as a result of the violence they have experienced. Legal interventions for battered women are often the first line of "treatment," and for this reason it is critical that they take into consideration the psychological, emotional, and physical consequences of abuse. When these are left unaddressed, jails and prisons become revolving doors for victims of domestic violence. The provision of treatment for substance abuse and mental health problems has increased, but the adoption of trauma-informed care in correctional facilities has lagged behind. Although several evidence-based trauma treatment programs are currently available and have been shown to be effective, the wide-scale adoption of these interventions throughout the criminal justice system has yet to be implemented. In the following sections, we discuss the main components of these treatment approaches and describe a strength-based and trauma-focused program that has been implemented with positive outcomes in both the community and correctional facilities in Broward County, Florida.

Trauma-Informed Treatment Approaches

The Substance Abuse and Mental Health Services Administration (2015) recommends the implementation of trauma-informed care for women with a history of abuse and with co-occurring substance-related and mental disorders. Principles of trauma-informed care include safety, trustworthiness, transparency, peer support, collaboration, mutuality, and empowerment (SAMHSA 2015). Effective treatment approaches are comprehensive and multidisciplinary, and address both the mental health consequences of domestic violence and the structural barriers that prevent escape from abuse. Battered women should be informed of the resources available to them in the community, such as safe housing and victim advocacy services. The provision of viable community resources is necessary so that women have options other than returning to the home of the abuser. Mental health interventions should be evidence-based, trauma-informed, sensitive to gender and cultural diversity, and based on principles of empowerment. To provide effective treatment, gender-sensitive and culturally competent training as well as interdisciplinary collaboration are critical and should include victim advocates, justice personnel, and mental health practitioners.

The Survivor Therapy Empowerment Program (STEP)

The Survivor Therapy Empowerment Program (STEP) is an evidence-based treatment model based on the principles of Survivor Therapy. Survivor Therapy is a strength-based and trauma-informed treatment approach to victims of domestic violence that is guided by feminist principles (Walker 2002). The overarching goal of Survivor Therapy is "re-empowerment"; it is achieved by (1) ensuring safety; (2) helping women explore alternatives to abuse; (3) validating their thoughts, feelings, and actions; (4) helping them regain cognitive clarity and judgment; (5) promoting personal decision-making abilities; (6) helping them heal from the effects of trauma; (7) helping them reestablish a sense of boundaries; (8) helping them develop supportive interpersonal relationships; (9) fostering an understanding of the broader sociocultural bases of oppression; and (10) modeling an egalitarian relationship in which both therapist and client work together to formulate and implement goals (Walker 2002).

STEP can be used as an individual or group intervention with women and girls in the community and in custody (Walker 2009). The program consists of twelve steps, and each two-hour session is divided into three parts: The first part involves a discussion of different trauma-related topics; it is followed by an examination of how the information applies to the personal experience of group members; lastly, women participate in skill-training exercises to practice and strengthen the tools they have gained during the psychoeducational part of the meeting.

The topics discussed in each session are defining gender violence; identifying physical, sexual, and psychological abuse; assertiveness training and relaxation therapy; clarifying cognitive confusion; regulating emotions; understanding the role of trauma triggers and learning to cope with PTSD symptoms; the impact of domestic violence on children and the introduction of positive parenting skills; letting go of old relationships and beginning new, positive, nonviolent relationships; and dealing with legal issues. Women receive information about the cycle of violence, learn to name the abuse, and develop assertiveness and relaxation skills. They also learn to separate thoughts, feelings, and actions, and to recognize what makes true friendships and intimacy. Women explore issues related to cultural diversity, substance abuse, and sexuality, together and openly. The facilitators are careful not to push women to talk before they are ready; they also monitor how discussion time is shared among group members.

The STEP program has been implemented in a battered women's shelter and several jails in Broward County, Florida. Quantitative data collected before and after each session provided evidence that women who participated in more sessions experienced lower levels of anxiety and better overall functioning (Groth et al. 2014). Qualitative data collected at the end of each session indicated that women enjoyed their participation in the group, left the sessions feeling supported and empowered, and viewed the program as instrumental to their healing and recovery.

As funding for justice and mental health programs has become increasingly scarce, it is necessary to identify cost-effective ways to support battered women both in the community and in the criminal justice system. The STEP program was developed, implemented, and evaluated with the resources of a major local university. At this university, students in the medical residency, forensic psychology, and mental health counseling programs provide trauma-informed multimodal services under the supervision of the faculty, in the local jails, in a battered women's shelter, and in the general community. Thanks to interdisciplinary collaboration, they have served hundreds of women and children who have survived domestic violence. In times of limited financial resources, it is possible to do more with less, when interprofessional networks are formed and maintained.

Conclusion and Recommendations

Battered women become involved in multiple arenas of the justice system as a direct or indirect result of domestic violence. The intersection of gender, race, ethnicity, class, sexual orientation, and socioeconomic status influences all aspects of their interactions with law enforcement and court officials, and creates unique barriers that account for many women's reluctance to pursue charges and seek help. Instead of receiving support, victims of domestic violence are often criminalized or stigmatized. Legal interventions and interactions further traumatize and disempower survivors of domestic violence.

The American Psychological Association (APA) has proposed a set of guidelines for mental health practitioners, to enhance gender and cultural sensitivity and address the specific treatment needs of women (2007). In line with feminist principles, APA highlights the importance of viewing the issues faced by women within a sociopolitical context and addressing the systemic and institutional biases within society that discourage women's initiative and empowerment. Practitioners must recognize how bias, oppression, and discrimination negatively impact the mental and physical health of women and how sex-role socialization reinforces power differentials. Interventions must be culturally sensitive, gender responsive, and evidence based; take into consideration women's intersecting identities; and promote self-sufficiency, recovery, and empowerment. APA emphasizes the role of trauma and other stressors faced by women in society and acknowledges the need for trauma-informed treatment strategies to address the unique experiences of women. For these strategies to be effective in both community and justice settings, it is essential that they adhere to the following recommendations.

Recommendation #1: Ensure physical and psychological safety.

In order to provide a therapeutic atmosphere that promotes psychological growth and healing, it is essential to first ensure the physical safety of each woman who has been abused. Physical safety can be ensured through the use of safety planning, collaboration with community agencies that provide victim advocacy or safe housing, or referrals to medical or legal professionals. Once physical safety is ensured, mental health providers should demonstrate hope, empathy, and positive regard, and develop an egalitarian relationship with each survivor in order to support psychological healing and maximize psychotherapeutic benefits.

Recommendation #2: Programs must acknowledge gender-specific issues and women's intersecting identities.

It is important for treatment programs to address the gender-based impact of violence along with the social, cultural, racial, and sexual biases that shape women's experiences. In order to provide validation and normalization, the unique experiences of each woman must be acknowledged and used to inform treatment approaches. In addition, it is necessary for society to recognize the systemic and institutional biases that prevent diverse women from seeking help within the mental health and legal arenas. Not only must services be culturally sensitive and gender responsive; there must be increased access to such services for women from marginalized and disadvantaged groups.

Recommendation #3: Treatment should be trauma-informed and promote traumatic healing.

Treatment programs must facilitate trauma processing in order to validate trauma reactions and address the cognitive, affective, and behavioral responses to traumatic experiences. For example, the trauma-processing component of the STEP program is augmented with skill building, which includes the introduction of techniques (e.g. cognitive restructuring, emotion reregulation, relaxation training) designed to facilitate adaptive coping skills and promote traumatic healing. Additionally, psychoeducation is utilized throughout STEP to provide women with insight into various types of abuse, in addition to normalizing the emotional, psychological, and behavioral manifestations of posttraumatic reactions.

Recommendation #4: Treatment should be strength-based and emphasize women's empowerment.

A survivor-focused approach, which emphasizes the woman's strengths and adaptive abilities, is necessary to promote empowerment and allow each woman to regain a sense of control over her life. Existing positive coping strategies should be accentuated and new coping skills should be introduced that allow the woman to overcome current obstacles within the various domains of her life with the goal to live a violence-free life.

Recommendation #5: Address the complex pathways of trauma through the provision of comprehensive mental health services.

Treatment should address the complexity of issues faced by survivors of domestic violence. Co-occurring issues such as substance abuse, the impact of abuse on parenting and children, mental health concerns, legal involvement, and the need for social services should be addressed and integrated into treatment according to the needs of the women seeking services.

Although these recommendations encompass the main tenets of trauma-informed treatment for survivors of domestic violence, it is important to remember that no two women are alike and that strategies may need to be adapted to address the unique experiences of each survivor. Furthermore, the pathways to healing are complex and go beyond the alleviation of PTSD and BWS; survivors may need additional assistance in overcoming barriers and rebuilding resiliency, self-sufficiency, and a sense of physical, psychological, and emotional well-being.

NOTE

1 Justice officials tend to refer to women who have experienced domestic violence as "victims," advocates prefer the term "survivor," and mental health professionals use the term "survivor" to describe women who were formerly victimized by a domestic partner but have made changes to protect themselves. One woman explained to us that her view of herself as a victim transitioned to that of a survivor after she left her abusive relationship and sought safety at a battered woman's shelter. Throughout this chapter, the terms "victim" and "survivor" are used interchangeably, although it is important to note that these labels have different meanings for different women.

REFERENCES

American Bar Association. 2010. "Domestic Violence Arrest Policies by State." American Bar Association Commission on Domestic Violence, http://www.americanbar.org.

American Psychological Association. 2007. "Guidelines for Psychological Practice with Girls and Women." *American Psychologist* 62 (9): 949–79. doi: 10.1037/0003-066X.62.9.949.

Amnesty International. 1975. *Amnesty International Report on Torture*. New York: Farrar, Straus, Giroux.

Anderson, Kristin L. 2015. "Victims' Voices and Victims' Choices in Three IPV Courts." *Violence Against Women* 21 (1): 105–24. doi: 10.1177/1077801214564166.

Anderson, Tanya R., and Ann M. Aviles. 2006. "Diverse Faces of Domestic Violence." *ABNF Journal* 17 (4): 129–32, http://people.umass.edu.

Barnett, Ola W. 2001. "Why Battered Women Do Not Leave, Part 2: External Inhibiting Factors—Social Support and Internal Inhibiting Factors." *Trauma, Violence, and Abuse* 2 (1): 3–35. doi: 10.1177/1524838001002001001.

Barnett, Ola W. 2000. "Why Battered Women Do Not Leave, Part 1: External Inhibiting Factors within Society." *Trauma, Violence, and Abuse* 1 (4): 343–71. doi: 10.1177/1524838000001004003.

Bennet, Larry W. 1998. *Substance Abuse and Woman Abuse by Male Partners*. Harrisburg, PA: VAWnet, a project of the National Resource Center on Domestic Violence/Pennsylvania. http://www.vawnet.org.

Bloom, Barbara, Barbara Owen, and Stephanie Covington. 2004. "Women Offenders and the Gendered Effects of Public Policy." *Review of Policy Research* 21 (1): 31–48. doi: 10.1111/j.1541-1338.2004.00056.x.

Bograd, Michele. 1999. "Strengthening Domestic Violence Theories: Intersections of Race, Class, Sexual Orientation, and Gender." *Journal of Marital and Family Therapy* 25 (3): 275–89. doi: 10.1111/j.1752-0606.1999.tb00248.x.

Breci, Michael G. 2014. "Police Response to Domestic Violence." In *Crisis Interventions in Criminal Justice/ Social Service*, 5th ed. Edited by James E. Hendricks and Cindy S. Hendricks, 129–65. Springfield, IL: Charles C. Thomas.

Brown, Geneva. 2012. "Ain't I a Victim? The Intersectionality of Race, Class, and Gender in Domestic Violence and the Courtroom." *Cardozo Journal of Law and Gender* 19: 147–83.

California Council on Gender. 2013. "Challenging Restrictive Gender Norms: A Key to Decreasing Partner Violence in at-Risk Communities." Report sponsored by True Child, Washington, DC, http://truechild.org.

Campbell, Jacquelyn C., and David Boyd. 2003. "Violence against Women: Synthesis of Research for Health Care Professionals." U.S. Department of Justice, NCJ 199761, https://www.ncjrs.gov.

Catalano, Shannon, Erica Smith, Howard Snyder, and Michael Rand. 2009. "Female Victims of Violence." NCJ 228356. Washington, DC: Bureau of Justice Statistics, http://www.bjs.gov.

Cattaneo, Lauren B., and Lisa A. Goodman. 2010. "Through the Lens of Therapeutic Jurisprudence: The Relationship between Empowerment in the Court System and Well-Being for Intimate Partner Violence." *Journal of Interpersonal Violence* 25 (3): 481–502. doi: 10.1177/0886260509334282.

Centers for Disease Control and Prevention. 2014. "Intimate Partner Violence: Definitions." Centers for Disease Control and Prevention, Injury Prevention and Control: Division of Violence Prevention, http://www.cdc.gov.

Chesney-Lind, Meda, and Lisa Pasko. 2013. *The Female Offender: Girls, Women, and Crime*, 3rd ed. Thousand Oaks, CA: Sage.

Coker, Ann L., Keith E. Davis, Ileana Arias, Sujata Desai, Maureen Sanderson, Heather M. Brandt, and Paige H. Smith. 2002. "Physical and Mental Health Effects of Intimate Partner Violence for Men and Women." *American Journal of Preventive Medicine* 23 (4): 260–68.

Conte, Carlye B., Stephen S. Grabner, and Lenore E. A. Walker. 2015. "The Inadmissibility of Expert Witness Testimony in Female False Confession Cases." Poster presented at the Annual Meeting of the American Psychology-Law Society, San Diego, CA.

Corsilles, Angela. 1994. "No-Drop Policies in the Prosecution of Domestic Violence Cases: Guarantee to Action or Dangerous Solution?" *Fordham Law Review* 63 (3): 854–81.

Crenshaw, Kimberle. 1991. "Mapping the Margins: Intersectionality, Identity Politics, and Violence against Women of Color." *Stanford Law Review* 43 (6): 1241–1300.

DeHart, Dana, Shannon Lynch, Joanne Belknap, Priscilla Dass-Brailsford, and Bonnie Green. 2014. "Life History Models of Female Offending: The Roles of Serious Mental Illness and Trauma in Women's Pathways to Jail." *Psychology of Women Quarterly* 38 (1): 138–51. doi: 10.1177/0361684313494357.

Dillon, Gina, Rafat Hussain, Deborah Loxton, and Saifur Rahman. 2013. "Mental and Physical Health and Intimate Partner Violence against Women: A Review of the Literature." *International Journal of Family Medicine* 13: 1–15. doi: 10.1155/2013/313909.

Edelson, Meredyth G., Audrey Hokoda, and Luciana Ramos-Lira. 2007. "Differences in Effects of Domestic Violence between Latina and Non-Latina Women." *Journal of Family Violence* 22 (1): 1–10. doi: 10.1007/s10896-006-9051-1.

Edwards, Susan M. 1996. *Sex and Gender in the Legal Process*. London: Blackstone.

Erez, Edna. 2002. "Domestic Violence and the Criminal Justice System: An Overview." *Online Journal of Issues in Nursing* 7 (1), http://www.nursingworld.org.

Erez, Edna, Madelaine Adelman, and Carol Gregory. 2009. "Intersections of Immigration and Domestic Violence: Voices of Battered Immigrant Women." *Feminist Criminology* 4 (1): 32–56. doi: 10.1177/1557085108325413.

Erez, Edna, and Joanne Belknap. 1998. "Battered Women and the Criminal Justice System: The Service Providers' Perspective." *European Journal on Criminal Policy and Research* 6 (1): 37–57.

Erez, Edna, and Carolyn C. Hartley. 2003. "Battered Immigrant Women and the Legal System: A Therapeutic Jurisprudence Perspective." *Western Criminology Review* 4 (2): 155–69.

Farley, Melissa. 2003. *Prostitution, Trafficking, and Traumatic Stress*. New York: Routledge.

Gilfus, Mary E. 2002. "Women's Experiences of Abuse as a Risk Factor for Incarceration." VAWnet, a project of the National Resource Center on Domestic Violence/ Pennsylvania Coalition Against Domestic Violence, http://www.vawnet.org.

Gilfus, Mary E. 1993. "From Victims to Survivors to Offenders: Women's Routes of Entry and Immersion into Street Crime." *Women and Criminal Justice* 4 (1): 63–89.

Golding, Jacqueline M. 1999. "Intimate Partner Violence as a Risk Factor for Mental Disorders: A Meta-Analysis." *Journal of Family Violence* 14: 99–132. doi: 10.1023/A:1022079418229.

Goodman, Lisa A., and Deborah Epstein, eds. 2008. "The Justice System Response." In *Listening to Battered Women: A Survivor-Centered Approach to Advocacy, Mental Health, and Justice*. Edited by Lias Goodman and Deborah Epstein, 71–87. Washington, DC: American Psychological Association.

Grabner, Stephen S., Carlye B. Conte, Cassandra M. Groth, Hunter Astor, Tatiana Hylton, and Lenore E. A. Walker. 2014. "False Confessions by Women with Histories of Trauma and Abuse." Poster presented at the Annual Meeting of the American Psychological Association, Washington, DC.

Green, Bonnie L., Jeanne Miranda, Anahita Daroowalla, and Juned Siddique. 2005. "Trauma Exposure, Mental Health Functioning, and Program Needs of Women in Jail." *Crime and Delinquency* 51 (1): 133–51. doi: 10.1177/0011128704267477.

Groth, Cassandra M., Carlye B. Conte, Catherine S. O'Neil, Lenore E. A. Walker, Ryan A. Black, and Tara S. Jungersen. 2014. "Empirically Supported Trauma Intervention in a Jail Setting." Poster presented at the Annual Meeting of the American Psychological Association, Washington, DC.

Han, Erin L. 2003. "Mandatory Arrest and No-Drop Policies: Victim Empowerment in Domestic Violence Cases." *Boston College Third World Law Journal* 23 (1): 159–91.

Hardesty, Jennifer L., Ramona F. Oswald, Lyndal Khaw, and Carol Fonseca. 2011. "Lesbian/Bisexual Mothers and Intimate Partner Violence: Help Seeking in the Context of Social and Legal Vulnerability." *Violence Against Women* 17 (1): 28–46. doi: 10.1177/1077801209347636.

Harlow, Caroline W. 1999. "Prior Abuse Reported by Inmates and Probationers, NCJ 172879." Washington, DC: Bureau of Justice Statistics, http://www.bjs.gov.

Hart, Barbara J. 1996. "Battered Women and the Criminal Justice System." In *Do Arrests and Restraining Orders Work?* Edited by Eve S. Buzawa and Carl G. Buzawa, 98–114. Thousand Oaks, CA: Sage.

Hartley, Carolyn C. 2003. "A Therapeutic Jurisprudence Approach to the Trial Process in Domestic Violence Felony Trials." *Violence Against Women* 9 (4): 410–37. doi: 10.1177/1077801202250954.

Hassouneh, Dena, and Nancy Glass. 2008. "The Influence of Gender Role Stereotyping on Women's Experiences of Female Same-Sex Intimate Partner Violence." *Violence Against Women* 14 (3): 310–25. doi: 10.1177/1077801207313734.

Heise, Lori. 2011. "What Works to Prevent Partner Violence? An Evidence Overview." Working Paper, London: Department for International Development, http://www.oecd.org.

Hirschel, David, Eve Buzawa, April Pattavina, and Don Faggiani. 2007. "Dual Arrest Laws: To What Extent Do They Influence Police Arrest Decisions." *Journal of Criminal Law and Criminology* 98 (1): 255–98.

Hoyle, Carolyn, and Andrew Sanders. 2000. "Police Response to Domestic Violence: From Victim Choice to Victim Empowerment?" *British Journal of Criminology* 40 (1): 14–36.

Huisman, Kimberly, Jeri Martinez, and Cathleen Wilson. 2005. "Training Police Officers on Domestic Violence and Racism: Challenges and Strategies." *Violence Against Women* 11 (6): 792–821. doi: 10.1177/1077801205276110.

James, Doris J., and Lauren E. Glaze. 2006. "Mental Health Problems of Prison and Jail Inmates." Washington, DC: Bureau of Justice Statistics, http://www.bjs.gov.

Jones, Loring, Margaret Hughes, and Ulrike Unterstaller. 2001. "Post-Traumatic Stress Disorder (PTSD) in Victims of Domestic Violence A Review of the Research." *Trauma, Violence, and Abuse* 2 (2): 99–119. doi: 10.1177/1524838001002002001.

Kasturirangan, Aarati, Sandhya Krishnan, and Stephanie Riger. 2004. "The Impact of Culture and Minority Status on Women's Experience of Domestic Violence." *Trauma, Violence, and Abuse* 5 (4): 318–32. doi: 10.1177/1524838004269487.

Lemon, Nancy K. D. 1999. "The Legal System's Response to Children Exposed to Domestic Violence." *Future of Children* 9 (3): 67–83.

Lynch, Shannon M., Dana D. DeHart, Joanne E. Belknap, Bonnie L. Green, Priscilla Dass-Brailsford, Kristine A. Johnson, and Elizabeth Whalley. 2012. "A Multisite Study of the Prevalence of Serious Mental Illness, PTSD, and Substance Use Disorders of Women in Jail." National Center on Domestic and Sexual Violence. doi: 10.1176/appi.ps.201300172.

Mallicoat, Stacy L. 2012. *Women and Crime: A Text/Reader.* Thousand Oaks, CA: Sage.

Mallicoat, Stacy L., and Connie E. Ireland. 2014. *Women and Crime: The Essentials.* Thousand Oaks, CA: Sage.

Miller, Susan L., and Michelle L. Meloy. 2006. "Women's Use of Force: Voices of Women Arrested for Domestic Violence." *Violence Against Women* 12 (1): 89–115.

Moe, Angela M. 2007. "Silenced Voices and Structured Survival: Battered Women's Help Seeking." *Violence Against Women* 13 (7): 676–99. doi: 10.1177/1077801207302041.

Nathanson, Alison M., Ryan C. Shorey, Vanessa Tirone, and Deborah L. Rhatigan. 2012. "The Prevalence of Mental Health Disorders in a Community Sample of Female Victims of Intimate Partner Violence." *Partner Abuse* 3 (1): 59–75. doi: 10.1891/1946-6560.3.1.59, http://www.vawnet.org.

Novisky, Meghan A., and Robert L. Peralta. 2015. "When Women Tell: Intimate Partner Violence and the Factors Related to Police Notification." *Violence Against Women* 21 (1): 65–86. doi: 10.1177/1077801214564078.

Platt, Melissa, Jocelyn Barton, and Jennifer J. Freyd. 2009. "A Betrayal Trauma Perspective on Domestic Violence." In *Violence Against Women in Families and Relationships*. Edited by Evan Stark and Eve S. Buzawa, 185–207. Westport, CT: Greenwood.

Potter, Hillary. 2007. "Battered Black Women's Use of Religious Services and Spirituality for Assistance in Leaving Abusive Relationships." *Violence Against Women* 13 (3): 262–84. doi: 10.1177/1077801206297438.

Richie, Beth E. 1996. *Compelled to Crime: The Gender Entrapment of Battered Black Women*. New York: Routledge.

Saunders, Daniel G., Kathleen Coulborn Faller, and Richard M. Tolman. 2011. "Child Custody Evaluators' Beliefs about Domestic Abuse Allegations: Their Relationship to Evaluator Demographics, Background, Domestic Violence Knowledge, and Custody-Visitation Recommendations." Washington, DC: National Institute of Justice, https://www.ncjrs.gov.

Schechter, Susan. 1982. *Women and Male Violence: The Visions and Struggles of the Battered Women's Movement*. Boston: South End.

Sherman, Lawrence W., and Richard A. Berk. 1984. "The Minneapolis Domestic Violence Experiment." Washington, DC: Police Foundation.

Shipway, Lyn. 2004. *Domestic Violence: A Handbook for Health Care Professionals*. New York: Routledge.

Stark, Evan, and Anne Flitcraft. 1996. *Women at Risk: Domestic Violence and Women's Health*. Thousand Oaks, CA: Sage.

Substance Abuse and Mental Health Services Administration (SAMHSA). 2015. "Trauma-Informed Approach and Trauma-Specific Interventions." *National Center for Trauma-Informed Care,* http://www.samhsa.gov.

Tjaden, Patricia, and Nancy Thoennes. 2000. "Extent, Nature, and Consequences of Intimate Partner Violence: Findings from the National Violence against Women Survey." NCJ181867. Washington, DC: National Institute of Justice, https://www.ncjrs.gov.

Truman, Jenifer L., and Rachel E. Morgan. 2014. "Nonfatal Domestic Violence, 2003–2012." NCJ244697. Washington, DC: Bureau of Justice Statistics, http://www.bjs.gov.

United Nations. 1993. "Declaration on the Elimination of Violence against Women." Resolution adopted by the General Assembly, 1993.

U.S. Department of Justice. 2011. Violence Against Women Act. Office on Violence Against Women, http://www.justice.gov.

Vidales, Guadalupe T. 2010. "Arrested Justice: The Multifaceted Plight of Immigrant Latinas Who Faced Domestic Violence." *Journal of Family Violence* 25 (6): 533–44. doi: 10.1007/s10896-010-9309-5.

Walker, Lenore E. A. 2009. *The Battered Woman Syndrome.* New York: Springer.

Walker, Lenore E. A. 2006. "Battered Woman Syndrome: Empirical Findings." *Annals of the New York Academy of Sciences* 1087: 142–57. doi: 10.1196/annals.1385.023.

Walker, Lenore E. A. 2002. "Politics, Psychology, and the Battered Woman's Movement." *Journal of Trauma Practice* 1 (1): 81–102. doi: 10.1300/J189v01n01_05.

Walker, Lenore E. A. 1984. *The Battered Woman Syndrome.* New York: Springer.

Walker, Lenore E. A. 1979. *The Battered Woman.* New York: Harper and Row.

Walker, Lenore E. A., and David L. Shapiro. 2003. *Introduction to Forensic Psychology: Clinical and Social Psychological Perspective.* New York: Kluwer Academic/Plenum.

Welle, Dorinda, and Gregory Falkin. 2000. "The Everyday Policing of Women with Romantic Codefendants: An Ethnographic Perspective." *Women and Criminal Justice* 11 (2): 45–65. doi: 10.1300/J012v11n02_03.

Williamson, Emma. 2010. "Living in the World of the Domestic Violence Perpetrator: Negotiating the Unreality of Coercive Control." *Violence Against Women* 16 (12): 1412–23. doi: 10.1177/1077801210389162.

World Health Organization. 2009. "Promoting Gender Equality to Prevent Violence against Women." Series of Briefings on Violence Prevention. Geneva: WHO Press, http://www.who.int.

World Health Organization. 2005. *WHO Multi-Country Study on Women's Health and Domestic Violence against Women: Summary Report of Initial Results on Prevalence, Health Outcomes, and Women's Responses.* Geneva: WHO, http://www.who.int.

Wren, Ginger Lerner. 2010. "Mental Health Courts: Serving Justice and Promoting Recovery." *Annals of Health Law* 19 (3): 577–93.

3

Women, Sex Trafficking, and the Justice System

From Victimization to Restoration

THEMA BRYANT-DAVIS, TYONNA ADAMS, AND ANTHEA GRAY

Maria is a client of the Coalition to Abolish Slavery and Trafficking–Los Angeles (CAST-LA). She is a survivor of sex slavery who was sold at the age of sixteen for two hundred dollars. She was raped, beaten, and tortured by her oppressor, who threatened to kill her and her family if she tried to escape.

Human sex trafficking takes many forms, including war-induced sexual slavery, ritual sexual slavery, forced marriage, and sexual servitude. Sex trafficking victims are persons who are compelled to trade sex by force, fraud, or coercion (see Trafficking Victims Protection Act. P.L. 106–386, codified at 22 U.S.C. § 7101, 2000). Trafficking survivors face multiple barriers that make accessing the judicial system difficult, including fear of violence, lack of awareness of resources, language barriers, fear of deportation, difficulty trusting, prior experience with corrupt government officials, constant monitoring from traffickers, fear of stigma, drug addiction, and pregnancy enforced by traffickers in attempts to control their movement (Rafferty 2008). To obtain services and legal protection, women and girls who have been trafficked often experience revictimization by being forced to disclose traumatic material multiple times in settings that are not emotionally supportive (Contreras and Farley 2011). They are harmed by being treated as criminals instead of victims, and may also be subjected to blaming statements and attitudes by agents of the justice system (Farley 2009).

This chapter will examine how social dynamics related to gender, class, and race shape the U.S. justice system's response to victims of sex trafficking, and will present implications for the clinical care of trafficking survivors, based on a critical review of the literature and the first author's clinical practice. It will focus on sex trafficking in the United States, although this is a global and national phenomenon. It will highlight issues of trust, oppression, and systemic and psychosocial barriers to safety and recovery. It will also propose guidelines for interprofessional collaboration and psycho-education for attorneys, evaluators, and judges concerning mental health issues of trafficking survivors.

An Overview of Sex Trafficking

The language used to identify commercial sex acts is varied and inconsistent. Commonly used terms such as "prostitution," "pornography," and "exotic dancing" refer to for-profit sex acts, while "sex trafficking" applies to sex acts that involve force, fraud, abduction, deception, control, and coercion (United Nations 2000). These are methods used to recruit, harbor, lure, transport, supply, or detain a person for the purpose of commercial sex (U.S. Department of State 2014). Debt bondage is yet another mechanism of subjugation whereby traffickers impose arbitrary fees on victims for things such as transport and housing, and do not permit them to leave the sex trade until they have paid off their "debt" (U.S. Department of State 2014). For these reasons, sex trafficking is a human rights violation (United Nations 2000). Regarding the use of language, it is also important to note that sex trafficking may or may not include transit across international or domestic borders, although the term "trafficking" implies movement (U.S. State Department 2014).

The United States government defines "commercial sex" as any sex act in which something of value is given or received (P.L. 106–386: § (3)). The question then arises as to how to determine whether a sex act is given willingly—consented to—or coerced. An adult might agree to participate in a commercial sex act, but there is truly no voluntary consent if that decision is motivated by any of the previously referenced external factors (e.g., force, fraud, coercion) (Contreras and Bryant-Davis 2011; U.S. Department of State 2014). With regard to children who may appear to willingly engage in commercial sex acts, "consent" is invalidated by the external variables listed above as well as the illegal status of sex acts with a minor (Hughes 2007). As for those who are inextricably born into the sex industry (e.g., individuals born into servitude), they are not in a position to provide consent (U.S. State Department 2014).

Prevalence Rates of Sex Trafficking

Statistics on sex trafficking vary greatly depending on the source (Clawson et al. 2009). This is due to limited pools of data and diverse methodological strategies for data collection. National reporting structures and barriers to disclosure are also factors that explain the dearth of demographic figures and variations in prevalence rates (Curtol et al. 2004; Hughes and Denisova 2001; U.S. Department of State 2014). Additionally, it is difficult to determine the incidence of sex trafficking because it is underreported. Underreporting is linked to (1) the fear of retribution from traffickers and law enforcement agencies (Curtol et al. 2004; Hughes and Denisova 2001), (2) the possible collusion and partnership of exploiters with authorities, who might return the victims to their traffickers (Hodge 2008), and (3) the social stigma commonly associated with commercial sex acts.

In 2013, the U.S. Department of State estimated that 44,758 individuals were trafficked across international borders, 9,460 were prosecuted, and 5,776 were convicted (U.S. Department of State 2014). Almost exclusively, these estimates represent the prevalence of international sex trafficking. National figures are less readily available (Laczko and Gozdziak 2005) and primarily account for the number of minors involved in the sex industry in the United States (U.S. Department of State 2009). According to the National Human Trafficking Resource Center (2014), in 2014 there were 3,598 reports of sexual trafficking—3,250 of which were women. Three of the most sexually trafficked cities were located in California: Los Angeles, San Francisco, and San Diego (U.S. Department of Justice 2009).

Hughes (2008) points out that economically strong, industrialized nations that either (1) permit prostitution or (2) have a preexisting, established sex industry, offer favorable conditions for commercialized sex activities. For example, the United States has the largest child pornography industry in the world (Flowers 2001), which makes the country highly attractive to traffickers. Estes and Weiner (2001) further explain that cities that are densely populated, particularly tourist and convention cities, are popular hubs for sex trafficking. As with any commercial market, the dominant driving force in keeping the commercial sex industry alive is demand for sex workers whom the traffickers supply to consumers (Hughes and Denisova 2001). Consumers of this profitable commerce include brothel owners, pornography producers, pimps, organized crime organizations (Hodge 2008), and everyday citizens.

Sex Trafficking Victims: Profile and Risk Factors

As a single mother in Mexico, Esperanza, a CAST-LA client, experienced the loss of a child due to starvation and decided she had to leave her children with her family and go to Los Angeles for a job as a seamstress. Following what she believed to be a legitimate job lead, Esperanza was sold into slavery, which separated her from her children and prevented her from sending home the money that she had gone to earn.

Each sex trafficking victim has a unique background; however, they share characteristics that place them at higher risk for sex trafficking. These characteristics include (1) poverty, (2) racial and ethnic marginalization, (3) being an undocumented immigrant, (4) identifying as lesbian, bisexual, transgender, and queer, (5) being disabled, (6) being a runaway and homeless, (7) being a survivor of childhood sexual abuse, (8) having little to no education, (9) having minimal vocational opportunities, and (10) coming from low-resource countries with little infrastructure to combat human trafficking (Contreras and Bryant-Davis 2011; Clawson et al. 2015). Trafficking recruiters are typically drawn to individuals who are impoverished and have very little access to social and economic opportunities (Clawson et al. 2015). Individuals who have limited access to opportunities such as education are often more susceptible to believing the empty promises of trafficking recruiters (Contreras and Bryant-Davis 2011). Another risk factor associated with domestic sex trafficking victims is age. Adolescents are particularly susceptible to recruitment (Flowers 2001; Clawson et al. 2015). The average age of entry into the commercial sex industry is twelve to fourteen for girls (Estes and Weiner 2001; Lloyd 2005), and eleven to thirteen for boys and transgendered youth (Estes and Weiner 2001). Being a runaway is also considered a risk factor for domestic sex trafficking. A significant portion of adult women with sexually exploitative prostitution histories reported being runaways during their youth (e.g., 72 percent in Boston) (Norton-Hawk 2002; Clawson et al. 2015). Identification as lesbian, gay, bisexual, transgendered, or questioning (LGBTQ) is an additional risk factor.

Victims of domestic trafficking are also likely to have a history of childhood sexual abuse (Clawson et al. 2015). In a meta-analysis of twenty studies, Raphael (2004) found that 33 to 84 percent of adult women who were exploited via prostitution were abused during their youth. Raphael (2004) also found increased rates of addiction and domestic violence within the homes of victims. Other thematic trends occurring among individuals involved in the commercial sex industry include low education rates (Aghatise 2004; Beyrer 2001), the presence of learning disabilities, and poor performance at school (Clawson et al. 2015), which correlate to low self-esteem (Harway and Liss 1999). The loss of a parent through abandonment, divorce, or death is also a risk factor (Clawson et al. 2015; Norton-Hawk 2002; Raphael and Shapiro 2002).

Recruitment into Sex Trafficking

There are four main pathways into the sex industry (Curtol et al. 2004): (1) false-front agencies, (2) local sex industries, (3) abduction, and (4) families living in poverty. Organizations known as false-front agencies offer employment, modeling, and even marriage to attract potential victims (Curtol et al. 2004). Recruiters will often lure prospects by offering promises of a better life. If the victim's recruitment involves travel, the accrued expenses will be used as debt (Curtol et al. 2004). Those individuals who are already engaged in the sex industry (e.g., exotic dancing, entertainment, prostitution) are also likely candidates for trafficking because they are somewhat familiar with the demands of the sex industry (Curtol et al. 2004). Those who are new to the sex industry might be eased into the field through the use of pornography—a socially legitimate form of entertainment whose message of female objectification may be propagated, tolerated, and portrayed as innocuous via media (e.g., social, print, online, music) (APA Division 35 2011). Traffickers might also present pornography as a means of gaining fame or notoriety, a stepping stone to reaching one's goals, or even an enjoyable, pleasurable experience (Lloyd 2005). Pornography may also be used as a means of psychological coercion, as these images are difficult to retract once posted on the Internet or printed (Estes and Weiner 2001; Raymond, Hughes, and Gomez 2001).

Individuals might also be abducted and forced into sexual exploitation (Curtol et al. 2004). Girls and women are most vulnerable to being abducted when they live in rural settings and urban areas with low levels of social cohesion. They may also be vulnerable when they are walking alone to and from work or school. Traffickers often send recruiters—a couple or a woman—to these low-resource communities to persuade impoverished families to let their young women and girls work for them (Curtol et al. 2004). The recruiters will promise the family members that they will secure employment for their young daughters, as a maid, nanny, or dancer, that they will take care of them, and that the young women and girls will earn enough money to provide for their relatives. Sometimes they also promise to assist the young women and girls in getting an education. These false promises are the mechanisms through which traffickers gain the trust of their victims' family members.

The manipulation also starts with the facade of a normal relationship: Recruiters attract girls and women into the sex industry through courtship. However, gradually, the caring boyfriend becomes a demanding and abusive pimp (Kotrla 2010). Once victims have been recruited, they have little control over the hours they work (Clawson et al. 2015) and over the sexual acts they participate in (Hodge 2008). Their work is often subject to quotas enforced through the threat of punishment (Hodge 2008).

Impact of Sex Trafficking on Victims' Functioning

Victims of the sex trade industry are impacted on a number of levels: physical, psychological, behavioral (Contreras and Bryant-Davis 2011), and social (APA Division 35 2011). Because sex trafficking victims are not able to advocate for safe-sex practices, their physical health is often compromised by sexually transmitted diseases (APA Division 35 2011). Other health problems include malnutrition (Rafferty 2008), physical injuries such as broken bones and head injuries (Rafferty 2008; Raymond, Hughes, and Gomez 2001), and gynecological complications like infertility and cervical cancer (APA Division 35 2011).

The psychological and behavioral sequelae of sex trafficking are pervasive. They may include guilt, depression, poor self-image, anxiety, social withdrawal, aggression, disorganized attachment, and isolation (Deb,

Mukherjee, and Mathews 2011; Watts-English et al. 2006). Victims are also more likely to utilize dissociation to escape—figuratively—and to cope with their experience (Dworkin 2002). They may develop eating-disordered behaviors that provide them with a false sense of control over their body and lives (Contreras and Bryant-Davis 2011). Lastly, it is not uncommon for sex traffickers to introduce women and girls to substances as a means of establishing control over their victims (Courtois 2008).

Sex trafficking victims may feel shunned and shamed by their respective cultural communities when they try to get out of "the life." Without treatment, even those individuals who are able to escape victimhood continue to experience the emotional and physical scars of domestic and international trafficking (Estes and Weiner 2001). The psychological and physical effects resulting from the mental and physical coercion of traffickers often leave women and girls at risk for continued victimization and exploitation.

Sex Trafficking and Entry into the Justice System

Lulu's story is an example of how anyone can become a victim of trafficking. Lulu, a CAST-LA client, is an educated woman who believed she was coming to America for a legitimate job opportunity, only to discover that she had been sold into slavery.

Women and girls who are victims of sex trafficking are often brought into the justice system as criminals instead of victims (Farley 2008). They are arrested more frequently than traffickers and consumers (Farley 2008) and are viewed by criminal justice workers, including police officers, attorneys, and judges, as empowered and consenting persons who willfully commit the crime of exchanging sexual acts for money. This ignores the fact that most sexually trafficked women entered the sex industry when they were minors, and came of age as trafficking victims. Legally, minors cannot consent to sexual acts and therefore should not be held responsible (Hughes 2007). However, prostitution laws criminalize juveniles who are sex trafficked by defining them as individuals who offer themselves as prostitutes rather than as victims of child sexual abuse and statutory rape perpetrated by the buyers and sellers of the sex trade (Mir 2013). What explains women's and girls' differential treatment in the criminal justice system?

Traditional gender norms support the perception that sex trafficking victims are consenting individuals who are committing a crime, in particular, the belief that girls and women are sexual gatekeepers and that boys and men should not be expected to control their sexual behaviors. Research has produced evidence that gender shapes individuals' attitudes towards sex trafficking. Menaker and Miller (2013) found that undergraduate college students who held sexist beliefs and who had little understanding of trauma were more likely to show lower empathy towards juvenile victims of sex trafficking, to place greater culpability on the youth, and to endorse punitive justice.

Socioeconomic status also has an influence on the differential treatment of sex trafficked individuals in the criminal justice system (Farley 2009): Female and male victims usually lack the information and resources necessary to defend themselves against police brutality or incarceration; they are without economic and political power and therefore are easier to police and prosecute than consumers and traffickers who have access to economic, social, and political resources.

Compared to white, middle-class women and girls, low-income, ethnic-minority women and girls are more likely to be criminalized and as a result incarcerated in a juvenile detention facility or placed on probation (Mauer 2013). Additionally, perpetrators of violence against ethnically and economically marginalized women are less likely to be prosecuted and convicted; when convicted, they often receive less time than those who violate white and economically advantaged women and girls (Kennedy 2006). Given their individual and collective experiences of discrimination, stigma, and stereotyping, women from marginalized communities may find it particularly difficult to report criminal acts against them (Bryant-Davis 2005). Mir (2013) notes that court professionals who endorse class and racial stereotypes are more likely to view impoverished, ethnic-minority sex trafficking victims as criminals, because racism and classism are built on the ideology that those who are racially and economically marginalized are immoral, untrustworthy, and thus less deserving of protection (Bryant-Davis 2005).

Victims of sex trafficking are exposed to diverse forms of violence. Kidnapping, robbery, sexual assault, battery, attempted homicide, and human trafficking are crimes that they are unlikely to report because they are afraid of coming into contact with the justice system and because they are not aware of their legal rights and of the community resources available to them (Deb, Mukherjee, and Mathews 2011; Watts-English et al. 2006). They suffer in silence for the many violations they have experienced, with psychological symptoms that include angry outbursts, self-harming behaviors, and self-medication with illicit substances.

Victims of sexual trafficking hesitate to report and participate in the criminal prosecution of their traffickers because they are worried the system will fail them. They fear social rejection, deportation, and retaliation against their loved ones and themselves. They are concerned about being charged with prostitution and deported (Mir 2013). Those who are mothers are also afraid they will lose their children. In addition, many victims have ambivalent feelings towards their pimps—attachment and fear of violent retaliation—that explain why they may not cooperate in criminal proceedings. Their concerns are legitimate, considering their exposure to numerous acts of violence, the barriers to safe employment and housing they experience after they become involved in the criminal justice system (Maxwell and Maxwell 2000), and the negative view many in society hold of sex trafficking victims as criminals who do not deserve public concern (Farley 2008; Farrell and Pfeffer 2014).

When women and girls come forward with their case and engage with the criminal justice system, they report their victimization directly or indirectly in their interactions with medical personnel, mental health professionals, advocates, or lawyers. This poses a number of challenges. First, the legal process requires that victims repeatedly tell their story, which is extremely difficult for women who experience trauma-related symptoms, such as shame, fear, self-blame, and lack of trust. In addition, the act of reporting is complicated by language barriers between the victims and the legal or health professionals, the victims' dissociation at the time of the event(s) or during the telling, and memory and speech impairment caused by reduced hippocampal and amygdala processing, physical injury, or substance use (Hayes et al. 2011; Deb, Mukherjee, and Mathews 2011; Watts-English et al. 2006). Disclosing and recounting the traumatic events are particularly taxing when victims are confronted by justice professionals who have received little or no training on trauma victims in general and human trafficking victims in particular, who as a result conduct insensitive questioning (Mir 2013), and who are victim blaming, hostile, and threatening.

Exploitation at the hands of justice workers and members of various helping professions is yet another predicament (Mir 2013). Female victims of sex trafficking have been the target of physical assault, rape, molestation, and sexual harassment by police officers, lawyers, probation officers, prison guards, and mental health professionals (Shannon et al. 2009; Odinokova et al. 2014). Violations by persons who identify themselves as helpers, such as mental health service providers, lawyers, and police officers, can be particularly traumatizing and result in victims experiencing increased distrust of people in general and helping professionals more specifically (Gonsiorek 1995).

Sex Trafficking Myths

The literature indicates that sex trafficking does occur domestically and internationally. Women and girls who are economically, politically, and psychologically vulnerable are preyed upon and through force, fraud, or coercion are cornered into sex trafficking. Sex trafficking victims, including those engaged in prostitution, can be raped, and are raped multiple times by traffickers, pimps, and consumers. And it is often hard to leave traffickers who use economic and legal pressures, violence, and threats of violence, including threats to one's family members (Contreras and Farley 2011). However, agents of the justice system and mental health professionals are often blind to this reality because they accept, or fail to question, the societal myths about sex trafficking victims that deny that violence and exploitation is an integral part of the trafficking process (NHTRC 2014). Among these myths are the beliefs that real human trafficking happens in other countries, not in the United States; that women and girls only become prostitutes because they want easy money; that prostitutes can't be raped because they are giving sex away; and that if women don't want to be sexually exploited they should just leave that life and start following the law.

These myths support the criminalization of trafficking victims and justify justice officials' hesitation and refusal to prosecute traffickers and consumers (Mir 2013). They create conditions that deprive human trafficking victims of the hope that they may find safety in the legal system (Contreras and Farley 2011). They support victim blaming and the view that women's and girls' bodies are insignificant and unworthy of protection. Last, they can also be used to justify the victims' further exploitation by justice workers. For all these reasons, myths about sex trafficking participate in the reproduction of an unjust justice system for victims of sex trafficking (Mir 2013).

Psychological and Justice Interventions for Sex Trafficking: Current Practices

Sex trafficking survivors and incarcerated women have often experienced pervasive and varied forms of trauma throughout their lives, conceptualized as complex trauma. Complex trauma is defined as reoccurring trauma, taking place over a period of time and within the context of specific relationships. It encompasses domestic violence, attachment trauma, witnessing death, experiencing rape, human trafficking, prostitution, and child abuse (Courtois 2008). Although experiences of complex trauma are prevalent, particularly for young urban women (Glass et al. 2007), there is little psychological research investigating what legal practices may minimize the harms experienced by victims of sex trafficking in the criminal justice system. At present, criminal proceedings do not take into consideration the developmental consequences of complex trauma for a person who transitions from childhood to adulthood (Deb, Mukherjee, and Mathews 2011; Watts-English et al. 2006). Without knowledge of complex trauma, court officials are not able to make decisions and create policies and procedures that are sensitive to survivors' struggles with identity, affect recognition and regulation, trust, and meaning making (Lanktree and Briere 2013).

Safe Harbor policies are a promising development in the criminal justice system: These policies are intended to rectify the criminalization of minors who were sexually exploited. Rather than prosecute youth, they provide protection to those who have been exploited through sex trafficking, and prioritize the provision of wrap-around mental health and social services (e.g., housing, education, vocational training, and medical care) (Mir 2013). These policies have the potential to limit the harms that youth and adult victims experience in the legal system. There have been other notable, state-level legislative efforts in the fight against human trafficking, including the introduction of greater penalties for those convicted of human trafficking, the rejection of defense arguments stating that the trafficker did not know the age of the victim, and the removal of statutes of limitation on charges against traffickers (Hill 2013).

A review of the psychological literature also shows limited knowledge regarding which mental health interventions may promote resilience, growth, and healing following sex trafficking and/or incarceration. The current research indicates that cognitive behavioral therapy (CBT) is an effective approach to the treatment of trauma (Bomyea and Lang 2012; Iverson et al. 2011; Seidler and Wagner 2006). For survivors of complex trauma, CBT-oriented treatment involves identifying core beliefs, challenging maladaptive thinking, and developing adaptive coping strategies. Trauma Focused CBT (TF-CBT), primarily associated with the treatment of children and adolescents, is a psychosocial treatment model that has demonstrated decreases in severity and duration of acute psychological disorders as well as long-term psychological outcomes of child sexual abuse (CSA) (Cohen, Mannarino, and Deblinger 2006). Given that TF-CBT is child focused, it could function as an early intervention for child and adolescent sex trafficked survivors.

Prolonged Exposure (PE) is another treatment model that has produced positive outcomes for clients with chronic posttraumatic stress disorder (PTSD; Bradley et al. 2014). However, evidence of its effectiveness in community-based clinics is limited. Feske (2008) found that the implementation of PE in community settings was associated with decreased symptoms of PTSD, general anxiety, and depression among low-income, minority women receiving services at a community clinic. Feske (2001) also recommended that PE include interventions aimed at improving interpersonal problems experienced by female survivors of complex trauma.

Culturally Congruent Responses to Sex Trafficking

Justice professionals need to respond to human sex trafficking in a gender-sensitive and culturally congruent manner. However, the literature on effective responses to sex trafficking is minimal, and the role and dynamics of culture have largely been ignored, thus leaving a major gap in research-based knowledge and guidelines for psychological and legal practice with sex trafficking victims. Understanding human trafficking and violence against women in general necessitates a framework that makes central the intersection of gender, race, class, and sexuality and how it perpetuates the victimization of women (Merry 2009). Such a framework would facilitate the development of culturally and gender-sensitive training for judicial and mental health professionals. This training would be ongoing and bidirectional and would include psycho-educational components on human trafficking and its social and individual consequences, as well as components that describe the context of intersecting identity markers, such as race, ethnicity, gender, and socioeconomic status (Bryant-Davis et al. 2009). It should make judicial professionals aware of the need for cultural humility, which is counter to culture blindness (i.e., inability to understand viewpoints or experiences of individuals from other cultural backgrounds) and/or cultural arrogance and silencing. It should also help them develop awareness of their own assumptions and identity as well as provide a framework for cultural sensitivity that is based on empirical knowledge and skills for working with culturally diverse trafficking survivors (Sue and Sue 2013). It is important that this training also foster an understanding of such key terms as "power," "privilege," "racism," "sexism," "heterosexism," "oppression," and "stigma" (Sue and Sue 2013) and such psychological constructs as depression, anxiety, substance dependence, panic attacks, traumatic triggers, dissociation, and posttraumatic stress.

It is essential that clinicians and justice officials know there is more to culture than the experience of cultural oppression—that they recognize the cultural strengths of their clients, not just their pathologies or deficits (Bryant-Davis 2005). It is also critical that they develop culturally congruent responses to trafficking victims in order to enhance trust and respect in ways that will foster retention and rehabilitation. At the most basic level, the offices of judicial employees should represent diversity in staffing and leadership positions and should utilize art, magazines, books, and supplies for clients' children that are culturally diverse and reflective of the various backgrounds of the survivors. Professionals should also be willing to speak directly about cultural issues and ask questions with respect and humility (Contreras and Farley 2011). These efforts will support the building of trust and the survivors' sense that they are being valued, respected, and heard. They can also bring about greater disclosures that are less retraumatizing, and thus facilitate case preparation to address human trafficking as well as recovery and pre-vention efforts. Additionally, mental health and justice professionals should learn how to make use of cultural community leaders, religious leaders, experts, and trained interpreters to serve as consultants and as-sist with the provision of culturally congruent communication and sup-port (Bryant-Davis 2005).

Project Rose provides a real-life example of the kind of partnerships that may develop to respond to sex trafficking. Created by an associate professor of social work and a police lieutenant, it is a community-based and interdisciplinary project that offers an alternative to arrest and de-tention (Roe-Sepowitz et al. 2014). Project Rose aims to alter victims' re-lationships with law enforcement by providing opportunities to interact with trained officers who are sympathetic and supportive and who do not see or treat them as criminals. In addition, when victims complete the program, their criminal record is expunged. Project Rose is also de-signed to empower victims through the provision of wrap-around social services that assist the participants in creating new, healthy, and legal options for socioeconomic independence. Victims are given referrals for housing, substance abuse, and medical and mental health treatment; they are connected with a mentor who has successfully exited trafficki-ng for at least a year, and with a police officer who orients them to the program. More than three hundred women, between the age of eigh-teen and fifty-eight, have participated in Project Rose since its incep-tion in 2011. Only 9 percent were rearrested at twelve months' follow-up, and participants in Project Rose were as likely as incarcerated women to show up to court. Critiques of Project Rose note that the program still threatens women with incarceration, which is disempowering (Roe-Sepowitz et al. 2014).

Recommendations for a Restorative Approach to Sex Trafficking

In order to adequately meet the unique needs of survivors of sex traf-ficking, it is critical that justice and mental health interventions be multifaceted, and that they target the multiple levels of this complex social issue. The following recommendations are derived from current knowledge of what works with trauma victims; they are intended to guide the development and implementation of effective strategies for women and girls who have been sex trafficked specifically. They are also grounded in the principles of the American Psychological Association's Guidelines for Psychological Practice with Girls and Women. These guidelines highlight the importance of attending to clients' context, including their cultural background, socioeconomic status, social support network, and the realities of oppression, stigma, and discrimination. They also recommend that those serving women and girls should engage in activities that are affirming and empowering, and that acknowledge and build on their strengths. Finally, it is critical for professionals serving women and girls to connect them with accessible, appropriate, effective community resources and for professionals to actively work to transform systems and not just individuals. Based on the APA guidelines described above, the following recommendations are made for providing services to women and girls who have been victims of sex trafficking in particular.

Recommendation #1: Adapt existing treatment approaches for use with sex-trafficking victims.

There is a dire need to develop therapeutic programs specifically designed for sex trafficking survivors. This may be accomplished by adapting already-existing models such as Prolonged Exposure (PE) in ways that are culturally syntonic. Developing and implementing culturally syntonic interventions would involve recognition of cultural variables such as language, socioeconomic status, and environmental factors.

Community studies have consistently shown that belonging to a minority group and having low socioeconomic status (SES) are associated with the use of fewer mental health services (Garcia and Weisz 2002). To address this issue, the underutilization of therapeutic services, it is essential to provide culturally informed treatment. Group modalities have been shown to be particularly effective for ethnically diverse populations, particularly when they integrate culturally syntonic values such as spirituality (Williams, Frame, and Green 1999). Engagement in group practices is based largely on the concept of establishing a community where reciprocal growth is plausible. Integration of group interventions is likely to be attractive to sex trafficked women who may feel a sense of isolation and loneliness. Through the sharing of stories, survivors can process their interpersonal traumas and receive compassion as well as validation from their peers. Creating a shared sense of community is particularly important when working in treatment settings where clients are vulnerable and/or suspicious of treatment.

It is equally important to tailor treatment to the needs of ethnically diverse survivors in ways that address gender-related concerns. Therapy approaches for female sex trafficking victims should aim to empower women and girls (Goodkind and Miller 2006); to accomplish this objective, attention must be given to improving body image and self-esteem and to developing adaptive coping strategies. It is also critical that clinicians build a strong therapeutic alliance and create a sense of safety for clients in order to promote recovery, rehabilitation, and, ultimately, reintegration.

Recommendation #2: Integrate adjunctive treatment approaches and advocacy.

Various adjunctive treatment approaches have been effective in fostering healing and resilience in survivors of complex trauma (Herman 1992; Kreuter and Reiter 2014). Herman (1992) suggests that healing occurs in three stages: safety, remembrance, and mourning. Culturally informed, adjunctive treatments such as expressive art therapy can support the healing process by helping survivors verbally express their trauma and make meaning of their experiences. For example, expressive writing, narrative journaling, poetry therapy, and art therapy are creative art interventions that aim to help victims transcend traumatization and thrive (Kreuter and Reiter 2014). Art therapy in particular has been found to promote biological as well as psychological change, to increase self-esteem, and to facilitate meaning making (Goodkind and Miller 2006), the integration of right- and left-brain functions, as well as the integration of traumatic memories and experiences (McNamee 2005; Talwar 2007). Implementation of expressive art therapies, if culturally syntonic, can provide survivors with a cathartic experience.

Like the creative arts, spirituality provides resources for healing. Helping women develop their own understanding of a higher power may stimulate the creation of meaning, a sense of wholeness, and self-transformation (Mattis 2000). Acknowledging the importance of spirituality and including spiritual ideals in treatment have proven to be culturally syntonic, particularly for ethnic minority populations (Covington 1998). Spiritual as well as religious beliefs are powerful agents of change for various ethnic minority groups, particularly African Americans, as they shape their understanding of justice, salvation, and coping with oppression (Mattis 2000). Religious beliefs can enhance an individual's ability to cope with negative life events, and negative life events can lead to enhanced religious faith (McIntosh 1995; Pargament 1990). For these reasons, the integration of spiritual and religious ideals in treatment with sex trafficked women and/or incarcerated women should be considered.

In many respects, advocacy is an adjunctive treatment component. Yet psychologists have often failed to acknowledge that advocacy is integral to their role as change agents (Radius, Galer-Unti, and Tappe 2009), unlike other professionals, such as physicians and nurses, who view client advocacy as essential to delivering quality services (DeLeon et al. 2006). There are several reasons why psychologists are less involved in advocacy-related activities: lack of time, lack of related training, and the idea that advocacy is a time-consuming, lofty endeavor (J. Hill 2013). Advocacy within the field of psychology is a multifaceted process involving the use of collaboration with other helping professions and organizations to foster change (Fox 2008), as well as informing decision makers through the process of promoting the interests of clients, health care systems, public health, and welfare issues (Lating, Barnett, and Horowitz 2010). Advocacy as an intervention is tied to justice practices in the sense that psychologists are able to take an active role in promoting just actions and rallying for change on behalf of their clients. In order to enact change and promote social justice, psychologists need to redefine their roles and intervene at multiple levels of the sociopolitical sphere (micro-level, meso-level, and macro-level).

The American Counseling Association (ACA) has defined advocacy competencies and provided a framework for understanding the roles and responsibilities of mental health professionals who wish to engage in social justice work (Lewis et al. 2003). These competencies highlight the importance of intervening at multiple levels: the micro-level, which refers to counselors' work with individual clients; the meso-level, which includes the client's support system or immediate community; and the macro-level, which corresponds to the client's social, cultural, or political context (Bradley, Werth, and Hastings 2011). Advocacy in support of sex trafficked women and girls in the judicial system should target all three levels of the client's ecology (Bronfenbrenner 1977). Multisystemic approaches that address the micro-, meso-, and macro-levels are necessary to prevent the exploitation of potential victims and to protect those who have been exploited from reentering the world of sex trafficking. The scope of the problem is much greater than the psychology of the victims, and therefore the solution needs to target diverse contributing factors, such as poverty, oppression, and victim-blaming attitudes held by many in society (Bryant-Davis 2005).

There are several ways in which psychologists can expand their role to participate in advocacy practices specific to the needs of sex trafficked women in the judicial system. One of the critical steps of advocating on behalf of sex trafficked women is to investigate the interplay of trauma histories and contextual and historical factors (e.g., age, ethnicity, setting, racism, sexism), all of which have an impact on well-being. Research that examines these factors is critical to identifying the specific needs of the population. Once this information is collected, psychologists can disseminate information to leaders and partner with organizations that meet the needs of the specific interest areas. Specifically, psychologists should strive to provide and interpret data in a manner that demonstrates urgency for change, collaborate with meso-level stakeholders to develop a vision for implementing change, and develop a detailed plan for implementing the change process (Lewis et al. 2003). Lastly, psychologists and stakeholders should be mindful of macrosystemic barriers and anticipate resistance.

Advocacy initiatives for the micro-level rehabilitation of sex trafficked women and girls may need to be innovative in order to transcend systemic barriers. These initiatives may include wrap-around services that address victims' needs for housing, education, employment, childcare, and legal advocacy. They may also involve collaboration with various meso-level helping professionals and psycho-education for members of the judicial system in order to increase attention to the mental health needs of sex trafficked survivors.

Recommendation #3: At the micro-level, identify and use self-care strategies to prevent burnout.

Psychologists, mental health practitioners, and justice personnel are particularly vulnerable to the negative consequences associated with working in helping professions, in particular compassion fatigue and burnout. While clinicians may exercise great care for others, they also may pay limited attention to their own well-being and experience greater levels of anxiety, depression, and emotional exhaustion than mental health researchers (Radeke and Mahoney 2000). Judicial system professionals may also develop symptoms of burnout, vicarious trauma, and occupational stress (Loo 1984; Chamberlain and Miller 2009). Hence the need for self-care strategies that protect against the development of adverse psychological conditions while serving victims of sex trafficking. Failure to engage in self-care practices could potentially lead to mental health impairment, which refers to an objective change in the professional's functioning or improper behavior such as crossing professional boundaries (e.g., inappropriate sexual conduct) (Wise, Hersh, and Gibson 2012).

Researchers have asserted that long-term exposure to trauma can alter psychologists' schemas about the world as well as result in intrusive thoughts and emotional reactions such as anxiety and anger (McCann and Pearlman 1990; Schauben and Frazier 1995; Jenkins and Baird 2002; Adams and Riggs 2008). It is imperative that mental health and justice providers of trauma-specific services adopt coping strategies aimed at helping them process work-related stress. Strategies that have been shown to be effective for psychologists include active coping (e.g., problem solving), seeking emotional support (e.g., from friends, family, or others), planning (i.e., making a plan of action), and seeking instrumental social support (i.e., getting advice from others) (Schauben and Frazier 1995).

Conclusion

Survivors of sex trafficking face psychological, social, medical, financial, and legal consequences (Farley 2008). The legal response to their victimization is usually one that criminalizes the trafficked person and minimizes consequences for the trafficker and consumer (Mir 2013). This chapter has made the case for a client-centered restorative process that addresses the multilayered needs of the survivors. It has also articulated recommendations for contextualized interventions that acknowledge the realities of oppression and the varied impact of long-term complex trauma. For justice to be served and to interrupt the cycle of human trafficking, there must be a shift in the guiding framework and procedures of the criminal justice system as relates to the treatment of victims of human trafficking. This shift would entail involving survivors of sex trafficking in the creation of policies and procedures that would assist and empower victims rather than criminalize them, and that would penalize traffickers and educate and train legal and helping professionals in order to promote justice models that focus on the restoration of victims psychologically, socially, and economically.

REFERENCES

Adams, Shelah A., and Shelley A. Riggs. 2008. "An Exploratory Study of Vicarious Trauma among Therapist Trainees." *Training and Education in Professional Psychology* 2 (1): 26–34. doi: 10.1037/1931-3918.2.1.26.

Aghatise, Esohe. 2004. "Trafficking for Prostitution in Italy: Possible Effects of Government Proposals for Legalization of Brothels." *Violence Against Women* 10 (10): 1126–55, https://www.ncjrs.gov.

Allen, Donald M. 1980. "Young Male Prostitutes: A Psychosocial Study." *Archives of Sexual Behavior* 9 (5): 399–426.

American Psychological Association Division 35, Special Committee on Violence Against Women. 2011. "Report on Trafficking of Women and Girls," http://www.apadivisions.org.

American Psychological Association Task Force on Evidence-Based Practice. 2006. "Evidence-Based Practice in Psychology." *American Psychologist* 61 (4): 271–85. doi: 10.103770003-066X61.4.271.

Beyrer, Chris. 2001. "Shan Women and Girls and the Sex Industry in Southeast Asia: Political Causes and Human Rights Implications." *Social Science and Medicine* 53 (4): 543–50. doi: 10.1016/S0277-9536(00)00358-0.

Bomyea, Jessica, and Ariel J. Lang. 2012. "Emerging Interventions for PTSD: Future Directions for Clinical Care and Research." *Neuropharmacology* 62 (2): 607–16. doi: 10.1016/j.neuropharm.2011.05.028.

Bradley, Joshua M., James L. Werth, and Sarah L. Hastings. 2011. "Social Justice Advocacy in Rural Communities: Practical Issues and Implications." *Counseling Psychologist* 40 (3): 607–16. doi: 10.1177/0011000011415697.

Bradley, Rebekah, Jamelle Greene, Eric Russ, Lissa Dutra, and Drew Westen. 2014. "A Multidimensional Meta-Analysis of Psychotherapy for PTSD." *American Journal of Psychiatry* 42 (2): 277–92, http://dx.doi.org.

Bronfenbrenner, Urie. 1977. "Toward an Experimental Ecology of Human Development." *American Psychologist* 32 (7): 513–31.

Bryant-Davis, Thema. 2005. *Thriving in the Wake of Trauma: A Multicultural Guide.* Westport, CT: Greenwood.

Bryant-Davis, Thema, Shaquita Tillman, Alison Marks, and Kimberly Smith. 2009. "Millennium Abolitionists: Addressing the Sexual Trafficking of African Women." *Beliefs and Values: Understanding the Global Implications of Human Nature* 1 (1): 69–78, http://bav.ibavi.org.

Chamberlain, Jared, and Monica K. Miller. 2009. "Evidence of Secondary Traumatic Stress, Safety Concerns, and Burnout among a Homogeneous Group of Judges in a Single Jurisdiction." *Journal of the American Academy of Psychiatry and the Law Online* 37 (2): 214–24, http://www.jaapl.org.

Clawson, Heather J., Nicole Dutch, Amy Solomon, and Lisa Goldblatt Grace. 2015. "Human Trafficking into and within the United States: A Review of the Literature." Accessed June 8, 2015, http://aspe.hhs.gov.

Cohen, Judith A., Anthony P. Mannarino, and Esther Deblinger. 2006. *Treating Trauma and Traumatic Grief in Children and Adolescents.* New York: Guilford.

Contreras, Michelle, and Thema Bryant-Davis. 2011. "The Psychology of Modern-Day Slavery" (film). American Psychological Association Division 35, http://www.apadivisions.org.

Contreras, Michelle, and Melissa Farley. 2011. "Human Trafficking: Not an Isolated Issue." In *Surviving Sexual Violence: A Guide to Recovery and Empowerment.* Edited by Thema Bryant-Davis, 22–36. Lanham, MD: Rowman & Littlefield.

Courtois, Christine A. 2008. "Complex Trauma, Complex Reactions: Assessment and Treatment." *Psychotherapy: Theory, Research, Practice, Training* 41 (4): 412–25. doi: 10.1037/0033–3204.41.4.412.

Covington, Stephanie S. 1998. "Women in Prison: Approaches in the Treatment of Our Most Invisible Population." *Women and Therapy* 21 (1): 141–55. doi: 10.1300/J015v21n01_03.

Curtol, Federica, Silvia Decarli, Andrea Di Nicola, and Ernesto Ugo Savona. 2004. "Victims of Human Trafficking in Italy: A Judicial Perspective." *International Review of Victimology* 11 (1): 111–41. doi: 10.1177/026975800401100107.

Deb, Sibnath, Aparna Mukherjee, and Ben Mathews. 2011. "Aggression in Sexually Abused Trafficked Girls and Efficacy of Intervention." *Journal of Interpersonal Violence* 26 (4): 745–68. doi: 10.1177/0886260510365875.

DeLeon, Patrick H., Christopher W. Loftis, Vicki Ball, and Michael J. Sullivan. 2006. "Navigating Politics, Policy, and Procedure: A Firsthand Perspective of Advocacy on Behalf of the Profession." *Professional Psychology: Research and Practice* 37 (2): 146–53. doi: 10.1037/0735–7028.37.2.146.

Dovydaitis, Tiffany. 2010. "Human Trafficking: The Role of the Health Care Provider." *Journal of Midwifery and Women's Health* 55 (5): 462–67. doi: 10.1016/j.jmwh.2009.12.017.

Dworkin, Andrea. 2002. *Heartbreak: The Political Memoir of a Feminist Militant.* New York: Basic Books.

Estes, Richard J., and Neil Alan Weiner. 2001. *The Commercial Sexual Exploitation of Children in the U.S., Canada, and Mexico.* University of Pennsylvania, School of Social Work, Center for the Study of Youth Policy. Philadelphia: University of Pennsylvania Press.

Farley, Melissa. 2009. "Theory versus Reality: Commentary on Four Articles about Trafficking for Prostitution." *Women's Studies International Forum* 32 (4): 311–15. doi: 10.1016/j.wsif.2009.07.001.

Farley, M. 2008. "Prostitution Policy Recommendations for the City of San Francisco," http://www.prostitutionresearch.com.

Farrell, Amy, and Rebecca Pfeffer. 2014. "Policing Human Trafficking: Cultural Blinders and Organizational Barriers." *Annals of the American Academy of Political and Social Science* 653 (1): 46–64. doi: 10.1177/0002716213515835.

Feske, Ulrike. 2008. "Treating Low-Income and Minority Women with Posttraumatic Stress Disorder: A Pilot Study Comparing Prolonged Exposure and Treatment as Usual Conducted by Community Therapists." *Journal of Interpersonal Violence* 23 (8): 1027–40. doi: 10.1177/0886260507313967.

Feske, Ulrike. 2001. "Treating Low-Income and African-American Women with Posttraumatic Stress Disorder: A Case Series." *Behavior Therapy* 32 (3): 585–601.

Flowers, Ronald B. 2001. *Runaway Kids and Teenage Prostitution: America's Lost, Abandoned, and Sexually Exploited Children.* Westport, CT: Greenwood.

Fox, Ronald E. 2008. "Advocacy: The Key to the Survival and Growth of Professional Psychology." *Professional Psychology: Research and Practice* 39 (6): 633–37. doi: 10.1037/00357-7028.39.6.633.

Garcia, Joe Albert, and John R. Weisz. 2002. "When Youth Mental Health Care Stops: Therapeutic Relationship Problems and Other Reasons for Ending Youth Outpatient Treatment." *Journal of Consulting and Clinical Psychology* 70 (2): 439–43. http://dx.doi.org/10.1037/0022-006X.70.2.439.

Glass, Nancy, Nancy Perrin, Jacquelyn C. Campbell, and Karen Soeken. 2007. "The Protective Role of Tangible Support on Post⬚Traumatic Stress Disorder Symptoms in Urban Women Survivors of Violence." *Research in Nursing and Health* 30 (5): 558–68. doi: 10.1002/nur.20207.

Gonsiorek, John C., ed. 1995. *Breach of Trust: Sexual Exploitation by Health Care Professionals and Clergy.* Thousand Oaks, CA: Sage.

Goodkind, Sara, and Diane Lynn Miller. 2006. "A Widening of the Net of Social Control? 'Gender-Specific' Treatment for Young Women in the US Juvenile Justice System." *Journal of Progressive Human Services* 17 (1): 45–70. doi: 10.1300/J059v17n01_04.

Harway, Michele, and Marsha Liss. 1999. "Dating Violence and Teen Prostitution: Adolescent Girls in the Justice System." In *Beyond Appearance: A New Look at Ado-*

lescent Girls. Edited by Norine G. Johnson, Michael C. Roberts, and Judith Worell, 277–300. Washington, DC: American Psychological Association.

Hayes, Jasmeet Pannu, Kevin S. LaBar, Gregory McCarthy, Elizabeth Selgrade, Jessica Nasser, Florin Dolcos, and Rajendra A. Morey. 2011. "Reduced Hippocampal and Amygdala Activity Predicts Memory Distortions for Trauma Reminders in Combat-Related PTSD." *Journal of Psychiatric Research* 45 (5): 660–69. doi: 10.1016/j.jpsychires.2010.10.007.

Herman, Judith. 1992. *Trauma and Recovery.* New York: Basic Books.

Hill, Calie. 2013. "Solutions to Human Trafficking: Exploring Local Alternatives." *Diplomatic Courier,* December 13, http://www.diplomaticcourier.com.

Hill, James K. 2013. "Partnering with a Purpose: Psychologists as Advocates in Organizations." *Professional Psychology: Research and Practice* 44 (4): 187–192, http://dx.doi.org.

Hodge, David R. 2008. "Sexual Trafficking in the United States: A Domestic Problem with Transnational Dimensions." *Social Work* 53 (2): 143–52. doi: 10.1093/sw/53.2.143

Hughes, Donna. 2007. "Enslaved in the USA." *National Review,* July 30, http://www.nationalreview.com.

Hughes, Donna M. 2000. "The 'Natasha' Trade: The Transnational Shadow Market of Trafficking in Women." *Journal of International Affairs* 53 (2): 625–51, http://www.uri.edu.

Hughes, Donna M., and Tatyana A. Denisova. 2001. "The Transnational Political Criminal Nexus of Trafficking in Women from Ukraine." *Trends in Organized Crime* 6 (3–4): 43–67. doi: 10.1007/s12117-001-1005-7.

Iverson, Katherine M., Jaimie L. Gradus, Patricia A. Resick, Michael K. Suvak, Kamala F. Smith, and Candice M. Monson. 2011. "Cognitive–Behavioral Therapy for PTSD and Depression Symptoms Reduces Risk for Future Intimate Partner Violence among Interpersonal Trauma Survivors." *Journal of Consulting and Clinical Psychology* 79 (2): 193–202. doi: 10.1037/a0022512.

Jenkins, Sharon Rae, and Stephanie Baird. 2002. "Secondary Traumatic Stress and Vicarious Trauma: A Validational Study." *Journal of Traumatic Stress* 15 (5): 423–32. doi: 10.1023/A:1020193526843.

Kennedy, Elizabeth. 2006. "Victim Race and Rape: A Review of Recent Literature" (student report, Brandeis University), http://www.brandeis.edu.

Kotrla, Kimberly. 2010. "Domestic Minor Sex Trafficking in the United States." *Social Work* 55 (2): 181–87. doi: 10.1093/sw/55.2.181.

Kreuter, Eric A., and Sherry Reiter. 2014. "Building Resilience in the Face of Loss and Irrelevance: Poetic Methods for Personal and Professional Transformation." *Journal of Poetry Therapy* 27 (1): 13–24. doi: 10.1080/08893675.2014.871808.

Laczko, Frank, and Elzbieta M. Gozdziak, eds. 2005. "Data and Research on Human Trafficking: A Global Survey," http://lastradainternational.org.

Lanktree, Cheryl, and John Briere. 2013. "Integrative Treatment of Complex Trauma." In *Treating Complex Traumatic Stress Disorders in Children and Adolescents: Scientific Foundations and Therapeutic Models.* Edited by Julian D. Ford and Christine A. Courtois, 143–61. New York: Guilford.

Lating, Jeffrey M., Jeffrey E. Barnett, and Michael Horowitz. 2010. "Creating a Culture of Advocacy." In *Competency-Based Education for Professional Psychology*. Edited by Mary Beth Kenkel and Roger L. Peterson, 201–8. Washington, DC: American Psychological Association.

Lewis, Judith A., Mary S. Arnold, Reese House, and Rebecca L. Toporek. 2003. "Advocacy Competencies: American Counseling Association Task Force on Advocacy Competencies," http://www.counseling.org.

Lloyd, Rachel. 2005. "Acceptable Victims? Sexually Exploited Youth in the US." *Encounter: Education for Meaning and Social Justice* 18 (3): 6–18.

Logan, T. K., Robert Walker, and Gretchen Hunt. 2009. "Understanding Human Trafficking in the United States." *Trauma, Violence, and Abuse* 10 (1): 3–30. doi: 10.1177/1524838008327262.

Loo, Robert. 1984. "Occupational Stress in the Law Enforcement Profession." *Canada's Mental Health* 32 (3): 10–13.

Mattis, Jacqueline S. 2000. "African American Women's Definitions of Spirituality and Religiosity." *Journal of Black Psychology* 26 (1): 101–22. doi: 10.1177/0095798400026001006.

Mauer, Mark. 2013. "The Changing Racial Dynamics of Women's Incarceration," http://sentencingproject.org.

Maxwell, Sheila R., and Christopher D. Maxwell. 2000. "Examining the 'Criminal Careers' of Prostitutes within the Nexus of Drug Use, Drug Selling, and Other Illicit Activities." *Criminology* 38 (3): 787–810. Doi: 10.1111/j.1745–9125.2000.tb00906.x.

McCann, Lisa I., and Laurie A. Pearlman. 1990. "Vicarious Traumatization: A Framework for Understanding the Psychological Effects of Working with Victims." *Journal of Traumatic Stress* 3 (1): 131–49. doi: 10.1007/BF00975140.

McIntosh, Daniel N. 1995. "Religion-as-Schema with Implications for the Relation between Religion and Coping." *International Journal for the Psychology of Religion* 5 (1): 1–16. doi: 10.1207/s15327582ijpr0501_1.

McKnight, Peter. 2006. "Male Prostitutes Face Enormous Risks." In *Prostitution and Sex Trafficking*. Edited by Louise Gerdes, 57–61. Detroit, MI: Gale.

McNamee, Carol M. 2005. "Bilateral Art: Integrating Art Therapy, Family Therapy, and Neuroscience." *Contemporary Family Therapy* 27 (4): 545–57. doi: 10.1007/s10591–005–8241-y.

Menaker, Tasha A., and Audrey K. Miller. 2013. "Culpability Attributions towards Juvenile Female Prostitutes." *Child Abuse Review* 22 (3): 169–81. doi: 10.1002/car.2204.

Merry, Sally E. 2009. *Gender Violence: A Cultural Perspective*. Malden, MA: Wiley-Blackwell.

Mir, Tanya. 2013. "Trick or Treat: Why Minors Engaged in Prostitution Should Be Treated as Victims, Not Criminals." *Family Court Review* 51 (1): 163–77. doi: 10.1111/fcre.12016.

Miranda, Jeanne, Bernal Guillermo, Lau Anna, Kohn Laura, Hwang Wei-Chin, and Teresa LaFromboise. 2005. "State of the Science on Psychosocial Interventions for Ethnic Minorities." *Annual Review of Clinical Psychology* 1 (1): 113–42. doi: 10.1146/annurev.clinpsy.1.102803.143822.

Mizus, Marisa, Maryam Moody, Cindy Privado, and Carol A. Douglas. 2003. "Germany, U.S. Receive Most Sex-Trafficked Women." *Off Our Backs* 33 (7/8): 4.

Monzini, Paola. 2004. "Trafficking in Women and Girls and the Involvement of Organized Crime in Western and Central Europe." *International Review of Victimology* 11 (1): 143–76. doi: 10.1177/026975800401100105.

National Human Trafficking Resource Center. 2014. "Myths and Misconceptions," http://www.traffickingresourcecenter.org.

Norton-Hawk, Maureen. 2002. "The Lifecourse of Prostitution." *Women, Girls, and Criminal Justice* 3 (1): 7–9.

Odinokova, Veronika, Maia Rusakova, Lianne A. Urada, Jay G. Silverman, and Anita Raj. 2014. "Police Sexual Coercion and Its Association with Risky Sex Work and Substance Use Behaviors among Female Sex Workers in St. Petersburg and Orenburg, Russia." *International Journal of Drug Policy* 25 (1): 96–104. doi: 10.1016/j.drugpo.2013.06.008.

Pargament, Kenneth. 1990. "God Help Me: Toward a Theoretical Framework of Coping for the Psychology of Religion." *Research in the Social Scientific Study of Religion* 2: 195–224.

Radeke, JoAnn T., and Michael J. Mahoney. 2000. "Comparing the Personal Lives of Psychotherapists and Research Psychologists." *Professional Psychology: Research and Practice* 31 (1): 82–84. doi: 10.1037/0735-7028.31.1.82.

Radius, Susan M., Regina A. Galer-Unti, and Marlene K. Tappe. 2009. "Educating for Advocacy: Recommendations for Professional Preparation and Development Based on a Needs and Capacity Assessment of Health Education Faculty." *Health Promotion Practice* 10 (1): 83–91. doi: 10.1177/1524839907306407.

Rafferty, Yvonne. 2008. "The Impact of Trafficking on Children: Psychological and Social Policy Perspectives." *Child Development Perspectives* 2 (1): 13–18. doi: 10.1111/j.1750-8606.2008.00035.x.

Raphael, Jody. 2004. *Listening to Olivia: Violence, Poverty, and Prostitution*. Boston, MA: Northeastern University Press.

Raphael, Jody, and Deborah Shapiro. 2002. *Sisters Speak Out: The Lives and Needs of Prostituted Women in Chicago: A Research Study*. Chicago: Center for Impact Research.

Raymond, Janice G., Donna M. Hughes, and Carol J. Gomez. 2001. *Sex Trafficking of Women in the United States: International and Domestic Trends*. North Amherst, MA: Coalition Against Trafficking in Women.

Roe-Sepowitz, Dominique E., James Gallagher, Kristine E. Hickle, Martha P. Loubert, and John Tutelman. 2014. "Project ROSE: An Arrest Alternative for Victims of Sex Trafficking and Prostitution." *Journal of Offender Rehabilitation* 53 (1): 57–74. doi: 10.1080/10509674.2013.861323.

Schauben, Laura J., and Patricia A. Frazier. 1995. "Vicarious Trauma: The Effects on Female Counselors of Working with Sexual Violence Survivors." *Psychology of Women Quarterly* 19 (1): 49–64. doi: 10.1111/j.1471-6402.1995.tb00278.x.

Seidler, Guenter H., and Frankie E. Wagner. 2006. "Comparing the Efficacy of EMDR and Trauma-Focused Cognitive-Behavioral Therapy in the Treatment of PTSD:

A Meta-Analytic Study." *Psychological Medicine* 36 (11): 1515–22. doi: http://dx.doi. org/10.1017/S0033291706007963.

Shannon, Kate, T. Kerr, S. A. Strathdee, J. Shoveller, J. S. Montaner, and M. W. Tyndall. 2009. "Prevalence and Structural Correlates of Gender-Based Violence among a Prospective Cohort of Female Sex Workers." *BMJ: British Medical Journal* 339 (7718): 442–45. doi: 10.1136/bmj.b2939.

Silbert, Mimi, and Ayala Pines. 1982. "Entrance into Prostitution." *Youth and Society* 13 (4): 471–500. doi: 10.1177/0044118X82013004005.

Sue, Derald W., and David Sue. 2013. *Counseling the Culturally Diverse: Theory and Practice*, 6th ed. Hoboken, NJ: Wiley.

Sue, Stanley, Nolan Zane, Gordan C. N. H. Hall, and Lauren K. Berger. 2009. "The Case for Cultural Competency in Psychotherapeutic Interventions." *Annual Review of Psychology* 60: 525–48. doi: 10.1146/annurev.psych.60.110707.163651.

Talwar, Savneet. 2007. "Accessing Traumatic Memory through Art Making: An Art Therapy Trauma Protocol (ATTP)." *Arts in Psychotherapy* 34 (1): 22–35. doi: 10.1016/j.aip.2006.09.001.

United Nations. 2000. "Article 3. Protocol to Prevent, Suppress, and Punish Trafficking in Persons, Especially Women and Children, Supplementing the United Nations Convention against Transnational Organized Crime," www.uncjin.org.

U.S. Department of Justice. 2009. "The Federal Bureau of Investigation's Efforts to Combat Crimes against Children," https://oig.justice.gov.

U.S. Department of Justice. 2007. "Fact Sheet: Civil Rights Division Efforts to Combat Modern-Day Slavery," http://www.usdoj.gov.

U.S. Department of Justice. 2006. "Assessment of U.S. Government Efforts to Combat Trafficking in Persons." Washington, DC: U.S. Government Printing Office.

U.S. Department of Justice. 2005. "Federal Bureau of Investigation Announce Arrests Targeting Child Prostitution Rings in Pennsylvania, New Jersey, and Michigan," http://www.fbi.gov.

U.S. Department of State. 2014. "Trafficking in Persons Report," http://www.state.gov.

U.S. Department of State. 2009. "Trafficking in Persons Report," http://www.state.gov.

Watts-English, Tiffany, Beverly L. Fortson, Nicole Gibler, Stephen R. Hooper, and Michael De Bellis. 2006. "The Psychobiology of Maltreatment in Childhood." *Journal of Social Sciences* 62 (4): 717–36. doi: 10.1111/j.1540-4560.2006.00484.x.

Williams, Carmen B., Marsha W. Frame, and Evelyn Green. 1999. "Counseling Groups for African American Women: A Focus on Spirituality." *Journal for Specialists in Group Work* 24 (3): 260–73. doi: 10.1080/01933929908411435.

Wise, Erica H., Matthew A. Hersh, and Clare M. Gibson. 2012. "Ethics, Self-Care, and Well-Being for Psychologists: Re-envisioning the Stress-Distress Continuum." *Professional Psychology: Research and Practice* 43 (5): 487–94. doi: 10.1037/a0029446.

4

Women and Adult Drug Treatment Courts

Surveillance, Social Conformity, and the Exercise of Agency

CORINNE C. DATCHI

I used for nineteen years so, you know, I never learned to be
honest until two years ago. . . . I've never succeeded or completed any probation or anything ever in my life. And when
the judge's seen I was begging for help, you know, that's not
the person that I really am, you know, I really want help.
Even though I could have got help in prison, I didn't want it
back then. I'm a grown-up woman now. I am married. I have
children. And I need to be at home with my children. And
she's seen that. . . . Drug court is like my last option of my
life. To save my life. And that's what it's done.
—Chelsea, 38, African American, married with children,
addiction to crack cocaine

Chelsea is among the 120,000 nonviolent substance-abusing offenders
who are served annually by drug treatment courts (DTC) in the United
States. DTCs are a criminal justice response to the problem of addiction
and drug-related crimes. They provide an alternative to traditional adjudication as well as a solution to the overcrowding of jails and prisons
with low-level drug offenders. The first DTC opened in Miami, Florida,
in 1989, and in June 2014, the U.S. justice system counted 2,968 drug
courts all over the nation (National Drug Court Resource Center 2014).
DTCs are federally funded diversion programs for nonviolent drug
offenders whose criminal behaviors primarily serve to support their
addiction (Hora 2002). Prosecutors identify potential candidates and
determine their eligibility for DTC (National Association of Drug Court
Professionals 2004). Violent crime and drug sale are exclusion criteria.
Participation is voluntary: Qualified defendants are given the option of
enrolling in the DTC program for an average of eighteen months. In

most jurisdictions, they must plead guilty to their current charges before they begin treatment in the community under the supervision of the court (National Association of Criminal Defense Lawyers 2009). If they comply and fulfill the requirements of the DTC program, their charges are dismissed; if they do not, they receive a prison sentence.

In the past decade, drug treatment courts have made the news headlines for giving addicts "a chance to straighten out" and "a free path" to a sober life outside prison (Eckholm 2008; Secret 2013). DTC judges and their team supervise drug offenders in the community: They hold defendants responsible for their criminal behaviors, and monitor their participation in substance-abuse treatment. Media images show compassionate judges shedding tears at a graduation ceremony and program participants thanking the court for saving them. As with Chelsea's story above, they are evidence that the criminal justice system is taking a new approach to addiction and crime: Rehabilitation is now again a priority after three decades of a punitive and unforgiving war on drugs.

Drug treatment courts (DTCs) constitute a significant departure from criminal justice courts: First, they adopt a nonadversarial, collaborative approach to justice, where judges, prosecutors, defense counsels, law enforcement, and mental health practitioners form a therapeutic team (Mackinem and Higgins 2009). They emphasize problem solving, rehabilitation, and accountability; monitor the behaviors and treatment of program participants in regular team meetings and status hearings; and use a system of rewards and sanctions to increase drug offenders' motivation for change (Berman 2009; Hora 2002; National Association of Criminal Defense Lawyers 2009). DTCs follow similar principles, yet vary in their implementation, routine practices, and type of services (Drug Policy Alliance 2011; National Association of Drug Court Professionals 2004). They operate within a theoretical framework that integrates the concepts of deterrence, therapeutic jurisprudence, and abstinence with the view that addiction is a disease of the brain (Brendel and Soulier 2009; Fentiman 2011). DTCs are designed to resolve the underlying causes of crime, shape pro-social attitudes and behaviors, compel drug offenders to enter and stay in treatment, and thus reduce recidivism and promote public safety. To accomplish these objectives, the role of the judge has been redefined from that of neutral facilitator of the adversarial justice process to team leader, service coordinator, and final authority in matters of treatment and legal interventions (Boldt 2009; Drug Policy Alliance 2011; Hora, Schma, and Rosenthal 1999). Informality has replaced professional distance in the courtroom; it also masks the judge's increased power to use sanctions in order to promote compliance and transform drug offenders into law-abiding citizens. In DTCs, punishment and fear are mixed with caring, benevolence, and the desire to save lives (Tiger 2013).

This chapter offers a careful examination of the theories that inform the exercise of problem-solving justice in drug treatment courts (DTCs). It evaluates the impact of DTC interventions on women participants, using qualitative data collected for a study of family involvement in DTC programming. The aim of this study was to identify the legal and social processes that promoted and hindered the participation of family members in the treatment of DTC offenders. In the summer of 2012, thirty-two individuals were interviewed. Their stories were analyzed using the critical methodology developed by Phil Francis Carspecken (1996). The term "critical" refers to the theoretical assumptions that guided the research, in particular the idea that reality is the product of individuals' agreement on what is and what is not true. The power that each individual holds determines the outcomes of such negotiations.

This chapter focuses on the stories of seven women who were arrested and prosecuted for nonviolent drug-related offenses (e.g., drunk driving, fraud, possession of illicit substances). These women, who faced possible prison penalties, pleaded guilty to their charges in order to enter the DTC program of their local community, located in a metropolitan area of the Midwest. They knew they would serve time in prison if they failed out of the program. At the time of their interviews, they had progressed to lower levels of court supervision and had remained sober for several months. Most of them expressed gratitude for the support of the DTC team and the opportunity to receive treatment in the community. Their stories illustrate the success of DTCs; yet, a careful reading reveals narratives of resistance that lie beneath the dominant discourse of "drug courts work" as promulgated by the National Association of Drug Court Professionals. These narratives show the need for more culturally and gender-sensitive interventions in the courtroom, and call for a redefinition of fairness in criminal justice. This chapter also considers how the intersection of race, gender, and class influences women's experiences of

DTC routine practices and of judges' judicial autonomy. The aim is to advance understanding of the unique concerns of diverse DTC participants, in order to improve the problem-solving model of justice and the use of psychological theories in the courtroom.

The Theoretical Framework of Adult Drug Treatment Courts

> There's a great poster of an addict. This is a picture of an addict, half woman, half man, four different colors, like the physician thing here, and the plumber's hat, or a construction hat, or hatch, or accountant thing.... I think what they have in common is they can't stop drinking even though they got into a lot of legal trouble, drinking or drug. (Charles, 66, Caucasian, addiction specialist and DTC team member)

> We're all the same. We're all there [in drug court] kind of for the same reasons. Yeah, we're all different on the surface, but we're all alcoholics and addicts. (Ruth, 40, Caucasian, single with children, addiction to opiates)

Drug treatment courts and problem-solving courts in general signal a return to the rehabilitative ideal of criminal justice and a concern for the therapeutic effects of legal interventions. The first DTCs were a pragmatic, atheoretical response to the overflow of drug cases in the criminal justice system. Today, they draw upon the principles of therapeutic jurisprudence, a field of inquiry that defines the law as a therapeutic agent (Boldt 2009; Hora 2002; Hora, Schma, and Rosenthal 1999; Winick 1997; Wiener et al. 2010).

In DTCs, the theories of two separate systems, psychology and criminal justice, are combined into hybrid practices designed to address the mental health needs as well as the criminogenic risks of drug offenders (Gonzales, Schofield, and Schmitt 2006; Volkow 2007). DTCs are therapeutic courts to the extent that they influence participants to accept treatment, facilitate access to appropriate social and psychological services, and target defendants' motivation at all stages of the program. In theory, the judge and the team use strategies that increase offenders' engagement with and responsibility for change (Hora 2002; Wiener et al. 2010). They recognize that enrollment in the DTC program is voluntary and refrain from exercising legal pressure. They tailor their interventions to the characteristics of the defendants, and use a system of immediate sanctions and incentives to promote desirable behaviors while in the program.

This system of reward and punishment is grounded in psychological theories of conditioning and operates to ensure compliance with the law (e.g., attending court hearings and twelve-step meetings, providing a valid urine sample). It also emphasizes defendants' ability to learn new ways of being and to adopt a new lifestyle. Paradoxically, it coexists with the court's definition of addiction as a chronic disease that reduces individuals' ability to control their behaviors but, unlike with other diseases, does not free drug-using offenders from their legal obligations (Boldt 2009; Larkin, Wood, and Griffiths 2006; Reinarman 2005).

The opening quotations highlight the widespread assumption that drug users and alcoholics are all equal before the disease of addiction regardless of race, gender, age, or class. Although addicts represent all walks of life, their differences blend together into one figure—the human shape of addiction. The construction of addiction as a disease supports the view that drug-using offenders are impaired, act compulsively, and thus have lost control over their capacity to take actions (Foddy 2010). It justifies DTCs' intervention in the everyday life of program participants and the provision of greater structure through mandated treatment, case management, twelve-step meetings, status hearings, and drug testing at least twice a week for the first several months. DTC participants may also have to submit weekly schedules of their activities and receive unplanned home visits from a field officer. These techniques of surveillance are specific ways DTCs participate in the growing reach of the criminal justice system into the private lives of drug offenders.

The framing of addiction as a disease of the brain and the use of conditioning techniques in DTC programs lay emphasis on the individual to the expense of relational and contextual factors. Yet, to understand human behaviors, it is critical to look at the natural environments in which they occur and to identify the social processes that account for problems related to substance use. Gender, race, and class, for example, have a prominent influence on individual experiences. For women in criminal justice settings, poverty, homelessness, lack of education, and health care, as well as cultural norms about motherhood and daily stressors associated with membership in a racial group, are issues that matter (Conner, Le Fauve, and Wallace 2009; Fentiman 2011).

The Relative Success of Drug Treatment Courts

Since their creation in the late 1980s, DTCs have attracted substantial interest from the political and scientific community at the national and local level. Their rapid expansion with the generous support of Congress is evidence that DTCs and other problem-solving courts are becoming a standard of justice that generates enthusiasm among correctional, court, and government officials. This enthusiasm is bolstered by empirical findings that DTC programs increase treatment retention and reduce general and drug-related recidivism by an average of 8 to 14 percent (Cosden et al. 2010; Franco 2010; Koetzle et al. 2015; Mackinem and Higgins 2009; Marlowe 2011; Mitchell et al. 2012). However, this interpretation of the evidence comes with caveats: Dropout rates (between 30 and 50 percent), inconsistent outcomes among different groups of DTC participants, variations in program implementation, the limitations of the studies, and the paucity of follow-up data make it difficult to draw firm conclusions about the effectiveness of DTCs in general (Gray and Saum 2005; NACDL 2009). A few studies have suggested that DTCs produced positive outcomes for those offenders who completed the program and had higher criminogenic risks, such as young adults with multiple past felonies who had not responded to community-based interventions (Marlowe 2011; Koetzle et al. 2015). In contrast, Larsen, Nylund-Gibson, and Cosden (2014) reported that high-risk individuals with a history of early involvement (before age sixteen) in criminal activities and substance use had a lower probability of successfully completing the drug court program. Female DTC participants may fare less well than men on social and mental health outcomes: Green and Rempel (2012) found that women were less likely to be employed, and more likely to report depressive symptoms eighteen months after the start of the program. Although initial evidence indicates that participant characteristics have a moderating influence on the outcomes of DTC programs, questions about who fails out of the program at what costs and who gets excluded still remain to be answered. In addition, there is still limited information about the differential effects of DTC procedures on diverse offenders. Judicial monitoring and the use of sanctions, in particular, are key DTC interventions that warrant more scrutiny in light of research showing that the severity of the first sanction may be linked to program completion (McRee and Drapela 2012).

Women's Experiences of DTC Interventions: Monitoring and Sanctions

> I knew that okay, every Wednesday I need to be in court at seven o'clock. I need to call every morning at five-thirty. I need to go to IOP and aftercare. Three meetings. . . . Mm. You know, I guess I just thought it was something that I would do and then carry on my activities of daily living and, you know, my life, which in a way I am. But in a way [the drug treatment court] comes first as far as me planning my day. . . . So it's more invasive than I thought it would be. (Leonore, 43, Caucasian, married with child, problems with alcohol)

> It was amazing to me how much they knew about each person. The more I went to those drug court sessions, I thought, "Boy, they know everything." . . . I learned to live in a glass house through all this. (Matilda, 44, Caucasian, married with children, addiction to opiates)

The women interviewed during the summer of 2012 used words such as "invasive," "a glass house," and "their eyes on me all the time" to describe their experience of surveillance in the drug court. Their stories indicated the extent to which the court had infiltrated their daily lives and made their affiliation with the program—and thus their identity as DTC participants—a priority over already existing relationships with families and friends. They also highlighted how graduated sanctions, or the use of more severe penalties in response to repeated violations, constituted a mechanism through which the court exercised legal control over their personal lives, and echoed existing worries about the predominance of punishment and the misuse of jail for minor violations such as being late or being obstinate (Boldt 2009; Drug Policy Alliance 2011).

> So I've been in jail so many times, but not because of drink[ing]. I've been in jail because my boyfriend is a drinker, and they don't want me to be with him. . . . I said, "Judge, I didn't put the money [in my boyfriend's jail account]." She said, "If you say you didn't put the money, I'm gonna put you back there [in jail]." I said, "Yes, I put the money." Now let me lie to you. (Samira, 68, African, single, problems with alcohol)

In Samira's case, jail time was used to deter her association with a drinker and, most likely, to minimize the risk factors that could contribute to her relapse. It also compelled her to take a one-down position in her interactions with the Caucasian female judge. This process was supported by the definition of addiction as a sickness that impaired her control and ability to make "rational" choices. It produced a relation of domination that strengthened the operations of gender, race, and class in the courtroom, and perpetuated a social system where lower-class Black women enjoy the least privilege and authority in the public and private spheres.

The women in the research project expressed their fear of sanctions and jail time in particular. Anxiety was a defining element of their experience in the courtroom: It resulted from their perception that punishment was inconsistent and unnecessary, and that jail ("the drunk tank") was a stressful and humiliating event that did not seem to fit the crime—being late and lying.

To me, it *is* horrifying. . . . I sit there and I know that I've done nothing that I'm gonna be in trouble for. But it's the people around you . . . they're talking about their kids and what's going on with their lives and work and this and that. And the next thing you know they're going to jail. (Leonore, 43, Caucasian, married with children, problems with alcohol)

It was very scary. It was very scary. [I was afraid of] being yelled at, you know, being yelled at in front of all these people. Or being thrown in jail. I've seen people come in there, who lie. . . . I think it's aggravating for [the judge] because she wants them to be honest. (Margaret, 27, Caucasian, married with children, addiction to heroin)

In fact the sanction for being late for checking in, . . . you spend the day in jail. . . . You sit in a room that is freezing cold . . . for about eight to ten hours. (Matilda, 44, Caucasian, married with children, addiction to opiates)

The drunk tank is cold, stinky. . . . The camera is there. The men can see you, whether you pee there or not. It's cold. . . . You don't have no clothes. . . . And you already talked, you're honest. (Samira, 68, African, single, problems with alcohol)

For Lenore, Margaret, Matilda, and Samira, jail was shaming and un-safe, and detention was associated with deprivation and vulnerability. Matilda and Samira described handing over their clothes in exchange for a jumpsuit, being confined with others in a "freezing cold" room, and being placed under the close watch of the men behind the camera. Exposed, they had to turn inwards for some sense of privacy.

Women's Experiences of Therapeutic Change in DTC: Autonomy and Agency

"Mandated treatment is effective," says Nora Volkow, director of the National Institute on Drug Abuse (2006), and the criminal justice sys-tem offers the "extraordinary opportunity to intervene and start treating people that are addicted." However, the women interviewed in 2012 indi-cated that forced participation in treatment was not synonymous with client engagement and therapeutic change, and when the use of judicial power was perceived as a threat to self-determination, DTC participants turned to various forms of resistance.

> You can tell when people are at meetings and they're on their phone, you know, they're going outside to smoke when you only have to sit there an hour. . . . Either they don't participate, you know, they don't share, they always, always pass. They're just there because they have to be. (Ruth, 40, Caucasian, single with children, addiction to opiates)

Being on the phone, going outside to smoke, and being silent in AA meetings were behaviors that defied the orders of the court but did not break the rule of compliance. They helped maintain a sense of inde-pendence in a context where individuals' rights to privacy and decision making were diminished. It was not judicial power per se but partici-pants' ability to take ownership of the treatment process that determined their level of engagement. For Margaret, Chelsea, Samira, Lenore, and Ruth, motivation for change was a matter of personal choice rather than the outcome of external pressure and intimidation.

> You know, it wasn't about me going to prison, it was about me, if I was ready to accept this, be ready to do what they're asking me to do, and

learn to love [myself]. . . . (Chelsea, 38, African American, married with children, addiction to crack cocaine)

But the drug court help you when you feel yourself that these things are gonna help me. It's like going to school, you know, you're not going to school for a teacher. You're going to school for yourself. (Samira, 68, African, single, problems with alcohol)

But for the most part the best [AA] meeting I go to is when I don't have to have proof that I was there. That I can go on my own. Nobody's making me go. I just go. (Lenore, 43, Caucasian, married with child, problems with alcohol)

Because if I don't have AA or a program of recovery in my life, then drug court does nothing for me. . . . Drug court, I mean it's there, but they can't get inside your thinking and your heart like the programs do. (Ruth, 40, Caucasian, married with children, addiction to opiates)

Chelsea, Samira, Lenore, and Ruth highlighted the role of agency and autonomy with regard to their sobriety and progress in the drug treatment court. They did not view the court as an agent of change; however, they recognized that it provided boundaries that helped them focus on their sobriety.

Female Drug Offenders Have Unique Concerns: Implications for DTCs

To hear about a woman or a sister that's a drug addict is one thing, but "Oh, she's got kids, two girls." You know. That's even worse. That's a lot worse. And it's just like, you know, my brother saying, "Your kids weren't even enough to stop." . . . Jail is a lot of shame for me. And shame does nothing for me, except make me feel worse. (Matilda, 44, Caucasian, married with children, addiction to opiates)

Female drug offenders face a dual form of marginalization: Their drug use and criminal behaviors defy both the law and gender norms, and challenge women's positioning in structures of social reproduction as well as the gendered organization of social relations (Campbell 2000). Women offenders who use substances have been portrayed as morally stained, irresponsible, sexually promiscuous, unfit, neglectful mothers who are preoccupied with self-gratification rather than their children's welfare (Anderson 2008; Fentiman 2011; Gueta and Addad 2013; Kendall 2010; Larkin, Wood, and Griffiths 2006). They have also been defined as powerless victims of addiction who lack agency and are unable to negotiate their environment (Anderson 2008).

Stigma and shame compound the negative legal consequences that women incur when they disclose their substance use (e.g., loss of child custody) and form a barrier to seeking treatment. They also intensify guilt, self-blame and low self-esteem, increase the risk of relapse, and make it more difficult to discuss drug use publicly, for example, in the courtroom of a drug treatment court where denial is viewed as a form of deceit and punished with sanctions. For female defendants, however, denial may be a coping strategy as much as a sign of addictive or criminal thinking, and a mechanism for managing the negative emotions that result from their interactions with the social environment.

Shame, guilt, and marginalization are some of the concerns women experience while in DTC programs. Compared to men, they have medical and psychological problems as well as family responsibilities that distract them from the priorities of the DTC program and the injunction that they focus on their recovery. They face greater economic challenges, are less educated, and are more likely to be unemployed and homeless and to use harder drugs such as crack and heroin (Ferdinand, Edwards, and Madonia 2012; D'Angelo and Wolf 2002; Glaze and Maruschak 2008). They are also two to four times more likely to report symptoms of depression and anxiety (Gray and Saum 2005).

Addiction research has highlighted other key sex differences that are important for treatment and legal decisions in adult drug courts (Center for Substance Abuse Treatment 2009; Fentiman 2011; Chen 2009; Hartman, Johnson Listwan, and Koetzle Shaffer 2007; Harvard Medical School 2010). First, biological factors (e.g., metabolism, water and body fat ratio, hormonal changes) explain women's greater vulnerability compared to men: Women may experience the rewarding effects of alcohol and drugs with more intensity, suffer more severe medical problems, find it more difficult to quit, develop symptoms of dependence more quickly, and be at a higher risk for relapse while in the DTC program.

In many cases, female addiction develops in the context of interpersonal and family violence where substance use functions as a strategy for coping with the psychological effects of past and/or present victimization (Covington 2008; Fentiman 2011; Chen 2009; Waldrop 2009). Women's exposure to sexual, physical, and emotional abuse results in lower feelings of safety and control over their body and their environment, and undermines their sense of agency. Boyfriends, partners, or spouses who use substances have a major influence on women's initiation to drugs and alcohol (Center for Substance Abuse Treatment 2009). Some women perceive substance use as a bonding activity that sustains their intimate relationship; they also experience relational conflict as a stressor and relapse trigger.

The psychological profile of women with addiction has important implications for therapeutic interventions in justice settings and drug treatment courts in particular. First, it is essential to underscore the link between trauma and addiction. Trauma is related to relapse in women but not in men (Heffner, Blom, and Anthenelli 2011). When drug courts emphasize abstinence and recovery as a treatment priority, they neglect women's unique need to address the effects of violence before they can imagine life without alcohol and drugs. When the treatment team uses jail time as a response to relapse, they also fail to consider whether this sanction may exacerbate women's trauma-related symptoms, including helplessness, self-blame, guilt, depression, and anxiety, and thus complicate women's progress towards sobriety. Jail weakens any sense of safety and power women may have gained during treatment. It may reduce trust and make it more difficulty to comply with the court's expectations for honesty and transparency. For female participants with a history of abuse, incarceration reinforces the belief that the person does not have control over herself, her body, and her environment. It reproduces the processes of disempowerment that occur in abusive relationships, and makes it less likely that women will address their trauma while in the DTC program. If addiction is not a choice and if substance use affects brain processes involved in the control of behaviors (Home Box Office 2007), then the threat and fear of incarceration will not prevent addicts from pursuing their drug of choice, even if they do not want to use.

However, it may have adverse consequences on the vast majority of female DTC participants who have a history of interpersonal violence and sexual trauma in particular.

Because incarceration is usually associated with criminal behaviors, it is a sign of deviance that supports the perception of substance-using women as unfit mothers. For female defendants involved in the child welfare system, jail time may pose a threat to their parental rights and place them further at risk of developing psychological problems that will undermine their recovery. Detention is also a significant disruption in the defendants' everyday life. It may result in loss of employment and income, limit the participant's ability to pay court fees, and therefore delay graduation from the program. This is an important concern given the wage gap between men and women in the United States (See chapter 9 in this book). The use of jail time may exacerbate already-existing gender disparities in income and thus further reduce women's ability to meet the requirements of the drug court program.

The Intersection of Gender, Class, and Race: Implications for DTCs

The focus of DTC programs on individual recovery, abstinence, fear, and deterrence conflicts with the multidimensional needs of substance-using women. In some cases, it may perpetuate the cycle of drug-using and law-breaking behaviors, as abstinence intensifies psychological distress, which in turn increases the likelihood of relapse for female offenders who use drugs and alcohol to self-medicate psychiatric symptoms. Trauma, relationships, and family roles are critical factors that may explain differences in outcomes between men and women. Likewise, considerations of race and class are critical to understanding the effects of DTC programs on diverse women.

Because African American women have the lowest retention rates in substance abuse treatment (Davis and Ancis 2012), and are three times as likely as White women to serve time behind bars for drug offenses (ACLU 2005, 2006; Glaze 2011; Mauer 2013), their culturally specific concerns warrant further consideration and offer an opportunity to highlight the intersection of class, race, and gender as relates to addiction and crime. Racism and sexism create persistent barriers to economic and social opportunities, perpetuate the lower status of African American women, and affect their well-being in ways that increase their vulnerability to substance use. Current research suggests that the stress associated with experiences of racial oppression has a direct impact on substance use; yet, the effects of racism are moderated by the strength of women's identification with and participation in African American culture (Stevens-Watkins et al. 2012). When African American women engage in the cultural practices of their racial community and connect with family and friends, they are better able to cope with racial aggressions and are at lower risk for drug use. Research also highlights the protective role of religion and spirituality, the link between feelings of powerlessness and experiences of racism, and the positive effects of trust, cultural sensitivity, and egalitarianism on treatment retention (Conner et al. 2009; Curtis-Boles and Jenkins-Monro 2000; Davis and Ancis 2012).

This knowledge may help explain why African American women in ten Missouri drug courts were more likely than all other groups to terminate early (Dannerbeck, Sundet, and Lloyd 2002). According to the National Association of Drug Court Professionals (2011), addiction to crack cocaine and lower socioeconomic status explained racial disparities in the study. This interpretation focuses on individual characteristics and does not recognize the importance of systemic processes in and outside of the courtroom. To enhance treatment outcomes, it is critical to integrate considerations of gender, class, and race. For example, it is possible that the demands of the DTC programs increased the stress associated with racial and gender oppression. Historically, African American women have been denied equal access to economic, political, and social resources; they have fewer opportunities for employment, which puts them at a disadvantage compared to their peers in DTC programs. Emphasis on individual recovery through regular attendance at case-management and twelve-step meetings, counseling sessions, and status hearings may represent a financial burden and limit their ability to engage in the activities of their racial community, to heal their relationships with family and friends, and to strengthen their racial identity in order to manage the effects of oppression. In their interactions with law officials and treatment providers, African American women are most likely exposed to racial and gender micro-aggressions, intentional or not, that reduce their chances of success (Nadal et al. 2014). These micro-aggressions shape their perception of the court as insensitive and untrustworthy, which in turn creates difficulties for treatment compliance and retention. Finally, ongoing monitoring and sanctions may increase their feelings of powerlessness and lead to avoidant behaviors in a context where active coping may result in more punishment (Stevens-Watkins et al. 2012). As a consequence, African American women may disengage from the DTC program, receive more sanctions, experience more stress, and be at higher risk for relapse and dropout.

Recommendations for Culturally and Gender-Responsive Justice

Cultural and gender responsiveness in adult drug treatment courts requires awareness of human differences and the way related social processes influence mental health and help-seeking behaviors as well as criminal justice practices (American Psychological Association 2007). It depends on the court's knowledge of the specific social, economic, and psychological needs of diverse populations and calls for appropriate program adaptations. Substance-using women in the criminal justice system face barriers that are unique to their social positioning: The majority are members of a racial/ethnic minority and are responsible for minor children; they are undereducated and have fewer job skills; they also have a history of victimization and high rates of medical and psychological problems (Bloom, Owen, and Covington 2002; Ney, Ramirez, and Van Dieten 2012). Their circumstances have important implications for the administration of the law in adult drug treatment courts.

Below are recommendations designed to promote the integration of psychological knowledge into legal practice and to enhance the cultural and gender responsiveness of DTC programs. These recommendations follow the American Psychological Association's Guidelines for Psychological Practice with Girls and Women (2007). In particular, they offer strategies to increase awareness of gender socialization and discrimination as they relate to mental health (APA Guideline numbers 1 and 3), to integrate information about human differences into DTC practices (APA Guideline number 2), and to support the use of gender- and culturally affirming interventions in adult drug treatment courts (APA Guideline number 4).

Recommendation # 1: Educate the DTC team about women's issues and integrate considerations of gender and race in treatment decisions.

Judges and staff should tailor their motivational strategies to address both addiction and trauma among women in adult drug treatment courts (Center for Substance Abuse Treatment 2005). Initial assessment of participants' risk factors should include questions about past and current abuse, trauma symptoms, and triggers. Survivors of interpersonal violence are sensitive to conditions that remind them of traumatic events, including tone of voice, body posture, and confrontational techniques. The court should adjust interventions to minimize trauma triggers and consider the need for more treatment rather than more punishment in response to relapse. Decisions about judicial sanctions and jail time in particular should take into account the participants' clinical profile, as detention may increase the risk of relapse among women with a history of abuse (Covington 2008). DTC staff should strive to create a supportive environment where women with trauma symptoms feel safe. If possible, they should minimize the use of punitive, shaming, and intrusive interventions. Women's specific concerns call for the development of new monitoring and behavior-management strategies. While this may pose a significant challenge for judicial settings that are primarily designed to handle male offenders, the tailored approach of DTCs creates conditions that are favorable to gender-responsive interventions.

Gender responsiveness is contingent upon the team's awareness that women's issues limit their ability to engage in treatment. Women's caregiving responsibilities are a critical factor as relates to treatment outcomes: Substance-using mothers fare better when they are able to participate in programming with their children; they are more likely to remain in treatment and maintain sobriety (Center for Substance Abuse Treatment 2009). Yet, very few facilities offer this opportunity: In 2003, 4 percent of residential programs had the capacity to serve mothers and their children, and 8 percent provided childcare services. When childcare is not available, mothers who have custody of their children are more likely to drop out of treatment (Brendel and Soulier 2009). Parenting is also a major stressor that complicates the recovery process (D'Angelo and Wolf 2002). For example, child and adolescent externalizing behaviors associated with parental substance abuse increase the caregiving burden. Women's restricted income exacerbates these family difficulties and is associated with a pattern of no-show or tardiness in therapy. These issues should inform the court's understanding of women's behaviors: Noncompliance may be the result of practical difficulties as much as criminal and addictive thinking. Appropriate responses to these problems include parenting classes, family therapy, and assistance with childcare and transportation.

Practical barriers, victimization, and higher rates of mental and medical disorders increase women's vulnerability to relapse. Repeated drug and alcohol use may result in more severe sanctions, which in turn may increase participants' burden and reduce their ability to meet program requirements, leading eventually to their termination and sentencing to prison. To avoid these iatrogenic outcomes, DTC judges and staff may consider alternatives to the model of abstinence. Medications are now available for the treatment of opiate and alcohol addiction; they can help DTC participants to manage the biological processes of relapse, early in the program, as they address the psychological and environmental factors that contribute to their substance-use disorder. Addiction medications offer an evidence-based strategy accepted by the National Institute on Drug Abuse but underutilized in justice settings (Volkow 2006). They have the potential to enhance DTC female participants' chances of success.

Recommendation #2: Adopt an empowerment approach to the rehabilitation of female participants.

In general, substance-using women enter treatment with a diminished sense of self and a history of self-neglect (Covington 2002). Their recovery depends on their ability to attain higher levels of self-esteem and to regain a sense of control over their lives. Empowering interventions aim to promote women's autonomy and agency. They help manage the effects of social inequalities and marginalization, and require the creation of an environment where women feel safe and respected, and where they can form meaningful connections with others.

In adult drug treatment courts, women's interactions with judges and case managers are opportunities for growth-fostering and empathic relationships, provided these interactions do not reproduce women's experiences of abuse and do offer a model of healthy relating based on reciprocal influence and trust (Bloom, Owen, and Covington 2002). Reciprocal influence and trust are characteristics of collaborative relationships. These are difficult yet not impossible in relations of power; they call for an empowerment approach to DTC procedures and for judges' readiness to share power in the courtroom. Power sharing may take different forms:

- *Behavorial contracts between participants and the court.* Similar to individualized plans in mental health services, these contracts would be discussed with all parties, and both the team and the participant would agree on their terms. They would specify which behaviors are unacceptable and how they will be sanctioned. They would be subject to change, and would replace discussions that happen behind closed doors, solely between the judge and the team (NACDL 2009). They would enable participants to assume greater responsibility in the court's treatment process.
- *Participants' role in making decisions.* The Honorable Peggy Fulton Hora (2002) suggests that it is possible for judges to modify their position in the courtroom and to allow participants to select their own sanctions, in order to enhance the therapeutic effects of DTC practices: "When participants themselves propose the sanctions, they are more likely to comply with them, and not feel coerced by the system or the judge. Persons who propose their own punishment can't help but think it's fair" (1477). When participants play a role in making decisions, they have a voice in the legal process; they are more likely to experience interactional fairness and to comply with judicial orders.
- *Empathy and positive regard* are important ingredients of therapeutic interactions. Judges communicate respect through nonverbal behaviors and their efforts to understand participants and explain their decisions. Their knowledge and consideration of gender and racial issues enhance their ability to deliver empathy and caring.
- *Emphasis on progress and rewards.* When DTC judges distribute sanctions, they highlight individual errors and faults as well as their legal and social consequences. Their goal is to deter noncompliance among all participants in the DTC program. However, if public punishment prevails in the courtroom, and if it is perceived as unfair, it may be less successful in producing long-term positive change than the use of rewards. To date, there has been

much debate, but little evidence, about the outcomes of graduated sanctions and jail time in particular (Marlowe 2012; Boldt 2009; McRee and Drapela 2012). Until research answers questions about the prevalence and effectiveness of punishment compared to rewards, it is important to consider the value of an empowerment approach to DTC interventions, where judges emphasize participants' strengths and reward progress in ways that increase women's self-esteem and self-efficacy.

In general, female offenders pose lower risks to public safety than men: They tend to engage in nonviolent criminal activities that involve drugs and property and that are driven by poverty and addiction (Bloom, Owen, and Covington 2002). These gender differences justify the adoption of an empowerment approach to justice interventions. Collaborative decision making, transparency, empathy, positive regard, and positive reinforcement promote agency, foster a sense of safety, and constitute a model of relating that values women's voices and experiences. They have the potential to enhance the outcomes of nonviolent female drug offenders in adult drug treatment courts.

Recommendation #3: Recognize the significance of relationships in women's lives, and adopt a relational approach to judicial interventions in and out of the courtroom.

Psychological research has shown that belongingness and connectedness are critical to women's identity development, and that the quality of women's relationships with others has an impact on their self-esteem and well-being (Covington 2002; Frey 2013). Relationships also play a major role in women's initiation of substance use and introduction to a criminal lifestyle (Bloom, Owen, and Covington 2002; Covington, 2002, 2008; Ney et al. 2012). In general, women engage in antisocial behaviors to provide for their children or to protect their connection with a significant other. Effective intervention programs take into consideration the relational pathways that lead to women's involvement in the criminal justice system (SAMHSA 2011a). They translate current knowledge about women's contextual risk factors into family and community-focused practices that help substance-using women form healthy relationships with their children, family members, and other social support systems.

A relational approach to judicial practices in adult drug treatment courts requires a careful assessment of the multiple systems that influence women's behaviors. It also calls for legal decisions that enhance connection in women's lives. For example, DTC judges and staff should consider referrals to couple and family-based substance-abuse treatment before they order female participants to avoid contact with significant others and relatives. They should promote family reunification, when it is safe for children, and provide assistance with legal procedures in family courts. Women's ability to regain custody of their children is a motivating factor for long-term rehabilitation. However, parenting and childcare challenges together with recovery needs may also increase the risk of relapse. For that reason, parenting programs should also be included in the treatment of female defendants, to reestablish their caregiving role and improve parent-child relationships.

Conclusion

Problem-solving courts represent a drastic and welcome change in the criminal justice system. The success of adult drug treatment courts, in particular, highlights the value of jail diversion and community-based rehabilitation. DTC programs integrate mental health treatment and criminal law in order to save lives. Their intent is both benevolent and noble. However, the blending of therapeutic and judicial principles constitutes a significant challenge in settings that have traditionally been punitive in practice. It is judges' responsibility to rule in favor of public safety. In drug treatment courts, they must combine public safety with treatment considerations in ways that produce positive outcomes for individual offenders and the community.

The therapeutic administration of the law depends on the justice system's sensitivity to the specific needs of diverse offender populations. This chapter has highlighted the concerns of substance-using women in criminal justice settings, and discussed how this knowledge might be used to enhance the therapeutic effects of DTC practices. In addition, this chapter has raised concerns about the court's increased power over participants, and nonviolent women defendants in particular, whose criminal activities (e.g., theft, drug possession, drunk driving) present a lower risk to public safety.

In adult drug treatment courts, caring and coercion coexist in ways that conceal the reproduction of social structures of domination. During status hearings, judges have the authority to override team decisions and to modify interventions in response to defendants' actions. Their challenge is to encourage participants to make healthy choices using coercive mechanisms that reproduce relations of domination. Their one-up position is strengthened by the use of punitive measures, jail time in particular. How disadvantaged individuals experience judges' exercise of power is important to treatment. When jail time is the consequence for being late, missing a meeting, lying, or being obstinate, then it is clear that the court's interventions are guided by an ideological discourse that emphasizes responsibility, hard work, truthfulness, and transparency. It is also apparent that change in DTC programs is a process of reformation: Adult drug treatment courts are not only a diversion program but a place where drug offenders should redeem themselves, shed their old self, and abide by the norms of society. When graduation from the DTC program is linked to social conformity, then there are important questions we must ask: Whose social norms and ideals must the participants embrace? To what extent are diverse participants equally able and willing to embrace these norms and ideals? And what are the consequences when they succeed or fail to meet these standards? Both the hierarchical organization of the court and the injunction to enact dominant social norms may compound the effects of women's subordinate status in society. Combined with the perception that sanctions are not fair, they may diminish women's sense of agency, level of motivation, and opportunity for success.

Therapeutic jurisprudence provides a theoretical and empirical framework for the ongoing assessment of drug court procedures. The key components of DTC programs offer broad guidelines for implementation (NADCP 2004). What happens in and out of the courtroom is subject to local variations, norms, beliefs, and broader social processes that should be examined in order to prevent undesirable outcomes. Evaluations of DTC programs should address questions about gender, class, and race, how they influence participants' interactions with DTC staff, the court's assessment of the participants' progress, and the selection of interventions. Research should also investigate the unintended consequences of defining drug offenders as sick and powerless, yet willful and responsible, and examine how structural inequalities get reproduced when judicial power is used to motivate DTC participants, to encourage them to accept their illness, to surrender to the demands of the court, and, if necessary, to give up their due process rights for the sake of recovery and rehabilitation. Answering these questions will enhance the implementation of problem-solving justice and promote fairness, impartiality, and collaborative decision making, which are key ingredients of change in offender rehabilitation.

Problem-solving courts offer a unique opportunity for psychologists to advance social justice by participating in the development, implementation, and evaluation of legal programs and interventions. Psychologists' expertise as relates to human behaviors, addiction, mental health, and person-environment interactions can help broaden the perspective of criminal courts and increase judges' responsiveness to diversity issues. However, the successful integration of treatment, psychology, and justice may require a fundamental shift in the structural organization of problem-solving courts and in the relations among judges, participants, and mental health professionals. In particular, this chapter proposed to increase women's involvement in decision making in order to support the development of women's autonomy and agency in DTC programs. This recommendation asks for the subversive redistribution of power in the courtroom, in order to make women's issues a treatment priority. It is also a major departure from the principle of parity and equal treatment in criminal justice, because it calls for the recognition that women's crimes and criminogenic needs (i.e., the risk factors that are amenable to change) warrant greater treatment consideration. Until judges and other legal staff acknowledge and integrate gender differences in judicial practices, problem-solving courts may fall short in implementing a tailored approach to justice.

REFERENCES

American Civil Liberties Union. 2006. *Cracks in the System: Twenty Years of the Unjust Federal Crack Cocaine Law*, http://www.aclu.org.

American Civil Liberties Union. 2005. *Caught in the Net: The Impact of Drug Policies on Women and Families*, http://www.aclu.org.

American Psychological Association. 2007. "Guidelines for Psychological Practice with Girls and Women." *American Psychologist* 62 (9): 949–79.

Anderson, Tammy L. 2008. "Introduction." In *Neither Villain nor Victim: Empowerment and Agency among Women Substance Abusers.* Edited by Tammy L. Anderson, 1–10. New Brunswick, NJ: Rutgers University Press.

Berman, Greg. 2009. "Problem-Solving Justice and the Moment of Truth." In *Problem-Solving Courts: Justice for the 21st Century?* Edited by Paul C. Higgins and Mitchell B. Mackinem, 1–11. Santa Barbara, CA: ABC-CLIO.

Bloom, Barbara, and Stephanie Covington. 2009. "Addressing the Mental Health Needs of Women Offenders." In *Women's Mental Health Issues across the Criminal Justice System.* Edited by Rosemary Gido and Lanette Dalley, 160–76. Columbus, OH: Prentice Hall.

Bloom, Barbara, Barbara Owen, and Stephanie Covington. 2002. *Gender-Responsive Strategies: Research, Practice, and Guiding Principles for Women Offenders,* http://static.nicic.gov.

Boldt, Richard C. 2009. "A Circumspect Look at Problem-Solving Courts." In *Problem-Solving Courts: Justice for the 21st century?* Edited by Paul C. Higgins and Mitchell B. Mackinem, 13–32. Santa Barbara, CA: ABC-CLIO.

Brendel, Rebecca W., and Matthew F. Soulier. 2009. "Legal Issues, Addiction, and Gender." In *Women and Addiction: A Comprehensive Handbook.* Edited by Kathleen T. Brady, Sudie E. Back, and Shelly F. Greenfield, 500–515. New York: Guilford.

Campbell, Nancy D. 2000. *Using Women: Gender, Drug Policy, and Social Justice.* New York: Routledge.

Carspecken, Phil F. 1996. *Critical Ethnography in Educational Research: A Theoretical and Practical Guide.* New York: Routledge.

Center for Substance Abuse Treatment. 2009. *Substance Abuse Treatment: Addressing the Specific Needs of Women (TIP 51),* http:// www.ncbi.nlm.nih.gov.

Center for Substance Abuse Treatment. 2005. *Substance Abuse Treatment for Adults in the Criminal Justice System (TIP 44),* http://www.ncbi.nlm.nih.gov.

Chen, Gila. 2009. "Gender Differences in Crime, Drug Addiction, Abstinence, Personality Characteristics, and Negative Emotions." *Journal of Psychoactive Drugs* 41 (3): 255–66.

Conner, Latoya C., Charlene E. Le Fauve, and Barbara C. Wallace. 2009. "Ethnic and Cultural Correlates of Addiction among Diverse Women." In *Women and Addiction: A Comprehensive Handbook.* Edited by Kathleen T. Brady, Sudie E. Back, and Shelly F. Greenfield, 453–74. New York: Guilford.

Cosden, Merith, Amber Baker, Cristina Benki, Sarah Patz, Sara Walker, and Kristen Sullivan. 2010. "Consumers' Perspectives on Successful and Unsuccessful Experiences in a Drug Treatment Court." *Substance Use and Misuse* 45: 1033–49.

Covington, Stephanie S. 2008. Women and Addiction: A Trauma-Informed Approach. *Journal of Psychoactive Drugs,* SARC Supplement 5: 377–85.

Covington, Stephanie S. 2002. "Helping Women Recover: Creating Gender-Responsive Treatment." In *The Handbook of Addiction Treatment for Women: Theory and Practice.* Edited by Shulamith L. Ashenberg Straussner and Stephanie Brown, 52–72. San Francisco: Jossey-Bass.

Curtis-Boles, Harriet, and Valata Jenkins-Monroe. 2000. "Substance Abuse in African American Women." *Journal of Black Psychology* 26 (4): 450–69.

D'Angelo, Laura, and Robert V. Wolf. 2002. "Women and Addiction: Challenges for Drug Court Practitioners." *Justice System Journal* 23 (3): 385–400.

Dannerbeck, Anne, Paul Sundet, and Kathy Lloyd. 2002. "Drug Courts: Gender Differences and Their Implications for Treatment Strategies." *Corrections Compendium* 27 (12): 1–26.

Davis, Telsie, and Julie Ancis. 2012. "Look to the Relationship: A Review of African American Women Substance Users' Poor Treatment Retention and Working Alliance Development." *Substance Use and Misuse* 47 (6): 662–72.

Drug Policy Alliance. 2011. *Drug Courts Are Not the Answer: Toward a Health-Centered Approach to Drug Use*, www.drugpolicy.org.

Eckholm, Erik. 2008. "Courts Give Addicts a Chance to Straighten Out." *New York Times*, October 14, http://www.nytimes.com.

Fentiman, Lisa C. 2011. "Rethinking Addiction: Drugs, Deterrence, and the Neuroscience Revolution." *University of Pennsylvania Journal of Law and Social Change* 233: 232–71.

Ferdinand, Jo A., Christine Edwards, and Joseph Madonia. 2012. *Addiction, Treatment, and Criminal Justice: An Inside View of the Brooklyn Treatment Court*, http://www.courtinnovation.org.

Foddy, Bennett. 2010. "Addiction and Its Sciences–Philosophy." *Addiction* 106 (1): 25–31.

Franco, Celinda. 2010. *Drug Courts: Background, Effectiveness, and Policy Issues for Congress*, http://www.fas.org.

Frey, Lisa L. 2013. "Relational-Cultural Therapy: Theory, Research, and Application to Counseling Competencies." *Professional Psychology: Research and Practice* 44 (3): 177–85.

Glaze, Lauren E. 2011. *Correctional Populations in the United States, 2010*, http://www.bjs.gov.

Glaze, Lauren E., and Laura Maruschak. 2008. *Parents in Prison and Their Minor Children*, http://www.bjs.gov.

Gonzales, Alberto R., Regina B. Schofield, and Glenn R. Schmitt. 2006. *Drug Courts: The Second Decade*, http://www.ndcrc.org

Gray, Alison R., and Christine A. Saum. 2005. "Mental Health, Gender, and Drug Court Completion." *American Journal of Criminal Justice* 30 (1): 55–69.

Green, Mia, and Michael Rempel. 2012. "Beyond Crime and Drug Use: Do Adult Drug Courts Produce Other Psychosocial Benefits?" *Journal of Drug Issues* 42 (2): 156–77.

Gueta, Keren, and Moshe Addad. 2013. "Moulding an Emancipatory Discourse: How Mothers Recovering from Addiction Build Their Own Discourse." *Addiction Research and Theory* 21 (1): 33–42.

Hartman, Jennifer L., Shelley Johnson Listwa, and Deborah Koetzle Shaffer. 2007. "Methamphetamine Users in a Community-Based Drug Court: Does Gender Matter?" *Journal of Offender Rehabilitation* 45 (3–4): 109–30.

Harvard Medical School. January 2010. "Addiction in Women." *Harvard Mental Health Letter* 26 (7): 1–3.

Heffner, Jaime, Thomas J. Blom, and Robert M. Anthenelli. 2011. "Gender Differences in Trauma History and Symptoms as Predictors of Relapse to Alcohol and Drug Use." *American Journal on Addictions* 20 (4): 307–11.

Home Box Office. 2007. "An Interview with Nora D. Volkow, M.D." *The Addiction Project: Why Can't They Stop? New Knowledge, New Treatment, New Hope*, http://www.hbo.com.

Hora, Peggy F. 2002. "A Dozen Years of Drug Treatment Courts: Uncovering Our Theoretical Foundation and the Construction of a Mainstream Paradigm." *Substance Use and Misuse* 37 (12–13): 1469–88.

Hora, Peggy F., William G. Schma, and John T. A. Rosenthal. 1999. "Therapeutic Jurisprudence and the Drug Treatment Court Movement: Revolutionizing the Criminal Justice System's Response to Drug Abuse." *Notre Dame Law Review* 74 (2): 439–537.

Kendall, Stephen R. 2010. "Women and Drug Addiction: A Historical Perspective." *Journal of Addictive Diseases* 29 (2): 117–26.

Koetzle, Deborah, Shelley Johnson Listwan, Wendy P. Guastaferro, and Kara Kobus. 2015. "Treating High-Risk Offenders in the Community: The Potential of Drug Courts." *International Journal of Offender Therapy and Comparative Criminology* 59 (5): 449–65.

Larkin, Michael, Richard T. A. Wood, and Mark D. Griffiths. 2006. "Towards Addiction as Relationship." *Addiction Research and Theory* 14 (3): 207–15.

Larsen, Jessica L., Karen Nylund-Gibson, and Merith Cosden. 2014. "Using Latent Class Analysis to Identify Participant Typologies in a Drug Treatment Court." *Drug and Alcohol Dependence* 138: 75–82.

Mackinem, Mitchell B., and Paul C. Higgins. 2009. "Adult Drug Courts: A Hope Realized?" In *Problem-Solving Courts: Justice for the 21st Century?* Edited by Paul Higgins and Mitchell B. Mackinem, 33–49. Santa Barbara: ABC-CLIO.

Marlowe, Douglas B. 2011. "The Verdict on Drug Courts and Other Problem-Solving Courts." *Chapman Journal of Criminal Justice* 2 (1): 57–96.

Mauer, Marc. 2013. *The Changing Racial Dynamics of Women's Incarceration*, http://sentencingproject.org.

McRee, Nick, and Laurie A. Drapela. 2012. "The Timing and Accumulation of Judicial Sanctions among Drug Court Clients." *Crime and Delinquency* 58 (6): 911–31.

Mitchell, Ojmarrh, David B. Wilson, Amy Eggers, and Doris L. MacKenzie. 2012. "Assessing the Effectiveness of Drug Courts on Recidivism: A Meta-Analytic Review of Traditional and Non-traditional Drug Courts." *Journal of Criminal Justice* 40 (1): 60–71.

Nadal, Kevin L, Katie E. Griffin, Yinglee Wong, Sahran Hamit, and Morgan Rasmus. 2014. "The Impact of Racial Microaggressions on Mental Health: Counseling Implications for Clients of Color." *Journal of Counseling and Development* 92: 57–66.

National Association of Criminal Defense Lawyers. 2009. *America's Problem Solving Courts: The Criminal Costs of Treatment and the Case for Reform*, http://www.nacdl.org.

National Association of Drug Court Professionals. 2011. *Drug Courts Save Lives and Money and for That They Are Attacked by Decriminalizers*, http://www.nadcp.org.

National Association of Drug Court Professionals. 2004. *Defining Drug Courts: The Key Components*, https://www.ncjrs.gov.

National Drug Court Resource Center. 2014. *How Many Drug Courts Are There?* http://www.ndcrc.org.

Ney, Becky, Rachelle Ramirez, and Marilyn Van Dieten, eds. 2012. *Ten Truths That Matter When Working with Justice-Involved Women*, http://nicic.gov.

Reinarman, Craig. 2005. "Addiction as Accomplishment: The Discursive Construction of Disease." *Addiction Research and Theory* 13 (4): 307–20.

Roberts, James C., and Loreen Wolfer. 2011. "Female Drug Offenders Reflect on Their Experiences with a County Drug Court Program." *Qualitative Report* 16 (1): 84–102.

Saum, Christine A., and Alison R. Gray. 2008. "Facilitating Change for Women? Exploring the Role of Therapeutic Jurisprudence in Drug Court." In *Neither Villain nor Victim: Empowerment and Agency among Women Substance Abusers*. Edited by Tammy L. Anderson, 102–16. New Brunswick, NJ: Rutgers University Press.

Secret, Mosi. 2013. "Outside Box, Federal Judges Offer Addicts a Free Path." *New York Times*, March 2, http://www.nytimes.com.

Stevens-Watkins, Danelle, Brea Perry, Kathy L. Harp, and Carrie B. Oser. 2012. "Racism and Illicit Drug Use among African American Women: The Protective Effects of Ethnic Identity, Affirmation, and Behavior." *Journal of Black Psychology* 38 (4): 471–96.

Substance Abuse and Mental Health Services Administration 2011a. *Addressing the Needs of Women and Girls: Developing Core Competencies for Mental Health and Substance Abuse Service Professionals*, http://store.samhsa.gov.

Substance Abuse and Mental Health Services Administration. 2011b. *Results from the 2010 National Survey on Drug Use and Health: Summary of National Findings*, http://www.oas.samhsa.gov.

Tiger, Rebecca. 2013. *Drug Courts and Coercion in the Justice System*. New York: NYU Press.

Volkow, Nora D. 2006. *An Examination of Drug Treatment Programs Needed to Ensure Successful Re-entry. Testimony to Congress*, http://www.drugabuse.gov.

Waldrop, Angela E. 2009. "Violence and Victimization among Women with Substance Use Disorders." In *Women and Addiction: A Comprehensive Handbook*. Edited by Kathleen T. Brady, Sudie E. Back, and Shelly F. Greenfield, 493–99. New York: Guilford.

Wiener, Richard, Bruce J. Winick, Leah Skovran Georges, and Anthony Castro. 2010. "A Testable Theory of Problem-Solving Courts: Avoiding Past Empirical and Legal Failures." *International Journal of Law and Psychiatry* 33 (5–6): 417–27.

Winick, Bruce J. 1997. "The Jurisprudence of Therapeutic Jurisprudence." *Psychology, Public Policy, and Law* 3 (1): 184–206.

5

Women, Incarceration, and Reentry

The Revolving Door of Prisons

ELIZABETH A. LILLIOTT, ELISE M. TROTT, NICOLE C. KEL-
LETT, AMY E. GREEN, AND CATHLEEN E. WILLGING

Women's incarceration rates have doubled since the 1990s (Rowan-Szal et al. 2009), as policies stemming from the War on Drugs result in higher arrest rates and longer sentences for women (Aday and Farney 2014), most of whom are imprisoned for nonviolent crimes (Smyth 2012; U.S. Department of Justice 2011). Women face myriad social and economic challenges upon release, especially when returning to rural areas where the intersecting challenges of poverty, social stigma, and resource scarcity constitute formidable impediments to their well-being and future life chances. Within this stressful context, women prisoners experience elevated risks for recidivism (Willging et al. 2013) and drug overdose and suicide in the weeks after release (Binswanger et al. 2007). In the rural state of New Mexico, women prisoners have commented on the cycle of reincarceration, claiming that inmates return to prison for the security of "three hots and a cot" or, as one inmate stated, "They are not afraid to come back because it's a roof and three squares."

In this chapter, we analyze the layered oppressions revealed in women inmates' description of conditions within prison and in their rural communities. We consider how their lives in rural areas are cast in a negative light in contrast to the presumed safety and predictability of existence in prison, while problematizing the facile conclusion that repeat offenders "prefer" prison. We also assess the complex challenges affecting women during and after incarceration, focusing on how negative ideologies, insufficient services and resources, and social support within and outside of prison influence well-being and chances for successful reentry.

To understand these experiences, we draw upon semistructured interview data collected between March and August 2009 from rural inmates of New Mexico's only women's prison. These data were collected as part of a larger multimethod study of women prisoners that included inmates in the general population who were scheduled to return to rural communities within the next six months. We interviewed a total of ninety-nine women who self-identified as Hispanic ($n = 33$), Native American ($n = 33$), non-Hispanic White ($n = 32$), and African American ($n = 1$). Interviewees ranged in age from twenty to fifty-six years old ($M = 35.2$, median = 34, $SD = 8.4$) with educational histories of four to sixteen years ($M = 11.0$, median = 11, $SD = 1.9$). Interviewees had been incarcerated from approximately nine months to three years, and almost half (47 percent) had been reincarcerated in the state prison (Willging et al. 2013).

In this chapter, we highlight our analysis of interview data. We used an iterative process of open and focused coding to analyze these data. First, segments of text ranging from a phrase to several paragraphs were assigned codes based a priori on the topics and questions that made up the interview guide. We then used *open coding* to identify and define new codes to capture information on emergent themes. Finally, we used *focused coding* to determine which themes surfaced frequently and which represented unusual or particular issues for rural women prisoners. After constantly comparing and contrasting codes, we grouped together those with similar content or meaning into broad themes that addressed the social and psychological concerns of women in prison, reentry planning, and factors that contribute to the phenomenon of reincarceration (Corbin and Strauss 2008).

Our goal is to show how the meager comforts of prison life, the stigma of being a felon, and the scarcity of resources within rural New Mexico are illustrative of the multiple oppressions that cause women released from prison to return to criminalized behavior and incarceration. We argue that the convergence of these overlapping forms of "structural violence" (Galtung 1993), combined with the effects and ideologies of neoliberalism, can prevent women from accessing resources to achieve a successful transition from prison while simultaneously facilitating the "revolving door" of reincarceration. We highlight the importance of a social justice psychology framework that attends to the structural inequities, system deficiencies, pervasive trauma, and health disparities that shape the lives of rural women prisoners. We also discuss psychologists' efforts to spearhead social justice– and trauma-informed reentry services in order to disrupt the pernicious cycle of rural women's incarceration and recidivism, and thereby improve their overall life chances.

Neoliberalism, Structural Violence, and Social Justice

The material conditions of rural life in New Mexico and the ideologies influencing both perceptions and social relationships of returning women prisoners are perpetuated through the socioeconomic structures and dominant discourses of neoliberalism. Neoliberalism—the guiding framework for economic and political processes in the United States since the 1970s—is characterized by the idea that human well-being is maximized through application of market exchange principles within all domains of human life. The role of the state is thus limited to the protection of free markets, private property rights, and free trade (Harvey 2005). This shifting in responsibilities is attributed to the contemporary neoliberal context and, as Marxist theorist David Harvey observes, is marked by "[d]eregulation, privatization, and withdrawal of the state from many areas of social provision" (Harvey 2005, 3). In New Mexico, for example, large-scale efforts to privatize state-funded mental health-care for low-income people has occurred concurrently with an influx of private and for-profit interests in the prison industry.

Structures of economic and political domination, such as neoliberalism, are bolstered by ideology. In this way, neoliberalism exerts "pervasive effects on ways of thought to the point where it has become incorporated into the common-sense way many of us interpret, live in, and understand the world" (Harvey 2005, 3). A salient neoliberal notion that has become a governing principle within systems of criminal justice and public assistance in the United States is the singular emphasis on individual choice and personal responsibility (Young 2011). This principle renders individuals exclusively responsible for making "good choices," regardless of the larger context of their everyday lives (Kellett and Willging 2011), thus absolving institutional or social structures of culpability for any harms suffered (Povinelli 2011).

We draw on scholarly understandings of "structural violence" to contest this neoliberal perspective (Farmer 2004; Galtung 1993). Structural violence refers to social conditions of racism, colonialism, gender oppression, and poverty that create unequal distributions of power. These conditions impair the capacity of individuals to ensure their own well-being by restricting allocation of resources to already privileged groups. Individuals may occupy multiple, cross-cutting positionalities (Collins 2000) through which inequality is reproduced. Feminist theories of intersectionality (Crenshaw 1991) examine these layers of inequality to advance "an intimate understanding of the multiplicative, overlapping, and cumulative effects of the simultaneous intersections of systems of oppression" (Bernard 2013, 3). Structures of violence can thus have compounded effects on individuals, such as the rural women in this chapter, who are also largely poor and Latina or Native American.

In this chapter, we point to the multidimensional effects of structural violence on rural women prisoners both within and outside of prison. To counter the ideological consequences of these oppressions, we advance a feminist read "against the grain" (hooks 1992) of dominant discourses, which posit that rural women prisoners "prefer" prison or are unwilling or unable to take responsibility for their own rehabilitation, and therefore constitute a drain on public resources. Instead, a social justice perspective allows us to elucidate the social causes of mental distress (Vasquez 2012) and to promote equality and justice in the distribution of basic human needs, such as housing, education, and medical attention (Kitchener and Anderson 2011).

Social justice psychology situates individuals within a larger social ecology that is shaped by multiple levels of influence, and seeks to engender positive change by attending to the social and political dynamics that impinge upon these different levels (Prilleltensky and Nelson 1997; Wolff 2014). Accordingly, the qualitative research described here highlights the intersecting oppressions that rural women prisoners experience and the broader structural and institutional factors that set them up for failure outside. For these women, violent legacies of colonialism, male domination, and economic marginalization (Garcia 2010; Trujillo 2009) couple with the disintegration of public assistance programs and privatization of healthcare services (Willging and Semansky 2014) to create a system of interconnected oppressions that limits material support, therapeutic resources, and, ultimately, a successful return home.

Rural Women and Incarceration

Due to the War on Drugs, rural women and girls come into contact with the criminal justice system primarily for nonviolent and drug-related offenses. Such contact also occurs under circumstances of social and economic hardship and significant physical and mental health disparities. Their positioning within historical structures of patriarchy exposes rural women to greater interlocking disadvantages, including inadequate housing, health insurance, formal education, and employment opportunities, compared to men and urban residents (Coward et al. 2006). Of the women prisoners we interviewed, only 33 percent had derived income from a job six months prior to incarceration. Forty-six percent lived in unstable housing; and 52 percent reported economic hardship during this period (Willging et al. 2013). Such disparities are compounded by serious health problems prevalent among women entering prison, including HIV, Hepatitis C, and reproductive diseases (Chandler 2003).

Rural women are also at heightened risk for mental distress (Coward et al. 2006), including depression and suicidality (Hauenstein and Peddada 2007), and have higher rates than men of co-occurring mental-health and substance-use issues (Vik 2007). While rural women in general are at higher risk for these issues, those in prison are exposed more often than the general population to adverse childhood events linked to poor physical and mental health outcomes (Bowles, DeHart, and Webb 2012). All study interviewees had experienced a traumatic event in their lifetimes, and 60 percent reported childhood physical or sexual abuse, with an average age of onset of eight years; 89 percent reported current substance dependence and/or major mental illness (Willging et al. 2013).

Rural women have a greater likelihood of intimate partner violence (IPV) (Dekeseredy, Dragiewicz, and Rennison 2012). Multiple studies document the extremely high rates of IPV among women prisoners in the year prior to incarceration (Green et al. 2005; Lake 1993; Lynch, Fritch, and Heath 2012). In fact, 91 percent of our interviewees reported experiences of IPV in the year preceding incarceration (Willging et al. 2013).

Rural women coming into contact with criminal justice systems may be further isolated and affected by high poverty rates and uneven economic expansion in their home communities. New Mexico has the second-highest poverty rate (21.9 percent in 2013) (U.S. Department of Commerce 2014) and greatest gap in income inequality between the top and bottom 5 percent in the nation (Center on Budget and Policy Priorities 2012). Its rural areas are often deficient in basic social services and suffer from chronic shortages of mental health professionals who commonly lack adequate training in culturally competent and evidence-based practices (Semansky et al. 2013). Rural women are thus burdened with interrelated physical, psychological, and socioeconomic disadvantages that undergird contact with criminal justice systems and affect their well-being before, during, and after incarceration.

Social and Psychological Concerns of Women in Prison

Within this trying context, rural women prisoners confront issues related to their physical and mental health, substance use, and social relationships. Ironically, women's descriptions of their prison experiences show that incarceration can be an opportunity to receive care and security as never before. In the following sections, we illustrate how women prisoners report improvements in their quality of life during incarceration, including better mental and physical health, safety, social support, food security, and shelter. However, incarceration can also aggravate their physical and psychological concerns. Prison-based services designed to address women's needs tend to be inconsistent, insufficient, and sometimes inappropriate, problems that have been linked to the privatization of prisons and prison services (Bondurant 2013). Women's experiences thus reveal a double-edged quality to the support, safety, and "three hots and a cot" rendered in prison that can negatively impact their overall health and well-being.

Mental and Physical Health and Healthcare

Although interviewees had high rates of trauma and abuse before incarceration, few partook in therapeutic services to deal with these experiences prior to imprisonment. Having struggled with cutting and suicidality since the age of nine, one interviewee asserted, "I never saw a doctor for them [mental health issues] until I came to prison." Other women described obtaining their first diagnoses and treatment for chronic medical conditions such as diabetes and high blood pressure. For some, routine medical checkups were experiences unique to prison. A second interviewee stated, "I had a pap smear when I came here, and the last one I had was when I was here last time." A third explained that her health was "better because I've had checkups and everything, which I didn't have [before] because I didn't have medical insurance."

Many women reportedly faced basic subsistence issues before incarceration. Consequently, prison provided some increased stability in diet and housing that positively affected their physical well-being. One woman made a stark comparison: "[My health] is better because I'm eating right, I'm taking vitamins, I'm doing a regular thing on a daily basis, whereas when I was out there I wasn't eating nothing but maybe a candy bar and a Coke twice a month."

Prison also provided access to pharmaceuticals, although many women we interviewed stated that these medications were primarily desirable for coping with prison life. One prisoner commented that without her medication, "I don't think I'd be sitting in here right now." A second explained, "If I don't take it, I'm lost. I cry a lot and I think a lot." Some women also found that medication helped curb addictions. For one inmate, Wellbutrin "took the cravings away and allowed me to actually get clean."

While women prisoners received healthcare in prison, changes to their health were not always positive. Women attributed health declines to the prison context, including lack of specialized care for ongoing conditions. Some complained of aches and pains as a consequence of hard beds and cement floors. Numerous women reported unhealthy weight gain after a diet rich in simple carbohydrates and a lack of exercise. They also critiqued long wait times and high turnover among primary care providers in prison. One individual described backsliding on her physical therapy initiated prior to incarceration because she did not qualify for such treatment in prison and was even denied the cane upon which her mobility depended. Another resorted to requesting urgent care for her persistent conditions: "They come up with excuses. But if I have something [urgent] at the last minute, that's when they'll see me. Other than that they just say, 'Put your slip in and we'll call you as soon as possible.' They call then two months later."

High caseloads and turnover in therapists, counselors, and case workers exacerbated difficulties obtaining individual counseling and related support services. Interviewees claimed that the prison's mental health unit was woefully understaffed in relation to demand, and that providers restricted what medications they could take, inadequately monitored their use, or prescribed them for pacification. Interviewees speculated that they were prescribed numbing psychotropic medications that "just dope you up and you're emotionless," transforming them into "walking zombies." Overall, they asserted that physical and mental health treatment was needed, but also judged these prison services as inconsistently available and largely inadequate.

Substance Use and Treatment Resources

Another way in which prison could provide a supportive and healthful environment for many interviewees was by reducing their exposure to alcohol and illicit drugs. One interviewee explained that without forced abstention from drinking during her various incarcerations, "I probably would have been dead by now with cirrhosis or something." She explained, "Out there I can do it [drink alcohol]. But I feel better here. I mean not to be wanting to be here, but I feel safer here because I can't get a hold of my alcohol."

Prison also offered substance use treatment resources, albeit in limited form. Moreover, such resources were rarely accessed by our interviewees prior to prison, despite their extremely high rates of addiction. Women generally valued prison-based self-help groups and psycho-educational classes, often describing them as safe places to reflect and consider change. However, many women lamented the limited availability of such classes. One interviewee explained, "The schooling is great, but they don't have enough therapists for the substance abuse classes. They don't have enough staff here period. So everything's always being canceled." Long wait lists for group therapy also restricted participation to those with longer sentences, excluding shorter-term prisoners serving time for nonviolent crimes related to mental distress or substance dependence. Confounding distinctions between who received these services and who did not appeared arbitrary. One woman described several attempts to participate in a psycho-educational class with no results: "I don't know.

I just gave up. They definitely have their favorites here." As with physical and mental healthcare, women's experiences with substance use services in prison reveal significant obstacles to any efforts at rehabilitation.

Social Support

In addition to secure food and shelter and the possibility of care and treatment, prison provided an environment where women found novel and much-needed social support. Although there were accounts of hostility, fighting, and violence, women more often described forming bonds with other inmates to cope with incarceration as well as to prepare for outside life. For instance, some explained how women swapped information about resources and places to go with others struggling with reentry planning. Often this information sharing represented the way women who had "been there" provided moral support to those facing first-time releases.

The shared experience of incarceration aided women in forming supportive connections that were distinct from those with kin on the outside, or with professional service providers inside. Of her fellow inmates, one interviewee said, "I can honestly say, they can relate. They know what I'm talking about when I'm distressed. After being locked up for so long they helped me out a lot, just striving to succeed." Another described a fellow inmate who was "more like a sister 'cause not even me and a sister have been that close." In this way, rural women inmates may experience the prison environment as a place where they can form positive social supports among understanding peers. These supports appeared valuable when compared to taxing social or kin relationships outside prison, which, as we describe later, could threaten reentry.

Rural women prisoners' descriptions of their incarceration thus reveal a contradictory experience. Coming from an intensely challenging socioeconomic context, these prisoners find a level of basic security and care that contrasts with their familiar subsistence, substance use, and mental distress. At the same time, they are able to form supportive relationships with peers. However, the care and support in prison is limited, sporadic, and overly reliant on powerful pharmaceuticals that may mute women's mental health symptoms without addressing their causes. Significantly, the provision of limited and inadequate resources within such closed institutional settings has been linked to the influx of private and for-profit interests into prisons and subsequent efforts to "economize" upon the escalating costs associated with incarceration (Bondurant 2013). The ill effects of prison care thus intersect with and compound the physical and mental health–related disparities that rural women prisoners commonly face. That incarcerated women experience these limited forms of prison-based care as improvements to their well-being highlights the dire conditions to which they are accustomed. Indeed, it is little surprise that rural women prisoners face their impending release with extreme trepidation.

The "Revolving Door": Contributions to Rural Women's Recidivism

As women prisoners prepared to reenter rural communities, their concerns about securing food and shelter, physical and mental healthcare, substance use treatment, and healthy social supports were accentuated. Women described anxiety and uncertainty about their lives outside prison, emotions influenced by the problematic dynamics of prison-based reentry-planning services and the increasing incidence of prolonged sentences and in-house parole. Once women were released into rural areas, they faced new oppressions that intersected with the socioeconomic and health-related disparities that affected them before incarceration. In the following sections, we describe how the synergy of inadequate reentry planning, social stigma, and punitive federal and state policies set women up for reentry failure.

Our interviewees' preparations for reentry were often frustrated by ambiguity about sentence lengths and release dates, and unproductive reentry planning. When collecting data, researchers and interviewees alike became perplexed with determining release dates. For our study, prison staff identified women eligible for release within the next six months, but sometimes these interviewees would express confusion when hearing of their imminent release. For example, when asked about her plans for release, one prisoner stated, "They give you four different out dates. They have it all messed up." Several of the women complained that they were unsure of their release dates because their cases were caught in the system. Others claimed that they had remained in prison past their release dates due to inaction by the parole board, missing or incorrect paperwork, or inability to locate safe and drug-free housing.

Prolonged length of stay (or stays in prison beyond the expected release date) affects growing numbers of women (New Mexico Sentencing Commission 2012). Vagueness about release dates undermined formal and informal reentry planning while in prison. It made it hard for women to formulate goals and strategies for the transition prior to release and complicated basic transportation arrangements for their impending return. For some inmates in New Mexico, a trip home could take eight hours, so arranging for someone to pick them up was a challenging prospect, especially in the absence of reliable release dates. Such uncertainties were inadequately addressed through the official discharge and reentry-planning meetings that were supposed to take place between prisoners and caseworkers, mental-health and substance-use counselors, medical representatives, and in-house parole officers. Such meetings were often delayed or truncated, with little opportunity for women to ask questions or give feedback. One interviewee summarized, "Once you're done, they just throw you out to the wolves, and they don't care."

Once released, most interviewees described difficulties finding jobs as known felons in rural communities. Few had work experience or training, and some had previously resorted to illicit forms of making a living. One woman explained, "Life gets hard out there. The money I make in two weeks working from nine to five is not even half the money I make in one day running the streets." This inability to meet basic needs probably contributed to relapse and reincarceration. Another woman recalled the conditions leading her back to prison: "I'm tired of living in a place with no lights, no gas. I'm tired of selling dope. I'm tired of trying to hustle to keep a roof over my head. . . . So I started smoking crack again, and I ended up back in prison. That's the sad thing."

Women also faced extreme difficulties in accessing healthcare. They most commonly described struggles obtaining insurance coverage, services, and the medications they were prescribed in prison. One recently reincarcerated woman explained, "To stay on my meds is hard out there, 'cause if you don't got a job or a medical card you can't get your meds, and meds for mental issues are very expensive." Several interviewees attributed their eventual return to prison to problems obtaining medications. When asked what events led to her reincarceration, one woman responded, "I couldn't get my meds. I have chronic nightmares. I have flashbacks, hear voices. Without the meds I go crazy. So I used heroin to stop the pain and the nightmares, and I got caught, so they sent me back." In this way, interviewees linked the scarcity of health resources in rural communities to their inability to establish successful lives outside of prison.

In addition to obstacles to treatment, the pervasiveness of alcohol and illicit drug use within rural communities was implicated in women's recidivism. One interviewee recounted a memory of a previous release: "When I walked out these doors it was not a good experience. It felt free to be released [but] my mom picked me up and we went straight to a dope house." In these challenging environments, women experienced multiple barriers to treatment. Stringent and often contradictory eligibility requirements for public treatment programs were known to confound even community-based providers. Women with criminal histories could be shut out of treatment, while other programs required criminalized behavior to qualify for them. For example, residential programs could require that patients be "dirty" in order to obtain a coveted bed, and some patients were only eligible for programs if they were court ordered. One woman's parole officer struggled to get her into treatment to avoid sending her back to prison for a violation but, "None of them accepted me because I have an assault [on my record]."

Rurality profoundly influences the ability to fulfill reentry needs. In rural New Mexico, neoliberal policies and practices have largely dismantled the mental healthcare safety net. Following privatization initiatives in recent years, the state has witnessed the disintegration of its mental healthcare system (Willging and Semansky 2014). This has a major effect on returning prisoners for whom deficient provider training and scarcity of resources has been linked to participation in criminalized activities, including substance use (Kellett and Willging 2011; Willging et al. 2013). These problems are particularly acute in rural areas, where returning prisoners already have less access to the more comprehensive reentry programs found in urban areas (Scroggins and Malley 2010).

Women in rural areas with few services were forced to travel elsewhere or to do without services altogether, increasing the likelihood of parole violations for those who were mandated to take part in treatment but who lacked reliable transportation. As with clinical services in prison, women found that the few rural treatment centers available in New Mexico were beleaguered by high turnover of clinical staff, long wait lists, and limited resources. Self-help groups were unreliable or difficult to access because of distance. Even when they were available, some of the interviewees did not consider these groups to be safe venues in which to disclose their thoughts, feelings, and experiences, especially related to trauma. Accordingly, the collision of punitive policies and resource scarcity in rural areas reportedly led many women needing assistance back to prison.

Social ties on the outside were another source of concern for returning women prisoners, many of whom found it difficult to break from harmful relationships. An interviewee worried about living with her mother, who struggled with alcohol issues: "[My mother] is like, 'I can't wait until you get out. We can just move in together.'" A second discussed the challenge of maintaining distance from friends who might contribute to relapse: "I don't think I could find a positive crowd in [town]. Because it's like once you're out and everybody knows you're out, they find out your number."

With social networks so small and encumbered, women explained that finding stigma- *and* drug-free associates was difficult. Inmates worried that "normal" individuals would avoid them because of their felony status, and feared that associating with the "wrong crowd" might lead to reincarceration. One woman elaborated on this predicament: "I don't wanna get caught for anything I wasn't even involved in. People would be saying, 'Oh, she just got out of prison, so she might've done it.' If my community finds out I got out of prison, I'm gonna be already labeled." Stigma from serving time and connections to others who were entrenched in behaviors that women sought to avoid thus made it extremely difficult to form prosocial bonds that they could rely upon for emotional and pragmatic support.

Given their high rate of reincarceration and recounting of their personal experiences, it appears clear that upon release rural women prisoners are commonly denied even the most basic assistance in finding employment, housing, education, and healthcare. In addition to the problems posed by stigma and the economic scarcity common to rural areas, federal and state policies can also restrict returning prisoners' access to public entitlement programs that could potentially assist them in fulfilling these needs (Freudenberg et al. 2005). At the same time, women may find themselves struggling to form supportive kin and peer relationships. Paradoxically, they are unable to maintain the supportive relationships they may have formed in prison, as parolees are typically not allowed to associate with one another.

Due to the intersection of material difficulties, the women we interviewed often pointed to the irony that prison life was "easier" for some. Yet, the descriptions presented by the women in their interviews also illustrate that their earnest and repeated attempts to access assistance and to meet the obligations of parole are frustrated by structural and institutional barriers that significantly limit their efforts to ensure their own well-being. Combined with the inadequate care that they receive during incarceration, these barriers set women up for failure on the outside.

Working Assumptions among Corrections and Mental Health Professionals

Stereotypes, prejudices, and ideologies of corrections officials and mental health providers, and within wider communities, make it possible to neglect the material disparities that rural women with incarceration histories may suffer. These ideologies often focus on specifically gendered characteristics, such as appearance and demeanor, and tend to perpetuate stereotypes of underclass femininity, including dependence in relationships and emotional instability. Parole officers, for example, may conceptualize women prisoners as "lost causes," unable to make the choices necessary to rehabilitate themselves after prison. Other ubiquitous gendered stereotypes include the ideas that these women are irresponsible parents, dependent on social welfare, and incapable of maintaining stable relationships and avoiding victimization (Willging, Lilliott, and Kellett 2015). Such views are not limited to correctional officers in New Mexico, as they have been documented in other settings as well (Appelbaum, Hickey, and Packer 2001). While mental health providers are also susceptible to patronizing and paternalistic attitudes (Willging et al. 2015), they have been described as being less punitive or judgmental in their perceptions (Appelbaum, Hickey, and Packer 2001).

The social dynamics of small communities, where entire families may be labeled as "criminal," reinforce these stereotypes and attitudes toward former women prisoners, engendering feelings of hopelessness and defeat among those released from prison (Willging et al. 2015). Other ethnographic research suggests that these dynamics reflect a pervasive attitude of "negativity" (Trujillo 2009) toward the poor, rural, and largely non-White areas of New Mexico. They are also fueled by the state's history of subjection to White American imperialism and the construction of these communities as dangerous, helpless, and mired in cultures unsuitable for modern life (Kosek 2006; Sanchez 1940).

Beliefs about the inferiority of women with incarceration histories also prevail in prisons, where health and behavioral interventions portray imprisonment as the result of poor choices rather than of structural violence begetting contexts of inequality. Interventions steeped in discourses of personal responsibility assign women the duty of their own rehabilitation without providing them with sufficient material and psychological resources to facilitate successful reentry (Kellett and Willging 2011). The appropriation of these neoliberal narratives of individual responsibility by women prisoners may contribute to complications during reentry. Women's rehabilitation becomes "up to them," and their possible failure will also be theirs alone.

Our previous research suggests that corrections and mental health professionals may mistake the structural inequities that impede women's life chances for innate qualities, casting them as irresponsible, helplessly victimized, and dependent on social welfare (Willging et al. 2015). Psychologists working in similar neoliberal contexts are also vulnerable to such ideologies. Although social justice is one of the core tenets of subfields such as feminist psychology (Brown 1997), multicultural counseling (Constantine et al. 2007), and community psychology (Prilleltensky and Nelson 1997; Wolff 2014), such work has yet to predominate in mainstream mental health services. For practices set in neoliberal service structures, these paradigms are less likely to shape the work of corrections officers, paraprofessionals, clinical psychologists, and psychiatrists with whom rural women prisoners may come into contact, resulting in less than ideal service provision.

Addressing Structural Violence and Intersectionality: Recommendations for Mental Health Professionals

Working effectively with rural women prisoners requires a comprehensive understanding of the interdependent nature of multiple levels of influence (e.g., gender/sexuality, race/ethnicity, and geography). Further, clinicians working within a social justice perspective recognize how contemporary systems of structural violence rooted in racism, colonialism, sexism, heterosexism, and classism facilitate and sustain the incarceration of rural women. They also become engaged in efforts to address larger societal and structural problems affecting these women. Increased integration of the concepts of structural violence and intersectionality into the everyday practice of mental health professionals is imperative to both understanding and helping rural women prisoners.

The social and psychological concerns of women described in this chapter reflect intersecting material and ideological oppressions. Structural disadvantages, including socioeconomic and health-related disparities, interact with institutional failures (notably the lack of reentry planning), the effects of systemic processes like the privatization of prison and mental health services, and a panoply of more diffused vulnerabilities common in rural areas, such as reduced availability of health and human services and transportation difficulties. Even when women leaving prison make every effort to find work, access public assistance, and get care, they are often thwarted by the intersection of these structural disadvantages.

Stigma and the cynical and prejudicial ideologies of professionals encountered in corrections and healthcare systems, and within communities, can exacerbate these oppressions, while reinforcing the notion that rural women prisoners "prefer" to be in a state of incarceration. Such ideologies burden women by uncritically drawing upon the gendered stereotypes described above. We argue that the history of colonialism also weighs on Latina and Native American prisoners in the form of prejudicial and paternalistic ideas of their cultural "backwardness" and lack of individual agency. It is the structural effects of these ideologies manifested in the unequal distribution of opportunities and resources that most concern women prisoners. At present, many mental health professionals may be ill prepared to tackle these effects.

Recommendation #1: Expand psychology's social justice framework.

Psychologists have called for expanding graduate training in race and multicultural issues to include concern for structural violence within a social justice framework that addresses issues such as gender/sexuality, race/ethnicity, and socioeconomic status from a perspective of power and privilege as part of case conceptualization, assessment, and treatment (Ali et al. 2008; Burnes and Singh 2010; Toporek and Vaughn 2010). Psychologists in prisons and rural service systems can expand a social justice framework that considers intersectionality and the larger contexts impacting rural women prisoners by incorporating these concepts not only into their own direct work with these women but also in their training, supervision, and mentoring of correctional officials and other mental health providers.

The American Psychological Association has published guidelines for psychological treatment with lesbian, gay, and bisexual clients; transgender and gender-nonconforming people; ethnically, linguistically, and culturally diverse populations; and girls and women (American Psychological Association n.d.). These guidelines address the need to attend to the impact of adverse social, environmental, and political factors in assessing and treating marginalized populations. In line with these guidelines, by forcefully challenging stereotypes about rural women prisoners through social justice praxis, psychologists can best arm themselves, trainees, and supervisees with effective and appropriate intervention strategies.

Recommendation #2: Adopt a trauma-informed and systemic approach to women's mental health before, during, and after incarceration.

The women quoted in this chapter discussed treatment primarily in the form of self-help and psycho-educational groups, and concerns about pharmaceuticals that render them "zombies" without addressing underlying issues. We suggest that rural women prisoners in New Mexico and probably elsewhere would benefit from a gender-responsive, trauma-informed approach implemented by mental health providers before, during, and after incarceration. This approach requires attention to the voices of rural women prisoners and system-level intervention. Service systems must be pressured to develop environments where practitioners can assess for and understand the impact of trauma and paths for recovery; recognize the signs of trauma for those involved with the system; integrate knowledge about trauma into policies, procedures, and practices; and seek to resist retraumatization (U.S. Substance Abuse and Mental Health Services Administration 2014).

Recommendation #3: Increase availability of services for women in rural areas.

Psychologists, in particular, can collaborate proactively with local, state, and federal governments for increased funding to expand the provider base within these service systems and to encourage greater utilization of existing loan-forgiveness programs to incentivize licensed mental health professionals to relocate to high-need, underserved areas. We also encourage psychologists to practice in rural areas, utilizing their unique skill sets to implement trauma-informed approaches initiated through specialized services within prisons and continued through coordination with community-based service providers. In rural communities, psychologists can take lead roles in facilitating support groups for women returnees, engaging families in the reentry process through education and direct services, and aiding women in cultivating strong social support networks that protect against substance use.

Recommendation #4: Advocate for additional training and broader systemic support for evidence-based clinical practice in rural areas.

For psychologists and other mental health providers in rural settings to wholly realize the social justice potential of a trauma-informed approach for empowerment, cultural relevance, and gender responsiveness, they may require additional training and systematic support. Seasoned psychologists can help by being vociferous in encouraging this training and support.

Rural women prisoners would benefit from integrated evidence-based, trauma-informed interventions that concertedly address substance use and prevention of relapse. Several evidence-based interventions for individuals undergoing reentry are already in extensive use in public service settings, including correctional systems and community settings (Lynch et al. 2012; Wallace, Conner, and Dass-Brailsford 2011). These models of intervention, including Seeking Safety (Najavits et al. 1998), the Addiction and Trauma Recovery Integration Model (Miller and Guidry 2001), and the Trauma Recovery and Empowerment Model (Harris 1998), combine empowerment principles with traditional clinical approaches (e.g., cognitive behavioral therapy and psychoeducation) to enhance coping skills, reduce self-harm behavior, navigate relationships, and explore connections between trauma and substance use. At the same time as such interventions promote change at the individual level, there is a need to continually challenge the social circumstances that can limit the life opportunities of rural women prisoners.

In each of these approaches to clinical practice, empowerment is a core treatment component. Each recognizes that trauma survivors may have lost their capacity to speak out against past and present injustices due to years of abuse, and encourages providers to learn skills to enable survivors to exercise their own voices and advocate for themselves (U.S. Substance Abuse and Mental Health Services Administration 2014). However, it is crucial to distinguish ideas of empowerment from neoliberal perspectives that emphasize individual responsibility apart from contextual factors engendered by structural violence. Evidence-based approaches will fail unless situated within a social justice framework that considers the broader impact of structural issues such as racism, sexism, and poverty on the outcomes of women prisoners. Providers of therapeutic services to these women in rural areas may need additional support and training in (a) administering appropriate treatments; (b) recognizing and contesting how neoliberal ideologies and gendered stereotypes about criminality can subtly infuse clinical work; and (c) engaging in policy-related advocacy efforts that target structural factors causing women to fall through the cracks both within and outside of prison. Only by regarding rural women as part of a larger social ecology, in which historically entrenched power inequities work against health and safety, will mental health professionals truly provide effective and holistic intervention for this marginalized population.

Conclusion

The experiences of rural women prisoners in this chapter illustrate the double-edged quality of the "three hots and a cot" offered in prison and the harsh realities of interlocking systems of structural violence that pave paths to incarceration. In response, psychologists and other professionals must heed the voices of these women, pursuing multilevel intervention strategies to address the layered oppressions of structural violence that adversely impact them, while remaining mindful of how their own attitudes and biases might also be steeped in neoliberal logics. This chapter suggests that geography should also be included as an issue of critical concern in relation to incarcerated women. Psychologists have a responsibility to engage in social justice praxis that encompasses (a) assessment, expansion, and coordination of health and other human services in prison and rural communities; (b) ongoing examination of connections among crime, incarceration, trauma, and structural inequities, such as poverty (Travis, Western, and Redburn 2014); and (c) development of supportive environments at the system level. This chapter points to the material and ideological barriers to empowered reentry and calls for psychologists to spearhead interventions in underserved rural communities to dismantle these barriers.

Acknowledgments

This research was funded by grant R34 MH082186 from the National Institute of Mental Health. The authors wish to thank Betty A. Bennalley, MA; Pamela Brown, RN, MPH; Patricia Hokanson, MPH; and Lara Gunderson, MA, for their contributions to this research.

REFERENCES

Aday, Ronald H., and Lori Farney. 2014. "Malign Neglect: Assessing Older Women's Health Care Experiences in Prison." *Journal of Bioethical Inquiry* 11 (3): 359–72. doi: 10.1007/s11673-014-9561-0.

Ali, Saba R., William M. Liu, Amina Mahmood, and JoAnna Arguello. 2008. "Social Justice and Applied Psychology: Practical Ideas for Training the Next Generation of Psychologists." *Journal for Social Action in Counseling and Psychology* 1 (2): 1–13.

American Psychological Association. n.d. APA Guidelines for Practitioners, http://www.apa.org.

Appelbaum, Kenneth L., James M. Hickey, and Ira Packer. 2001. "The Role of Correctional Officers in Multidisciplinary Mental Health Care in Prisons." *Psychiatric Services* 52 (10): 1343–47.

Arfken, Michael, and Jeffery Yen. 2014. "Psychology and Social Justice: Theoretical and Philosophical Engagements." *Journal of Theoretical and Philosophical Psychology* 34 (1): 1–13. doi: 10.1037/a0033578.

Bernard, April. 2013. "The Intersectional Alternative: Explaining Female Criminality." *Feminist Criminology* 8 (1): 3–19.

Binswanger, Ingrid A., Marc F. Stern, Richard A. Deyo, Patrick J. Heagerty, Allen Cheadle, Joann G. Elmore, and Thomas D. Koepsell. 2007. "Release from Prison: A High Risk of Death among Former Inmates." *New England Journal of Medicine* 356 (2): 157–65. doi: 10.1056/NEJMsa064115.

Bondurant, Brittany. 2013. "The Privatization of Prisons and Prisoner Healthcare: Addressing the Extent of Prisoners' Right to Healthcare." *New England Journal on Criminal and Civil Confinement* 39: 407.

Bowleg, Lisa. 2012. "The Problem with the Phrase 'Women and Minorities': Intersectionality—an Important Theoretical Framework for Public Health." *American Journal of Public Health* 102 (7): 1267–73. doi: 10.2105/AJPH.2012.300750.

Bowles, Melissa A., Dana DeHart, and Jennifer R. Webb. 2012. "Family Influences on Female Offenders' Substance Use: The Role of Adverse Childhood Events among Incarcerated Women." *Journal of Family Violence* 27 (7): 681–86. doi: 10.1007/s10896-012-9450-4.

Brown, Laura S. 1997. "The Private Practice of Subversion: Psychology as Tikkun Olam." *American Psychologist* 52 (4): 449–62. doi: 10.1037/0003-066X.52.4.449.

Burnes, Theodore R., and Anneliese A. Singh. 2010. "Integrating Social Justice Training into the Practicum Experience for Psychology Trainees: Starting Earlier." *Training and Education in Professional Psychology* 4 (3): 153–62. doi: 10.1037/a0019385.

Center on Budget and Policy Priorities. Economic Policy Institute. 2012. *Pulling Apart: A State-by-State Analysis of Income Trends.* Washington, DC: GPO, 2012, http://www.cbpp.org.

Chandler, Cynthia. 2003. "Death and Dying in America: The Prison Industrial Complex's Impact on Women's Health." *Berkeley Women's Law Journal* 18: 40–60, http://scholarship.law.berkeley.edu.

Cole, Elizabeth R. 2009. "Intersectionality and Research in Psychology." *American Psychologist* 64 (3): 170–80. doi: 10.1037/a0014564.

Collins, Patricia H. 2000. *Black Feminist Thought: Knowledge, Consciousness, and the Politics of Empowerment,* 2nd ed. New York: Routledge.

Constantine, Madonna G., Sally M. Hage, Mai M. Kindaichi, and Rhonda M. Bryant. 2007. "Social Justice and Multicultural Issues: Implications for the Practice and Training of Counselors and Counseling Psychologists." *Journal of Counseling and Development* 85: 24–29. doi: 10.1002/j.1556-6678.2007.tb00440.x.

Corbin, Juliet, and Anselm Strauss. 2008. *Basics of Qualitative Research: Techniques and Procedures for Developing Grounded Theory,* 3rd ed. Thousand Oaks, CA: Sage.

Coward, Raymond T., Lisa A. Davis, Carol H. Gold, Helen Smiciklas-Wright, Luanne E. Thorndyke, and Fred W. Vondracek, eds. 2006. *Rural Women's Health: Mental, Behavioral, and Physical Issues.* New York: Springer.

Crenshaw, Kimberle. 1991. "Mapping the Margins: Intersectionality, Identity Politics, and Violence against Women of Color." *Stanford Law Review* 43 (6): 1241–99.

Dekeseredy, Walter S., Molly Dragiewicz, and Callie M. Rennison. 2012. "Racial/Ethnic Variations in Violence against Women: Urban, Suburban, and Rural Differences." *International Journal of Rural Criminology* 1 (2): 184–202.

Farmer, Paul. 2004. "An Anthropology of Structural Violence." *Current Anthropology* 45 (3): 305–25.

Freudenberg, Nicholas, Jessie Daniels, Martha Crum, Tiffany Perkins, and Beth E. Richie. 2005. "Coming Home from Jail: The Social and Health Consequences of Community Reentry for Women, Male Adolescents, and Their Families and Communities." *American Journal of Public Health* 95 (10): 1725–36. doi: 10.2105/AJPH.2004.056325.

Galtung, Johan. 1993. "Violence Typology: Direct, Structural, and Cultural Violence." *Kulturelle Gewalt, in Der Burger im Staat* 43 (2): 106.

Garcia, Angela. 2010. *The Pastoral Clinic: Addiction and Dispossession along the Rio Grande.* Berkeley: University of California Press.

Green, Bonnie L., Jeanne Miranda, Anahita Daroowala, and Juned Siddique. 2005. "Trauma Exposure, Mental Health Functioning, and Program Needs of Women in Jail." *Crime and Delinquency* 51: 133–51.

Harris, Maxine. 1998. *Trauma Recovery and Empowerment: A Clinician's Guide for Working with Women in Groups.* New York: Free Press.

Harvey, David. 2005. *A Brief History of Neoliberalism.* New York: Oxford University Press.

Hauenstein, Emily J., and Shyamal Peddada. 2007. "Prevalence of Major Depressive Episodes in Rural Women Using Primary Care." *Journal of Health Care for the Poor and Underserved* 18: 185–202. doi: 10.1353/hpu.2007.0010.

hooks, bell. 1992. *Black Looks: Race and Representation.* Boston: South End Press, 1992.

Jones, Nicole T., Peter Ji, Mary Beck, and Niels Beck. 2002. "The Reliability and Validity of the Revised Conflict Tactics Scale (CTS2) in a Female Incarcerated Population." *Journal of Family Issues* 23 (3): 441–57. doi: 10.1177/0192513X02023003006.

Kellett, Nicole C., and Cathleen E. Willging. 2011. "Pedagogy of Individual Choice and Female Inmate Reentry in the U.S. Southwest." *International Journal of Law and Psychiatry* 34 (4): 256–63. doi: 10.1016/j.ijlp.2011.07.003.

Kitchener, Karen S., and Sharon K. Anderson. 2011. *Foundations of Ethical Practice, Research, and Teaching in Psychology,* 2nd ed. New York: Taylor and Francis.

Kosek, Jake. 2006. *Understories: The Political Life of Forests in Northern New Mexico.* Durham, NC: Duke University Press.

Lake, Elise S. 1993. "An Exploration of the Violent Victim Experiences of Female Offenders." *Violence and Victims* 8: 41–51.

Lynch, Shannon M., April Fritch, and Nicole M. Heath. 2012. "Looking beneath the Surface: The Nature of Incarcerated Women's Experiences of Interpersonal Vio-

lence, Mental Health, and Treatment Needs." *Feminist Criminology* 7 (4): 381–400.
doi: 10.1177/1557085112439224.

Lynch, Shannon M., Nicole M. Heath, Kathleen C. Mathews, and Galatia J. Cepeda.
2012. "Seeking Safety: An Intervention for Trauma-Exposed Incarcerated Women?"
Journal of Trauma and Dissociation 13: 88–101. doi: 10.1080/15299732.2011.608780.

Miller, Dusty, and Laurie Guidry. 2001. *Addictions and Trauma Recovery: Healing the
Body, Mind, and Spirit*. New York: Norton.

Najavits, Lisa M., Roger D. Weiss, Sarah R. Shaw, and Larry R. Muenz. 1998. "Seeking
Safety: Outcome of a New Cognitive-Behavioral Psychotherapy for Women with
Posttraumatic Stress Disorder and Substance Dependence." *Journal of Traumatic
Stress* 11 (3): 437–56. doi: 10.1023/A:1024496427434.

New Mexico Sentencing Commission. 2012. *New Mexico's Female Prisoners: Exploring
Recent Increases in the Inmate Population: Report in Brief*, http://nmsc.unm.edu.

Povinelli, Elizabeth A. 2011. *Economies of Abandonment: Social Belonging and Endur-
ance in Late Liberalism*. Durham, NC: Duke University Press.

Prilleltensky, Isaac, and Geoffrey Nelson. 1997. "Community Psychology: Reclaiming
Social Justice." In *Critical Psychology: An Introduction*. Edited by Dennis Fox and
Isaac Prilleltensky, 166–84. Thousand Oaks, CA: Sage.

Rowan-Szal, Grace A., George W. Joe, D. Dwayne Simpson, Jack M. Greener, and Jerry
Vance. 2009. "During-Treatment Outcomes among Female Methamphetamine-
Using Offenders in Prison-Based Treatments." *Journal of Offender Rehabilitation* 48
(5): 388–401. doi: 10.1080/10509670902979496.

Sanchez, George I. 1940. *Forgotten People: A Study of New Mexicans*. Albuquerque:
University of New Mexico Press.

Scroggins, Jennifer R., and Sara Malley. 2010. "Reentry and the (Unmet)
Needs of Women." *Journal of Offender Rehabilitation* 49 (2): 146–63. doi:
10.1080/10509670903546864.

Semansky, Rafael M., Jessica Goodkind, David H. Sommerfeld, and Cathleen E.
Willging. 2013. "Culturally Competent Services within a Statewide Behavioral
Healthcare Transformation: A Mixed-Method Assessment." *Journal of Community
Psychology* 41 (3): 378–93. doi: 10.1002/jcop.21544.

Smyth, Julie. 2012. "Dual Punishment: Incarcerated Mothers and Their Children."
Columbia Social Work Review 3: 33–45.

Toporek, Rebecca L., and Shemya R. Vaughn. 2010. "Social Justice in the Training of
Professional Psychologists: Moving Forward." *Training and Education in Professional Psychology* 4 (3): 177–82. doi: 10.1037/a0019874.

Travis, Jeremy, Bruce Western, and Steve Redburn, eds. 2014. *The Growth of Incarceration in the United States: Exploring Causes and Consequences*. Washington, DC:
National Academies Press.

Trujillo, Michael L. 2009. *Land of Disenchantment: Latina/o Identities and Transformations in Northern New Mexico*. Albuquerque: University of New Mexico Press.

U.S. Department of Commerce. United States Census Bureau. 2014. *Poverty: 2012 and
2013 American Community Survey Briefs*. Washington, DC: GPO, https://www.cen-

sus.gov. U.S. Department of Justice. 2011. *Prisoners in 2010 (NCJ 236096)*. Washington, DC: GPO, http://www.bjs.gov.

U.S. Substance Abuse and Mental Health Services Administration. 2014. *Trauma-Informed Approach and Trauma-Specific Interventions*, http://www.samhsa.gov.

Vasquez, Melba J. 2012. "Psychology and Social Justice: Why We Do What We Do." *American Psychologist* 67 (5): 337–46. doi: 10.1037/a0029232.

Vik, Peter W. 2007. "Methamphetamine Use by Incarcerated Women: Comorbid Mood and Anxiety Problems." *Women's Health Issues* 17 (4): 256–63. doi: 10.1016/j. whi.2006.12.004.

Wallace, Barbara C., Latoya C. Conner, and Priscilla Dass-Brailsford. 2011. "Integrated Trauma Treatment in Correctional Health Care and Community-Based Treatment upon Reentry." *Journal of Correctional Health Care* 17 (4): 329–43. doi: 10.1177/1078345811413091.

Willging, Cathleen E., Elizabeth Lilliott, and Nicole C. Kellett. 2015. "Gendered Ideologies of Community Reentry: Contrasting the Perspectives of Rural Women Prisoners, Parole Officers, and Mental Healthcare Personnel." In *Reentry Planning for Offenders with Mental Disorders*. Edited by Henry A. Dlugacz, 11.1–11.19. New York: Civic Research.

Willging, Cathleen E., Lorraine H. Malcoe, Shilo St. Cyr, William H. Zywiak, and Sandra C. Lapham. 2013. "Behavioral Health and Social Correlates of Reincarceration among Hispanic, Native American, and White Rural Women." *Psychiatric Services* 64 (6): 590–93. doi: 10.1176/appi.ps.201200120.

Willging, Cathleen E., and Rafael Semansky. 2014. "State Mental Health Policy: Back to the Future; New Mexico Returns to the Early Days of Medicaid Managed Care." *Psychiatric Services* 65 (8): 970–72. doi: 10.1176/appi.ps.201400102.

Wolff, Tom. 2014. "Community Psychology Practice: Expanding the Impact of Psychology's Work." *American Psychologist* 69 (8): 803–13. doi: 10.1037/a0037426.

Young, Iris M. 2011. *Responsibility for Justice*. New York: Oxford University Press.

6

Girls in Juvenile Detention Facilities

Zones of Abandonment

KENDRA R. BREWSTER AND KATHLEEN M. CUMISKEY

Fighting the soul of the city is hard. When you fight the soul of the city you are destroying evil. Fighting the soul of the city is dramatic. It is dramatic because you see people getting hurt and dying. Fighting the soul of the city is hurtful because you lose your most precious loved ones. Fighting the soul of the city can be a positive way to go because you can't help prevent "forest fires." Fighting the soul of the city can be a wonderful thing . . . because you can learn about different people, culture, attitudes, and the way they adapt to the society. That is what fighting the soul of the city means to me.
—Kimaya, incarcerated girl, 2008

Kimaya's words above say something about her sense of isolation. They also indicate that her feelings and agency—the thoughts and actions she engages in to adapt to her sociocultural contexts (Jenkins 2001)—are not hers alone; they are shared with many other girls who emerge from urban environments that feel largely out of their control. Kimaya represents the voice of one of the hundreds of girls in confinement who participated in a course called Mentoring and Adolescent Development, between 1999 and 2012, at the College of Staten Island, City University of New York (CUNY). This course took place within a nonsecure/limited-secure facility run by the New York State Office of Children and Family Services.

Incarcerated girls occupy marginalized positions in society that severely restrict their access to material and social resources. The value society grants them is dependent on their perceived racial, class, and gendered statuses. These statuses are the foundation for the uneven trauma and unequal treatment that girls experience (Morton and Leslie 2005; Sangoi and Goshin 2013). Despite these circumstances, court-involved girls are agents who try to make meaning and take responsibility for their individual situations and behaviors.

Kimaya reminds us that poor girls and girls of color are not criminal personalities but agents struggling with social isolation and abandonment. They lose their loved ones, and witness or experience trauma. They also survive "the soul of the city" and need to continue struggling to survive as long as structural inequalities remain. These inequalities are at play in the daily operations of juvenile detention facilities, in the therapeutic relationships girls develop with service providers behind bars, and in the various kinds of programming that are offered to them during incarceration. It is important to note that those who work with incarcerated girls form temporary relationships that do not buffer the girls from the losses and deficits they experience. Although these relationships may be the only lifeline in a context of mass deprivation, they are not solutions to the underlying causes of girls' displacement and social abandonment. When service providers, decision makers, and other stakeholders recognize the political dimension of their role in relation to the girls, only then can they directly address social inequality in every arena, from the interactions they have with those they serve to opportunities for social activism and civic engagement within communities and organizations.

In this chapter, we define the juvenile justice system as a zone of social abandonment and examine how it makes some girls more vulnerable to harm and further victimization. Zones of social abandonment are places where already-marginalized groups are further disenfranchised (Harvey 2014; Marrow and Lurhmann 2012). Jails, hospitals, many public housing developments, and refuges are examples of zones of social abandonment where people live a "bare life," that is, a life focused on basic necessities (Marrow and Lurhmann 2012). Bare life is the condition of securing food, shelter, safety; however, it does not guarantee that the person will have social value, a voice, or authentic relationships (Marrow and Lurhmann 2012). People in zones of social abandonment have very little control over what happens to them and are the least respected members of society. They are often poor, non-White, female, and/or living with a disability. They struggle with mental health issues, have a criminal history, are homeless or precariously housed, may identify as lesbian, gay, bisexual, transgender, or queer, may be pregnant, or may have vulnerable immigration statuses. In zones of social abandonment, people face additional physical harm because they are devalued and placed in precarious situations, where sexual abuse, familial violence, and commercial exploitation are all intensified by social inequalities and deprivation (Eisenstein, Heinigeri, and Bezerra De Melloi 2010).

Zones of social abandonment may be characterized as continuous because they often are identified in families and spread to other social contexts where individuals undergo various types of neglect (e.g., relational, educational, legal). At the community level, this neglect is experienced as lack of resources or opportunity (e.g., unemployment, closing of community centers, poor transportation options) (National Scientific Council on the Developing Child 2012). Policies related to crime control and criminological theories strengthen the boundaries of these zones of abandonment. Kelling and Wilson's "Broken Windows" theory (1982), for example, suggests that visible signs of abandonment in neighborhoods encourage crime and signal the need for more aggressive policing. In the family, interpersonal abandonment occurs when relatives hand their "troubled" ones (i.e., children with disabilities or family members with mental illness) over to institutions such as psychiatric hospitals. This results in further isolating the "troubled" person from broader social support by separating them from the outside world and from their social networks (Marrow and Luhrmann 2012). The institution itself may be built on a culture of power, predictability, and control that may impose reinforcement for rule following and an overreliance on restraints and medication. Lack of resources for state- and city-run facilities may trickle down to the consumer as the experience of neglect and abuse (Hartocollis 2009). At a macro-systemic level, professional discourses that promote the myth that independent individuals are wholly responsible for their fate mask structural inequalities in ways that compound the experience of social abandonment.

In this chapter, we examine our own experiences with incarcerated girls and student mentors, whom we came to know through CUNY's Mentoring and Adolescent Development course. We review the relevant literature, discuss the multidimensional factors that lead to girls' incarceration, and highlight the psychological and social concerns of abandoned girls. Then we examine "what works" for girls and discuss the key tenets of gender-responsive programming. We argue that deficits in theory and practice might be filled by the intentional inclusion of incarcerated girls' voices. We close by highlighting the directions that research and programming can take in order to maintain a deeper commitment to serving girls in zones of social abandonment.

The voices of girls and mentors who participated in the course come from multiple sources. The girls' voices come from art projects they completed as part of the course, and the mentors' voices, from a study about intergroup relationships. We did not ask girls to indicate their demographic descriptions in their art projects. The mentors' demographic descriptions were captured since they come from a formal, rather than archival, study. We are withholding all demographic descriptions in this chapter so that girls and mentors are addressed in equal terms. We analyzed the data from the girls and mentors using grounded theory practices (Corbin and Strauss 2007; Strauss and Corbin 1994). We used a start-list of words and subthemes that fit the primary areas of interest as highlighted in the literature about incarcerated girls' social and psychological concerns and their experiences of incarceration and release. The resultant start list of codes, subcodes, and specific words was then used as a scheme for hand coding the data. In this chapter, we present data to show where girls' voices are missing and, alternatively, where they affirm and challenge research findings, and offer insight.

Framing Our Course

The course Mentoring and Adolescent Development occupies a unique position in the history of the College of Staten Island at CUNY. The course was founded by Drs. Judith Kuppersmith and Rima Blair, who sought to provide unique, female, and adolescent-centered experiences to the girls in the facility. They also sought to provide students who were interested in becoming clinicians an opportunity to develop an understanding of therapeutic interventions with a forensic population and to examine the larger social contexts of devaluation and abandonment that had the potential to restrict girls' opportunity and impact their self-concept. As we taught the course, we considered it an opportunity to offer critical analyses and ways of relating to others and to extend professional worldviews to include a view of the person-in-context. In the classroom, we taught students some basic counseling skills and discussed critical social-psychological approaches to juvenile justice. We coordinated the students' weekly visits, and designed ten facility-wide workshops open to all the girls, staff, and mentors. We (faculty and student mentors) also sought to be active community members outside of the realm of the course, and therefore went to the facility to lead expressive arts and support/social groups (i.e., we led a Girl Scout troop, created a cheer/dance team, and conducted a knitting grief group). We attended Family Day when girls' families came for routine visits, which often featured a group meal and an activity (e.g., girls showed films they made about their lives from a digital journaling class and were recognized for their school work). We also participated in the Community Advisory Board meetings at the facility.

The mentors were mostly White and middle class, and the girls resided in an all-female facility that primarily housed Black and Latina girls from poor and gentrifying neighborhoods. The demographic differences between the girls and the mentors provided the opportunity to recognize inequality and to challenge stereotypic perceptions about the girls. The average age of the college student mentors was twenty-two, while the girls were fifteen years old and had on average a ninth-grade education level. Given these differences, we attempted to help the college students and the girls develop a critical consciousness and acknowledge that differences in race, class, gender, and sexuality shape everyone's life. This consciousness often began to take shape when we had the college students theorize why they themselves or people they knew weren't incarcerated for doing some of the same things the girls had done (e.g., truancy and theft). While we followed the institutional directive to not ask why any one girl was incarcerated, girls' self-disclosures indicated that they entered the detention facility for various reasons, including excessive truancy, noncompliance in other residential settings, and getting caught up in rings of street gangs and related crimes. The majority were victims of sexual violence that led to their involvement in survival crimes. Often the girls were incarcerated simply because there was no other residential placement or responsible, willing adult available for their care.

Instead of focusing on girls as "juvenile delinquents," we acknowl-edged them as adolescents who had sometimes made mistakes and were often abandoned by people and institutions. Rather than positioning ourselves as "saviors," we framed ourselves as a community who some-times shared elements of the girls' histories. We approached the course as a journey towards mutual self-discovery that involved learning about inequality and disrupting discourses of individual criminality through self-reflection. With this frame, students were able to see girls in context and to view incarceration as a zone of social abandonment, as illustrated in the quotation below:

> They [most people] should know that the girls all have a story to tell, and that they should not be dismissed from society or our minds just because they are in the facility. It should be brought to light the impact that pov-erty, parental neglect, education, and abuse have on their lives. (Sarah, student mentor)

Girls' Social and Psychological Concerns in Zones of Social Abandonment

Practitioners in the field of child and family, clinical, and counseling psychology understand the importance of embracing an ecological approach when working with clients who have had some contact with the juvenile justice system. Within the ecological model, the child is in the center, and the contexts within which this child is nested are taken into consideration in attempts to address behavioral issues (Stormshak and Dishion 2002). The ecological approach moves away from a focus on the "criminal personality" to a focus on individual behaviors in con-text. The ecological approach also attempts to address community and societal dynamics like racism, sexism, and classism as factors that have an impact on individuals' lives.

Ecological models explain how racism, sexism, and classism posi-tion certain girls as targets for differential treatment. Gender norms and racial stereotypes influence girls' representations, which in turn deter-mine the kinds of interactions they have with the legal, penal, and edu-cational systems (Neville and Mobley 2001; Welch, Roberts-Lewis, and Parker 2009). For example, gender norms define women's true nature as innocent, peaceful, warm, weak, and worthy of protection. Girls who are seen as breaking these gender norms are targeted for incarceration and other forms of "treatment" designed to "refeminize" them (Godsoe 2014). There is a "cost" to violating gender norms: Girls may be characterized as cold, sexually promiscuous, gender-nonconforming and, perhaps, lesbian (Carr 1998). They may also be judged more harshly within the justice system.

Gender norms influence which behaviors are seen as criminal. Status offenses are the most explicit illustrations of the way gender norms contribute to girls' incarceration. Behaviors that would not be considered a crime in an adult court, like truancy, running away, disobeying parents, or breaking curfew, become criminalized (Hockenberry and Puzzanchera 2014). Up to half of girls' arrests are for status offenses, and girls are punished more harshly than boys for similar offenses (MacDonald and Chesney-Lind 2001). The criminalization of girls' behaviors has been described not only as a means of "taking care" of girls but also as a way of ensuring their conformity to gender norms (Dohrn 2004; Kempf-Leonard and Johansson 2007). Even being pregnant as a disenfranchised youth can be criminalized or, worse, be ignored as a life event that is important to the young mother. Our facility was the only one in the state of New York that allowed pregnant girls to keep their babies with them after they gave birth.

Girls of color and poor girls stand out against dominant societal representations of femininity in ways that contribute to their targeting for policing and incarceration (Holsinger and Holsinger 2005; Schaffner 2006). Gender, class, and racialized stereotypes blend and produce different images for different girls: White girls are cast as passive and in need of protection, Black girls as sexual, independent, and crime prone, and Latinas as sexual, dependent, and family oriented (Nanda 2012). Similarly, representations of poor people suggest that they are unable to plan or uninterested in planning for their future, and are prone to laziness (Lott and Saxon 2002). These stereotypes impact girls because they communicate messages about why girls deserve to be locked up and how they might be reformed into "good girls" (i.e. feminine, "White-acting," docile, and quiet—with the promise of entry into the dominant culture) and whether or not the origins of their crime are a result of their inherent nature or a byproduct of their primary social worlds (Nanda 2012). Some suggest that the juvenile justice system seeks to control the gender and sexual expressions of low-income girls (Goodkind 2009; Pasko 2010). Racial, class, and gender stereotypes also "justify the policy of abandonment of this segment of society by public authorities" (Wacquant 2004, 96), which is illustrated in both the prevalence of policing and the relative absence of services within poor communities of color.

Poverty is a primary determinant in girls' incarceration, even when the contribution of race is taken out of the equation (Chauhan et al. 2010). Poverty is linked to criminal activities through concentrated disadvantage, victimization, and discrimination (Acoca and Dedel 1998; Kaufman et al. 2008). A large number of girls involved in the criminal justice system run away to escape abuse or neglect within the home (Chesney-Lind and Sheldon 2003; Sangoi and Goshin 2013). They comprise an estimated 53 percent of runaway petitions in courts (Hockenberry and Puzzanchera 2014). Girls experience active and passive forms of neglect and find themselves left alone because their parents are working, are struggling with their own mental health and physical needs, or are incarcerated. Girls may have to take care of the household, their siblings, their own children, and even their parents by themselves, and thus endure further neglect and abandonment (Schaffner 2006). Lesbian, bisexual, and transgender youth are particularly vulnerable to physical and sexual abuse and homelessness, which contribute to their higher rates of incarceration (Curtin 2002; Graziano and Wagner 2011; see also Irvine, Canfield, and Roa, chapter 8 in this book).

Girls often attempt to survive poverty by committing crimes in order to secure basic needs for safety, shelter, food, clothes, and medication (Kempf-Leonard and Johansson 2007). Beyond sheer need, in a class-based society that emphasizes monetary success, girls may also use crime as an instrument to obtain material goods that would otherwise be unattainable (Giordano, Deines, and Cernkovich 2006).

What Works in Girls' Mental Health and Juvenile Justice Programming?

Ecological explanations of female crime and incarceration are an important first step towards bringing mental health and criminal justice interventions into closer alignment with gender-sensitive practices. At present, many mental health and criminal justice programs limit service providers in their ability to fully contextualize the lives of incarcerated people (Pollack 2004). Failure to take into account the contexts of girls' lives and to adapt the delivery of services to their realities is the way the voices of incarcerated girls are silenced.

Ecological treatment models like Multisystemic Therapy (MST) have been empirically documented as effective (Evans-Chase and Zhou 2014; Latimer 2005). Only a few models, however, explicitly address the issue of systemic inequality rather than focus on the "criminal personality" (Neville and Mobley 2001; Welch, Roberts-Lewis, and Parker 2009). Addressing girls' needs from an ecological perspective requires that mental health and criminal justice practitioners develop a more complex understanding of what defines girls' agency. Service providers are decision makers in every aspect of girls' incarceration, from treatment through exit planning. Although they may develop a great deal of empathy towards those in their care, and use multisystemic theories and approaches to treat them, they must still self-consciously think of their role as that of "interventionists" in order to examine the ways in which service delivery may contribute to girls' social abandonment. The term "interventionist" refers to the ways in which service providers become involved in individual lives and communities as outsiders who dictate what the problem and the solution are from a dominant frame that may or may not take into consideration the girls' culture and values. Below we highlight how mental health and criminal justice practitioners can pay attention to girls' immediate and diverse needs during incarceration and to their ongoing conditions of social abandonment in ways that enhance service as well as gender and multicultural sensitivity (Sherman 2005).

Recommendation #1: Programming should be empowering.

Gender-responsive approaches to programming stress the value of empowering girls to find and use their voices. Girls should have the ability to provide their perspectives on their service needs and placements (Dorhn 2004). For example, they should make choices about whether to participate in individual or group therapy and what issues to address in treatment (Bloom et al. 2002a, 2002b). When girls take part in decision making, they feel validated and develop a sense of engagement and accountability. They also experience greater success in treatment. Zahn and colleagues (2009) found that 85 percent of girls reported achieving the desired outcomes they themselves had defined. Making choices and exercising agency is a crucial part of adolescent development that is often only acknowledged and rewarded when incarcerated young people choose to be compliant with the punitive aspects of living in a residential setting (e.g., deciding not to speak out if something seems unfair to avoid challenging power, withholding feelings or attempting to say what therapists want to hear in order to appear to be healing/healed) (Polvere 2014; Tosouni 2010).

In the Mentoring and Adolescent Development course, we engaged girls in the design of our program in order to decrease the sense of uncertainty they carried around with them each day. Girls in the juvenile detention facility never knew when their exact release dates were and had limited control over their aftercare planning, which often went awry for a multitude of reasons. Girls would literally feel trapped in not knowing, in asking questions and not getting answers. Uncertainty about what would happen to them intensified their sense of instability and abandonment. A few girls thought their aftercare social worker had forgotten about them, or that facility staff had forgotten about or refused to complete their paperwork. These dynamics intensified girls' experiences of mistrust.

By contrast, our course provided girls with opportunities for control and recognition: Girls routinely voted which topics they wanted to learn about, discuss, or explore more deeply in the workshops and weekly visits with mentors (see figure 6.1). They also decided which subtopics we should address and the format of the exploration (e.g., discussion, fishbowl, talking, anonymous question box, poetry, and role play). Having choices seemed to engage girls who were enthusiastic about integrating their life experiences with what they learned. We also allowed them to guide us in what they wanted to gain from our "mentoring" relationship. This included researching college options, applying to college, studying for the GED, learning about various careers, and getting into nontraditional job training programs.

Table 6.1: Topic Selection Survey

TOPICS FOR FALL WORKSHOPS

HEALTH

Hygiene STDs/Teen Pregnancy/OB/ GYN care Fitness/Obesity	Mental illness/Suicide Bad influences Drugs/Drinking and driving	Lack of social services Neglect and abuse Pollution Medical/Health services/ Insurance/Overmedicating Children Conditions of hospital/ Lack of quality healthcare

SCHOOL AND EDUCATION

Higher education Importance of education Career paths/Educational goals (what is a BA, MA, PhD?)	Dropping out/Being pushed out Truancy and social promotion Special education/I.E.P. Diploma Safety in schools/Drugs in schools	High school diploma/ OCFS education School-to-jail pipeline No Child Left Behind Military recruitment

Recommendation #2: Programming should be relational.

A relational approach to treatment is gender responsive because it attends to girls' tendency to draw their self-concept from their relationships with others (Gilligan 1982). This is essential given the high incidence of exploitative relationships in the histories of incarcerated girls (Chesney-Lind and Shelden 2003). Some suggest, however, that correctional contexts discourage positive, relational dynamics (Ashkar and Kenny 2008; Gaarder, Rodriguez, and Zatz 2004). Correctional staff may perceive girls as manipulators who tell stories to get attention and who avoid responsibility for their actions (Gaarder, Rodriguez, and Zatz 2004). Such perceptions increase their inclination to establish control over girls (Ashkar and Kenny 2008).

Relationships between girls and staff range from indifference to aggression: Girls may be shouted at, demeaned, threatened, or physically restrained (Dierkhising, Lane, and Natsuaki 2014). Girls have reported that they would be "punished" with hostility if they advocated for better treatment (Belknap, Holsinger, and Dunn 1997; Tosouni 2010). Girls seem to be painfully aware that they do not have a voice, and often think it is unfair that they should have to be respectful to adults when they are not given the same regard (Belknap, Holsinger, and Dunn 1997). Our experience affirms that girls feel singled out, silenced, and punished in relationships with staff. Some girls even indicated that these relationships matched their family dynamics and left them feeling scared or retraumatized.

Positive interactions between staff and girls are rarely discussed in the literature, but our experience provides some examples. Nekesha's story indicates the importance of having the staff and girls participate in authentic, caring relationships:

> Some facilities is positive because there staff and other residents that are willing to work together and help another that is goin thru problems. Just listen when they need a ear, talk when they need advice. Just keep it real at all times good and bad. (Nekesha, incarcerated girl)

Nekesha focuses on the everyday support girls can receive from staff and community members (e.g., volunteers who facilitated classes in art or yoga). We observed such support when staff helped girls with homework after their workday was over, or talked to them gently about their behavior or relationships outside. Administrators also shared fond memories of former residents, kept mementos like portraits of girls that were hand sketched before they were released, or stayed in contact with them well into their adulthood. This suggests that there is room for supportive and authentic relationships between incarcerated girls and juvenile justice staff, where problem solving and positivity replaces mistrust and hostility (Ashkar and Kenny 2008).

Many of the mentors in our program witnessed girls looking out for one another, advising each other to calm down so they wouldn't get written up, or warning each other not to play basketball too passionately to avoid personal injury. In our course, we realized the importance, for girls, of developing reliable and trusting relationships with us as well as with each other: They would loudly exclaim to other girls, "Oh look, there is *my* mentor!"—thus expressing their excitement as well as their sense of connection with the mentors. On the other hand, when a meeting with the mentors was missed, they would respond with disappointment. Through the course activities, we—the mentors included—strove to foster authentic relationships; we also provided structured opportunities for girls to develop trusting and reliable relationships with one another. For example, Della facilitated a cheer/dance squad with two other classmates:

> Although at first it was a struggle to get them to work together, little by little egos disappeared and teamwork emerged. We were able to get the girls to trust each other enough to learn stunts and gymnastics. They were able to learn an entire routine and performed it during Family Day. The difference between the first practice and the Family Day performance was night and day. Incredible. I cried tears of joy as they performed. (Della, student mentor)

Other mentors observed a similar sense of community as they participated in mentor-initiated programs at the facility (e.g., Girl Scouts Behind Bars or No Child Left Inside—a nature exploration program), or as they collaboratively made art or completed participatory research projects.

Recommendation #3: Programming should be culturally relevant.

A culturally sensitive approach to gender-sensitive programming stresses three dimensions of girls' experience. First, girls contend with structural disadvantages based on their racial, class, gender, and sexual identities and related social positioning (Mattews and Hubbard 2008). Second, girls of color are overrepresented within the juvenile justice system; they receive harsher treatment, and are exposed to the unconscious biases of staff and practitioners (Mattews and Hubbard 2008). Third, the needs of justice-involved girls call for criminal justice and mental health programming that affirms their identities. Addressing these considerations will allow service providers to validate girls' experiences, to interpret their behaviors in context, to understand girls' experience in terms of resistance rather than unruly character, and to identify how they can intervene not only in girls' lives but also in their communities. When service providers acknowledge the importance of belonging and group membership and display an affirmative attitude towards the communities from which girls come, they foster girls' positive identification with their gender, race, class, and sexual orientation (National Council on Crime and Delinquency 2012; Walker, Muno, and Sullivan-Colgazier 2012).

To meet the needs of incarcerated girls, mental health and criminal justice programming should attend to components that help girls (1) recognize everyday instances of racism, (2) contest biased social representations of their communities, (3) identify their cultural strengths, and (4) develop their own perspectives on society and history (Fejes and Miller 2002; Roberts and Welch-Brewer 2008; Valentine Foundation 1990). Naming inequalities can help girls discuss and "talk back to" representations that prescribe who they are or who they can be (DeFinney, Loiselle, and Mackenzie 2011).

In the Mentoring and Adolescent Development course, we strove towards culturally relevant programming by inviting the girls to explore a variety of topics related to race and gender. For example, we focused on Afrocentric rites of passage and autobiographical exploration exercises. We organized a unit on gendered violence that addressed relational and sexual health. We also led a research project where girls and mentors examined and analyzed images of Black and White women using a protocol designed to foster their interpretation of symbols of power and their understanding of women's placement relative to men in the images. In another participatory action research project, girls and mentors interviewed one another. They asked questions about social support, community resources, and basic goods available in their neighborhoods. They also discussed why there might be differences in the resources available to girls and mentors. The project engaged the girls in a roundtable discussion about the relationship among schools, policing, and incarceration. The aim of this discussion was to address the racial dimension of girls' experiences of being profiled. We found that unless race and culture were the explicit focus of the conversation, girls and mentors rarely addressed their cultural differences. By contrast, they acknowledged cultural similarities (e.g., "we're both Latinas") more readily. Therefore, we strove to create a safe environment and provided ample opportunities for mentors and girls to embrace both differences and similarities. Last, it is important to note that we looked primarily towards the girls for their perspectives on the discussion topics, before adding our own to the conversation. Our objective was to avoid imposing our meanings and interpretations before the girls had voiced their own.

Recommendation #4: Programming should be comprehensive.

Community-based and residential interventions with a comprehensive and ecological approach to the needs of at-risk girls have the most promise. They often share the same definition of desirable outcomes for girls—reduced recidivism, increased education, and improved relationships. Among them are residential treatment models with positive results that offer individualized intervention planning, case management, educational programming, and relational and life skills training (Zahn et al. 2009). AMICUS Girls' Restorative Program, Southern Oaks Girls School, and Girls and Boys Town USA, for example, are interventions that have been found to enhance family reunification, to reduce disruptive behaviors, and to promote maturity and compassion (see also Gordon 2004). Community- and school-based programs for formerly incarcerated girls, such as Reaffirming Young Sister's Excellence (RYSE), Working to Insure and Nurture Girls Success (WINGS), and Practical Academic Cultural Education (PACE), aim to strengthen girls' social, academic, and vocational skills as well as familial and community connections (National Council on Crime and Delinquency 2012; Roman et al. 2006; Zahn et al. 2009). They also provide assistance with transportation and emergency financial support. SafeFutures, a five-year demonstration project implemented in several cities in the United States, provided girls with individualized services, life and parenting skills training, mentoring, mental health treatment, and basic and vocational education (Roman et al. 2006). The effectiveness of the program varied across sites; however, SafeFutures was found to reduce girls' justice involvement and to increase their school attendance (Roman et al. 2006).

Recommendation #5: Girls need multifaceted mental healthcare.

Access to mental-health and substance-abuse treatment inside juvenile detention facilities is limited, and when programs are available, they have been described as too impersonal or too superficial (Tosouni 2010). The girls who participated in our course confirmed the one-size-fits-all nature of mental health programming in the detention facility:

The negative effect that can occur is that facility usually have groups and programs that they use to serve different types of behaviors at one time. Facilities usually use it as "the cure" to all behaviors. Which means that one child behavior can never get the right attention they need or right care. They have to be half-assed with they problems and get consequences for not doing things the "right way." (Tracee, incarcerated girl)

Girls also critiqued the use of psychiatric medication as ineffective or harmful (Polvere 2014). For example, Tracee indicated that medications did not address core issues, but caused other problems:

They label the residents and diagnose them with problems and give them meds that they think is going to heal them. Which they don't pay attention to is that most meds heal one thing and has more dangerous side effects and causes other problems. One main side effect of most drugs is suicide. How is that helping youngins and teens? (Tracee, incarcerated girl)

Cognitive behavioral therapies (CBT) hold a position of prominence in correctional programming. CBT has been documented to decrease negative emotional and behavioral responses and to reduce juvenile recidivism and substance abuse by changing the thoughts that are linked to problematic feelings and behaviors (Milkman and Wanberg 2007; National Mental Health Association 2004). CBT interventions for justice-involved youth include Anger Replacement Therapy, Moral Reconation Therapy, and Thinking for a Change (Mahoney et al. 2004; Milkman and Wanberg 2007; National Mental Health Association 2004). Despite evidence of their effectiveness, these CBT programs have been heartily critiqued for focusing on the "criminal personality" as the target of treatment (Pollack 2004; Van Wormer 2010) and for not considering how classism, racism, and sexism affect girls' mental health (Myers 2013; Pollack 2014). For example, critics have argued that CBT is inappropriate for use with diverse clients because it emphasizes dominant cultural worldviews like science, logic, and rationality, while claiming it is value neutral (David 2009). Others have also noted that the implementation of CBT often places emphasis on intrapersonal factors, and discounts the external, oppressive dynamics that non-White, non-Western clients experience, ranging from micro-aggressions and differential treatment to structural and institutional barriers (David 2009; Sue 2015).

However, the American Psychological Association's policy statement on evidence-based practice in psychology suggests that it is possible to deliver CBT programs for justice-involved youth with multicultural responsivity by matching treatment to clients' characteristics and culture. The therapeutic process of matching opens an avenue for addressing oppression and privilege in treatment (David 2009; Kelly 2006) because it calls for a conceptualization of clients' distress and therapeutic change in the social environments where they occur. Additionally, emphasizing clients' strengths with a view to empowerment is a core clinical process of multicultural counseling that is equally important to gender-sensitive programming in juvenile justice settings. Strengths-based treatment contrasts with traditional justice interventions in several ways (see for example Van Wormer's model; Van Wormer 2010). First, it emphasizes the self as resilient, rational, and situated in social contexts, rather than focusing on the criminal personality. Second, it defines women and girls as active participants in a collaborative therapeutic process, rather than as people who are either resistant to or compliant with treatment. Third, it targets women's and girls' fulfillment and well-being rather than recidivism. It also considers the structural factors that contribute to women's and girls' participation in criminal activities, and supports women's and girls' initiatives to become effective and supportive community members. Contextual and strength-based approaches to justice interventions for girls are in line with the American Psychological Association's Guidelines for Psychological Practice with Girls and Women, which call for practitioners' attention to oppression and privilege, gender socialization and stereotypes, and institutional and systemic bias in clinical practice (American Psychological Association 2007).

Girls' Last Days in the Detention Facility: Reentry or Social Abandonment?

> This is my last day in here. In one way I'm happy and in another scared but it's my time to go and leave but now it's all about me and what I need to do. I do want to cry cuz I been with them . . . six months and I'm out the door. So the ball is in my court. (Charlene, an incarcerated girl)

On her last day in the facility, Charlene suggested that she alone was responsible for herself when she stated, "it's all about me and what I need to do." While this is a statement of autonomy, it also speaks to the dearth of personal, social, or institutional support that girls have after incarceration (Belknap, Holsinger, and Dunn 1997). Upon discharge from detention facilities, girls are concerned with large and small issues, "fears about how to handle everyday occurrences they had missed or forgotten, such as what it would be like to drive, attend a regular school, take a bus, cook, buy groceries, date boys, and get along with people" (Belknap, Holsinger, and Dunn 1997, Key Finding Number Five). Programs that seek to help girls expand their sense of agency may inadvertently intensify their sense of social abandonment: When girls return to their communities with the belief that they, and only they, are responsible for their lives, they are ill equipped to recognize and deal with the structural inequalities that remain intact outside of juvenile justice facilities (Myers 2013).

An ecological approach to juvenile justice interventions is a good first step to help girls address their everyday concerns in ways that also acknowledge systemic disadvantages. Treatment for incarcerated girls must integrate the personal and the social and foster girls' ability to address everyday injustice. Treatment should also foster mental health and justice practitioners' understanding that girls' needs emerge from contexts of deprivation (Polvere 2014; Smith and Romero 2010).

The principles of scientism have predominated in the field of psychology in ways that have prevented practitioners from producing complex multidimensional analyses of systemic oppression (Sue 2015). Scientism is the overvaluation of post-positivistic scientific methods as a way to find solutions to problems, while lived experience is undervalued or invalidated as a base for knowledge production. Scientism is often regarded as a reductionist approach with a focus on individual variables as the cause of problems (Fox 1996). Practitioners can minimize the likelihood that they will reproduce oppression by widening their therapeutic worldview from scientism to a complex and multilevel understanding of individuals in contexts, by engaging in critical self-reflexive practice, by sharing power and voice with court-involved youth, and by working together with incarcerated girls to build on strengths and hone tools for social change (Chesney-Lind and Shelden 2003; Dohrn 2004;

Goodman et al. 2004; Van Wormer 2010), so that no girl continues to be abandoned.

REFERENCES

Acoca, Leslie, and Kelly Dedel. 1998. "No Place to Hide: Understanding and Meeting the Needs of Girls in the California Juvenile Justice System," http://www.nccdg-lobal.org.

American Psychological Association (APA). 2007. Guidelines for Psychological Practice with Girls and Women, http://www.apa.org.

Ashkar, Peter J., and Dianna Theadora Kenny. 2008. "Views from the Inside: Young Offenders' Subjective Experiences of Incarceration." *International Journal of Offender Therapy and Comparative Criminology* 52 (5): 584–97. doi: 10.1177/0306624X08314181.

Belknap, Joanne, Kristi Holsinger, and Melissa Dunn. 1997. "Understanding Incarcerated Girls: The Results of a Focus Group Study." *Prison Journal* 77 (4): 381–405.

Blair, Irene V., Kristine M. Chapleau, and Charles Judd. 2005. "The Use of Afrocentric Features as Cues for Judgment in the Presence of Diagnostic Information." *European Journal of Social Psychology* 35 (1): 59–68.

Bloom, Barbara, Barbara Owen, Elizabeth Piper Deschenes, and Jill Rosenbaum. 2002a. "Improving Juvenile Justice for Females: A Statewide Assessment in California." *Crime and Delinquency* 48 (4): 526–52.

Bloom, Barbara, Barbara Owen, Elizabeth Piper Deschenes, and Jill Rosenbaum. 2002b. "Moving toward Justice for Female Juvenile Offenders in the New Millennium: Modeling Gender-Specific Policies and Programs." *Journal of Contemporary Criminal Justice* 18 (10): 37–56.

Carr, C. Lynn. 1998. "Tomboy Resistance and Conformity: Agency in Social Psychological Gender Theory." *Gender and Society* 12 (5): 528–33. doi: 10.1177/0891243980120050003.

Chauhan, Pretti, N. Dickon Reppucci, Mandi Burnette, and Scott Reiner. 2010. "Race, Neighborhood Disadvantage, and Antisocial Behavior among Female Juvenile Offenders." *Journal of Community Psychology* 38 (4): 532–40.

Chesney-Lind, Meda, and Randall G. Shelden. 2003. *Girls, Delinquency, and Juvenile Justice*. Belmont, CA: West and Wadsworth.

Corbin, Juliet M., and Anselm Strauss. 2007. *Basics of Qualitative Research: Techniques and Procedures for Developing Grounded Theory*. Thousand Oaks, CA: Sage.

Curtin, Mary. 2002. "Lesbian and Bisexual Girls in the Juvenile Justice System." *Child and Adolescent Social Work Journal* 19 (4): 285–301.

David, E. J. R. 2009."Internalized Oppression, Psychopathology, and Cognitive-Behavioral Therapy among Historically Oppressed Groups." *Journal of Psychological Practice* 15 (1): 71–103.

DeFinney, Sandrina, Elicia Loiselle, and Dean Mackenzie. 2011. "The Minoritization of Girls in Child and Youth Care." In *Child and Youth Care: Critical Perspectives on*

Pedagogy, Practice, and Policy. Edited by Alan Pence and Jennifer White, 70–94. Vancouver: University of British Columbia Press.

Dierkhising, Carly B., Andrea Lane, and Misaki N. Natsuka. 2014. "Victims behind Bars: A Preliminary Study of Abuse during Juvenile Incarceration and Post-Release Social and Emotional Functioning." *Psychology, Public Policy, and Law* 20 (2): 181–90.

Dohrn, Bernadine. 2004. "All Ellas: Girls Locked Up." *Feminist Studies* 30 (2): 302–24.

Eisenstein, Evelyn, Sabine Heinigeri, and Yvonne Bezerra De Melloi. 2011. "Child and Adolescent Sexual Abuse: Intervention and Prevention in Brazil." In *Psychology Research Progress: Psychological Impact of Living under Violence and Poverty in Brazil.* Edited by Lovisi Giovanni Marcos, Jair De Jesus Mari, and Elie S. Valencia, 61–69. New York: Nova Science.

Evans-Chase, Michelle, and Huiquan Zhou. 2014. "A Systematic Review of the Juvenile Justice Intervention Literature: What It Can (and Cannot) Tell Us about What Works with Delinquent Youth." *Crime and Delinquency* 60 (3): 451–70.

Fejes, Kathy E., and Darcy Miller. 2002. "Assessing Gender-Specific Programming for Juvenile Female Offenders: Creating Ownership, Voice, and Growth." *Journal of Correctional Education* 53 (2): 58–64.

Fox, Ronald E. 1996. "Charlatanism, Scientism, and Psychology's Social Contract." *American Psychologist* 51 (8): 777–84.

Gaarder, Emily, Nancy Rodriguez, and Marjorie S. Zatz. 2004. "Criers, Liars, and Manipulators: Probation Officers' View of Girls." *Justice Quarterly* 21 (3): 547–78.

Gilligan, Carol. 1982. *In a Different Voice.* Cambridge, MA: Harvard University Press.

Giordano, Peggy, Jill Deines, and Stephen Cernkovich. 2006. "In and out of Crime: A Life Course Perspective on Girls' Delinquency." In *Gender and Crime: Patterns of Victimization and Offending.* Edited by Karen Heimer and Candace Kruttschnitt, 31–81. New York: NYU Press.

Godsoe, Cynthia. 2014. "Contempt, Status, and the Criminalization of Non-conforming Girls." *Cardozo Law Review* 35 (3): 1091–1116.

Goodkind, Sara. 2009. "'You can be anything you want, but you have to believe it': Commercialized Feminism in Gender-Specific Programs for Girls." *Signs: Journal of Women in Culture and Society* 34 (2): 397–422.

Goodman, Lisa A., Belle Liang, Janet E. Helms, Rachel E. Latta, Elizabeth Sparks, and Sarah R. Weintraub. 2004. "Training Counseling Psychologists as Social Justice Agents: Feminist and Multicultural Principals in Action." *Counseling Psychologist* 32 (6): 793–837.

Gordon, Katya G. 2004. *From Corrections to Connections: A Report on the Amicus Girls Restorative Program.* St. Paul, MN: Amicus.

Graziano, Juliette Noel, and Eric F. Wagner. 2011. "Trauma among Lesbians and Bisexual Girls in the Juvenile Justice System." *Traumatology* 12 (2): 45–55.

Hartocollis, Anemona. 2009. "For Families of Mentally Ill, Mixed Feelings over Push Away from Adult Homes." *New York Times*, October 8, 2009.

Harvey, Daina C. 2014. "Disasters as Hyper-marginalization: Social Abandonment in the Lower Ninth Ward of New Orleans." In *Urban Ills: Twenty-first Century*

Complexities of Urban Living in Global Contexts. Edited by Carol C. Yeakey, Velta L. Sanders Thompson, and Anjanette Wells, 281–308. Boston: Lexington Books.

Hockenberry, Sarah, and Charles Puzzanchera. 2014. "Juvenile Court Statistics 2011," http://www.ojjdp.gov.

Holsinger, Kristi, and Alexander M. Holsinger. 2005. "Differential Pathways to Violence and Self-Injurious Behavior: African American and White Girls in the Juvenile Justice System." *Journal of Research in Crime and Delinquency* 42 (2): 211–42.

Jenkins, Adelbert H. 2001. "Individuality in Social Context: The Case for Psychological Agency." *Theory and Psychology* 11 (3): 347–62.

Kaufman, Joanne M., Cesar J. Rebellon, Sherod Thaxton, and Robert Agnew. 2008. "A General Strain Theory of Racial Differences in Criminal Offending." *Australian and New Zealand Journal of Criminology* 41 (3): 421–37.

Kelling, George L., and James Q. Wilson. 1982. "Broken Windows: The Police and Neighborhood Safety." *Atlantic*, March, http://www.theatlantic.com.

Kelly, Shalonda. 2006. "Cognitive-Behavioral Therapy with African Americans." In *Culturally Responsive Cognitive-Behavioral Therapy: Assessment, Practice, and Supervision.* Edited by Pamela Hays and Gayle Y. Iwamasa, 97–116. Washington, DC: American Psychological Association.

Kempf-Leonard, Kimberly, and Pernilla Johansson. 2007. "Gender and Runaways: Risk Factors, Delinquency, and Juvenile Justice Experiences." *Youth Violence and Juvenile Justice* 5 (3): 308–27.

Kerig, Patricia K., and Sheryl R. Schindler. 2013. "Engendering the Evidence Base: A Critical Review of the Conceptual and Empirical Foundations of Gender-Responsive Interventions for Girls' Delinquency." *Laws* 2 (1): 244–82.

Latimer, Jeffery. 2005. "Multisystemic Therapy as a Response to Serious Youth Delinquency," http://www.justice.gc.ca.

Lott, Bernice, and Susan Saxon. 2002. "The Influence of Ethnicity, Social Class, and Context on Judgments about U.S. Women." *Journal of Social Psychology* 142 (4): 481–99.

MacDonald, John M., and Meda Chesney-Lind. 2001. "Gender Bias and Juvenile Justice Revisited: Multiyear Analysis." *Crime and Delinquency* 47 (2): 173–95.

Mahoney, Karen, Julian D. Ford, Susan J. Ko, and Christine B. Siegfried. 2004. "Trauma-Focused Interventions for Youth in the Juvenile Justice System," http://www.nctsnet.org.

Marrow, Jocelyn, and Tanya Marie Lurhmann. 2012. "The Zone of Social Abandonment in Cultural Geography: On the Street in the United States, inside the Family in India." *Culture, Medicine, and Psychiatry* 36 (3): 493–513.

Mattews, Betsy, and Dana Jones Hubbard. 2008. "Moving Ahead: Five Essential Elements for Working Effectively with Girls." *Journal of Criminal Justice* 36 (6): 494–502.

Milkman, Harvey, and Kenneth Wanberg. 2007. "Cognitive Behavioral Treatment: A Review and Discussion for Corrections Professionals," http://static.nicic.gov.

Morton, Goldie M., and Leigh A. Leslie. 2005. "The Adolescent Female Delinquent: A Feminist Developmental Analysis." *Journal of Feminist Family Therapy* 17 (1): 17–50.

Murray, Rallie. 2013. "Invisible Bodies: The Politics of Control and Health in Maximum Security Prisons." *Trans-Scripts* 3 (1): 76–90.

Myers, Randolph R. 2013. "The Biographical and Psychic Consequences of 'Welfare Inaction' for Young Women in Trouble with the Law." *Youth Justice* 13 (3): 218–33.

Nanda, Jyoti. 2012. "Blind Discretion: Girls of Color and Delinquency in the Juvenile Justice System." *UCLA Law Review* 59 (6): 1502–39.

National Council on Crime and Delinquency. 2012. "Voices from the Field: Findings from the NGI Listening Sessions," http://www.nccdglobal.org.

National Mental Health Association. 2004. "Mental Health Treatment for Youth in the Juvenile Justice System: A Compendium of Promising Practices," https://www.nttac.org.

National Scientific Council on the Developing Child. 2012. "The Science of Neglect: The Persistent Absence of Responsive Care Disrupts the Developing Brain," http://developingchild.harvard.edu.

Neville, Helen A., and Michael Mobley. 2001. "Social Identities in Contexts: An Ecological Model of Multicultural Counseling Psychology Processes." *Counseling Psychologist* 29 (4): 471–86.

Pasko, Lisa. 2010. "Damaged Daughters: The History of Girls' Sexuality and the Juvenile Justice System." *Journal of Criminal Law and Criminology* 100 (3): 1099–1130.

Pollack, Shoshana. 2004. "Anti-oppressive Social Work Practice with Women in Prison: Discursive Reconstructions and Alternative Practices." *British Journal of Social Work* 34 (5): 693–707.

Polvere, Lauren. 2014. "Agency in Institutionalized Youth: A Critical Inquiry." *Children and Society* 28 (3): 182–93.

Roberts, Amelia, and Chiquita L. Welch-Brewer. 2008. "Incarcerated Teens and Substance Abuse: The Holistic Enrichment for at-Risk Teens (HEART) Program." In *Handbook of Prevention and Intervention Programs for Adolescent Girls*. Edited by Joyce Elizabeth Mann and Craig W. Le Croy, 269–304. Hoboken, NJ: Wiley.

Roberts-Lewis, Amelia, Chiquita L. Welch-Brewer, Mary S. Jackson, Raymond Kirk, and O. Martin Pharr. 2010. "Assessing Change in Psychosocial Functioning of Incarcerated Girls with a Substance Use Disorder: Gender-Sensitive Substance Abuse Intervention." *Journal of Offender Rehabilitation* 49 (7): 479–94.

Roman, Caterina G., Rebecca Naser, Shelley B. Rossman, Jennifer Yahner, and Jennifer Lynn-Whaley. 2006. *At-Risk and Delinquent Girls Programs in the SafeFutures Demonstration*. Washington, DC: Urban Institute Justice Policy Center.

Sangoi, Lisa K., and Lorie S. Goshin. 2013. "Women and Girls' Experiences before, during, and after Incarceration: A Narrative of Gender-Based Violence and an Analysis of the Criminal Justice Laws and Policies That Perpetuate This Narrative." *UCLA Women's Law Journal* 20 (2): 137–67.

Schaffner, Laurie. 2006. *Girls in Trouble with the Law*. New Brunswick, NJ: Rutgers University Press.

Sherman, Francine T. 2005. *Making Detention Reform Work for Girls: A Guide to Juvenile Detention Reform*, http://www.aecf.org.

Smith, Laura, and LeLaina Romero. 2010. "Psychological Interventions in the Context of Poverty: Participatory Action Research as Practice." *American Journal of Orthopsychiatry* 80 (1): 12–25.

Stormshak, Elizabeth, and Thomas Dishion. 2002. "An Ecological Approach to Child and Family Clinical and Counseling Psychology." *Clinical Child and Family Psychology Review* 5 (3): 197–215.

Strauss, Anselm, and Juliet M. Corbin. 1994. "Grounded Theory Methodology: An Overview." In *Handbook of Qualitative Research*. Edited by Norman K. Denzin and Yvonne S. Lincoln, 273–85. Thousand Oaks, CA: Sage.

Sue, Derald Wing. 2015. "Therapeutic Harm and Cultural Oppression." *Counseling Psychologist* 43 (3): 359–69.

Sue, Derald Wing, Joseph E. Bernier, Anna Durran, Lawrence Feinberg, Paul Pedersen, Elsie J. Smith, and Ena Vasquez-Nuttall. 1982. "Position Paper: Cross-cultural Counseling Competencies." *Counseling Psychologist* 10 (2): 45–52.

Tosouni, Anastasia. 2010. "Who's Bad? An Ethnographic Study of Incarcerated Girls." PhD diss., University of California. ProQuest [821454802].

Valentine Foundation and Women's Way. 1990. *A Conversation about Girls*. Bryn Mawr, PA: Valentine Foundation.

Van Wormer, Katherine. 2010. *Working with Female Offenders*. Hoboken, NJ: Wiley.

Wacquant, Loic. 2004. "Decivilizing and Demonizing: The Remaking of the Black American Ghetto." In *The Sociology of Norbert Elias*. Edited by Steven Loyal and Stephen Quilley, 95–121. Boston: Cambridge University Press.

Walker, Sarah Cusworth, Ann Muno, and Cheryl Sullivan-Colgazier. 2012. "Principles in Practice: A Multistate Study of Gender-Responsive Reforms in the Juvenile Justice System." *Crime and Delinquency* 58 (1): 1–25.

Welch, Chiquita L., Amelia Roberts-Lewis, and Sharon Parker. 2009. "Incorporating Gender-Specific Approaches for Incarcerated Female Adolescents: Multilevel Risk Model for Practice." *Journal of Offender Rehabilitation* 48 (1): 67–83.

Zahn, Margaret A., Jacob C. Day, Sharon F. Mihalic, and Lisa Tichavsky. 2009. "Determining What Works for Girls in the Juvenile Justice System: A Summary of Evaluation Evidence." *Crime and Delinquency* 55 (2): 266–93.

PART II

Specific Populations of Justice-Involved Women and Girls

7

Transwomen in the Criminal Justice System

Sans Justice

ALEXIS FORBES AND KEVIN L. NADAL

Transgender Women and the Police: Denise's First Encounter

Denise is an eighteen-year-old Latina transgender male-to-female (MTF) woman who just graduated from high school in a large metropolitan city. Denise, who was born a biological male named Dennis, began to explore her transgender identity when she was fourteen years old. She had always felt like a girl for as long as she could remember. For instance, when she was younger, she had liked to play with her sisters' dolls and sometimes liked to wear her mother's dresses, jewelry, and makeup in private. Because she was her parents' only "boy" and because she had never met any transgender people in her life, she knew she would not be accepted. So she hid this part of her identity as best as she could. Just a few months before her fifteenth birthday, she told her parents that she was transgender and that she preferred to be called "Denise." Her father exploded when he heard this announcement and kicked her out of the house; her mother began to cry, but did not stop her father from disowning and humiliating Denise.

Denise immediately ran to her childhood friend Claire—an African American female. With Claire's parents' permission, Denise stayed at their home and continued to resume her life as a high school student. After weeks went by, Claire's mother tried to talk to Denise and ask her what her options were, but did not want Denise to be living on the streets. Denise felt as though she was being a burden, so she decided to leave in the middle of the night while Claire's family was sleeping.

The next day, Denise decided to contact Lorial—a Latina transgender woman whom she had befriended on the Internet. Lorial, who is in her early twenties, had been kicked out of her house when she was around Denise's age. Lorial gladly took Denise in, but she asked Denise to help pay the rent. Denise agreed and realized that she would have to drop out of school in order to find a full-time job so that she could support herself.

Lorial became the mentor that Denise needed in her life. She validated Denise's experiences and shared her own story of how her own parents were violent when she came out to them. Lorial also gave Denise some of her old clothes, so that Denise could start wearing women's clothing openly for the first time in her life. Denise was grateful to have Lorial in her life and was especially grateful that she could finally have a close friend whom she could relate to.

After a few weeks, Denise asked Lorial about her own transitioning process, as it was clear that Lorial was "passing" as a cisgender woman (i.e., she had visible breasts and long hair, she dressed femininely, and she had a higher-pitched voice). Because Denise was a minor (and thus her parents would have to consent to her acquiring hormones), she would be unable to legally begin her physical transition into her true gender identity. Lorial offered Denise some of her hormone injections and told her to find a good job, so that she could get her own hormones. Lorial also encouraged Denise to save money for breast implants, which was the first gender-affirming surgery that Lorial got when she was eighteen years old.

Denise began to apply for any job that she saw was available, including retail, restaurant, and other service jobs. During this search, she started to notice that people treated her differently and realized that it was because of the way she presented. For example, when she walked through the shopping mall in her feminine clothing, she heard people yelling "she-male" and "tranny" as they passed her. When she inquired about "hiring" signs in store windows, employees would quickly tell her that they were no longer hiring. When she asked one store manager why their "hiring" signs were still hanging, he told her, "Oh, we'll take them down later."

Two months went by, and Denise was not able to find a job. Lorial was patient with her, but reminded her that she needed to help pay for the rent. Lorial suggested that Denise could "walk the stroll" and see if she could make any money that way. Denise was terrified of the idea of becoming a sex worker, but she viewed it as the only viable way to make money quickly. Lorial told her that she had been a sex worker off and on for the past several years and that it was a guaranteed way to make money. Denise reluctantly agreed and decided it was her only option.

The first time that Denise walked the stroll, she was terrified. When a client approached her, she was hesitant, but she did her best to appear confident. She managed to get through the incident without any injury and decided to try it again. She met a few new clients every other night or so. A few clients became regulars and she found herself making a steady income.

After several months, Denise was walking to her regular spot when a man pulled his car over and asked her to come home with him. When she approached his car, the man asked her, "How much for what?" Denise replied, "Fifty dollars for a blowjob and a hundred dollars for the whole thing." The man revealed that he was an undercover police officer and arrested her.

When they arrived at the police station, the officer announced to his friends, "Just picked up another tranny." The other officers began to laugh, when another one said, "Where are you gonna put him?" They knew that they were not supposed to lock her up with the male inmates, but they did not want to put Denise with the female inmates either. The officer decided to handcuff Denise to a bench while he consulted with his supervisor.

As exemplified through Denise's story, transgender women and girls endure discrimination and maltreatment in almost all aspects of their lives. Their interactions with the justice system often expose the institutionalized transphobic discrimination by police, correctional systems, judges, and discriminatory laws. While there have been some landmark legal cases that have improved living conditions for transgender women in America (for a review see Forbes 2014), many aspects of the criminal justice system retain some inherent transphobia and expose the extent to which legal remedies can benefit transgender women and girls. In this chapter, we outline the experiences of transwomen (i.e., transgender MTF women) in their interactions with the justice system. We use statistics and qualitative research from peer-reviewed journal articles, research findings, national surveys, and publications from advocacy groups who provide services to transgender women who have been perpetrators or victims of crime. We argue that the criminal justice system harms transwomen and transgirls more than it helps them, by highlighting how the criminal justice system (i.e., police, prisons, and the courts) are inherently incompatible with the needs of transwomen in the United States. We first provide definitions about gender nonconformity and transgender identity, while reviewing the current circumstances of transgender Americans. Second, we explore the discriminatory experiences of transgender women, including acts of intimate partner violence and hate crimes. Third, we discuss the problems common within transwomen's interactions with police officers and within correctional and detention facilities. Finally, we examine the mental health aspect of transgender identity and recognized treatment and therapy practices.

Definitions

The complications in describing the trans-identified and gender-nonconforming (GNC) community arise because individuals' labels of their gender, gender identity, and sexual orientation are often reliant on context. However, the term "sex" has been consistently defined as having a biological basis in that individuals' sex is determined through internal reproductive organs and sex chromosomes. With the exception of intersex people, who may have both male and female sex characteristics (Hughes et al. 2006), the majority of Americans are classified at birth as either male or female.

Gender is comprised of a set of culturally constructed norms, feelings, attitudes, and behaviors that are stereotypically associated with the biological sexes, male and female (American Psychological Association Council of Representatives 2011). The way in which these gender norms present or manifest is reliant, to a certain extent, on an individual's level of identification with the male or female gender. Gender is not a biological condition; therefore, anyone can identify as male or female.

Gender nonconformity (GNC) occurs when someone exhibits behaviors that are "incompatible" with the gender-normative behaviors that are expected of their birth-assigned sex. For example, if someone's birth-assigned sex is male, it is GNC for that person to wear a dress or to have stereotypically feminine interests. In addition to endorsing or expressing sex-incompatible norms, GNC people may view gender as a set of characteristics on a spectrum as opposed to viewing gender as discretely masculine or discretely feminine. In fact, many GNC individuals identify as having a combination of characteristics that correspond to both male and female gender identities. GNC people may sometimes report that they identify as "genderqueer," which means that they have no absolute gender identity and/or they identify as neither male nor female (Marksamer 2011).

Having an understanding of the complexities and lack of restrictions on norms and behaviors associated with sex and sexual orientation is a necessity when working with or describing the transgender population. As the fight for equal civil rights and protections for transgender people intensifies, so does the validation of the complex sexual and gender identities that are most evident in the transgender and GNC (TGNC) group.

Experiences and Demographics of Transgender People

The National Transgender Discrimination Survey (NTDS) (Grant et al. 2011) has provided comprehensive information about the lives of TGNC people in America, and is an invaluable resource for researchers, advocates, and members of the TGNC community. Information was gathered from 6,450 TGNC people about a range of topics, including gender identity, sexual orientation, poverty and homelessness, mental health, HIV, social and systemic discrimination, and experiences with the criminal justice system. The complexity of gender and sex among those in the TGNC community was evident in the NTDS participants' reporting of their gender identity and in their labels for their gender identity (Grant et al. 2011). Sixty percent of the people sampled in the NTDS were assigned male sex at birth, and the largest portion of respondents (41 percent) primarily identified as female. The other 58 percent identified either as male (26 percent), as "both genders" (20 percent), or as "self-identified" (13 percent). Other than the term "transgender," which was the most popularly used term, participants reported strongly identifying with terms such as "MTF" (male-to-female), "transsexual," "gender-nonconforming," "FTM" (female-to-male), "genderqueer," "two-spirit," "cross-dresser," "androgynous," "third gender," "feminine male," "masculine female," "intersex," and "drag king" or "drag queen" (Grant et al. 2011). These terms stand in strong contrast to the more popularized concept of cisgender people (i.e., those individuals who identify with their birth sex), who tend to recognize only the dichotomous categories of male and female. Transgender identity does not determine sexual orientation. Transgender people might identify in multiple ways, with 31 percent identifying as bisexual, 29 percent as lesbian, 23 percent as heterosexual, 7 percent as queer, and 7 percent as asexual. Two percent of them used other terms to describe their sexual orientation.

High rates of unemployment and underemployment contribute to the high rates of homelessness for transgender people (Grant et al. 2011; Mottet and Ohle 2003; Quintana et al. 2010; Xavier 2002). Many transgender people report not feeling safe in their housing situations and receiving hostility and insensitivity from neighbors and housing staff. An overwhelming number of transwomen who have sought help from homeless shelters were denied access and/or benefits that the shelter readily provides to cisgender women (Mottet and Ohle 2003). When transgender women were accepted at homeless shelters, they were typically housed with and harassed by cisgender men. Homeless shelters are not centers of refuge for transgender women. After being accepted at a shelter, transgender people experience harassment (55 percent), physical assault (25 percent), and sexual assault (22 percent) (Grant et al. 2011).

Discrimination against Transgender People

Because most Western societies accept and promote a gender binary on systemic, institutional, group, and individual levels, many cisgender people are less accepting of the diverse ways in which others experience or express gender. This gender binary may promote heteronormativity, in which all people are expected to act in accordance with their birth sex and subsequent gender roles. As a result of this, TGNC people are discriminated against in a spectrum of ways—judged, mocked, or punished when they behave in GNC ways; ridiculed or assaulted when they don't "pass" as the gender they identify with; or harassed or questioned when they do not match what is traditionally "male" or "female."

"Transphobia" can be defined as "an emotional disgust toward individuals who do not conform to society's gender expectations" (Hill and Willoughby 2005, 533), while "genderism" is "an ideology that reinforces the negative evaluation of gender non-conformity or an incongruence between sex and gender" (Hill and Willoughby 2005, 534). "Transphobia" is often viewed as a parallel term to "homophobia," in which individuals are fearful of gay, bisexual, and lesbian people, while "genderism" may be a parallel term to "heterosexism," which describes the subtle ways in which individuals may be prejudiced towards gay, bisexual, and transgender persons.

Transphobic and genderist discrimination may manifest in an array of ways. These types of discrimination may at times be more overt (e.g., hate crimes), and at other times the discrimination may be more subtle. Transphobic and genderist discrimination may manifest interpersonally (e.g., by cisgender people) as well as systemically (e.g., through institutions and the media).

While there has been a dearth of literature involving antitransgender hate crimes, one study revealed two major findings: (1) hate crimes toward TGNC people are especially violent, in comparison to hate crimes against other groups, and (2) transgender victims are targeted for more complex reasons than their gender variance alone (Stotzer 2008). Another report found that from the beginning of 2008 to the middle of 2009, there were more than two hundred antitransgender murders worldwide, equaling approximately nineteen transgender murders per month (Nadal, Skolnik, and Wong 2012). The Transgender Violence Tracking Portal (TVTP 2014) indicated that there were 102 reports of antitransgender violence worldwide from January 1, 2014, to April 30, 2014. The report specified that almost 10 percent of all reported violence against transgender people targeted transgender young people under the age of eighteen years. The report also cited that out of the 102 antitransgender murders, thirty-six persons were shot multiple times, fourteen were stabbed multiple times, eleven were beaten to death, three were burned to death, three were dismembered/mutilated, two were tortured, two were strangled, and one was hanged. One had her throat cut, and one was stoned to death.

The gender binary may impact the way discrimination may manifest for the various subgroups under the transgender umbrella. First, gender presentation is one determining factor that may influence the types of discrimination a TGNC person may experience. Pre-op transgender people (i.e., those individuals who do not complete gender-affirming treatment like hormonal treatment or surgeries) may have difficulty in "passing" as their self-identified gender identity (i.e., their physical appearance does not match the gender that they identify with or feel most comfortable with), which may result in everything from hate crime violence to subtle stares or biased behavior. Conversely, post-op transgender people (i.e., those individuals who do complete gender-affirming treatment like hormonal treatment or surgeries) may have an easier time "passing" in that their physical bodies may match the way they identify psychologically and emotionally. However, these individuals may still experience discrimination if they still do not "pass" as the gender they identify with or when people discover that they are transgender. Finally, it is necessary to acknowledge that other multiple marginalized identities may further exacerbate the types of discrimination that a transgender person may experience. For example, most of the known antitransgender murders in 2013 and 2014 were of transgender women of color, particularly Black transwomen. When TGNC people are also members of other marginalized groups (e.g., people of color, people with disabilities, etc.), they may experience multiple levels of discrimination that may affect the way they are treated, as well as the way they cope with various stressors in their lives.

Transgender Women and the Criminal Justice System

While discrimination may occur towards transgender people in all aspects of their lives, discrimination within the criminal justice system may especially prevent transgender women from having access to justice. For instance, when transwomen are victimized by hate crimes, these crimes are often underreported because of fear of being retraumatized or fear of being mistreated by police officers. Similarly, when transgender women experience micro-aggressions by judges, lawyers, and police officers, they may view the criminal justice system as being unfair, biased, or cruel, preventing them from seeking justice in the future.

Transwomen Survivors of Intimate Partner Violence and Hate Crimes

The National Coalition of Anti-Violence Programs (NCAVP 2013) reports that transgender people, especially transgender people of color, are disproportionately affected by intimate partner violence (IPV) in at least two ways. First, transgender people were 2.5 times more likely than nontransgender survivors to experience IPV in public places. Second, transgender people were almost twice as likely as nontransgender people to experience physical violence in cases of IPV.

Transwomen are also disproportionately affected by hate violence, also known as hate crime (NCAVP 2014). Types of hate violence include threats and intimidation, sexual assault, verbal harassment, and physical violence. One sample of data collected in 2013 (n = 2,001) indicates that there are at least six ways in which hate crime impacted transwomen at higher rates than it impacted cisgender survivors. First, transgender women were more likely to experience discrimination as a form of hate violence than cisgender people, while also experiencing harassment at rates 1.8 times higher than cisgender survivors. Additionally, threats and intimidation were reported at rates 1.5 times higher for transwomen than for cisgender survivors, while transwomen were victims of sexual-violence hate crimes 1.8 times more than cisgender people. Further, transwomen were four times more likely than cisgender survivors to report hate violence from police officers, while transgender women were six times more likely than cisgender survivors to experience hate crimes in the form of physical violence from police officers. In light of this police misconduct, it is not surprising that many of the transwomen surveyed were not likely to seek police assistance with hate violence.

Transwomen's Encounters with Police Officers

A growing body of quantitative and qualitative data suggests that police abuse, harassment, and mistreatment of transwomen occur under other circumstances and with high frequency. Many transwomen's interactions with the police are preceded by circumstances in which the transgender woman has not committed a crime. Police harassment includes profiling transgender women as sex workers, detaining transwomen who do not have matching identity documents, or stopping transwomen just because of their GNC appearance. These incidents of harassment, false arrests, and unwarranted detainment of law-abiding transwomen is detrimental to the women and is arguably a waste of law enforcement's time. It fosters transwomen's fear and distrust of the law officers in their community, putting them at risk for further victimization. Moreover, even when transgender people are victims, police officers mistreat them in biased and hurtful ways. One transgender woman described how detectives treated her when she was trying to report a crime: "The detectives were passing by and they said . . . [singing] 'Transformers . . . men up in disguise'" (Nadal, Skolnik, and Wong 2012, 73).

Walking while Trans

The pattern of police harassment of transwomen, and especially transwomen of color, is sometimes known as "walking while trans." Advocates and agencies that support transwomen have noted high rates of police profiling and improper detainment of transgender women under the discriminatory policy called "stop-and-frisk," which disproportionately criminalizes racial, ethnic, and gender-identity minorities through police profiling and detainment. Police frequently stop, search, and arrest transwomen for seemingly no reason but later attribute the stop to the transwoman's appearance of loitering or to the suspicion of prostitution. Other than being unlawfully stopped, transwomen have reported that the stops entail verbal harassment, humiliation, inappropriate touching of their genitals, and arrests for prostitution. A 2012 report from Make the Road New York (MRNY) surveyed 305 residents of Jackson Heights, NY, to investigate the pattern of stopping and frisking people of color. Of the residents who had reported being stopped by the police, transgender residents reported the highest rates of verbal (51 percent) and physical (46 percent) harassment from law enforcement officers. In contrast, approximately one-third of nontransgender LGBQ and approximately one-quarter of cisgender heterosexuals report those same types of verbal and physical police harassment. The MRNY report provides dozens of testimonials from transgender Latina women who had been harassed by police, profiled as sex workers, and arrested under the suspicion of manifesting prostitution.

While being arrested is a generally unpleasant experience for anyone, the process of arrest and detainment for transwomen is especially traumatic. Many of the women arrested under the suspicion of sex work report being humiliated by police officers who demand that they empty their purses, remove prosthetic breasts, and take off their wigs. In the process of the transwoman complying with these demands, police often damage their property and make antitransgender comments. The police snatched their wigs off, threw the wigs to the ground, and stomped on them. Aside from being humiliating, these encounters are abusive and contribute to transwomen's distrust of law enforcement. For example, one transgender woman describes an experience she had when she was arrested:

> I remember the first comment: "Oh, look at this one! This is a gorgeous one. We haven't had one like you in a long time," starting with the commanding officers. Then the [inmates start] yelling, "Put it in our cell. C'mon, we'll have some fun tearing up that asshole." You all get into a line and you're going to get strip searched. . . . They have like five guys go into this room and strip in front of them and then put their clothes into a bin through a metal detector and to shower. I started stripping right in front of all the guys. I mean. . . . It put me. . . . I felt very uncomfortable. (Nadal, Skolnik, and Wong 2012, 73)

Transwomen in Detention Facilities

From the moment when they are arrested until the time when they are released from custody, transwomen are subject to discrimination regarding their gender identity. In detention facilities, like jails and prisons, transwomen are subject to violent physical and sexual assaults from inmates and facility staff, and are denied medical care and supplies to support their gender affirmation. Previous legal cases have helped to require protections for transwomen in detention facilities (see *Farmer v. Brennan*, 511 U.S. 825 [1994]); however, there remain three major detention issues that are unique to transwomen. First, transwomen often have problems with methods of sex classification in prison, which informs administrative decisions about facility placement and administrative or protective segregation. Second, transwomen are victimized at rates that are up to thirteen times higher than male-identified inmates in the same detention facilities (Emmer, Lowe, and Marshall 2011; Grant et al. 2011; Jenness et al. 2007). Finally, the healthcare needs of transwomen, including gender-affirming hormones, are often delayed, diminished, or altogether denied. In a study on transgender sex workers, one former transgender inmate describes her experiences behind bars:

> I mean it was hard for me being there because I was transgender. . . . It's worse because they look at you not only because of what you're doing— they judge you for that—but they also judge you for who you are. . . . I don't know how to explain it but it was something that like—there was a lot of abuse involved. You know, I was abused—verbally abused, physically abused and even sexually abused. (Nadal et al. 2012, 131)

Classification

Sex-segregated prisons are inherently incompatible with transgender identity (for a review see Sumner and Jenness 2014). As of 2014, jails and prisons in many jurisdictions classify prisoners as male or female according to the sex that they were assigned at birth (Sumner and Jenness 2014). More often than not, law enforcement staff place transwomen with cisgender men. In a landmark case involving placement of a transwoman in a cisgender male prison, *Farmer v. Brennan* (511 U.S. 825 [1994]), the court ruled that prison staff had violated a transwoman's Eighth Amendment right (freedom from cruel and unusual punishment) by having "deliberate indifference" to her safety in an all-male prison. Dee Farmer, a transwoman, was beaten and sexually assaulted in her cell by another inmate. The court ruled that Dee's transgender identity should have signaled that she was a vulnerable prisoner, and the prison should have taken steps to prevent violence against her.

Within the male detention facilities, staff place transwomen in administrative segregation to protect them from victimization. Administrative segregation can mean that the transwoman is placed in a "vulnerable male" unit or solitary confinement. Administrative segregation reduces the risk that other inmates will victimize a transwoman, but it also increases the risk that she will suffer from mistreatment and abuse from the detention and correctional officers. Additionally, administrative segregation prevents transwomen from interacting with other inmates and from participating in and benefiting from prison programs and activities that have been shown to improve inmates' mental health. In a victory for transwomen, *Tates v. Blanas* (U.S. Dist. LEXIS 26029 [E.D. Cal. Mar. 6, 2003]) ruled that a prison policy of placing all transgender inmates in total separation from other inmates is an Eighth Amendment violation.

A new case has initiated the conversation about the classification and placement of transgirls in detention facilities. *Jane Doe v. Connecticut Department of Correction* (Case No. 3:14CV469 [RNC] filed October 20, 2014) is a civil rights case of a sixteen-year-old transgender Latina girl who, after being removed from a group home, was placed in three different types of detention facilities: one for girls, one for boys, and another for women. Jane's time in each of these facilities has involved her being put in solitary confinement, being denied access to her wigs and makeup, or being called by her birth-assigned male name and male pronouns. Jane's case is unique and complex because it involves issues related to her minor age, her being a ward of the state, and the fact that she is being detained in these facilities without being charged with a crime. It will be interesting to study the outcomes for Jane and to follow the legal arguments raised by her situation. A legal precedent that supports Jane's case is *R.G. v. Koller* (415 F. Supp. 2d 1129, 1154 [D. Haw. 2006]), wherein the court ruled that isolating juvenile offenders who identify as LGBT is a violation of their due process rights, even if that isolation is for their own protection from other inmates.

Violence and Victimization in Jails and Prisons

Greene v. Bowles (361 F.3d 290 [6th Circuit 2004]) found that placing a transwoman inmate in a protective-custody unit alongside a "predatory inmate" was an instance of deliberate indifference to the transwoman's safety and therefore a possible violation of her Eighth Amendment right. Much of the research on the abuse and violence that transwomen endure indicates that they are more likely to be sexually and physically victimized in jails and prisons than other gender identities. MTF report a higher incidence of sexual assault (20 percent) than FTM (6 percent) and GNC (8 percent) (Grant et al. 2011). Black MTF have higher rates of sexual assault (38 percent) than MTF overall (20 percent). One report from Jenness and colleagues (2007) detailed sex-assault statistics for

California prisoners. Fifty-nine percent of transgender inmates reported that they had been sexually assaulted, while the rate of sexual assault reported by other inmates was 4.4 percent.

Victimization in correctional facilities is multifaceted. *Murray v. U.S. Bureau of Prisons* (106 F.3d 401, 1997 WL 34677 [6th Cir. 1997]) stated that the prison staff's verbal abuse and harassment of an MTF inmate based on her gender identity is not an Eighth Amendment violation; while inappropriate, it did not amount to cruel and unusual punishment under the law. In addition to the physical and emotional pain from assault and discrimination, transwomen are reluctant to report victimization because they will lose access to activities and programs, as they will probably be placed in administrative segregation for their own protection. Many times, these "ad-seg" conditions are identical or akin to solitary confinement. The emotional stress associated with solitary confinement can exacerbate mental and physical illnesses. Another side effect of solitary confinement is that it places transgender inmates at an increased risk for sexual assault and misconduct perpetrated by male corrections officers (American Civil Liberties Union 2014).

The Prison Rape Elimination Act (PREA) (U.S. Department of Justice 2012) is a set of federal guidelines for the prevention of inmate sexual assault. In addition to preventing sexual assault, PREA aims to improve detention facilities' methods of responding to incidents of inmate rape (National PREA Resource Center 2014). The behaviors required or prohibited by this act have specific relevance to transgender prisoners. First, PREA forbids cross-gender searches. This includes prohibiting the search of transwomen inmates by male guards. Additionally, the act states that guards must be trained on how to conduct respectful searches of transgender inmates, preventing physical searches aimed at determining the inmate's genitalia. The act allows transwomen to shower separately from the other inmates to prevent disclosure of the inmate's genitalia and transgender identity to other inmates. PREA allows inmates to request protective custody if they are concerned about their safety. PREA also states that inmates should have access to ways of reporting sexual assault to internal facility sources as well as external sources without fear of retaliation by other inmates or staff. These standards apply to all of the prisons, jails, juvenile detention centers, halfway houses, and short-term confinement facilities like police stations.

Gender-Affirming Care in Detention Facilities

The goal of gaining access to gender-affirming care has been met with mixed success across the country. Barriers to treatment include limited or no access to the following resources: counseling, physicians who are competent to handle the medical needs of transgender women, supplies for grooming, female undergarments, and cosmetics to maintain their gender-affirming appearance. In most facilities, transwomen must have a medical diagnosis of gender dysphoria (previously referred to as "gender identity disorder") in order to initiate hormone therapy or any other type of gender-affirming therapy in prison. Gender dysphoria (GD) refers to the depression, anxiety, and stress associated with being in the body of the wrong sex.

For transgender women who seek to begin or continue their transition while in prison, hormone therapy is a popularly recognized medical treatment. In *Fields v. Smith* (653 F. 3f 550 [7th Circuit 2011]), the court overturned Wisconsin's Inmate Sex Change Prevention Act and allowed prisoners to get transition-related treatment and care. The *Fields* ruling allows doctors to prescribe hormones and gender-reassignment surgery to Wisconsin inmates. Despite landmark legal decisions ordering some prisons to provide hormone therapy to its transgender prisoners, some facilities continue to stall or outright deny treatment to transwomen in their custody. Transwomen who received hormone therapy in prison complained that they received reduced dosages or that their treatment did not allow them to increase or decrease dosages as prescribed by their own medical provider. Not all transgender women pursue all of the available treatments. For instance, many choose not to have genital reconstruction as part of their gender affirmation and sex reassignment. Their capacity to choose is acknowledged in *Kosilek v. Maloney* (221 F. Supp. 2d 156 [2002]), which states that prisons must use "individualized medical evaluation" to determine the treatment of a prisoner's gender dysphoria as opposed to a single, "freeze-frame" rule about continuing hormone therapy. The *Kosilek* decision, as well as the other cases involving transwomen in prisons, only provides resolutions for the inmate or the facility identified in the case. Transwomen in other facilities still have to litigate to gain the medical evaluation and treatment that they need.

Other Mental Health Experiences of Transwomen in Detention Facilities

Mental health professionals have acknowledged the need for specialized treatments aimed at treating co-occurring mental and physical health conditions such as depression and HIV in transgender women. In their Personalized Cognitive Counseling (PCC) model, the University of California–San Francisco Center for Excellence for Trans Health and Center for AIDS Prevention Studies (2013) recommends that providers abandon judgmental attitudes about high-risk sexual behaviors of their MTF clients. Instead, the PCC calls for high levels of competency as it relates to mental health issues specific to transwomen living with HIV. The "T-SISTA" protocol (Gutierrez-Mock et al. 2009) provides mental health recommendations for transwomen of color. The "T-SISTA" program teaches transwomen of color to rely on other transwomen of color and other healthy sources of social support to recognize and reduce internalized transphobia while also curbing the behaviors that put transwomen at risk for contracting HIV.

The World Professional Association for Transgender Health (WPATH) (2012) Standards of Care offer guidelines for diagnosing and treating GD. They recommend that providers try to eliminate their clients' GD mental health symptoms by affirming the client's gender identity through psychosocial and medical treatments. Despite the mental health diagnosis of GD, WPATH recommends that providers refrain from pathologizing transwomen's gender identity and instead focus on resolving the symptoms that are associated with transgender identity. The WPATH Standards of Care emphasize the importance of a network of culturally competent providers who can assist the transgender woman in different aspects of her gender affirmation. These providers may offer counseling, medical care, funding, and logistical support for the transwoman's access to care. WPATH recognizes that providing care for transwomen often includes treating other coexisting medical (i.e., HIV) or mental health (i.e., depression) conditions. In the Standards of Care, WPATH also offers detailed information about the protocols associated with hormone therapy and surgery. In keeping with the Standards of Care, *Kosilek v. Spencer* (No. 12–2194 [1st Cir.

Jan. 17, 2014]) ruled that transgender inmate Michelle Kosilek must be given gender-reassignment surgery in order to treat her severe GD. After reviewing testimony from a variety of medical experts, the court agreed that the only acceptable and effective treatment for Kosilek was gender-reassignment surgery. This is the first case where a department of corrections has been ordered to provide surgical gender-affirmation treatment to an inmate.

Lessons Learned from Denise's Story

In order to understand all of these aforementioned issues affecting transwomen and the criminal justice system, let us revisit Denise's story. Because Denise wanted to live truthfully in the gender that she identified with, she decided to tell her parents. Her parents' reactions were similar to what many transgender people, particularly transgender youth, experience. When many transgender youth are not supported by their parents, they often find themselves getting kicked out of their homes by their parents or running away from home as a result of an abusive or hostile environment (Nadal 2013). In general, transgender people tend be disproportionately homeless compared to the general population. This is often correlated with other difficulties like poverty, unemployment, educational disparities, and health problems (National Center for Transgender Equality and the National Gay and Lesbian Task Force 2009).

After getting kicked out of her home, Denise was able to a find a mentor in another transgender woman named Lorial. Having someone to relate to was very validating for Denise, who appeared to have not met anyone else who identified as transgender. Lorial provided advice on transitioning (e.g., gender-affirming surgeries) as well as practical support (e.g., allowing Denise to stay at her home). While the relationship was positive in many ways, it also represented a risk when Lorial offered to share her hormones with Denise. Because Denise was a minor and legally could not obtain any hormones on her own, she viewed sharing hormones as a viable option. If there had been systemic or institutional assistance that Denise could turn to, she might have been able to access necessary hormonal treatments in a healthy (and legal) way. For instance, there are youth programs in various urban areas that assist transgender youth with hormonal treatments. If Denise had been aware of these programs, she would have met a physician who could monitor her treatment; she would have been prescribed the appropriate amount of hormones, and she would have avoided sharing needles with Lorial (or anyone else who offers to share their hormones with her).

Denise's struggles in finding a job were due to multiple factors: her young age, her lack of experience or skills, and her transgender identity. When she was unable to find a job, she decided to "walk the stroll," which was a code for sex work. Many studies have revealed that due to the rampant discrimination transgender people experience from both employers and prospective employers, many transwomen turn to sex work as their only perceived feasible option (Nadal et al. 2012; Sausa, Keatley, and Operario 2007). When they become sex workers, they also put themselves at risk for other dangers, including violence, poor sexual health, drug use, and incarceration (Rekart 2005). Even if Denise had secured traditional employment, she might have been susceptible to micro-aggressions and other forms of interpersonal discrimination, ranging from transphobic language to overt harassment (Nadal, Davidoff, and Fuji-Doe 2014).

When Denise was arrested, she experienced several forms of blatant discrimination from the police officers. As noted earlier, transwomen who are sex workers, as well as those who are not sex workers, often experience harassment and other forms of discrimination from police officers and other members of the criminal justice system. Because transgender women are often stereotyped as sex workers, there have been many reports of transwomen who are profiled by police officers, leading to false arrests and detainment (Nadal 2013). Sometimes this mistreatment may appear to be harmless or minimal in nature; however, many transgender people have reported that they have been abused and assaulted by police officers and by other inmates who were not punished for their actions (Nadal et al. 2012).

Finally, Denise's story tells us that individuals' decisions to participate in criminal activities (e.g., sex work) may not be the result of malicious intent or immoral character. Denise entered the world of sex work for multiple reasons. First, she was kicked out of her home by her parents, which eventually led to Denise becoming homeless. Living on her own at sixteen, she was forced to drop out of school in order to pay for her basic needs. She could not find a traditional job and had to turn to sex work as a last resort. While sex work in itself should not be viewed as a deviant act, the fact that she was a young person who was being paid for sex is potentially troubling. Not only did she put herself at risk for sexual health problems and violence, but also it is very likely that she was not mature enough to make decisions about her own sexuality and best interests.

Recommendations and Conclusion

Throughout the chapter, we described the various obstacles that transgender women and transgender girls may experience in the criminal justice system as a result of their gender identities. This last section will focus on potential recommendations for systemic, institutional, and interpersonal change.

Recommendation #1: Increase awareness of transgender issues through education of the public, school personnel, and justice officials.

Systemically, there are many obstacles that transgender people experience, including disparities in unemployment, educational attainment, health, and homelessness. Such disparities may be the result of stigma and lack of advocacy for transgender people. Both educational programming and increased positive visibility of transgender issues in government, media, and education could help to minimize this stigma. Institutionally, it would be important for employers and schools to promote inclusivity and cultural competence for transgender people in their mission and everyday practices. For instance, if employers were more open to hiring transgender employees (or at least had antidiscrimination policies in place that protect transgender people), perhaps there would be more career opportunities for transgender people. If school systems promote transgender inclusion, this may bolster teachers' efforts to support transgender students and result in less bullying or lower dropout rates for transgender high school students.

Recommendation #2: Promote inclusivity and cultural competence in the criminal justice system.

The criminal justice system needs to make several changes in order to support and advocate for transgender people, particularly transgender women and girls. First, transgender inclusivity and cultural competence need to be promoted and practiced at all levels, from police officers to correctional officers to public attorneys and judges. Individuals who work with transgender people need to be aware of micro-aggressive language and behaviors that promote an unsafe and hostile environment for transgender people. Federal, state, and local laws must change in order to better protect the rights of transgender people. For instance, prison facilities and police stations need to have more options for transgender inmates and detainees. Transgender people should be housed in facilities based on the gender they identify with, and their safety should be guaranteed not only with other inmates but also with correctional officers.

Recommendation #3: Assist families in creating transgender-affirming environments.

Finally, interpersonally, there are many things that individuals can do in their families and communities to ensure that transgender people receive the support they need. First, because families are where children first acquire knowledge about values and where they initially start to develop their personality, parents may promote the importance of being accepting and open-minded towards those different from them. Parents and other family members may also consider being mindful about gender-role norms and how these may affect children's mental health. For instance, when a young boy is told, "Dresses are only for girls!" or "Be a man!" the child learns explicitly that there is a rigid way for boys (or men) to be. If the child is transgender, messages like these can take a negative toll on the child's mental health and self-esteem, perhaps even impacting the child's development as an adult. For cisgender children, statements like these reinforce the stereotypes of what boys are "supposed to be" and give permission to discriminate against transgender people.

The recommendations made in this chapter are congruent with the APA's Guidelines for Psychological Practice with Transgender and Gender Nonconforming People (American Psychological Association 2015). These guidelines describe the level of competence psychologists should attain in order to work with transgender and gender-nonconforming clients, and offer incremental yet comprehensive changes in providers' understanding of transgender issues, from the fluidity and dynamic nature of gender identity to the importance of individualized directives that address the needs of transgender youth. By adopting policies and procedures that agree with these APA guidelines, police, judges, social workers, and other administrators of justice can make a difference in the lives of transwomen and in transwomen's confidence in the justice system throughout their life cycle.

REFERENCES

American Civil Liberties Union. 2014. "Worse Than Second Class: Solitary Confinement of Women in the United States," https://www.aclu.org.

American Psychological Association. 2015. Guidelines for Psychological Practice with Transgender and Gender-Nonconforming People, http://www.apa.org.

American Psychological Association Council of Representatives. 2011. Guidelines for Psychological Practice with Lesbian, Gay, and Bisexual Clients. Adopted by the APA Council of Representatives, February 18–20, 2011, http://www.apa.org.

Emmer, Pascal, Adrian Lowe, and R. Barrett Marshall. 2011. This Is a Prison, Glitter Is Not Allowed: Experiences of Trans and Gender-Variant People in Pennsylvania's Prison Systems, http://socialproblems.voices.wooster.edu.

Forbes, Alexis. 2014. "Define 'Sex': Legal Outcomes for Transgender Individuals in the United States." In Handbook of LGBT Communities, Crime, and Justice. Edited by Dana Peterson and Vanessa R. Panfil, 387–403. New York: Springer Science + Business Media.

Grant, Jaime M., Lisa A. Mottet, Justin Tanis, Jack Harrison, Jody L. Herman, and Mara Keisling. 2011. "Injustice at Every Turn: A Report of the National Transgender Discrimination Survey," http://www.thetaskforce.org.

Gutierrez-Mock, Luis, Yavanté Thomas-Guess, Jae Sevelius, JoAnne Keatley, Paul Cotten, and Susan Kegeles. 2009. "T-SISTA: A Resource Guide for Adapting SISTA for Transwomen of Color," http://www.aidsnet.org.

Hill, Darryl B., and Brian L. B. Willoughby. 2005. "The Development and Validation of the Genderism and Transphobia Scale." Sex Roles 53 (7–8): 531–44. doi: 10.1007/s11199-005-7140-x.

Hughes, Ieuan A., Christopher Houk, S. F. Ahmend, Peter A. Lee, and Consensus Group. 2006. "Consensus Statement on Management of Intersex Disorders." Archives of Disease in Childhood 91: 554–62. doi: 10.1136/adc.2006.098319.

Human Rights Watch. 2012. "Sex Workers at Risk: Condoms as Evidence of Prostitution in Four U.S. Cities," http://www.hrw.org.

Jenness, Valerie, Cheryl Maxson, Kristy N. Matsuda, and Jennifer M. Sumner. 2007. "Violence in California Correctional Facilities: An Empirical Examination of Sexual Assault," http://www.wcl.american.edu.

Lambda Legal. 2014. "Transgender Rights Toolkit: A Legal Guide for Transpeople and Their Advocates," http://www.lambdalegal.org.

Make the Road New York. 2012. "Transgressive Policing: Police Abuse of LGBTQ Communities of Color in Jackson Heights," http://www.maketheroad.org.

Marksamer, Jody. 2011. "A Place of Respect: A Guide for Group Care Facilities Serving Transgender and Gender Non-conforming Youth," http://www.nclrights.org.

Mottet, Lisa, and John M. Ohle. 2003. "Transitioning Our Shelters. A Guide to Making Homeless Shelters Safe for Transgender People," http://srlp.org.

Nadal, Kevin L. 2013. *That's So Gay! Microaggressions and the Lesbian, Gay, Bisexual, and Transgender Community.* Washington, DC: American Psychological Association.

Nadal, Kevin L., Kristin C. Davidoff, and Whitney Fujii-Doe. 2014. "Transgender Women and the Sex Work Industry: Roots in Systemic, Institutional, and Interpersonal Discrimination." *Journal of Trauma and Dissociation* 15 (2): 169–83.

Nadal, Kevin L., Avy Skolnik, and Yinglee Wong. 2012. "Interpersonal and Systemic Microaggressions: Psychological Impacts on Transgender Individuals and Communities." *Journal of LGBT Issues in Counseling* 6 (1): 55–82.

Nadal, Kevin L., Vivian Vargas, Vanessa Meterko, Sahran Hamit, and Katherine Mclean. 2012. "Transgender Female Sex Workers: Personal Perspectives, Gender Identity Development, and Psychological Processes." In *Managing Diversity in Today's Workplace: Strategies for Employees and Employers.* Vol. 1, *Gender, Race, Sexual Orientation, Ethnicity, and Power.* Edited by M. A. Paludi. Santa Barbara, CA: Praeger.

National Center for Transgender Equality and the National Gay and Lesbian Task Force. 2009. "National Transgender Discrimination Survey: Preliminary Findings," http://www.thetaskforce.org.

National Coalition of Anti-Violence Programs. 2014. "Hate Violence against Lesbian, Gay, Bisexual, Transgender, Queer, and HIV-Affected Communities in the United States in 2013: A Report from the National Coalition of Anti-Violence Programs," http://www.avp.org.

National Coalition of Anti-Violence Programs. 2013. "Lesbian, Gay, Bisexual, Transgender, Queer, and HIV-Affected Intimate Partner Violence: A Report from the National Coalition of Anti-Violence Programs," http://www.avp.org.

National Institute of Corrections. 2012. "A Quick Guide for LGBTI Policy Development for Adult Prisons and Jails," https://s3.amazonaws.com.

National PREA Resource Center. 2014. "Frequently Asked Questions," http://www.prearesourcecenter.org.

Quintana, Nico Sifra, Josh Rosenthal, and Jeff Krehely. 2010. "On the Streets. The Federal Response to Gay and Transgender Homeless Youth," https://cdn.american-progress.org.

Rekart, Michael L. 2005. "Sex-Work Harm Reduction." *Lancet* 366: 2123–34. doi: 10.1016/S0140–6736(05)67732-X.

Rorvig, Leah B. 2013. "'We Have a Hard Time Treating Your Kind Here': Negative Health Care Experiences of Transgender Women in San Francisco." Paper presented at 2013 National Transgender Health Summit, http://transhealth.ucsf.edu.

San Francisco Human Rights Commission. 2014. "The San Francisco Human Rights Commission Commends NYPD on Decision to Limit Use of Condoms as Evidence in Prostitution-Related Cases," http://sf-hrc.org.

Sausa, Lydia A., JoAnne Keatley, and Don Operario. 2007. "Perceived Risks and Benefits of Sex Work among Transgender Women of Color in San Francisco." *Archives of Sexual Behavior* 36: 768–77.

Stotzer, Rebecca L. 2008. "Gender Identity and Hate Crimes: Violence against Transgender People in Los Angeles County." *Sexuality Research and Social Policy: A Journal of the NSRC* 5 (1): 43–52.

Sumner, Jennifer, and Valerie Jenness. 2014. "Gender Integration in Sex-segregated U.S. Prisons: The Paradox of Transgender Correctional Policy." In *Handbook of LGBT Communities, Crime, and Justice*. Edited by Dana Peterson and Vanessa R. Panfil, 229–60. New York: Springer Science + Business Media.

Transgender Violence Tracking Portal. 2014. "International Day against Homophobia and Transphobia (IDAHOT)," http://www.transviolencetracker.org.

U.S. Department of Justice. 2012. "National Standards to Prevent, Detect, and Respond to Prison Rape (28 CFR Part 115) (RIN 1105-AB34)," http://ojp.gov.

World Professional Association for Transgender Health. 2012. "Standards of Care for the Health of Transsexual, Transgender, and Gender-nonconforming People," http://admin.associationsonline.com.

Xavier, Jessica. 2002. "The Washington Transgender Needs Assessment Survey (WT-NAS)," http://dctranscoalition.files.wordpress.com.

8

Lesbian, Bisexual, Questioning, Gender-Nonconforming, and Transgender (LBQ/GNCT) Girls in the Juvenile Justice System

Using an Intersectional Lens to Develop Gender-Responsive Programming

ANGELA IRVINE, AISHA CANFIELD, AND JESSICA ROA

Over the past twenty-five years, feminist criminologists have done an exceptional job documenting the way girls were entering the juvenile justice system at growing rates, and explaining why services originally designed for boys could not serve this new female population (Chesney-Lind 2002; Sherman 2005; Acoca 1998). Advocates have argued that drug and alcohol use, past histories of sexual and physical abuse, family chaos, domestic assault, persistent running away from home, and commercial sexual exploitation were all driving girls into the juvenile justice system. Empirical review of case files shows that these factors hold for many girls. However, when researchers and advocates take the intersections of race, sexual orientation, and gender identity into consideration, different patterns emerge (Crenshaw 2014; Jones 2009; Morris 2013, 2012).

New research reinforces the need for an updated paradigm on girls in the juvenile justice system. Data from a recently completed survey of seven detention halls around the country shows that 86 percent of detained girls are of color, 32 percent are lesbian, bisexual, or questioning, and 17 percent are gender-nonconforming or transgender (Irvine and Canfield 2014).[1] This chapter argues that, in order to be effective, mental and behavioral health services must begin to affirm the many dimensions of girls' identities as well as the multiple layers of oppression that girls have experienced on the pathway to the juvenile justice system.

Programming for all youth must be developed with an intersectional lens that takes race and sexual orientation, gender identity and gender expression (SOGIE) into consideration. Our arguments are based on a review of existing literature as well as an analysis of original survey and interview data collected from seven counties and parishes across the country.[2]

This chapter provides three case studies of girls in the juvenile justice system and illustrates why mental and behavioral health services must develop an intersectional lens. We then provide literature reviews and empirical data on how birth sex, sexual orientation, gender identity, gender expression, and race drive girls into the juvenile justice system, as well as a literature review on the mental and behavioral health needs of LBQ/GNCT girls. We end with recommendations for how mental and behavioral health services working with justice-involved girls can better serve the LBQ/GNCT population.

The Lived Experiences of Girls Illustrate the Need for an Expanded Paradigm

Over the last three years, the authors completed 145 interviews with youth nationally who were justice–involved. The following three stories illustrate the need for expanded programming for girls in the juvenile justice system that considers the intersection of race and ethnicity, sexual orientation, gender identity, and gender expression.

Diana

Diana is a fifteen-year-old Latina living in Chicago. She was arrested and charged with assault. She and her friends got into a fight that they did not initiate with some other girls outside a pizza parlor in the neighborhood of Humboldt Park. She and her friends are gender nonconforming, while the other girls involved in the fight are not. Diana and her friends wear hoodies, loose pants, and large t-shirts and typically wear their hair cut short or pulled behind hats and beanies. The prosecutor argued that Diana and her friends belong to a gang despite being unaffiliated—a stereotype not atypical for gender-nonconforming Latinas and Latinas with tattoos who come from certain neighborhoods. As a foster child,

Diana was already living in a group home. Convicted of assault, she was placed for a year in a residential facility designed for juvenile justice–involved youth. She successfully completed her probation and has just recently returned to the group home she was living in before the fight.

Erica

Erica is a sixteen-year-old Black girl living in Oakland, California, who ran away from home and was arrested for solicitation with intent to perform a lewd act. Her case was reviewed by the Alameda County girls' court, and Erica was sent to a camp for girls who are commercially sexually exploited (CSE) in Arizona. She stayed in the camp for twelve months and has just returned to Oakland but cannot move back in with her mother and her mother's boyfriend. She is serving three years of formal probation, which requires her to receive services for CSE girls, counseling, drug and alcohol treatment, and job development. She is living with an aunt who is very involved with her church. Everyone who has worked with Erica—probation officers, community-based services, as well as her family—has assumed that she is straight. In actuality, she is a lesbian, but is only out to her mother, with whom she is no longer in contact, and her friends at the school she attended prior to her conviction.

Bebe

Bebe is a seventeen-year-old Black transgender girl living in Birmingham, Alabama. She was recently arrested and charged for shoplifting a dress from a local department store. She was not required to stay in detention or an out-of-home placement, but was placed on formal probation. One evening when Bebe was walking home from an after-school program, a White police officer in a marked police car approached her. He requested she stay put and proceeded to get out of his vehicle and question her. He wanted to know what she was out doing "walking the streets" alone. This was not Bebe's first experience with a police officer assuming she was engaging in prostitution. After she told him she was walking home, the officer asked if he could take her out one night. He then began to describe what a night out with him would consist of, including the sexual acts he would like her to perform on him. Once she told him she was not interested, the officer demanded that she provide him with identification and sit on the curb. Upon looking at her identification and running her record, the officer discovered that she was a minor and on probation for the shoplifting incident. The officer warned her that she would be violating probation if she did not get home by curfew and that he would take her down to the station should he see her out again that night. The officer left, leaving Bebe terrified and angry.

How Do Girls Like Diana, Erica, and Bebe End Up in the Juvenile Justice System?

The empirical framework explaining girls' involvement in the juvenile justice system has grown over the past ten years, though more research is needed to fully explain how intersecting identities and forms of oppression place different girls at risk for juvenile justice system involvement.

Understanding How Birth Sex Drives Girls into Juvenile Justice

Concerns about girls in the juvenile justice system began to rise as the use of secure detention for girls increased.[3] The percentage of girls in detention increased from 12 percent to 18 percent from 1991 to 2003 (Sherman 2005). Also, between 1995 and 2005, the number of girls involved in the juvenile justice system grew by 49 percent compared with a 7 percent increase for boys (Berkeley Center for Criminal Justice 2010).

To understand this increase, researchers have studied the effects of policy changes and youths' risk factors for juvenile justice system involvement. Several policy changes have expanded the number of girls getting disciplined or arrested for behaviors that were not previously formally punished (Steffensmeier et al. 2005). For example, increased punishments for school-based fights and family conflicts pulled girls into the juvenile justice system in greater numbers (Steffensmeier et al. 2005). Girls in the juvenile justice system experience high levels of conflict within their home. For example, while girls' arrests for simple assault increased 36 percent between 1994 and 2003, case analysis shows that many of these assaults occur when there is conflict with family members or guardians about curfew or truancy (Sherman, Mendel, and Irvine 2013). As a result of family conflict, nearly one-third of girls in the California juvenile justice system reported being kicked out of their homes at least once, and 25 percent reported being shot or stabbed at least once (Acoca 1998).

The correlation between trauma and system involvement for girls is increasingly being studied. While there is a lack of consensus on whether girls experience trauma at higher rates than boys, studies show that girls experience very high levels of abuse and neglect. One study found that 75 percent of girls in the California Youth Authority (now called the Division of Juvenile Justice) reported histories of physical abuse; another 46 percent reported histories of sexual abuse (Berkeley Center for Criminal Justice 2010). Acoca (1998) reported that 92 percent of girls in the California juvenile justice system reported histories of physical, sexual, or emotional abuse.

Abuse and family conflict increase girls' risk of engaging in behaviors that may land them in the juvenile justice system. Girls who have been abused often run away from home or out of home placement (Chesney-Lind 2002; Chesney-Lind and Sheldon 1992; Luke 2008). When girls run away from home or are kicked out, they often have to resort to crimes such as theft or prostitution to survive (Majd, Marksamer, and Reyes 2009; Sherman 2005). Girls on the streets are also more likely to get involved in fights as a survival strategy (Luke 2008). These particular survival strategies often lead to arrest and involvement in the juvenile justice system as well as placement outside the home (Chesney-Lind 2002; Luke 2008). Once girls are arrested, they are more likely to be detained while awaiting adjudication because juvenile justice professionals want to protect them from returning to the street (Gilfus 1992; Sherman 2005). Moreover, girls are more likely to be placed outside their home after running away (American Bar Association and the National Bar Association 2001; Chesney-Lind and Shelden 1992). Parent-child conflict explains why parents are more likely not to take custody of their daughters after arrest and booking. As a consequence, girls are sent to out-of-home placement, and serve longer detention times compared to boys with similar offenses (Sherman 2005).

The concept of trauma has helped to link delinquent behaviors to abuse. It also has helped to redefine the very behaviors that lead to girls' involvement in the criminal justice system. Running away and conflict are no longer perceived as symptoms of conduct or personality disorders; they are framed as coping mechanisms for extreme levels of disruption and violence within the home. However, this paradigm shift has almost exclusively been used in support of the needs of White, cisgender, and straight girls. Given the alarming rate at which Black, Latina, and LBQ/GNCT girls are becoming involved in the justice system, it is urgent that research move beyond birth sex and consider gender identity, gender expression, race, and ethnicity.

How Sexual Orientation, Gender Identity, and Gender Expression Drive Girls' Involvement in the Juvenile Justice System

Lesbian, bisexual, and transgender or gender-nonconforming (LBT/GNC) girls constitute a significant proportion of girls in the juvenile justice system. Irvine (2010) found that 15 percent of the justice-involved youth who participated in an anonymous survey indicated that they identified as lesbian, gay, or bisexual (LGB), were questioning their sexual orientation (Q), had nonconforming gender identities (GNC), or were transgender (T). The response rates varied by gender: While 11 percent of boys indicated they were GBQ/GNCT, 28 percent of girls indicated they were LBQ/GNCT (Irvine 2010).[4] In a more recent survey, 20 percent of all youth and 40 percent of all girls reported being LGBQ/GNCT (Irvine and Canfield 2014). Of those girls, 32 percent disclosed their LBQ orientation and 17 percent their transgender or GNC identity. In both studies, the rates were the same for White, African American, and Latino youth (Irvine 2010; Irvine and Canfield 2014). It is likely these percentages underestimate the actual number of LGBQ/GNCT youth behind bars; those are often aware of the risks of harm associated with disclosing a nonheterosexual identity while in detention, and they may choose to not come out to protect themselves. However, these rates reveal the disproportionate representation of LGBQ/GNCT youth in the justice system; it is estimated that 7 to 8 percent of all adolescents in the general population identify as LGBQ/GNCT. With regard to LBQ/GNCT girls in particular, the numbers for justice-involved teens are four to five times higher than those for the general population.

LBQ/GNCT girls are overrepresented in the youth justice system because they are more likely than straight and cisgender girls to have been suspended or expelled from school, to have been removed from their home for abuse and neglect, or to have been homeless (Garnette et al. 2011; Irvine and Canfield 2014; Irvine 2010; Majd et al. 2009). LBQ/ GNCT girls are also discriminated against by law enforcement officials and youth justice stakeholders. For example, youth who experience same-sex attraction and youth who self-identify as lesbian, gay, or bisexual are more likely to be stopped by the police, arrested, and convicted of crimes when engaging in the same behaviors as straight youth (Himmelstein and Brückner 2011).

Juvenile justice staff are ill equipped to serve LBQ/GNCT girls who enter the system. In most jurisdictions across the country, when adolescents are booked into detention, probation officers assess the youths' risks and needs and evaluate the youths' likelihood of committing a new offense. They use actuarial instruments to collect data about romantic relationships, linkages to school, and family conflict. This information is designed to guide the selection of treatment programs that can help address the difficulties youth are facing. However, the risks and needs assessment usually fails to consider that youth may have same-sex relationships, that truancy may be linked to homophobic bullying, or that family conflict may be connected to relatives' disapproval of a young person's sexual orientation or gender expression (Garnette et al. 2011).

During detention in jail and other secure facilities, LGBQ/GNCT youth are vulnerable to verbal harassment and other forms of discrimination by institutional staff (Valentine 2008). Beck, Harrison, and Guerino (2010) found that 10 percent were sexually assaulted by other peers in secure facilities, compared to 1.5 percent of straight youth. LGBT youth are more likely to languish in detention for longer lengths of time (Garnette et al. 2011). This places them at a heightened risk of abuse, injury, and suicide (Majd et al. 2009). LBQ and GNCT girls are also subject to inappropriate use of solitary confinement or alternative housing based on their SOGIE.

Once released from detention or secure confinement, LGBT youth experience the adverse effects of formal and informal probation terms, which generally require that youth obey all laws, follow their parents'/ guardians' directions, participate in counseling and other community-based programs, and attend school (Garnette et al. 2011). Given that LGBT youth are subject to school bullying and family conflict and rejection based on their SOGIE, they are more likely to skip school, run away, and break curfew, and thus accumulate probation violations and new offenses that will delay successful exit from the juvenile justice system (Clatts et al. 1999; Cochran et al. 2002; Garnette et al. 2011; Hyde 2005; Kosciw 2004; Kosciw, Diaz, and Greytak 2007; Massachusetts Department of Elementary and Secondary Education 2006; Owen, Heineman, and Gerrard 2007; Ray 2007; Robson 2001; Saewyc, Pettingell, and Skay 2006; Valentine 2008; Witbeck et al. 2004).

Taking Race into Consideration

The proportion of youth of color in the juvenile justice system has been growing at an alarming rate, while the total number of youth held in secure detention has decreased since 1995 (Davis, Irvine, and Ziedenberg 2014a; Mariscal and Bell 2011). In 1985, youth of color represented 43 percent of detained youth. By 1995, they represented 56 percent of the juvenile population behind bars. Their number has continued to grow in proportions that suggest youth of color have become victims of mass incarceration. In 2002, 66.8 percent of all youth receiving dispositions in juvenile court were youth of color being sentenced to probation, out-of-home placement, and secure facilities. This proportion grew to 80.4 percent in 2012 (Davis et al. 2014a).

These growing disparities are linked to unfair treatment at many points of contact in the juvenile justice system. Criminologists have documented differences in arrests for Black and Brown people (Alexander 2010; Mauer 2010). While African Americans are subject to traffic stops at the same rate as White people, they are three times more likely to be searched once they are stopped (Alexander 2010; Mauer 2010). Additionally, the New York Civil Liberties Union has tracked police stops and interrogations in New York City since 2002. The most recent data show that the New York Police Department stopped people 191,558 times in 2013 (New York Civil Liberties Union 2014). Fifty-six percent of these stops involved Black individuals, 29 percent Latino, and 11 percent White (New York Civil Liberties Union 2014). In most cases (88 percent), people who were stopped were innocent. This information suggests police officers are disproportionately targeting African Americans and Latinos, and police stops are not a necessary intervention to maintain public safety (New York Civil Liberties Union 2014).

The court system reinforces disparities in arrests. Data reveal that White youth are more likely to be diverted from formal processing into detention and less likely to receive probation violations compared with youth of color who are charged with the same crimes (Mariscal and Bell 2011). Once a case makes it to court, Blacks and Latinos receive harsher sentences than White people (Johnson and Johnson 2012; Nelson 2008; Schlesinger 2005; Demuth 2003; Steffensmeier and Demuth 2001). Moreover, the majority of these sentences are for nonviolent offenses. In 2006, only 31 percent of all youth, including youth of color, were detained for violent crimes (Mendel 2009). This means that 69 percent of youth were detained for property crimes, drug offenses, probation violations, or status offenses such as curfew violations and truancy (Mendel 2009).

Gang enhancements place Black and Latino defendants at risk of longer court sentences than their White peers. Gang enhancements require that judges declare longer sentences, if a defendant commits a felony for the benefit of a street gang or to assist a gang member. The rules around enhancements vary across cities. In Los Angeles, a crime is considered gang related if either the victim or the perpetrator is associated with a gang. In Chicago, a crime is considered gang related only if gang membership drives the motive for the crime. Either way, these gang enhancements have been disproportionately applied to Black and Latino people (Van Hofwegen 2009).

There are few studies specifically focusing on how both gender and race are linked to involvement in the juvenile justice system. The research that exists shows that girls of color are overrepresented in the juvenile justice system (Morris 2013). Black girls experience some of the highest rates of juvenile detention and are the fastest-growing segment of the juvenile justice population (Morris 2013). This is largely due to the fact that Black girls are viewed as more masculine and therefore more aggressive and violent than White girls (Morris 2013). Discrimination against Black girls becomes even more extreme when Black girls are gender nonconforming.

The research that compares the experiences of White and Black girls shows some important differences and highlights the need to consider race and culture when providing services. For example, two studies show that physical abuse is linked to violent behavior for White girls, while witnessing violence is related to violent and delinquent behaviors for African American girls (Chauhan and Repucci 2009; Chauhan, Repucci, and Turkheier 2009). Another study suggests that African American girls are less likely than White girls to become suicidal after witnessing domestic violence, and therefore may have different mental health needs (Holsinger and Holsinger 2005).

Addressing Multiple Forms of Identity and Oppression within Mental and Behavioral Health Services for Youth in the Juvenile Justice System

LGBQ/GNCT youth have a sullied relationship with the mental and behavioral health professions. Historically, same-sex attraction, nonconforming gender expression, and the pursuit of gender transition were classified as psychopathology in multiple editions of the *Diagnostic and Statistical Manual of Mental Disorders* (DSM) (Dresher 2009; Fox 1988). "Homosexuality" was included in early editions of the DSM under the category of "sexual disorders." It was removed in 1973 and later replaced, in 1980, with a new diagnosis called "ego-dystonic homosexuality." The criteria for "ego-dystonic homosexuality" included a persistent lack of "heterosexual arousal" and persistent distress about "homosexual arousal." "Ego-dystonic homosexuality" was removed from the DSM in 1986. Yet, in 1994 and 2000, two gender disorders— "transvestic fetishism" and "gender identity disorder"—were added to the list of mental conditions and used to diagnose and treat transgender men and women. In 2012, the American Psychiatric Association combined these two terms into a new label: "gender dysphoria." In order to minimize the pathologizing effect of addressing gender expression in the DSM, gender-related disorders are no longer grouped with other sexual dysfunctions. Transgender advocates and other members of the LGBTQ community see these changes as a move in the right direction, but remain concerned about the unintended consequences of having a gender-identity diagnosis in the DSM-5, with good reason (Toscano and Maynard 2014; Dresher 2009). The definition and classification of nonheterosexual orientation and non-gender-conforming identity as mental pathology resulted in the development of programs aimed at reversing or curing same-sex attraction and gender nonconformity. These programs, which include reparative and aversion techniques, have been rejected as harmful and unethical by the medical and psychological professions (Israel and Tarver 1997; Mallon 1999).

Changes in the classification and treatment of non-gender-conforming identity and nonheterosexual orientation reflect the now-dominant view of sexuality and gender as normal developmental processes whereby individuals form multilayered identities. Gender identity, for both cisgender and transgender children, is established before kindergarten (Brill and Pepper 2008; Mallon and DeCrescenzo 2006; Wilber, Ryan, and Marksamer 2006). Sexual orientation develops around the same age for lesbian, gay, bisexual, questioning, and straight youth. The first experience of same- or cross-sex attraction occurs, on average, around the age of ten. Youth can identify as lesbian and gay as early as the age of thirteen (Ryan and Diaz 2005). Further, having same-sex attraction or being gender nonconforming do not cause mental disorders or emotional or social problems; nor are they linked to prior sexual abuse or other trauma (American Psychological Association 2004; Herek and Garnets 2007). However, the marginalized social positions of LGBQ/GNCT youth create debilitating chronic stress that puts them at higher risk for depression, suicidality, self-harm, and substance abuse (Bostwick et al. 2014; Marmot 2004; Ryan and Diaz 2005).

LBQ/GNCT girls are stigmatized and maltreated because of their sexual orientation and/or gender identity and expression. For example, LBQ/GNCT girls experience high rates of family neglect, rejection, and abuse (up to 30 percent, according to Sullivan and colleagues) (Cochran et al. 2002; Earls 2002; Saewyc et al. 2006; Savin-Williams 1994; Sullivan et al. 2001; Valentine 2008; Witbeck et al. 2004). Kosciw (2004) found that 90 percent of LGBT youth were frequently the target of homophobic comments from peers at school; 20 percent reported homophobic comments from teachers. Of greater concern, 86 percent of LGBT youth were subjected to harassment at school, and 60 percent felt unsafe (Kosciw, Diaz, and Greytak 2007). LBQ/GNCT girls, in particular girls of color, encounter multiple forms of discrimination and violence outside of the home—homophobia, transphobia, and/or racism (Hill and Willoughby 2005; Martin 1995). The ways in which their social identities intersect determine their unique experience of maltreatment and influence their biopsychosocial outcomes (Hill Collins 1998; Hurtado 1996; Hurtado and Gurin 2004). For most LBQ/GNCT girls, contact with the juvenile justice system, in particular detention in secure facilities, perpetuates trauma and intensifies their experience of oppression (Schaefer 2008).

LBQ/GNCT girls' responses to adversity are varied and complex and depend on the social contexts in which they are embedded. In schools, foster homes, juvenile detention halls, and behavioral health programs, girls engage in both assimilative and resistant behaviors: There are times when they follow rules and exhibit emotional attachment to facilitators of support groups. There are also times when they fail to show up to appointments or scheduled groups, disagree with group facilitators, or have conflicts with their peers (Irvine and Roa 2010).

Gender, race, and class shape the ways girls behave in these diverse social contexts (Jones 2009). African American girls in poor, violent communities often perform "unapologetic expression of female strength which contrasts with traditional White, middle class conceptions of femininity and the gendered expectations embedded in Black respectability" (Jones 2009, 19). These forms of self-expression can easily be misinterpreted as acts of aggression and result in harsh punishment from the juvenile justice system.

How Do Programs Need to Change to Serve Diana, Erica, and Bebe?

LBQ/GNCT girls of color like Diana, Erica, and Bebe face multiple oppressions, disproportionate punishment, and physical, verbal, and mental abuse inside and outside of the juvenile justice system (Garnette et al. 2011; Majd et al. 2009; Valentine 2008). Accordingly, it is essential that justice and mental health programming be sensitive to LBQ/GNCT girls' unique experiences (Greene et. al. 1998). Research is needed to define what culturally competent or responsive programming might be for these girls (Holsinger and Holsinger 2005). An important first step is to collect SOGIE data during the implementation of behavioral health services in juvenile justice settings.

It is equally important that justice and mental health professionals participate in training that fosters awareness of racial, gender, class, and sexual biases, increases multicultural competence for working with diverse LBQ/GNCT girls, and supports the implementation of antidiscrimination policies. Carefully trained staff should understand the multiple sources of oppression that impact the lives of LBQ/GNCT girls. This is critical to the development of therapeutic relationships that will keep girls from being pulled deeper into the juvenile justice system.

Recommendation #1: Collect SOGIE data.

Data collection is a critical component of better serving LBQ/GNCT girls in the juvenile justice system. This is particularly important given that 22.9 percent of LGB girls in the juvenile justice system are gender conforming (Irvine and Canfield 2014)—meaning, they do not give visual cues indicating that they *may* identify as LGBT. Essentially, these girls are invisible unless they decide to "out" themselves to adults in the justice system. As a consequence, they may slip through the cracks and not receive gender- and culturally responsive mental health and social services. To meet the unique needs of these vulnerable youth, mental and behavioral health service organizations must collect data from juvenile clients each time they enter their facility or program. While this may seem redundant, it is important to remember that SOGIE is part of adolescent development, and needs are subject to change as their identities do.

Collecting SOGIE data increases the visibility of gender-conforming LBT girls, and thus makes it possible to conduct assessment that is appropriate to their needs and to provide treatment that is affirmative of their LGBTQ identity and housing that is safe. Because probation departments often believe they only serve a handful of LGBTQ or GNC youth (Irvine 2010), little intentionality is given to lining up services for them or ensuring that organizations provide unique programming that addresses SOGIE-related needs. Collecting SOGIE data will not only benefit gender-conforming LBT girls but also help justice and mental health organizations recognize that some girls of color are LBT too, which is crucial to making referrals that are appropriate and affirming of both SOGIE and race/ethnicity.

Several community-based organizations and probation departments in central and northern California have begun collecting SOGIE data from their youth using a simple, anonymous survey instrument administered by intake, medical, or program staff. Youth are given the opportunity to complete the survey, and can opt out without repercussions. The survey asks similar questions, with slight differences across juvenile justice agencies, and this makes it possible to compare the data across settings. The youth are prompted to describe their gender, gender expression, sex assigned at birth, and sexual orientation. Questions about gender and sexuality are interwoven with other basic demographic items so as to normalize the topics. Notably, they are not placed in the section of the survey that inquires about abuse so that sexual orientation may not be confused with and linked to abusive or predatory behavior. The data will be used to yield understanding of the populations and create an appropriate continuum of care.

Recommendation #2: Develop antidiscrimination policies.

The American Psychological Association's Guidelines for Psychological Practice with Lesbian, Gay, and Bisexual Clients (American Psychological Association 2011) emphasize the importance of recognizing personal attitudes and beliefs about sexual orientation and gender identity, to reduce the risk that these attitudes and beliefs will interfere with the assessment and treatment of LGB/GNCT clients. The guidelines recommend that practitioners "seek consultation or make appropriate referrals when indicated" (American Psychological Association 2011). Additionally, the authors of this chapter promote the creation and adoption of LGB/GNCT antidiscrimination policies in order to ensure the safety of LGB/GNCT youth in the juvenile justice system. These policies are intended to promote the fair treatment of LGBT and GNC youth as well as to prevent unnecessary harsh punishment and other forms of discrimination due to actual or perceived SOGIE status. For example, it is important that these policies protect LBQ/GNCT girls from unnecessary arrests. Whether a justice department decides to create or adopt antidiscrimination policies from another organization, it is important that a collaborative process be put in place. In particular, staff from each part of the department should contribute to decision making. This is essential to achieve staff buy-in and to foster the successful implementation of antidiscrimination policies.

Antidiscrimination policies also require the expertise and support of community-based service providers who work with LBQ/GNCT girls in the juvenile justice system. These providers are able to build deeper relationships with LBQ/GNCT girls outside of confinement. They understand the girls' experiences in the context of their home and community, and therefore offer valuable insight into the unique needs of these youth. For these reasons, they should contribute to the development and implementation of gender- and culturally responsive policies for working with LBQ/GNCT girls in the justice system. Increasing interprofessional collaboration and communication will ensure better outcomes for LBQ/GNCT girls.

Agencies and organizations may consider looking to state and federal laws and regulations for guidance when creating an antidiscrimination policy. For example, the Prison Rape Elimination Act (PREA) highlights LGBTI adult inmates and juvenile residents in confinement as priority populations for protection from sexual victimization. It provides guidance on properly housing LGB and GNCT youth, the use of showers and restrooms, transportation, searches, clothing, medical treatment, and access to and participation in programs and activities. Whether or not institutions decide to adopt PREA or draft their own policy, Garnette and colleagues (2011) stress the importance of giving *all* youth, and not just those perceived to be LGB or GNCT, "a copy of the policy in a form they can understand" (169). Additionally, any policy, created or adopted, must include a confidentiality clause that gives youth the power to decide if, when, and how their SOGIE information is disclosed.

Recommendation #3: Provide training.

Juvenile justice reform that prioritizes culturally affirming programming cannot be implemented without proper education. Juvenile justice stakeholders need training that will increase their general knowledge of research on risk factors associated with diverse LBQ and GNCT girls' involvement in the justice system.

Training should also improve staff's knowledge of identity development, introduce them to the terms that describe LGB/GNCT youth, and include recommendations for effective, individualized interventions. As staff become familiar with concepts and theories relevant to LGBTQ communities, they should also explore myths and stereotypes, learn about the coming-out process, and become informed about "how stigma related to sexual orientation and gender identity can be related to the reason youth are involved in the juvenile justice system" (Garnette et al. 2011, 169). It is important that staff first learn the vocabulary that is most appropriate to describe the experiences of LGB/GNCT youth. This recommendation is in line with the Guidelines for Psychological Practice with Lesbian, Gay, and Bisexual Clients, in particular the call for clinicians to "increase their knowledge and understanding of homosexuality[5] and bisexuality through continuing education, training, supervision, and consultation" (American Psychological Association 2011).

Training that emphasizes the use of respectful language regarding LGB/GNCT youth promotes staff's cultural sensitivity and understanding of intersectionality. In addition, LGBTQI language empowers staff to confidently and competently engage with LGB/GNCT youth and build rapport and relationships that are critical in LB/GNCT girls' successful and permanent exit from the system. When stakeholders are equipped to not only hear, but also use, language that is affirming of LB/GNCT girls, they will be better prepared to effectively manage their responses to girls' self-disclosure. This is particularly important because LGB/GNCT youth evaluate their level of safety and determine whether or not an adult is an ally by listening for supportive language and reading nonverbal responses.

A number of programs provide education on LGBT youth and the obstacles they face, including juvenile justice involvement (Irvine, Canfield, and Bradford 2015). However, few integrate issues of race/ethnicity with SOGIE-specific concerns (Irvine et al. 2015). Unintentionally, yet harmfully, they only train professionals to serve a small segment of the LGBTQ youth population—i.e., White and gender conforming—that experiences lower risks of being swept up in the juvenile justice system (Irvine et al. 2015). Likewise, diversion programs are biased in favor of low-risk, White, cisgender, and straight youth who are less likely to recidivate due to cultural/societal assumptions that they do not break the law, despite engaging in the same transgressive behaviors as other youth (Cochran and Mears 2015). It is particularly essential to address racial issues in the training of juvenile justice agents who work with diverse girls so that they can avoid potentially harmful decisions, for example, sending a system-involved Black lesbian to an LGBT youth center in a predominantly White neighborhood with no culturally competent staff or program participants of color.

Conclusion

Diana, Erica, and Bebe and other girls like them struggle to exit the juvenile justice system. In the absence of intersectional mental and behavioral health programming, they are at risk of being rearrested for running away, of engaging in survival crimes, or of being stopped and searched by police.

Despite her lack of gang affiliation, Diana's gender expression and ethnicity will continue to be considered a threat to public safety by police officers, judges, and community-based organizations that do not have the capacity to serve juvenile justice–involved GNC girls of color. She is likely to be referred to a local care provider that has not been trained to collect SOGIE data or intentionally address SOGIE in their programming. She may be required to attend anger management; but without a culturally competent and SOGIE-trained facilitator, she will not be able to discuss that she and her friends were profiled for their gender expression, and she will not explore the consequences of the way law enforcement perceived them.

Erica will not come out to her probation officer, social worker, or aunt, because she is afraid this will upset them and disrupt another placement, which happened when she told her mother. The program she attends for commercially sexually exploited girls and their counselors is heavily focused on teaching women how to have healthy relationships with men, which is irrelevant to Erica, who is firm in her identity as a lesbian. She considers skipping the program because she does not like the pressure of talking about her plans to avoid abusive (heterosexual) relationships, which is a program requisite. Concurrently, rumors of her sexual orientation have been spread at her new school, making it difficult for her to make new, supportive friends. This has resulted in her avoiding school and hanging out with other Black lesbians in her community, who are also no longer attending school.

Bebe is fortunate to have a family that is supportive of her transition as a Black transwoman. They are aware of her shoplifting incident and have been consistent in making sure she observes the terms of her probation, which include attending school regularly. However, they have had a difficult time finding a counselor with experience serving transgender youth. Bebe's brother knows about the recent incident with the officer, in addition to other, similar incidents she has had with male, White police officers. Bebe's brother has vowed to walk with her more, especially at night, but she fears that as a Black male, he may bring more negative attention to them, exacerbating her stress. Further, she fears that his reaction to a future incident may escalate the situation. Bebe has heard that there is an LGBT center in a nearby city that works against the criminalization of transgender women and serves as a support network, but it is inaccessible by public transportation, and her family resources are already strained. Bebe would like to get a job through a youth center that is close to her house—she wants to save up for a car to begin attending the LGBT center—but she knows that other transwomen have been ridiculed when they seek assistance.

System-involved lesbian, bisexual, transgender, and gender-nonconforming girls will continue to remain marginalized as long as the adults who are serving them continue to assume that only White youth are gay, to link gender nonconformity with gang affiliation and hyperaggressivity, and to view youth of color as hypersexual and predatory. Mental and behavioral health professionals must undergo training to better understand how to identify and dismantle these negative and harmful associations in their institutions, facilities, and programs. Adopting an antidiscrimination policy formalizes fair and equitable treatment of LGBQ and GNCT youth, and provides more support for staff already doing the work to provide gender-responsive, culturally appropriate interventions and case plans for their youth. Data collection further highlights the need for a continuum of services and heightens the urgency to get system-involved LGBQ and GNCT girls of color the services and resources they need to successfully and permanently leave the juvenile justice system.

NOTES

1 For the purpose of this chapter, "lesbian" is defined as a girl or woman who is emotionally, romantically, or sexually attracted to girls or women. "Gay" is defined as a person who is emotionally, romantically, and sexually attracted to individuals of the same sex, typically in reference to boys and men but also used to described women. "Bisexual" is defined as a person who is emotionally, romantically, and sexually attracted to both males and females. "Transgender" is defined as a person whose gender identity (understanding of himself or herself as male or female) does not correspond with the person's birth sex. "Gender identity" is defined as a person's

internal sense of being a man, boy, woman, or girl. "Gender expression" describes how someone chooses to perform his or her gender identity, usually through clothing, hair, and chosen name. The term "gender nonconforming" refers to people who express their gender in a way that is not consistent with their birth sex.

2 Fourteen hundred surveys were collected from straight and LGBQ/GNCT youth in Alameda County, CA; Cook County, IL; Jefferson County, AL; Jefferson Parish, LA; Maricopa County, AZ; Orleans Parish, LA; and Santa Clara County, CA. All surveys were analyzed using descriptive statistics, analysis of variance, and binary logistic regression tests. One hundred and thirty interviews were collected from straight and LGBQ/GNCT youth in Chicago, IL; Oakland, CA; New Orleans, LA, and the surrounding metropolitan area; New York, NY; and Santa Clara, CA. All interviews were transcribed and coded for common themes.

3 The authors intentionally use the term "birth sex" for this section. The construction of girls and boys on a binary is based on the assignment of sex at birth. In contrast, the authors see "gender identity" on a spectrum between female and male. Individual youth may choose one end of the spectrum or another. Youth may also choose to identify as both or as "gender queer," an identity that does not fall into either "female" or "male." Similarly, "gender expression" also falls on a spectrum from feminine to masculine.

4 The authors do not know why these differences across gender were captured by our research. These differences could occur because LBQ/GNCT girls are incarcerated at higher rates or because they are more likely to respond truthfully to the survey. Further research is required to enable us to understand the differences.

5 The authors do not use the term "homosexuality" and recognize that it may be offensive to members of the LGBT community.

REFERENCES

Acoca, Leslie. 1998. "Outside/Inside: The Violation of American Girls at Home, on the Streets, and in the Juvenile Justice System." *Crime and Delinquency* 44: 561–89.

Alexander, Michelle. 2010. *The New Jim Crow: Mass Incarceration in the Age of Color Blindness.* New York: New Press.

American Bar Association and the National Bar Association (ARANBA). 2001. "Justice by Gender: The Lack of Appropriate Prevention, Diversion, and Treatment Alternatives for Girls in the Juvenile Justice System." Accessed September 1, 2010, http://www.abanet.org.

American Psychiatric Association. 2013. "'Gender Dysphoria' Fact Sheet." www.dsm5.org.

American Psychological Association. 2011. Guidelines for Psychological Practice with Lesbian, Gay, and Bisexual Clients. Accessed December 15, 2015, www.apa.org.

American Psychological Association. 2004. "Sexual Orientation and Homosexuality," www.apa.org.

Annie E. Casey Foundation. 2008. "A Road Map for Juvenile Justice Reform, Annie E. Casey Foundation 2008 Kids Count Data Book." Accessed September 2, 2010, http://datacenter.kidscount.org.

Beck, Allen J., Paige M. Harrison, and Paul Guerino. 2010. "Sexual Victimization in Juvenile Facilities Reported by Youth 2008–09," http://bjs.ojp.usdoj.gov.

Beirne, Piers, and James Messerschmidt. 2000. *Criminology.* 3rd ed. Boulder, CO: Westview.

Belknap, Joanne, and Kristi Holsinger. 2006. "The Gendered Nature of Risk Factors for Delinquency." *Feminist Criminology* 1 (1): 48–71.

Berkeley Center for Criminal Justice. 2010. "Gender Responsiveness and Equity in California's Juvenile Justice System, Juvenile Justice Policy Brief Series." Accessed September 1, 2010, http://www.law.berkeley.edu.

Bostwick, Wendy B., Nan Meyer, Frances Aranda, Stephen Russell, Tonda Hughes, Michelle Birkett, and Brian Mustanski. 2014. "Mental Health and Suicidality among Racially/Ethnically Diverse Sexual-Minority Youths." *American Journal of Public Health* 104: 1129–36. doi: 10.2105/AJPH.2013.301749.

Brill, Stephanie, and Rachel Pepper. 2008. *The Transgender Child: A Handbook for Families and Professionals.* San Francisco: Cleis Press.

California Endowment. 2009. "Healing the Hurt: Trauma-Informed Approaches to the Health of Boys and Young Men of Color." Accessed August 6, 2010, http://www.calendow.org.

Chauhan, Preeti, and Dickon N. Reppucci. 2009. "The Impact of Neighborhood Disadvantage and Exposure to Violence on Self-Report of Antisocial Behavior among Girls in the Juvenile Justice System." *Journal of Youth and Adolescence* 38: 401–16.

Chauhan, Preeti, Dickon N. Reppucci, and Eric Turkheimer. 2009. "Racial Differences in the Associations of Neighborhood Disadvantage, Exposure to Violence, and Criminal Recidivism among Female Juvenile Offenders." *Behavioral Sciences and the Law* 27: 531–52.

Chesney-Lind, Meda. 2002. "Criminalizing Victimization: The Unintended Consequences of Pro-Arrest Policies for Girls and Women." *Criminology and Public Policy* 2: 81–90.

Chesney-Lind, Meda, and Randall Shelden. 1992. *Girls, Delinquency, and Juvenile Justice.* Belmont, CA: Wadsworth.

Clatts, Michelle C., Reese W. Davis, J. L. Sotheran, and Aylin Atillasoy. 1999. "Correlates and Distribution of HIV Risk Behaviors among Homeless Youth in New York City." In *Children and HIV/AIDS*, edited by G. Anderson, C. Ryan, S. Taylor-Brown, and M. White-Gray, 95–107. Piscataway, NJ: Transaction.

Cochran, Bryan N., Angela J. Stewart, Joshua A. Ginzler, and Ana M. Cauce. 2002. "Challenges Faced by Homeless Sexual Minorities: Comparison of Gay, Lesbian, Bisexual, and Transgender Homeless Adolescents with their Heterosexual Counterparts." *American Journal of Public Health* 92 (5): 773–77.

Cochran, Joshua C., and Daniel P. Mears. 2015. "Race, Ethnic, and Gender Divides in Juvenile Court Sanctioning and Rehabilitative Intervention." *Journal of Research in Crime and Delinquency* 52 (2): 181–212.

Crenshaw, Kimberlé. 2014. "The Girls Obama Forgot: My Brother's Keeper Ignores Young Black Women." *New York Times*, July 29.

Davis, Antoinette, Angela Irvine, and Jason Ziedenberg. 2014a. "Stakeholder Views on the Movement to Reduce Youth Incarceration," http://www.nccdglobal.org.

Davis, Antoinette, Angela Irvine, and Jason Ziedenberg. 2014b. "Supervision Strategies for Justice-Involved Youth," http://www.nccdglobal.org.

Demuth, Stephen. 2003. "Racial and Ethnic Differences in Pretrial Release Decisions and Outcomes: A Comparison of Hispanic, Black, and White Felony Arrestees." *Criminology* 41 (3): 873–908. doi:10.1111/j.1745-9125.2003.tb01007.x.

Dresher, Jack. 2009. "Queer Diagnoses: Parallels and Contrasts in the History of Homosexuality, Gender Variance, and the *Diagnostic and Statistical Manual*." *Archives of Sexual Behavior* 39 (2): 427–60. doi: 10.1007/s10508-009-9531-5.

Earls, Meg. 2002. "Stressors in the Lives of GLBTQ Youth." *Transitions* 14 (4): 1–3, http://www .advocatesforyouth.org.

Fazal, Shaena M. 2014. "Safely Home: Reducing Youth Incarceration and Achieving Positive Outcomes for High- and Complex-Need Youth through Effective Community-Based Programming," http://www.yapinc.org.

Fox, Ronald E. 1988. "Proceedings of the American Psychological Association, Incorporated, for the Year 1987: Minutes of the Annual meeting of the Council of Representatives." *American Psychologist* 43: 508–31.

Gabarino, James. 2006. *See Jane Hit: Why Girls Are Growing More Violent and What Can Be Done about It*. New York: Penguin.

Garnette, Laura, Angela Irvine, Carolyn Reyes, and Shannan Wilber. 2011. "Lesbian, Gay, Bisexual, and Transgender (LGBT) Youth." In *Juvenile Justice: Advancing Research, Policy, and Practice*. Edited by Francine Sherman and Francine Jacobs. Hoboken, NJ: Wiley.

Gilfus, Mary. 1992. "From Victims to Survivors to Offenders: Women's Routes of Entry and Immersion into Street Crime." *Women and Criminal Justice* 4 (1): 63–89. doi: 10.1300/J012v04n01_04.

Greene, Peters, and Associates. 1998. "Guiding Principles for Promising Female Programming: An Inventory of Best Practices," http://www.ojjdp.gov.

Herek, Gregory M., and Linda D. Garnets. 2007. "Sexual Orientation and Mental Health." *Annual Review of Clinical Psychology* 3 (1): 353–59. doi: 10.1146/annurev.clinpsy.3.022806.091510.

Hill, Darryl B., and Brian L. B. Willoughby. 2005. "The Development and Validation of the Genderism and Transphobia Scale." *Sex Roles*. 53: 531–44.

Hill Collins, Patricia. 1998. *Black Feminist Thought: Knowledge, Consciousness, and the Politics of Empowerment*. New York: Routledge.

Himmelstein, Kathryn E. W., and Hannah Brückner. 2011. "Criminal Justice and School Sanctions against Nonheterosexual Youth: A National Longitudinal Study." *Pediatrics* 127 (1): 48–56.

Holsinger, Kristi, and Alexander M. Holsinger. 2005. "Differential Pathways to Violence and Self-Injurious Behavior: African American and White Girls in the Juvenile Justice System." *Journal of Research in Crime and Delinquency* 42 (2): 211–42.

Hoytt, Eleanor H., Vincent Schiraldi, Brenda Smith, and Jason Ziedenberg. 2001. "Reducing Racial Disparities in Juvenile Detention." *Pathways to Juvenile Detention Reform. Number 8,* http://www.aecf.org.

Hurtado, Aida. 1996. *The Color of Privilege: Three Blasphemies on Race and Feminism.* Ann Arbor: University of Michigan Press.

Hurtado, Aida, and Patricia Gurin. 2004. *Chicana/o Identity in a Changing Society.* Tucson: University of Arizona Press.

Hyde, Justeen. 2005. "From Home to Street: Understanding Young People's Transitions into Homelessness." *Journal of Adolescence* 28: 171–83.

Irvine, Angela. 2010. "'We've Had Three of Them': Addressing the Invisibility of Lesbian, Gay, Bisexual, and Gender-Nonconforming Youth in the Juvenile Justice System." *Columbia Journal of Gender and Law* 19 (3): 675–701.

Irvine, Angela, and Aisha Canfield. 2014. "Survey of National Juvenile Detention Facilities." Unpublished raw data.

Irvine, Angela, Aisha Canfield, and Akiba Bradford. 2015. "Providing Culturally Affirming Programs for LGBT Youth of Color in the Juvenile Justice System." Policy brief, Impact Justice, Oakland, CA.

Irvine, Angela, and Jessica Roa. 2010. "When Gender-Specific Programs for Girls Are Not Culturally Competent Enough." Policy brief, Ceres Policy Research, Santa Cruz, CA.

Israel, Gianna E., and Donald E. Tarver. 1997. *Transgender Care: Recommended Guidelines, Practical Information, and Personal Accounts.* Philadelphia: Temple University Press.

Johnson, Marcia, and Luckett A. Johnson. 2012. "Bail: Reforming Policies to Address Overcrowded Jails, the Impact of Race on Detention, and Community Revival in Harris County, TX." *Northwestern Journal of Law and Social Policy* 7 (1): 42–87.

Jones, Camara P. 2000. "Levels of Racism: A Theoretic Framework and a Gardener's Tale." *American Journal of Public Health* 90 (8): 1212–15.

Jones, Nikki. 2009. *Between Good and Ghetto: African American Girls and Inner-City Violence.* Newark, NJ: Rutgers University Press.

Kosciw, Joseph G. 2004. "The 2003 National School Climate Survey," http://www.glsen.org.

Kosciw, Joseph G., Elizabeth M. Diaz, and Emily A. Greytak. 2007. "The 2007 National School Climate Survey: The Experiences of Lesbian, Gay, Bisexual, and Transgender Youth in our Nation's Schools," http://www.glsen.org.

Krisberg, Barry. 2005. *Juvenile Justice: Redeeming Our Children.* Thousand Oaks, CA: Sage.

Luke, Katherine P. 2008. "Are Girls Really Becoming More Violent? A Critical Analysis." *Affilia: Journal of Women and Social Work* 23 (1): 38–50.

Majd, Katayoon, Jody Marksamer, and Carolyn Reyes. 2009. "Hidden Injustice: Lesbian, Gay, Bisexual, and Transgender Youth in Juvenile Courts; The Equity Project," http://www.hivlawandpolicy.org.

Mallon, Gary P. 1999. "Gay and Lesbian Adolescents and Their Families." *Journal of Gay and Lesbian Social Services* 11 (1/2): 23–33.

Mallon, Gary P., and Terry DeCrescenzo. 2006. "Transgender Children and Youth: A Child Welfare Practice Perspective." *Child Welfare* 85 (2): 215–41.

Mariscal, Raquel, and James Bell. 2011. "Race, Ethnicity, and Ancestry in Juvenile Justice." In *Juvenile Justice: Advancing Research, Policy, and Practice.* Edited by Francine Sherman and Francine Jacobs, 111–30. Hoboken, NJ: Wiley.

Marmot, Michael. 2004. *The Status Syndrome: How Social Standing Affects Our Health and Longevity.* New York: Henry Holt.

Martin, Carol L. 1995. "Stereotypes about Children with Traditional and Non-Traditional Gender Roles." *Sex Roles* 33 (11–12): 727–51. doi: 10.1007/BF01544776.

Massachusetts Department of Elementary and Secondary Education. 2006. "2005 Massachusetts Youth Risk Behavior Survey Results," http://www.doe.mass.edu.

Mauer, Marc. 2010. "Race, Class, and the Development of Criminal Justice Policy." *Review of Policy Research* 21 (1): 79–92.

Mendel, Richard. 2009. "Two Decades of the Juvenile Detention Alternatives Initiative: From Demonstration Project to National Standard." Accessed August 6, 2010, http://www.aecf.org.

Morris, Monique. 2013. *Searching for Black Girls in the School-to-Prison Pipeline* (blog), http://www.nccdglobal.org.

Morris, Monique. 2012. "Race, Gender, and the School-to-Prison Pipeline: Expanding Our Discussion to Include Black Girls; Report for the African American Policy Forum," http://www.otlcampaign.org.

Mustanski, Brian S., Robert Garofalo, and Erin M. Emerson. 2010. "Mental Health Disorders, Psychological Distress, and Suicidality in a Diverse Sample of Lesbian, Gay, Bisexual, and Transgender Youths." *American Journal of Public Health* 100: 2426–32. doi: 10.2105/AJPH.2009.178319.

Nelson, Douglas W. 2008. "Essay: A Road Map for Juvenile Justice Reform." *Annie E. Casey Foundation 2008 Kids Count Data Book*, http://datacenter.kidscount.org.

New York Civil Liberties Union. 2014. "Stop-and-Frisk Data," http://www.nyclu.org

Owen, Greg, June Heineman, and Michael D. Gerrard. 2007. "Overview of Homelessness in Minnesota, 2006: Key Facts from the Statewide Survey," http://www.wilder.org.

Ray, Nicholas. 2007. "Lesbian, Gay, Bisexual, and Transgender Youth: An Epidemic of Homelessness," http://www.thetaskforce.org.

Robson, Ruthann. 2001. "Our Children: Kids of Queer Parents and Kids Who Are Queer: Looking at Sexual-Minority Rights from a Different Perspective." *Albany Law Review* 64: 915–24.

Ryan, C., and R. M. Diaz. 2005. "Family Responses as a Source of Risk and Resiliency for LGBT Youth." Paper presented at the pre-conference Institute on LGBT Youth, Child Welfare League of America National Conference, Washington, DC.

Saewyc, Elizabeth, Sandra Pettingel, and Carol Skay. 2006. "Hazards of Stigma: The Sexual and Physical Abuse of Gay, Lesbian, and Bisexual Adolescents in the United States and Canada." *Journal of Adolescent Health* 34 (2): 115–16.

Sarri, Rosemary. 1999. "The Female Offender: Girls, Women, and Crime." *Social Service Review* 73: 265–67.

Savin-Williams, Ritch C. 1994. "Verbal and Physical Abuse as Stressors in the Lives of Lesbian, Gay Male, and Bisexual Youths: Associations with School Problems, Running Away, Substance Abuse, Prostitution, and Suicide." *Journal of Consulting and Clinical Psychology* 62 (2): 261–69.

Schaefer, Paula. 2008. "Gender-Responsive Programs for Girls." Presentation to the Santa Cruz County Probation Department.

Schlesinger, Traci. 2005. "Racial and Ethnic Disparity in Pretrial Criminal Processing." *Justice Quarterly* 22: 170–92.

Schwarzer, Ralf, and Urte Scholz. 2000. "Cross-Cultural Assessment of Coping Resources: The General Perceived Self-Efficacy Scale." Paper presented at the First Asian Congress of Health Psychology: Health Psychology and Culture, Tokyo, Japan.

Sherman, Francine. 2005. "Pathways to Juvenile Detention Reform—Detention Reform and Girls: Challenges and Solutions. Accessed August 6, 2010, http://www.aecf.org.

Sherman, Francine, Richard Mendel, and Angela Irvine. 2013. "Making Detention Reform Work for Girls: A Guide to Juvenile Justice Reform," http://www.aecf.org.

Steffensmeier, Darrell, and Stephen Demuth. 2001. "Ethnicity and Judges' Sentencing Decision: Hispanic-Black-White Comparisons." Criminology 39 (1): 145–178.

Steffensmeier, Darrel, Jennifer Schwartz, Hua Zhong, and Jeff Ackerman. 2005. "An Assessment of Recent Trends in Girls' Violence Using Diverse Longitudinal Sources: Is the Gender Gap Closing?" *Criminology* 43 (2): 355–405.

Sullivan, Colleen, Susan Sommer, and Jason Moff. 2001. "Youth in the Margins: A Report on the Unmet Needs of Lesbian, Gay, Bisexual, and Transgender Adolescents in Foster Care," http://www.lambdalegal.org.

Toscano, Marion E., and Elizabeth Maynard. 2014. "Understanding the Link: 'Homosexuality,' Gender Identity, and the DSM." *Journal of LGBT Issues in Counseling* 8 (3): 248–63.

Valentine, Sarah E. 2008. "Traditional Advocacy for Non-Traditional Youth: Rethinking Best Interest for the Queer Child." *Michigan State Law Review* 1053 (4): 1054–1113.

Van Hofwegen, Sara L. 2009. "Unjust and Ineffective: A Critical Look at California's STEP Act." *Southern California Interdisciplinary Law Journal* 18: 679–702.

Wilber, Shannan, Caitlyn Ryan, and Jody Marksamer. 2006. "CWLA Best Practice Guidelines: Serving LGBT Youth in Out-of- Home Care," http://www.nclrights.org.

Witbeck, Les, Xiaojin Chen, Dan R. Hoyt, Kimberly A. Tyler, and Kurt D. Johnson. 2004. "Mental Disorder, Subsistence Strategies, and Victimization among Gay, Lesbian, and Bisexual Homeless and Runaway Adolescents." *Journal of Sex Research* 41: 329–42.

9

Women, Poverty, and the Criminal Justice System

Cyclical Linkages

ERICA G. ROJAS, LAURA SMITH, AND
RANDOLPH M. SCOTT-MCLAUGHLIN II

A volatile, complicated journey into the nature of relationships at the intersections of race, gender and gender
identity, culture, class, and sexuality. It's about the interdependent nature of our day-to-day social, economic, political,
and spiritual relationships with one another. The journey
takes us straight into the heart of the inhumanity inherent
in declaring vast numbers of people to be expendable—
overwhelmingly people of color, poor people, women,
youth, and people with mental illness. It is a journey not
only into the violence individuals do to one another but also
into the systemic violence of the state.
—Solinger et al. 2010

With this passage describing Kay Whitlock's experience of incarceration in the United States, Solinger and colleagues (2010) highlighted
the political, economic, and social underpinnings that perpetuate the
oppression of marginalized populations—and specifically poor women
of color—through mass incarceration. Women represent a significant proportion of offenders under criminal justice supervision in the
United States. In 2001, over one million women were under some form
of correctional sanction—making up 17 percent of all offenders (Bloom,
Owen, and Covington 2004). Nationally, in 2011, sixty-five out of every
one hundred thousand women were in prison, and over two hundred
thousand women were incarcerated in correctional facilities (Carson
and Sabol 2012). Although men comprise the majority of the population

of incarcerated individuals, women are the fastest-growing population of inmates. The number of women in prison increased by 587 percent between 1980 and 2011, nearly 1.5 times the rate of men (Cahalan 1986; Carson and Golinelli 2013). Moreover, current statistics support an inverse relationship between the rates of incarceration based on gender. Between 2010 and 2013, the female inmate population increased 10.9 percent, while the male inmate population declined 4.2 percent during the same time frame (Golinelli and Minton 2014).

An overwhelming commonality shared by many incarcerated women is a disadvantaged socioeconomic status. Pearce (1978) referred to the overrepresentation of women living in poverty as "the feminization of poverty"—a trend with important implications for the economic and political status of women. Although poverty may not constitute a cause of crime in and of itself, it can indeed be considered a *source* of crime in that it leaves people in positions where they have fewer legal alternatives for meeting legitimate needs (Reiman 2007). Women are particularly vulnerable to finding themselves in these positions: In the United States, women are 32 percent more likely to live in poverty than are men (Legal Momentum 2010). The National Women's Law Center analyzed the U.S. Census's 2014 figures to determine that, among the nearly eighteen million poor women (or one American woman in seven) who lived in poverty in 2013, about 43 percent lived in extreme poverty, with incomes at under half the federal poverty rate. Moreover, poverty rates were especially high, at about one in four, among Black women (25.3 percent), Latinas (23.1 percent), and Native American women (26.8 percent); rates for Asian American women were closer (11 percent) to the poverty rates for White women (10.7 percent). Poverty rates for all racial groups of adult women were higher than for their male counterparts (Entmacher et al. 2014).

Women in poverty, therefore, find themselves at the nexus of powerful, oppressive societal forces—including classism, gender discrimination, and racism—as they encounter the criminal justice system. What do we know about the nearly one million women now involved with that system (Ney 2015), and what are the implications for the psychologists and other professionals who wish to serve them? We begin this chapter by introducing a critical review of the psychological and criminological literature using an intersectional framework to explore racial-ethnic identity, gender, and criminal justice encounters (Barak, Leighton, and Flavin 2010; Cole 2009; Gabbidon 2010; McCall 2005). We then introduce the feminization of poverty as a contextual framework (Smith 2010; Smith, Appio, and Cho 2010) in which to understand the marginalization of female offenders and outline the cyclical, mutually perpetuating linkages between poverty and criminal involvement in low-income women's lives. We conclude our chapter with directions for developing socially just research and practices for use among diverse women in prison populations.

Levels of Intersectionality: Factoring in Racial-Ethnic Identity

Before foregrounding the topics of gender and class, it is essential to note race as an overarching factor in U.S. citizens' experiences with the justice system. Black defendants are more likely to be incarcerated during pretrial proceedings, more likely to be convicted of their crimes, and more likely to receive harsher sentencing as compared to White defendants of similar charges (Mitchell 2005). Moreover, while 95 percent of felony criminal cases never see trial and result in plea bargains (Cohen and Reaves 2006), most bargained outcomes benefit White and middle-class individuals (Donziger 1996). Zatz (2000) observed that White defendants are the least likely to enter the stage in criminal justice proceedings that would put them at risk for incarceration, let alone to a point where they would be involved in a trial. These statistics dovetail with the fact that adjudicated women are more likely to have lived in poverty, with the consequence that poor women of color are more likely to comprise the low-income female defendants represented in legal proceedings, who remain within the legal system. Until recently, psychologists have contributed little to the psychological theories and assumptions that have informed the responses of justice officials and mental health practitioners, as theorists in the field of criminology have largely contributed to the critical overview of women and crime. In this section, we offer a critique of both the psychological and the criminological literature using an intersectional framework, and comment on some of the implications of the gender-race-class intersection.

Intersectionality and Criminal Justice

The introduction of mandatory minimum sentencing laws has spurred scholars to address the fact that certain races and social classes are consistently overrepresented in the criminal justice system (Gabbidon 2010). Criminologists Barak, Leighton, and Flavin (2010) posited four assumptions that underlie all integrative approaches to understanding the manner in which identity status and criminal justice intersect. These assumptions are based on the understandings that (a) all categories of social difference share the ability to provide both privilege *and* marginalization in one capacity or another, inherently naturalizing (or masking) the privilege that members of advantaged social groups may be experiencing; (b) multiple forms of oppression do not have a simple additive effect, with certain combinations having a stronger effect than others; (c) ethnicity creates variation in the manner in which oppression is experienced, due in part to the invisibility of power and the uniqueness of individual identity; and (d) since the social roles of oppressor and oppressed are not mutually exclusive, the overlap of such roles provides for a complex experience in which it may be easier for individuals to be more aware of their oppression than their privilege.

Intersectionality is a complex, multifaceted topic that defies many of the researchers who support its theoretical importance (Cole 2009). McCall (2005) helpfully suggested three frameworks by which to organize and choose among emerging approaches to intersectionality: (a) anticategorical, (b) intercategorical, and (c) intracategorical. In the anticategorical approach, no form of labeling or categorization is used, in that adherents are interested in the fluid, individualized nature of social interactions, which they see as incompatible with labeling systems that are inevitably limited in their ability to capture these interactions. At the other end of the continuum, intercategorical theorists accept the need to use current social group–labeling methods, imperfect though they may be, in order to document "relationships of inequality among social groups and changing configurations of inequity" (1773). The third approach, intracategorical, is an intermediate approach that emphasizes the flawed nature of systems of social categorization yet draws upon them in order to critique them and discuss categorical boundary challenges. In the present discussion, we primarily make use of an intercategorical structure, in that we do rely on existing social group categories to discuss the circumstances of women in different racial-ethnic groups, yet, like the intracategorical theorists, we acknowledge the imperfect, nonabsolute nature of such labels.

Poor Women of Color and Criminal Justice Encounters

Given the trends explicated above, it stands to reason that race is a determining factor in low-income women's experiences of adjudication. In fact, the great majority of incarcerated women are poor women of color. As one woman in prison described,

> Most of the women are poor. In all the time I was there I didn't meet one wealthy woman. A large percentage of Black and Chicana are there. Most of us were defended by the public defenders and couldn't afford good attorneys. We would hear about middle-class crimes on the TV or in the papers but we never saw the women who had committed the offenses come into the prison. They had good attorneys and connections with the judges. Their charges would be dropped or they would pay fines, which they could well afford, or go into rehab, or just minimum probation sentences. (Faith and Near 2006, 16)

Statistics support this depiction: In 2010, Black women were incarcerated at nearly three times the rate of White women (133 versus 47 per 100,000), and Latinas were incarcerated at 1.6 times the rate of White women (77 versus 47 per 100,000) (Porter 2012). White women charged with crimes are more likely to be referred to drug rehabilitation services, while Black women are more likely to have their sentences lead to incarceration (Barak et al. 2010). Zatz (2000) found that during sentencing procedures for similar offenses, White women received less harsh punishments than Black women.

The experiences of poor women of color with the criminal justice system are not only distinguished by their quantity; they can also differ in quality, often beginning with the ways in which their communities are policed. The practice of overpolicing and underpolicing within economically disempowered communities of color has created a contentious relationship between the police and the people they serve (Russell-Brown 1998).

African Americans, Latino/as, and Native Americans are stopped by officers more often than Whites, and these stops more often lead to arrests (Perry 2009). As a result, people of color have reported feeling disempowered and "unwilling to cooperate with a system that reinforces their oppression" (Perry 2009, 78). Along these lines, the policy stance known as the "war on drugs"—a term commonly applied to a set of drug policies used to reduce the illegal drug trade—has been critiqued as a form of social control that criminalizes drug use via an inflexible set of procedures targeted at low-income urban African American communities. These rigid drug policies have catalyzed the imprisonment of racial minorities to such a large extent that they have been considered a contemporary version of Jim Crow laws (Alexander 2012). Similarly, Zatz (2000) contended that mandatory minimum sentencing procedures for nonviolent drug offenses serve to marginalize low-income women and men of color. For instance, prior to the Fair Sentencing Act of 2010, the possession of five grams of *crack* cocaine (more commonly used in poorer communities of color) has yielded a mandatory minimum of five years in prison, while the ruling for fifty grams of *powdered* cocaine (more commonly used by more affluent Whites) amounted to only one one-hundredth the prison time (Gabbidon and Greene 2013). Low-income African American communities have been devastated by mass incarnation as a result of these policies (Alexander 2012), adding to the social marginalization and stigmatization of the women and their families who live there.

Racism exists, therefore, as a catalyst that is crucial to the operations of classism and gender discrimination that perpetuate the cyclical involvement of poor women in the criminal justice system. Within this cycle, the feminization of poverty influences how and why women come into contact with the law, how likely they are to remain incarcerated after arrest, and how they experience further marginalization as a result of institutional practices during and after incarceration.

The Feminization of Poverty: A Contextual Framework

The moral condemnation of poor women sentenced to prison continues to permeate public perception and policy. In 1994, a warden of an unnamed state prison for women elaborated on the prevailing attitude towards incarcerated women:

Poor men stick somebody up or sell drugs. To me, as strange as this may sound coming from a warden, that is understandable. I can see how you would make that choice. Women degrade themselves. Selling themselves, you should hear some of the stuff they do. There is no sense of self-respect, of dignity. . . . There is something wrong on the inside that makes an individual take up those kinds of behavior and choices. (Law 2009, 12)

As the quotation above indicates, poor women who fail to conform to prescribed societal gender roles are often the recipients of increased disdain. *Patriarchy* and *classism* are two forms of oppression whose operations intersect in the feminization of poverty (Smith, Appio, and Cho 2010). "Patriarchy" refers to the degree to which society is *male-dominated, male-identified*, and *male-centered* (Johnson 1997). Therefore, patriarchal societies tend to have positions of power that are occupied by men, and tend to consider qualities associated with men to be good or normal. "Classism" refers to the discriminatory actions and attitudes associated with social class privilege (Smith, Appio, and Cho 2010). Heather E. Bullock explicated classism as "the oppression of the poor through a network of everyday practices, attitudes, assumptions, behaviors, and institutional rules" (Bullock 1995, 119). Like women across the social spectrum, women in poverty contend with the impact of patriarchy, and classism adds an additional dimension of oppression to their experience (Smith 2010).

These intersecting forms of oppression result in financial deprivation and gender discrimination that increase women's vulnerability to poverty. Perhaps the most frequently cited example of this intersection is the longstanding wage gap between men and women in the United States (Entmacher et al. 2014). In 2013, median annual earnings in the United States for women and men working full-time, year-round, were $39,157 and $50,033, respectively—resulting in women earning just 78 percent of what men earned for similar jobs (American Association of University Women 2014).

Moreover, women are more likely than men to be supporting children as single parents on these diminished incomes, and the necessary demands of childcare subsequently preclude women's abilities to work as much as would otherwise be possible (e.g., Albelda and Tilly 1997; Maume 1991). The clear financial deprivation that results from societal gender discrimination and women's impoverishment is further accompanied by concomitant psychological harm. The mental health research has repeatedly confirmed the damaging impact of poverty upon many aspects of physical and emotional well-being (e.g., Siefert et al. 2000; Siefert et al. 2004).

In addition to their financial deprivation, poor women also face negative attitudes and discriminatory actions as the result of social-class bias. Specifically, social institutions and their policies and procedures function to perpetuate the deprivation and low status of poor people through *institutional classism.* Individual prejudice, stereotyping, and discrimination are perpetuated through *interpersonal classism* (Lott and Bullock 2007).

Discriminatory practices related to classism can be traced throughout the criminal justice system. A particularly blatant example of classism can be found in the setting of bail, a common practice through which poor people occupy prison cells while affluent people accused of the same crimes go home. Other examples can be gathered from basic assumptions about crime: Reiman (2007) has argued that the criminal justice system is classist in some of its deepest assumptions about what crime *is.* Crimes tend to be portrayed to the public as the crimes of poverty—burglary, theft, selling drugs, and other street crimes. According to Reiman, these are not, however, the crimes that cause the most death, destruction, and suffering in our country. Rather, those crimes include corporate fraud, hazardous working conditions, the creation of toxic pollutants, profiteering from unhealthy or unsafe products, and risky high-level financial services ventures in which the American public ends up bearing the consequences of the risk—which are, of course, crimes of the affluent. By defining crime in the popular imagination as street crime, and by promulgating images of criminals as poor people (especially poor people of color), the system deflects societal attention away from class-privileged groups and toward the poor (Reiman 2007).

The Feminization of Poverty and Crime: Cycles of Dispossession

Classism and patriarchal oppression operate together and have a profound influence on *how* women become involved in the criminal justice system. From the beginning, women in prisons and jails are more likely to have been socioeconomically disadvantaged and to have had less access to education before their arrests. For example, nearly half (44 percent) of women in state prisons in 1998 had not completed high school (Bureau of Justice Statistics 1999). Diminished access to education erodes opportunity in the workplace, and inequitable work opportunities maintain women in lower-paying jobs, preventing them from being as able to move up the economic ladder (Albelda and Tilly 1997; Goldberg and Kremen 1990). As noted earlier, gender discrepancies in wage earnings factor into the equation at this point as well.

Other statistics affirm the significant relationship among poverty, unemployment, and crime. In 2000, the Bureau of Justice Statistics reported that incarcerated women were twice as likely as the general population to grow up in single-parent households, making them more likely to live in poverty. Only four out of ten women were employed full-time at the time of their offense (Bureau of Justice Statistics 2000), with 80 percent of women in prison reporting incomes of less than two thousand dollars per year and 92 percent reporting incomes of less than ten thousand dollars per year (Fosado 2007). Furthermore, 53 percent of female inmates in prison and 74 percent of female inmates in jail were unemployed when arrested (Fosado 2007). The majority of incarcerated women lived below the poverty level, a circumstance that can create vulnerability to criminal involvement as the result of reduced legal options for family support (Richie 1996). For this reason, *any* discussion of women in the criminal justice system is largely a discussion of poor women in the criminal justice system.

Women's limited socioeconomic conditions are further reflected in the *types* of crimes that they commit. Because women offenders are primarily poor, low-income, undereducated, and unskilled, they are more likely to have been convicted of nonviolent crimes involving drugs or property—crimes that reflect their limited socioeconomic circumstances (Bloom, Owen, and Covington 2004). As one incarcerated woman described her introduction to crime, "Our 'apartment' cost $14 a week and we loved it. I stole a couple of credit cards and a few linens from my mother. . . . When the rent was due again I went home and took an air conditioner and a stereo and hocked them to pay the rent" (Faith and Near 2006). In 2009 the Bureau of Justice Statistics reported that the most frequently charged offenses among female felony defendants were fraud (37 percent), forgery (34 percent), and larceny/theft (31 percent) (Bureau of Justice Statistics 2013). In general, women are primarily arrested and incarcerated for property and drug offenses, with property offenses comprising 29 percent and drug offenses comprising 25 percent of the female population in state prison in 2010 (Bureau of Justice Statistics 2013).

Low-Income Women in Custody

Upon arrest, women offenders enter an organization whose institutional policies, regulations, and sentencing procedures reflect a patriarchal sociopolitical structure. According to Judge Patricia Wald (2001),

> The circumstances surrounding the commission of a crime vary significantly between men and women. Yet penalties are most often based on the circumstances of crimes committed by men, creating a male norm in sentencing which makes the much-touted gender neutrality of guideline sentencing very problematic. (Wald 2001, 12)

As Judge Wald indicated, the majority of current judicial rules and regulations were developed originally for men and, moreover, for more violent male samples. For example, women are required to post the same amount of bail as men in order to stay out of jail despite their relative economic disadvantages. In a study of female pretrial jail detainees, Teplin, Abram, and McClelland (1996) concluded that the majority of women who remained in jail were nonviolent offenders who could not afford to pay bail. Although maintaining uniform bail postings across gender may initially seem to be an equitable state of affairs, it actually penalizes the poorer, less violent group of offenders, women, who are held to the same dollar amounts. In other words, when bail is set equally for women and men, women are more likely to remain in custody for less violent offenses than men.

Legislative efforts to control crime have significantly increased the number of women in state and federal prisons. Tough-on-crime legislation was initially enforced to prohibit violent male offenders from posing a risk in the community (Covington and Bloom 2003). However, these legislative policies have ultimately targeted women, as women who would have previously been given community sanctions are increasingly being sentenced to prison as a result of mandatory minimum sentencing statutes and increased sentence lengths (Bloom, Owen, and Covington 2004; Covington and Bloom 2003). For instance, twenty years ago, nearly two-thirds of the women convicted of federal felonies were granted probation, compared to 36 percent of women given probation in 2010 (Maruschak and Bonczar 2013).

One of the most detrimental trends in sentencing policies for women has been the war on drugs. Since its inception in 1971, the war on drugs has inadvertently become a war on women (Bloom, Chesney-Lind, and Owen 1994), and more specifically, on poor women whose means of entry into the legal economy were limited. These policies have led to an upsurge in women arrested for nonviolent, drug-related offenses. For instance, in 1979 approximately one in every ten women in U.S. prisons was serving a sentence for a drug conviction. In 1999, this figure skyrocketed to approximately one in three. Moreover, the number of women incarcerated for drug offenses rose a staggering 888 percent between 1986 and 1996 (Mauer, Potler, and Wolf 1999). Stricter sentencing laws regarding drug-related offenses distinctively target female offenders, as the literature has consistently revealed that women are more likely than men to have reported drug use at the time of their offenses (Bureau of Justice Statistics 1999), to have committed crimes in order to obtain money to purchase drugs, and to have used more drugs while in prison than men (Morash, Bynum, and Koons 1998). Since women have always represented the minority of individuals who commit violent crimes, the increasing number of women in prison would not have grown as dramatically if not for the changes in drug enforcement policies and practices (Mauer 2013).

Wanted: Adequate, Relevant Services for Incarcerated Low-Income Women

Once women are sentenced to serve their terms in correctional facilities, they encounter yet another environment that serves to perpetuate patriarchal and classist trends in society at large. Correctional treatment has historically adopted a male-oriented focus, with programs, policies, and services that were created to treat the needs of men in the criminal justice system. The past twenty years have witnessed an increase in research regarding the lack of appropriate services available to women in the fields of mental health, substance abuse, and trauma treatment (Covington and Bloom 2003). In an effort to rectify such disparities, the U.S. Congress and the courts have mandated that female offenders be given access to services of the same quality as those designed and provided for incarcerated men (Collins and Collins 1996). However, forcing women to take part in services that are identical to those offered to men can serve to marginalize women further, as such programs are not gender- or culturally responsive to the unique needs and issues that women face.

Well-Being and Mental Health

Issues that contribute to the marginalization of low-income incarcerated women are intricately connected with issues of health and well-being (Jose-Kampfner 1997). Richie (2001) reported that health care needs are among the most common challenges for incarcerated women. In particular, incarcerated women possess many distinct needs that require specialized treatment services. For example, incarcerated women require mental health services, as they consistently reveal high rates of psychiatric disorders and substance use issues (Battle et al. 2003; Jordan et al. 1996; Sanders et al. 1997; Teplin, Abram, and McClelland 1996). Yet the few available treatment programs that do exist are inconsistent or subpar:

> Inside, there were some treatment groups, but they only met every once in a while. I'd try to get there, but sometimes the officers forgot to call me out of my housing area. Or, I'd get there and the group would be cancelled for some reason. Other times, we'd just be there talking, but not getting very deep. It was good to get a distraction, but I wouldn't say I worked on my issues. I'm an addict and have been for 8 years. I really need help, but didn't get it in jail. (Richie 2001, 372)

The majority of female offenders in the United States are incarcerated for drug-related offenses and were using illegal substances at the time of arrest (Richie 2001). As in the case of the woman quoted above, their struggles with addiction often go untreated and continue to create difficulties during their incarceration. Green and colleagues (2005) found that 32 percent of female inmates in a county correctional facility in Maryland were classified as having an alcohol problem, with nearly 72 percent reporting recent use of an illicit substance and 74 percent reporting either an alcohol or a substance abuse problem. Female inmates were also significantly more likely to have met the criteria for dependence on or abuse of drugs (61 percent) than their male counterparts (Karberg and James 2005).

Due to increased funding and the development of gender-specific programs, services that address incarcerated women's needs have become more prevalent over the past twenty-five years (White 2008). For instance, the Federal Bureau of Prisons (2009) asserted that the importance of treatment should be emphasized for female offenders through skill-building activities, education, vocational training, and release preparation. This treatment includes drug education, nonresidential programs, the Residential Drug Abuse Program (RDAP), follow-up treatment, transitional drug abuse treatment, and counseling for all female inmates who are eligible and willing to volunteer for treatment (Federal Bureau of Prisons 2009).

Nevertheless, the implementation of these programs has proven to be inconsistent, as eligibility standards and enforcement policies are vague and differ across various correctional institutions. The Federal Bureau of Prisons (2000) reported that over 92 percent of female offenders who are eligible volunteer to participate in these programs, with 15 percent less likely to recidivate following release from prison after three years of treatment. Other statistics paint a different picture, asserting that it is estimated that no more than 10 percent of drug-abusing women are offered drug treatment in jail or prison (Freudenberg 2001; Prendergast, Wellisch, and Falkin 1995), with only 20 percent of substance-dependent or -abusing female inmates participating in treatment ever while in prison or jail (Karberg and James 2005). Koons and colleagues (1997) conducted a comprehensive survey of state and federal settings where women were incarcerated to examine mental health treatment programs that were in place. Only 47 percent included substance abuse treatment and 44 percent included parenting interventions. Only 7 percent of the programs addressed other areas, such as mental health. In spite of mandates to provide basic mental health treatment in the criminal justice system, only a portion offered a comprehensive range of services (Steadman, Barbera, and Dennis 1994). Morris, Steadman, and Veysey (1997) concluded, in a study of health services in jails serving men and women, that 50 percent of the jails surveyed provided crisis intervention and psychotropic medication, while other services such as counseling were only offered in about one-third of programs. Research consistently supports that female offenders have experienced a history of serious traumatic experiences (Felitti and Anda 2010; Felitti et al. 1998; Messina and Grella 2006), yet this is rarely taken into account within treatment services to address women's physical and mental health issues (Covington 2012). Few, if any, prisons are able to offer a comprehensive array of mental health services for all inmates. Limited staffing and resources force prison officials to direct their attention to inmates with the most severe impairments—most of which present with dangerous and disruptive symptoms. Inmates with difficulties deemed less severe may end up waiting long periods of time for treatment, if they receive such treatment at all (Hills, Siegfried, and Ickowitz 2004).

Given that women in prison have frequently come from low-income backgrounds where they have limited access to health care, the unavailability of adequate treatment behind bars builds upon a lifetime of unaddressed mental health needs. Women enter correctional facilities already suffering from treatable diseases such as asthma, diabetes, cancer, late-term miscarriages, and seizures. Prisons may be the first circumstance where poor women have access to adequate health care; however, understaffing, long delays, and poor quality of treatment severely limit the medical attention they receive. Furthermore, many prisons and jails charge inmates for medical visits, making health care even less accessible for already-poor women. Female inmates serving sentences in super–maximum security prisons, where prisoners are not allowed to work for wages, often find it impossible to get adequate treatment (Amnesty International USA 2001).

For women prisoners who receive mental health services, many are routinely given psychotropic medication without the opportunity to undergo psychotherapeutic treatment (Amnesty International USA 2001). This inevitably causes difficulties for poor women who suffer from mental health problems: When they return to the community and do not have access to affordable outpatient services, they run out of medication (Zaitzow 2010) and are at higher risk of rearrest. These women (sometimes referred to as "frequent flyers") return to prison or jail as a result of not obtaining adequate care to treat their mental illnesses.

Poverty itself has consistently been associated with adverse mental and physical health outcomes of many kinds (e.g., Blazer et al. 1994; Brown and Moran 1997; Siefert et al. 2000). For poor women, the experience of navigating overt experiences of classism and sexism (as well as other forms of oppression they may face on the basis of their race, ethnicity, ability status, or sexual orientation) can be especially depleting and stressful; in fact, Belle and Doucet (2003) referred to poverty in the lives of women as *depressogenic*. At the same time, as vulnerable as poor women are to emotional distress, they are one of the groups least well served by mental health professionals (Smyth, Goodman, and Glenn 2006).

Given the lack of treatment for poor women in general, and for adjudicated women in particular, it follows that rates of psychiatric disorders among female inmates are higher than would be expected in the community (Green et al. 2005). Incarcerated women have an even higher rate of mental health problems than incarcerated men, with women in state prisons or local jails diagnosed with mental health disorders at three times the rate of their male counterparts (James and Glaze 2006). According to preliminary findings from a national study of women in jail, Dehart et al. (2014) asserted that women offenders self-medicated with drugs to cope with overwhelming trauma, loss, depression, and mental health struggles. Findings indicated that 66 percent of women had histories of substance dependence, 55 percent met criteria for lifetime posttraumatic stress disorder (PTSD), 31 percent for major depressive disorder (MDD), 16 percent for bipolar disorder, 5 percent for schizophrenia spectrum, and 13 percent met criteria for brief psychotic disorder (Dehart et al. 2014).

Depression itself is often associated with violence and early trauma (National Alliance on Mental Illness 2011). Female prisoners have been shown to have very high exposure to a variety of traumatic experiences, especially to interpersonal violence, including childhood physical and sexual abuse (Battle et al. 2003; Browne, Miller, and Maguin 1999; Greene et al. 2000; Jordan et al. 1996; Owen and Bloom 1995; Teplin,

Abram, and McClelland 1996). A recent review suggests that exposure to traumatic events may be nearly universal among incarcerated women, with studies showing ranges of trauma exposure to be between 77 percent and 90 percent (Battle et al. 2003). In a study of female incarcerated offenders, Green et al. (2005) found that 98 percent of the women surveyed had been exposed to at least one category of trauma, with childhood trauma reported in 62 percent and interpersonal trauma reported in 90 percent of women. Rates of exposure to lifetime trauma and violence among incarcerated women consistently exceed those of the general population (Kessler et al. 1995). Despite the multiple mental health needs of incarcerated women, treatment programs often fall short in addressing their needs.

Poverty, Incarceration, and Motherhood

The efforts of incarcerated women to mother their children show clearly the impact of poverty-related obstacles. Imprisoned women are continually exposed to noninclusive legislative policies that fail to address their specific and unique needs as caregivers. Halperin and Harris (2004) reported that child welfare policies regarding children of incarcerated women have not been modified despite the rapidly increasing rates of female incarceration. Legislation such as the 1997 Adoption and Safe Families Act (ASFA) mandates the termination of parental rights once a child has been in foster care for fifteen or more of the preceding twenty-two months—especially detrimental for incarcerated women, as they serve an average of eighteen months (Jacobs 2001). In many cases, the forced separation that results in mothers being imprisoned leads to a permanent termination of parental rights (Genty 1995). Even alternative resources available to imprisoned mothers prove difficult to access. Placing children with relatives instead of in foster homes to avoid the ASFA mandate can be challenging, as state policies provide less financial aid to relatives who are caregivers than nonrelative foster caregivers (Bloom, Owen, and Covington 2004). Consulting with the child welfare caseworkers available to female offenders can also prove problematic or impossible, as they are often overworked, underresourced, and lacking the training to serve incarcerated mothers adequately. These obstacles create obvious disadvantages for imprisoned mothers, as they ultimately impact their chances of reunifying with their children (Correctional Association of New York 2006).

Relatedly, in a study of incarcerated mothers, Allen, Flaherty, and Ely (2010) reported that a remarkably high number of women were homeless prior to incarceration—their rate of homelessness was twenty-five times higher than that of other local citizens. As the population of female offenders increases, so does the number of incarcerated mothers and familial caregivers. Approximately 70 percent of imprisoned women are mothers, most of whom were the primary caretakers for their children prior to their incarceration (Greenfeld and Snell 1999; Mumola 2000; Phillips and Harm 1997). Incarcerated women and their children experience a lack of support via inadequate, or most often nonexistent, policies within correctional facilities that exacerbate the difficulties associated with separation. A report by the Correctional Association of New York (2006) emphasized the lack of resources available for female offenders, including inefficient visitation and parenting programs, inadequate legal representation, and lack of proximity of a mother's location to that of her child. For example, Bloom and Steinhart (1993) reported that over half of children were found to have never visited their mothers while incarcerated. Among the reasons most cited for the lack of contact with children is geographical distance from the prison (Bureau of Justice Statistics 2000). The consequences of incarceration for mothers and their children are detrimental. As one incarcerated woman described,

> Your children look at you like a stranger. When my son's grandma left him with me he started crying because he didn't know me, and he felt he was being deserted by the only mother he knew. My little girl was older— she was six when I got out. She remembered me a little, but she has never been able to live with me. She and my sister had grown so attached to each other that it would be unfair of me to snatch my daughter up. (Faith and Near 2006, 18)

Low-Income Women and Societal Reentry

The consequences of institutional marginalization persist and continue to influence the lives of female offenders—especially those living in poverty—long after a jail or prison term has been served. Instead of helping women transition into their communities, many state and federal laws impede access to basic necessities, including education and financial assistance:

> Since I was convicted for marijuana, I have to register with the police department in any town I live. When you first come to a new town, in the hope of making a fresh start, it is really frustrating to have to march straight to the police and let them know you are a bad one. You want to make a good impression on a prospective employer, but if you admit that you have been in prison you probably won't be hired, and it's against the law to not admit it. (Faith and Near 2006, 17)

Education

As mentioned, a significant number of incarcerated women have a history of low educational access before entering the criminal justice system. As low-income female offenders reenter the community, the few financial resources previously available to them become even more limited. Legislative policies such as the Higher Education Act of 1998, which was created with the intention of providing accessible financial assistance to disadvantaged students pursuing higher education, denies eligibility for any grant, loan, or work-study assistance to students convicted of drug offenses. Most states even allow employers to deny jobs to anyone with a criminal record, regardless of how much time has passed or the individual's work history or personal circumstances (American Civil Liberties Union 2006).

Public Assistance

Many low-income women released from prison turn to public assistance to help support their reentry into the community, only to find that these resources are unavailable or significantly limited. For example, the Welfare Reform Bill of 1996 not only imposed time limits on the aid that women can receive but has denied services and resources for women with a criminal record, particularly in cases of women convicted on a felony drug-related charge (Mallicoat 2014). Section 115 of the 1996 Welfare Reform Bill, Temporary Assistance for Needy Families

(TANF), stipulates that persons convicted of a state or federal felony offense involving the use or sale of drugs are subject to a lifetime ban on receiving cash assistance and food stamps. This provision applies only to those who are convicted of a drug offense (Allard 2002). The lifetime welfare ban has had a disproportionate impact on female offenders, as women are more susceptible to poverty and are therefore disproportionately represented in the welfare system (Allard 2002). Women who are denied this transitional assistance may not be able to provide shelter and food for themselves and their children while engaging in job training and placement (Mallicoat 2014).

Housing

Low-income women who relied upon public housing for their families before their incarceration are often released to discover that their only opportunities for shelter have disappeared. Women convicted of a drug offense are barred from living in public housing developments and, in some areas, a criminal record can limit the availability of Section 8 housing options (Mallicoat 2014). In 1996, the U.S. federal government implemented the "One Strike Initiative" authorizing local public housing authorities to obtain the criminal conviction records of all adult applicants or tenants. Federal housing policies permit (and in some cases require) public housing authorities, Section 8 providers, and other federally assisted housing programs to deny housing to individuals who have a drug conviction or are suspected of drug involvement (Allard 2002). Drug charges are the only offense type subjected to this ban—even convicted murderers can apply for and receive government benefits following their release (Porter 2012). Mallicoat (2014) estimates that the lifetime ban on assistance affects more than 92,000 women, placing more than 135,000 children of these mothers at risk for future contact with the criminal justice system due to economic struggles. Therefore, female offenders end up resorting to behaviors that led to their interactions with the criminal justice system in the first place. The statistics on recidivism provide evidence in support for this: The 2009 recidivism rate for female offenders in New York State was at 30 percent within three years of release (Correctional Association of New York 2009).

Concluding Comments: Directions for Research and Practice

One of the most obvious ways in which psychologists can support poor adjudicated women is to strengthen their own research contributions in this area. The vulnerability of women in poverty to criminal justice involvement is clear, as is the damaging impact of poverty, incarceration, and their sequellae. More research to document these trends is *not*, therefore, a vital need. Rather, we suggest that psychologists direct their efforts in other directions.

Recommendation #1: Work to highlight the need for gender-sensitive correctional policies and practices.

As summarized by Ney (2015), such practices have evolved in keeping with empirical research focused on male offenders, and do not address the needs and risk factors relevant to women. Incarcerated women face unique discriminatory practices that impact their access to gender-specific treatment while incarcerated, such as access to appropriate health care, mental health needs, and legislative burdens that impact their ability to mother their children. Poverty-related obstacles specific to incarcerated women prevent successful reentry into society, which impacts access to education, public assistance, and housing.

Recommendation #2: Study the current experiences and outcomes of poor women with mental health service providers within the criminal justice system.

Little systematic psychological knowledge currently exists with regard to this work, and the limited research that does exist suggests that service providers are not contributing as much as they could. Recently, a growing body of research has utilized a pathways framework to better understand female criminality. This type of research typically collects data, usually through qualitative interviews, that provide retrospective inquiry into women's life experiences (Schram and Tibetts 2014). This theoretical approach serves to explore incarcerated women's own perspectives on the life factors that have led them to jail or prison, and allows for the identification of themes regarding potential pathways to crime. Mental health practitioners stand to gain a deeper understanding of the needs of incarcerated women through this perspective. Studies utilizing a pathways perspective have reported themes within female offenders' stories, such as lack of familial and social networks, corrupt role models, living conditions permeated with poverty and violence, and multiple forms of ongoing victimization (DeHart 2008). Justice officials can also gain further insight into policy reform via the pathways framework, as many incarcerated women are aware of how their needs could be better met while serving their sentences. Singer and colleagues (1995) found that, when questioned, an overwhelming number of incarcerated women mentioned a need for services such as drug treatment or rehabilitation, mental health counseling, and alcohol counseling within correctional facilities. Similarly, most women described a willingness to participate in drug education/treatment programs, individual mental health counseling, stress management, and health education if these services were available (Green et al. 2005).

Recommendation #3: Develop innovative, socially just practices for use with diverse women that are central to their historical realities.

Van Wormer (2010) emphasized that understanding the familial cultural orientation of female offenders is essential for practitioners working with African American and Latina women in a clinical context. Practitioners must form a personal connection with the women with whom they work, and small-group therapy services can act as a beneficial medium in which clinicians can achieve this type of rapport. Failure to recognize this cultural difference can result in clinicians facing a potentially impenetrable barrier, jeopardizing their ability to experience the client's reality, to understand which services are most needed, and to deliver these services most effectively to women during incarceration (van Wormer 2010). The incorporation of spirituality in working from the Afrocentric framework has also been explored as essential to working with African American women who value tradition, community, and values taught in the church (van Wormer 2010). Faith (1993) outlined methods of Native American ceremonies and healing circles as a means to reinvigorate imprisoned women. Accordingly, the Correctional Service of Canada (2005) allows indigenous people who are incarcerated to practice culturally specific modes of helping. This program includes a peer mentorship system that includes elders in their native community attending parole hearings and assisting in prisoner reentry upon their release from prison.

One of the most detrimental effects of imprisonment on women and their children is the inability to develop close attachments. Programs such as the Parenting Program at the Nebraska Correctional Center for Women (Carlson 1998) was developed in an effort to facilitate secure, healthy attachments between incarcerated women and their children. This program allows incarcerated women to spend an entire day with their children in an uncrowded and private area. These days are spent exclusively between mother and child, creating experiences that are otherwise impossible during general visiting hours, which are supervised, noisy, crowded, and may not allow for mothers to touch or hug their children. Mothers are given the opportunity to develop relationships with their children by spending the day engaged in activities such as baking or playing games. The program also allows for overnight visits. One incarcerated mother explained, "If it weren't for this program, I think I would have left here much the same person I was when I came in—detached, distracted, lost, and broken. . . . My children don't just have their old mom back. They have a much better mother and human being in their lives" (Solinger et al. 2010, 96). Such programs serve as models for innovative psychological interventions in prisons that speak to the realities of diverse women. Developing such services can lead to more effective rehabilitation for women *while* incarcerated, and also allow them to develop social support systems that are necessary for aiding in their successful reentry into society.

Recommendation #4: Use research and practice to combine psychological services with other supports for poor women who are transitioning from incarceration to the community.

Incarcerated women often have family and/or childcare responsibilities as well as diminished employment histories, which helps to explain the 58 percent of women who are rearrested (Cimino et al. 2015). Rearrests often stem from survival needs that are associated with poverty itself, such as difficulty meeting financial obligations or the inability to secure safe housing (Ney 2015). By addressing these issues directly, educational and vocational programming may also serve to improve psychological well-being among poor women in transition. Such a linkage was suggested by focus group members in Foley's (2012) study of incarcerated women, who spoke of such programming as an empowering and hope-inspiring experience: "Being able to start college and have the revelation that I could make it through, that's something that I picked up here. That's been the most beneficial for me" (Foley 2012, 26).

Recommendation #5: Initiate cross-disciplinary collaborations to assess the dynamics of women's criminal justice interactions.

Historically, much of this knowledge has resided in the field of criminology. However, criminologists have often accepted a legal definition of crime that centers on the idea of an individual, male offender, and much of the literature fails to acknowledge the need for gender-sensitive policies, treatment programs, and legislation. Therefore, the unique needs of poor and incarcerated women of color are often overlooked. Fields such as criminology could strengthen their own investigations through the adoption of counseling psychology's approach to understanding the well-being of marginalized groups. Racism exists as a driving force in facilitating the marginalization of women, and is even more detrimental when compounded by the operations of classism and gender discrimination, which perpetuate the cyclical involvement of poor women in the criminal justice system. Counseling psychology research focusing on racial-cultural analyses and social justice–based treatment approaches could contribute greatly to the field of criminology in helping to develop these just practices. Strengthening our research involvements in these new directions can allow psychologists to extend their social justice practice in support of some of society's most vulnerable members: adjudicated women living in poverty, whose crimes are often those of "desperation or survival" (United Way of Calgary 2008, 6).

The recommendations above directly support the implementation of the American Psychological Association's Guidelines for Psychological Practice with Girls and Women, hereafter referred to as the "APA Guidelines" (American Psychological Association 2015). Specifically, Recommendations #1, #2, and #4 support the application of Section (A) of the

APA Guidelines—Diversity, Social Context and Power—which necessitates a framework for the exploration of social identity and gender role socialization issues in diverse areas such as health, education, employment, research, and legal systems. Recommendation #3 supports the implementation of Section (B)—Professional Responsibility—including principles that facilitate culturally sensitive and affirming practices for girls and women. Lastly, Recommendation #5 directly links to Section (C) of the APA Guidelines—Practice Applications—which encourages practitioners to consider the problems of girls and women within the broader sociopolitical context and to employ gender-specific interventions.

As previously discussed, women are the fastest-growing population of inmates in the United States, with an overrepresentation of women living in poverty before their arrest (Golinelli and Minton 2014). Because women in poverty find themselves at the nexus of oppressive societal forces such as classism, gender discrimination, and racism, the feminization of poverty provides a contextual framework in which to understand the marginalization of female offenders. The feminization of poverty influences how and why women come into contact with the law, how likely they are to remain incarcerated after arrest, and how they experience further marginalization as a result of patriarchal and discriminatory institutional practices during and after incarceration. Adequate, gender-specific services for female offenders that address the unique challenges faced at these intersections are necessary to strengthen research contributions in this area and inform gender-sensitive corrections policies and practices. Strengthening our research involvements in these and other new directions can allow psychologists to extend their social justice practice in support of adjudicated women.

REFERENCES

Albelda, Randy, and Chris Tilly. 1997. *Glass Ceilings and Bottomless Pits: Women's Work, Women's Poverty.* Boston: South End.

Alexander, Michelle. 2012. *The New Jim Crow: Mass Incarceration in the Age of Colorblindness.* New York: New Press.

Allard, Patricia. 2002. "Life Sentences: Denying Welfare Benefits to Women Convicted of Drug Offenses," http://www.sentencingproject.org.

Allen, Suzanna, Chris Flaherty, and Gretchen Ely. 2010. "Throwaway Moms: Maternal Incarceration and the Criminalization of Female Poverty." *Journal of Women and Social Work* 25: 160–72.

American Association of University Women. 2014. "The Simple Truth about the Gender Pay Gap," http://www.aauw.org.

American Civil Liberties Union. 2006. "Words from Prison: The Collateral Consequences of Incarceration," https://www.aclu.org.

American Psychological Association. 2015. Guidelines for Psychological Practice with Girls and Women, http://www.apa.org.

Amnesty International USA. 2001. "Women in Prison: A Fact Sheet," http://www.prisonpolicy.org.

Barak, Greg, Paul Leighton, and Jeanne Flavin. 2010. Class, Race, Gender, and Crime: The Social Realities of Justice in America. Lanham, MD: Rowman and Littlefield.

Battle, Cynthia L., Caron Zlotnick, Lisa M. Najavits, Marysol Guttierrez, and Celia Winsor. 2003. "Posttraumatic Stress Disorder and Substance Use Disorder among Incarcerated Women." In Trauma and Substance Abuse: Causes, Consequences, and Treatment of Comorbid Disorders. Edited by Paige Ouimette and Pamela J. Brown, 209–25. Washington, DC: American Psychological Association.

Belle, Deborah, and Joanne Doucet. 2003. "Poverty, Inequality, and Discrimination as Sources of Depression among U.S. Women." Psychology of Women Quarterly 27: 101–13.

Blazer, Daniel G., Ronald C. Kessler, Katherine A. McGonagle, and Marvin S. Swartz. 1994. "The Prevalence and Distribution of Major Depression in a National Community Sample: The National Comorbidity Survey." American Journal of Psychiatry 151: 979–86.

Bloom, Barbara, Meda Chesney-Lind, and Barbara Owen. 1994. "Women in California Prisons: Hidden Victims of the War on Drugs," http://www.cjcj.org.

Bloom, Barbara, Barbara Owen, and Stephanie Covington. 2004. "Women Offenders and the Gendered Effects of Public Policy." Review of Policy Research 21: 31–48.

Bloom, Barbara, and David Steinhart. 1993. "Why Punish the Children? A Reappraisal of Incarcerated Mothers in America," http://www.nccdglobal.org.

Brown, George W., and Patricia M. Moran. 1997. "Single Mothers, Poverty, and Depression." Psychological Medicine 27: 21–33.

Browne, Angela, Brenda Miller, and Eugene Maguin. 1999. "Prevalence and Severity of Lifetime Physical and Sexual Victimization among Incarcerated Women." International Journal of Law and Psychiatry 22: 301–22.

Bullock, Heather E. 1995. "Class Acts: Middle-Class Responses to the Poor." In The Social Psychology of Interpersonal Discrimination. Edited by Bernice E. Lott and Diane Maluso, 118–59. New York: Guilford.

Bureau of Justice Statistics. 2013. "Felony Defendants in Large Urban Counties, 2009 Statistical Tables," http://bjs.gov.

Bureau of Justice Statistics. 2000. "Women Offenders," http://bjs.gov.

Bureau of Justice Statistics. 1999. "Prisoners in 1999," http://www.bjs.gov.

Cahalan, Margaret W. 1986. "Historical Corrections Statistics in the United States, 1850–1984," http://www.bjs.gov.

Carlson, Joseph R. 1998. "Evaluating the Effectiveness of a Live-In Nursery within a Women's Prison." Journal of Offender Rehabilitation 27: 73–85.

Carson, Ann E., and Daniela Golinelli. 2013. "Prisoners in 2012," http://www.bjs.gov.

Carson, Ann E., and William J. Sabol. 2012. "Prisoners in 2011," http://bjs.gov.

Cimino, Andrea N., Natasha Mendoza, Kara Thieleman, Randy Shively, and Kami Kunz. 2015. "Women Reentering the Community: Understanding Addiction and Trauma-Related Characteristics of Recidivism." *Journal of Human Behavior in the Social Environment* 25: 468–76.

Cohen, Thomas H., and Brian A. Reaves. 2006. "Felony Defendants in Large Urban Counties, 2002," http://www.bjs.gov.

Cole, Elizabeth R. 2009. "Intersectionality and Research in Psychology." *American Psychologist* 64: 170–80.

Collins, William C., and Andrew W. Collins. 1996. "Women in Jail: Legal Issues," http://static.nicic.gov.

Correctional Association of New York. 2009. "Women in Prison Project: Women in Prison Fact Sheet," http://www.correctionalassociation.org.

Correctional Association of New York. 2006. "Women in Prison Project: The Punitiveness Report—Hard Hit: The Growth in Imprisonment of Women, 1977–2004," http://csdp.org.

Correctional Service Canada. 2005. "CSC Action Plan in Response to the Report of the Canadian Human Rights Commission," http://www.csc-scc.gc.ca.

Covington, Stephanie S. 2012. "Curricula to Support Trauma-Informed Practice with Women." In *Becoming Trauma Informed*. Edited by Nancy Poole and Lorraine Greaves, 1–8. Toronto: Centre for Addiction and Mental Health.

Covington, Stephanie S., and Barbara Bloom. 2003. "Gendered Justice: Women in the Criminal Justice System." In *Gendered Justice: Addressing Female Offenders*. Edited by Barbara Bloom, 3–23. Durham, NC: Carolina Academic Press.

DeHart, Dana. 2008. "Pathways to Prison: Impact of Victimization in the Lives of Incarcerated Women." *Violence Against Women* 14: 1362–81.

DeHart, Dana, Shannon Lynch, Joanne Belknap, Priscilla Dass-Brailsford, and Bonnie Green. 2014. "Life History of Female Offending: The Roles of Serious Mental Illness and Trauma in Women's Pathways to Jail." *Psychology of Women Quarterly* 8: 138–51.

Donziger, Steven R. 1996. *The Real War on Crime: The Report of the National Criminal Justice Commission*. New York: Harper Perennial.

Entmacher, Joan, Katherine Gallagher Robbins, Julie Vogtman, and Anne Morrison. 2014. "Insecure and Unequal: Poverty and Income among Women and Families, 2000–2013," http://www.nwlc.org.

Faith, Karlene. 1993. *Unruly Women: The Politics of Confinement and Resistance*. Vancouver: Press Gang.

Faith, Karlene, and Anne Near. 2006. *13 Women: Parables from Prison*. Vancouver: Douglas and McIntyre.

Federal Bureau of Prisons. 2009. "State of the Bureau 2009," http://www.bop.gov.

Federal Bureau of Prisons. 2000. "TRIAD Drug Treatment Evaluation Project Final Report of Three-Year Outcomes: Part I," http://www.bop.gov.

Felitti, Vincent J., and Robert F. Anda. 2010. "The Relationship of Adverse Childhood Experiences to Adult Medical Disease, Psychiatric Disorders, and Sexual Behaviour: Implications for Healthcare." In *The Effects of Early Life Trauma on Health and Disease: The Hidden Epidemic.* Edited by Ruth A. Lanius and Eric Vermetten, 77–87. New York: Cambridge University Press.

Felitti, Vincent J., Robert F. Anda, Dale Nordenberg, David F. Williamson, Alison M. Spitz, Valerie Edwards, Mary P. Koss, and James S. Marks. 1998. "Relationship of Childhood Abuse and Household Dysfunction to Many of the Leading Causes of Death in Adults: The Adverse Childhood Experiences (ACE) Study." *American Journal of Preventive Medicine* 14: 245–58.

Foley, Jillian. 2012. "Gender-Responsive Policies and Practices in Maine: What Incarcerated Women at the Women's Center Say They Need from the Criminal Justice System," http://usm.maine.edu.

Fosado, Gisela. 2007. "Women, Prisons, and Change." *Scholar and Feminist Online: The Barnard Center for Research on Women* 5 (3), http://sfonline.barnard.edu.

Freudenberg, Nicholas. 2001. "Jails, Prisons, and the Health of Urban Populations: A Review of the Impact of the Correctional System on Community Health." *Journal of Urban Health* 78: 214–35.

Gabbidon, Shaun L. 2010. *Criminological Perspectives on Race and Crime.* New York: Routledge.

Gabbidon, Shaun L., and Helen T. Greene. 2013. *Race and Crime.* Thousand Oaks, CA: Sage.

Genty, Philip M. 1995. "Termination of Parental Rights among Prisoners: A National Perspective." In *Children of Incarcerated Parents.* Edited by Katherine Gabel and Denise Johnston, 167–82. Lanham, MD: Lexington Books.

Goldberg, Gertrude S., and Eleanor Kremen. 1990. *The Feminization of Poverty: Only in America?* Santa Barbara, CA: Greenwood.

Golinelli, Daniela, and Todd D. Minton. 2014. "Jail Inmates at Midyear 2013—Statistical Tables (Revised)," http://www.bjs.gov.

Green, Bonnie L., Jeanne Miranda, Anahita Daroowalla, and Juned Siddique. 2005. "Trauma Exposure, Mental Health Functioning, and Program Needs of Women in Jail." *Crime and Delinquency* 51: 133–51.

Greene, Susan, Craig Haney, and Aida Hurtado. 2000. "Cycles of Pain: Risk Factors in the Lives of Incarcerated Mothers and Their Children." *Prison Journal* 80: 3–23.

Greenfeld, Lawrence A., and Tracy L. Snell. 1999. "Women Offenders," http://www.bjs.gov.

Halperin, Ronnie, and Jennifer L. Harris. 2004. "Parental Rights of Incarcerated Mothers with Children in Foster Care: A Policy Vacuum." *Feminist Studies* 30: 339–52.

Hills, Holly, Christine Siegfried, and Alan Ickowitz. 2004. "Effective Prison Mental Health Services: Guidelines to Expand and Improve Treatment," http://static.nicic.gov.

Jacobs, Ann L. 2001. "Give 'Em a Fighting Chance: Women Offenders Reenter Society." *Criminal Justice Magazine* 16 (1), http://www.americanbar.org.

James, Doris J., and Lauren E. Glaze. 2006. *Mental Health Problems of Prison and Jail Inmates*, http://bjs.gov.

Johnson, Allan G. 1997. *The Gender Knot: Unraveling Our Patriarchal Legacy*. Philadelphia: Temple University Press.

Jordan, Kathleen B., William E. Schlenger, John A. Fairbank, and Juesta M. Caddell. 1996. "Prevalence of Psychiatric Disorders among Incarcerated Women." *Archives of General Psychiatry* 53: 1048–60.

Jose-Kampfner, Christina. 1995. "Health Care on the Inside." In *Health Issues for Women of Color: A Cultural Diversity Perspective*. Edited by Diane Adams, 164–84. Thousand Oaks, CA: Sage.

Karberg, Jennifer C., and Doris J. James. 2005. *Substance Dependence, Abuse, and Treatment of Jail Inmates, 2002*, http://www.bjs.gov.

Kessler, Ronald C., Amanda Sonnega, Evelyn Bromet, Michael Hughes, and Christopher B. Nelson. 1995. "Posttraumatic Stress Disorder in the National Comorbidity Survey." *Archives of General Psychiatry* 52 (12): 1048–60. doi: 10.1001/archpsyc.1995.03950240066012.

Koons, Barbara A., Josh D. Burrow, Merry Morash, and Tim Bynum. 1997. "Expert and Offender Perceptions of Program Elements Linked to Successful Outcomes for Incarcerated Women." *Crime and Delinquency* 43: 515–32.

Law, Victoria. 2009. *Resistance behind Bars: The Struggles of Incarcerated Women*. Oakland, CA: PM Press.

Legal Momentum: The Women's Legal Defense and Education Fund. 2010. "Ensuring the Economic and Personal Security of Women and Girls," http://www.legalmomentum.org.

Lott, Bernice, and Heather E. Bullock. 2007. *Psychology and Economic Injustice: Personal, Professional, and Political Intersections*. Washington, DC: American Psychological Association.

Mallicoat, Stacy L. 2014. *Women and Crime: A Text/Reader*, 2nd ed. Sage Text/Reader Series in Criminology and Criminal Justice. Thousand Oaks, CA: Sage.

Maruschak, Laura M., and Thomas P. Bonczar. 2013. "Probation and Parole in the United States, 2012." Revised January 21, 2015, http://www.bjs.gov.

Mauer, Marc. 2013. "The Changing Racial Dynamics of Women's Incarceration," http://sentencingproject.org.

Mauer, Marc, Cathy Potler, and Richard Wolf. 1999. "Gender and Justice: Women, Drugs, and Sentencing Policy," http://www.drugpolicy.org.

Maume, David J. 1991. "Child-Care Expenditures and Women's Employment Turnover." *Social Forces* 70: 495–508.

McCall, Leslie. 2005. "The Complexity of Intersectionality." *Signs* 30: 1771–1800.

Messina, Nena, and Christine Grella. 2006. "Childhood Trauma and Women's Health Outcomes: A California Prison Population." *American Journal of Public Health* 96: 1842–48.

Mitchell, Ojmarrh. 2005. "A Meta-Analysis of Race and Sentencing Research: Explaining the Inconsistencies." *Journal of Quantitative Criminology* 21: 439–66.

Morash, Merry, Timothy S. Bynum, and Barbara A. Koons. 1998. "Women Offenders: Programming Needs and Promising Approaches," https://www.ncjrs.gov.

Morris, Suzanne M., Henry J. Steadman, and Bonita M. Veysey. 1997. "Mental Health Services in United States Jails: A Survey of Innovative Practices." *Criminal Justice and Behavior* 24: 3–19.

Mumola, Christopher J. 2000. "Incarcerated Parents and Their Children," http://www.bjs.gov.

National Alliance on Mental Illness. 2011. "Posttraumatic Stress Disorder," http://www.nami.org.

Ney, Becki. 2015. "10 Facts about Women in Jails," http://www.americanjail.org.

Owen, Barbara, and Barbara Bloom. 1995. "Profiling Women Prisoners: Findings from National Surveys and a California Sample." *Prison Journal* 75: 165–85.

Pearce, Diana. 1978. "The Feminization of Poverty: Women, Work, and Welfare." *Urban and Social Change Review* 11: 28–36.

Perry, Barbara. 2009. *Policing Race and Place in Indian Country: Over- and Under-Enforcement.* Critical Perspectives on Crime and Inequality Series. Lanham, MD: Lexington Books.

Phillips, Susan D., and Nancy J. Harm. 1997. "Women Prisoners: A Contextual Framework." *Women and Therapy* 20: 1–9.

Porter, Nicole D. 2012. "The State of Sentencing 2011: Developments in Policy and Practice," http://sentencingproject.org.

Prendergast, Michael L., Jean Wellisch, and Gregory P. Falkin. 1995. "Assessment of and Services for Substance-Abusing Women Offenders in Community and Correctional Settings." *Prison Journal* 75: 240–56.

Reiman, Jeffrey H. 2007. *The Rich Get Richer and the Poor Get Prison.* New York: Pearson.

Richie, Beth E. 2001. "Challenges Incarcerated Women Face as They Return to Their Communities: Findings from Life History Interviews." *Crime and Delinquency* 47: 368–89.

Richie, Beth. 1996. *Compelled to Crime: The Gender Entrapment of Black Battered Women.* New York: Routledge.

Russell-Brown, Katheryn. 1998. *The Color of Crime: Racial Hoaxes, White Fear, Black Protectionism, Police Harassment, and Other Macroaggressions.* New York: NYU Press.

Sanders, Jeannette F., Kevin F. McNeill, Beth M. Rienzi, and Tara-Nicholle B. DeLouth. 1997. "The Incarcerated Female Felon and Substance Abuse: Demographics, Needs Assessment, and Program Planning for a Neglected Population." *Journal of Addictions and Offender Counseling* 18: 41–51.

Schram, Pamela J., and Stephen G. Tibetts. 2014. *Introduction to Criminology: Why Do They Do It?* Thousand Oaks, CA: Sage.

Siefert, Kristine, Phillip J. Bowman, Colleen M. Heflin, Sheldon Danziger, and David R. Williams. 2000. "Social and Environmental Predictors of Maternal Depression in Current and Recent Welfare Recipients." *American Journal of Orthopsychiatry* 70: 510–22.

Siefert, Kristine, Colleen M. Heflin, Mary E. Corcoran, and David R. Williams. 2004. "Food Insufficiency and Physical and Mental Health in Longitudinal Survey of Welfare Recipients." *Journal of Health and Social Behavior* 45: 171–86.

Singer, Mark L., Janet Bussey, Li-Yu Song, and Lisa Lunghofer. 1995. "The Psychosocial Issues of Women Serving Time in Jail." *Social Work* 40: 103–13.

Smith, Laura. 2010. *Psychology, Poverty, and the End of Social Exclusion: Putting Our Practice to Work*. New York: Teachers College Press.

Smith, Laura, Lauren Appio, and Rosa Cho. 2010. "The Feminization of Poverty: Implications for Mental Health Practice." *Women and Mental Disorders* 1: 99–117.

Smyth, Katya Fels, Lisa Goodman, and Catherine Glenn. 2006. "The Full-Frame Approach: A New Response to Marginalized Women Left Behind by Specialized Services." *American Journal of Orthopsychiatry* 76: 489–502.

Solinger, Rickie, Paula C. Johnson, Martha L. Raimon, Tina Reynolds, and Ruby C. Tapia. 2010. *Interrupted Life: Experiences of Incarcerated Women in the United States*. Berkeley: University of California Press.

Steadman, Henry J., Sharon S. Barbera, and Deborah L. Dennis. 1994. "A National Survey of Jail Mental Health Diversion Programs." *Hospital and Community Psychiatry* 45: 1109–13.

Teplin, Linda A., Karen M. Abram, and Gary M. McClelland. 1996. "Prevalence of Psychiatric Disorders among Incarcerated Women: 1. Pretrial Jail Detainees." *Archives of General Psychiatry* 53: 505–12.

United Way of Calgary. 2008. "Crimes of Desperation: The Truth about Poverty-Related Crime," http://www.calgaryunitedway.org.

van Wormer, Katherine. 2010. *Working with Female Offenders: A Gender-Sensitive Approach*. Hoboken, NJ: Wiley.

Wald, Patricia M. 2001. "Why Focus on Women Offenders?" *Criminal Justice* 16: 10–16.

White, Kim. 2008. "Women in Federal Prison: Pathways In, Programs Out." *William and Mary Journal of Women and the Law* 14 (2): 305–18, http://scholarship.law.wm.edu.

Zaitzow, Barbara H. 2010. "Psychotropic Control of Women Prisoners: The Perpetuation of Abuse of Imprisoned Women." *Justice Policy Journal* 7: 2.

Zatz, Marjorie S. 2000. "The Convergence of Race, Ethnicity, Gender, and Class on Court Decision Making: Looking Toward the 21st Century." *Criminal Justice* 3: 503–52.

10

Undocumented Mexican Women in the U.S. Justice System

Immigration, Illegality, and Law Enforcement

ANNA OCHOA O'LEARY

While in detention, the women asked for food and milk
for their children but received nothing. The cells were cold.
Their children trembled with cold: "Mis hijos temblando de
frio." [My children trembled with cold.] For two days they
were with their children, after which the official made good
his threat and their children were taken away. At first their
feelings were mixed. At least their children would be warm,
they consoled themselves.
—Betita and Irma, Nogales, 2007

Undocumented immigrant women, such as Betita and Irma, are increasingly coming into contact with the U.S. justice system. This is due to
ramped-up immigration enforcement efforts throughout the entire
nation (Rocha Romero and Ocegueda Hernández 2013) and the rise in
the number of immigrant women entering the United States since the
late 1990s (Cerrutti and Massey 2001; Donato 1994). The 1994 neoliberal
economic agreement among Mexico, the United States, and Canada—
the North American Free Trade Agreement (NAFTA)—disrupted
subsistence economies in Mexico (Hing 2010; Koulish 2010), which set
into motion one of the largest migrations of undocumented immigrants
in U.S. history. Women were disproportionately impacted by the economic disruption in Mexico brought about by NAFTA (McCarty 2007;
McGuire 2007). This is reflected in the greater rates of women migrating
through Nogales, from 4.9 percent of all immigrants in 1994–1995 to 37.1
percent in 1998 (Castro Luque et al. 2006).

Subsequently, in what is widely acknowledged as a backlash to the dramatic rise in undocumented immigration, thousands of state and municipal-level immigration-control laws have been proposed and/or passed in the United States since 2005 (Harnett 2008; Hing 2014) (see figure 10.1).[1] The anti-immigrant sentiment that this trend reflects has served to normalize general and long-standing disrespect and suspicion towards mostly Mexican immigrants (Romero 2008) and the pervasive and insidious social construction of immigrants as "illegals." The social construction of "illegals" is a product of ideas expressed outside the legal arena, through various discursive practices within the wider society that increasingly couple immigration with criminality, and immigration law with criminal law (Menjívar and Kanstroom 2014; Plascencia 2009; Romero 2008). These ideas contribute to immigration enforcement practices and the harshness immigrants experience when they come in contact with law enforcement (Orraca Romano, Paulo, and Corona Villavivencio 2014; Juby and Kaplan 2011; Capps et al. 2007).

The intersection of the U.S. justice and immigration systems is a significant recent development that has impacted a great number of individuals. It is visible in the implementation of so-called consequence programs such as Operation Streamline. Operation Streamline is a "fast-track" legal procedure that requires the federal criminal prosecution and imprisonment of immigrants in certain jurisdictions as a way to dissuade unlawful entry and reentry into the United States (Lydgate 2010). Through this program, over 17,850 immigrants a year have been prosecuted and have entered the U.S. immigration detention system (Williams 2008). Those prosecuted include immigrants who have been in the United States for many years (Slack et al. 2013). About 7–10 percent of these are women.[2]

Operation Streamline was first put into effect in 2005 in a limited segment of the Del Rio U.S. Border Patrol sector in Texas. Since then, it has been expanded to seven of the nine southern U.S. Border Patrol sectors, including the busiest one, the Tucson sector. Operation Streamline cases are heard *en masse* in federal courts. For example, every day in Tucson Arizona, seventy migrants go through the process of initial appearance, arraignment, plea, and sentencing in a matter of a few hours. During this time, they are shackled at the feet, waist, and wrists (Slack et al.

2013). For their initial appearance in court, they wear the same clothes they wore crossing the border, and are undernourished (Nazarian 2011). The Streamline program has been sharply criticized for eroding due process guarantees (Nazarian 2011).

For immigrant women, the long-term psychological implications of arrest, prosecution, detention, criminalization, and repatriation by the U.S. justice system continue to be underresearched. This is due to several related reasons. One is that after their repatriation or removal from the country, women may return to their communities of origin, where few support services may be available to them. Similarly, for those who successfully make it across the border into the United States and settle into communities as "undocumented,"[3] immigration status complicates their ability to access health services in general (Kaltman et al. 2010; O'Mahony and Donnelly 2013). In such circumstances, silence, minimization, and suppression of traumatic events that are known to produce psychological distress may be the only way to cope. They may also explain the dearth of information about mental health disorders for these populations.

This chapter examines the experiences of recently deported Mexican immigrant women whose encounter with immigration enforcement officials came primarily through arrests by agents and agencies responsible for enforcing U.S. immigration laws. Most of these women came to Albergue San Juan Bosco, a migrant shelter in Nogales, Sonora, Mexico, as a result of their repatriation or deportation, either because they were living in the United States for any number of years and were detained by either the police, the U.S. Border Patrol, or both, or because they were detained as they attempted to cross into the United States. These women shared their stories in the context of a research project carried out in 2006–2007 that aimed to investigate the nature of their interaction with arresting officers (O'Leary 2008, 2009c).

The shelter Albergue San Juan Bosco is located in Nogales, Sonora, Mexico, a border city fifty-five miles south of Tucson, Arizona. Nogales lies within the busiest migration corridor that links Mexico to the United States. The shelter provides housing and food to repatriated migrants who, upon their release from the custody of U.S. immigration enforcement authorities, often find themselves without a support system in the area. It accommodates both male and female migrants who typi-

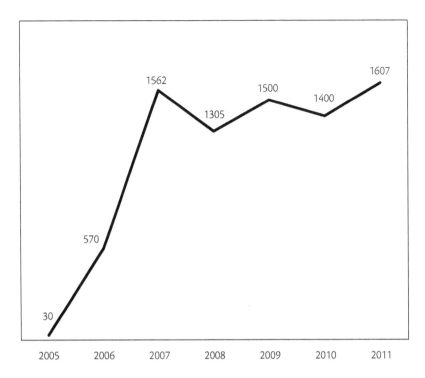

Figure 10.1: Number of State Immigration Laws, Proposed or Passed, 2005–2011. Data compiled from Immigrant Policy Project of the National Conference of State Legislatures.

cally stay only one to two nights before either attempting to reenter the United States or returning to their communities of origin.

Given the transient status of migrants at the shelter, I chose Rapid Appraisal (RA) techniques for the research (Beebe 2001). A semistructured topic guide was used to interview migrant women who arrived at the shelter. This topic guide was designed to investigate women's encounters with the system of immigration enforcement laws, the agents responsible for carrying them out, and their practices. It also helped document more fully the various systems that simultaneously facilitate migration, such as social networks (O'Leary 2012), employer/employee relations, and the organization of the unauthorized crossing of the U.S.-Mexico border (O'Leary 2009a), and those systems intended to impede migration, such as border enforcement (Cunningham and Heyman 2004; O'Leary

2009c). The U.S. system of immigration-control laws and corresponding punitive measures are designed to dissuade and impede the unlawful movement of migrants across the U.S.-Mexico border. For example, in Arizona, migrants who reenter the United States without authorization and are reapprehended serve progressively longer prison terms in the state's immigration detention centers (Alvarado 2004), or may be repatriated to places distant from where they were apprehended, a practice known as the Alien Transfer Exit Program (ATEP) (De Leon 2013).

The interviews with the migrant women captured the different ways in which they experienced the system of immigration enforcement laws, and thus provided the opportunity to reflect on the possible long-term mental health effects of these experiences. Between February 2006 and June 2007, 129 migrant women were interviewed at the shelter. With the consent of those interviewed, the majority of these interviews were tape recorded. Other information-gathering activities included informal conversations during quotidian activities with migrant women, such as eating or assisting with shelter tasks. Interviewing the women was challenging due to the limitations on the time that I had to solicit their cooperation and establish a measure of trust.[4] The shelter opened its doors at 7:00 every evening, and during a span of about three hours, migrants had to register, eat, wash, and bed down for the night. Few stayed beyond one night, virtually eliminating chances to meet anyone a second time to ask follow-up questions. A few women were reluctant to be tape recorded, in which case I wrote notes during the interviews and attempted to write down as many quotations as possible. Fortunately, most were willing if not eager to relate their experiences on a variety of topics. During these months, I visited the shelter every two weeks to conduct interviews.

The profile of the sample of women I interviewed showed that an overwhelming majority were fleeing poverty. They came from Mexico's most economically "disadvantaged" states, which primarily rely on subsistence agriculture (O'Leary 2012): 35.7 percent came from Chiapas, Guerrero, Oaxaca, ranked as the most disadvantaged according to Mexico's Instituto Nacional de Estadística Geografía e Informática (INEGI)[5] and 37.2 percent came from Campeche, Hidalgo, Puebla, San Luis Potosí, Tabasco, Veracruz, ranked as the second most economically disadvantaged group of states (O'Leary 2012). This demographic profile is important for understanding how the U.S. immigration enforcement

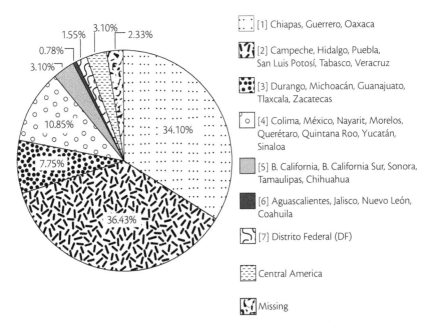

Figure 10.2: Distribution of Sample (N=129), by State Ranking (1–7) from Most Disadvantaged to Least.

system intersects not only with gender but also with class. Moreover, an analysis of data gathered from repatriated migrants along the border in another study found that those who are more likely to be victims of aggression during apprehension are less economically advantaged (Orraca Romano, Paulo, and Corona Villavivencio 2014).

Violent Encounters with U.S. Immigration and Justice Officials

A content analysis of the interviews with migrant women revealed several patterns of mistreatment by immigration enforcement agents after women had been arrested and while under custody in detention facilities:

- 7.14 percent expressed complaints about the manner in which they had been transported to the detention center;
- 25.71 percent expressed complaints about the conditions in the detention center facility;

- 10 percent were physically abused by a U.S. Border Patrol agent;
- 21.43 percent witnessed someone else being physically abused by a U.S. Border Patrol agent;
- 10 percent were verbally abused by a U.S. Border Patrol agent;
- 10.71 percent witnessed someone else being verbally abused by U.S. Border Patrol.

The narratives, translated from Spanish, revealed that the women experienced both physical and psychological trauma. The sample included a total of forty-five reported incidents in which they witnessed or were victim of some form of physical or psychological abuse while under U.S. Border Patrol custody. They also reported fifty-five negative experiences in U.S. detention centers, mostly related to the lack of food, extreme cold, and unsanitary conditions. For example, one migrant woman, Elizabeth, witnessed the physical abuse of her husband at the hands of a border patrol agent, and she herself was subjected to abusive conditions while in detention. She explained that after the group of migrants that she and her husband had been a part of crossed near Sásabe, Arizona, they caught their ride, but while on the way to Phoenix they were stopped by a U.S. Border Patrol agent. At that time she witnessed a border patrol agent beat up her husband because he tried to run. Later, in detention, she observed that the officers seemed to enjoy making migrants suffer by ignoring their requests to go to the bathroom. She and others were detained for about nine hours and were not given any food.

In a separate incident, another migrant woman, Isabel, related that when the border patrol agent found them in the desert, some of the women and men tried to run, and that the agents beat them up, threw them to the ground, and kicked them and punched them. They too were denied food and drink at the detention center. Isabel referred to the detention center as the *"perrera,"* Spanish for "kennel"—a metaphor commonly used by migrants. The border patrol truck has also been referred to by this name. Migrants have also referred to the outdoor detention yards as *"gallineras,"* Spanish for "chicken coops." The coyotes who guide them through the desert are often referred to as *"polleros,"* Spanish for "those who care for chickens" (O'Leary 2009a). The self-deprecating nature of these metaphors indicates the extent to which migrants have become dehumanized (Santa Ana 1999). This discursive practice is known

to occur in racialized spaces where inequality is articulated and reproduced. Placed in historical context, labeling used to dehumanize and
objectify Mexican migrant populations can be traced to the end of the
Bracero Program when it became common to refer to those who entered
the United States to work in ranches and fields as "wetbacks" (Plascencia
2009), "muds," or "illegals" (Rodriguez and Paredes 2014). As Rodriguez
and Paredes (2014) argue, such derogatory labeling strips migrants of
their human qualities, normalizes their harsh and cruel treatment by
immigration-control officers, and prepares them for large-scale criminal
processing in justice systems designed to achieve expediency by operat-
ing in assembly-line fashion.

The narratives of the immigrant women I interviewed at the shelter
illustrate how ideas about immigrants and immigration materialize in
callous disregard and rough treatment by agents when they arrest migrants. Antonia and Cecilia[6] were two women from the Mexican state
of Puebla who crossed into the United States at a remote place in the
desert near Sásabe, Arizona. Sásabe is one of six ports of entry in Arizona. Much of the area north and east of Sásabe is within the remote and
isolated Buenos Aires National Wildlife Refuge. For this reason, Sásabe
has been a major gateway for unauthorized border crossers. On the evening we met, the women described their encounter with the U.S. Border
Patrol and their experience in short-term detention.

> ANTONIA: We were all resting, a total of sixty persons, when the Bor-
> der Patrol came walking through the desert, and, well, they caught us
> sleeping. We were only about ten minutes from where we would be
> picked up, or so the guide told us. We had walked three nights and
> three days. First four of them came. They were very angry and they
> treated us very badly. They spit on us, yelled at us, they spoke among
> themselves, humiliating us. One grabbed me by my hair and they
> threw me down and kicked me in the stomach. I think that because
> women were mixed in with the men, I think that he thought I was
> a man. I complained, telling him that I was not a man, but he just
> shoved me down and yelled at me. They also beat up a young man
> terribly, and his friend. Even one of their own fellow officers scolded
> him and told him to let us alone.
>
> O'LEARY: Can you tell me what the officer looked like?

ANTONIA: He wasn't very tall. He looked like a Chicano and all he
said were vulgarities. There were two Chicanos because they spoke
Spanish.

CECILIA: There were two persons who were Latino. It is the Latinos
who devalue being Latino. When I was detained the first time, it was
a Chicano *migra* [border patrol agent], and he hit me against a pipe,
and I heard him say "son of a bitch," and he put his knee on my waist
to handcuff me.

O'LEARY: So then what happened?

ANTONIA: So then they put us all together and told us to spread our
legs, as much as we could, then they stuck us all together, one behind
another, men and women alike, and they dragged us along the
ground, with the dogs at our side.

CECILIA: That is how they brought us down the hill, so that we would
be picked up, and to count us, they sat us all down. There everyone
was equal.

ANTONIA (incredulously): But opening up our legs? And putting
one man inside of the other, one behind and one in front, men and
women?

CECILIA: And that is how they dragged us, on our *nalgas* [rear ends],
for about five minutes.

ANTONIA: That is how they detained us until about two, three in the
morning. Then we asked them for water when we were inside the
detention yard, and they told us to drink out of the hose. And then
when we were hungry . . . the truth is that food didn't come until
very late, about three in the afternoon. They fed us at around three,
and they would say that if we asked for food, that they would throw
us in prison because it is only there that we would be fed because
they did not have food for us. The truth is that we were treated very
badly.

The case of Betita and Irma, whose story was introduced at the beginning of this chapter, illustrates the psychological trauma that may
result from detention. Betita and Irma, both from the Mexican state of
Veracruz, left their communities fleeing poverty. They did not know
each other prior to departing Veracruz. Neither had family in the United
States, but Irma had a friend in Phoenix, Arizona, who had encour-

aged her to come to the North where she could work and make enough money to support her children. The two women had been walking near Sásabe, Arizona, for about fifteen minutes when they were picked up by the car that would take them to Phoenix. Betita had her small daughter with her, and Irma had her four small children. After about five minutes of being on the road, the car was stopped by a border patrol agent, who then arrested them and transported them to a detention center.

When I met the two women at the shelter, they had just been released after twenty-eight days in detention. They were tearful, confused, and upset. When they were apprehended, their hands and feet were tied up, with chains around their hands, waist, and feet. She says the immigration officers did not care that the chains were really tight. When they pleaded to be released, the officer replied that they deserved their punishment for coming to this country illegally.

Because of their distressed state, it took me a while to understand that they had been detained to serve as material "witnesses" in the legal case against their smuggler. The driver of the auto in which they were passengers was supposedly testifying against the smuggler. In 2005, lawmakers in Arizona passed an "anti-coyote" smuggling law[7] in response to the increase in smuggling activity through the state, some of which had resulted in a growing number of migrants being stranded in the desert, many of whom succumbed to death due to dehydration. The case of these two women may represent one of the first attempts to implement this law.

While in detention, Betita and Irma were pressed for information about the smuggler, a woman whom they had never met. At first, immigration officials threatened them with taking their children as a way to elicit their cooperation. While in detention, the women asked for food and milk for their children but received nothing. The cells were cold. Their children trembled with cold: "Mis hijos temblando de frio." For two days they were with their children, after which the official made good his threat. Their children were taken away. They were told that the kids were going to be placed with families (presumably with foster parents). Irma protested, telling them that they could not do that with her kids because they were Mexicanos. The women were tormented by their children's cries, which continued to ring in their ears. Another woman in detention, who was later released, contacted the Mexican consulate about Betita and

Irma's children. The Mexican consulate was able to locate Irma's children and to turn them over to Irma's mother. Irma was relieved at this news. She was able to contact one of her children with a calling card that she was given. Betita, on the other hand, said that she had signed off custody of her daughter to her father; however, she was worried about what was going to happen because he was so poor that it was uncertain whether he would be able to travel to the border to pick up her daughter. She later heard that Irma's mom had taken her daughter.

According to the women, the immigration officer told them they were going to release the driver who had transported them (a young "gringo") because he was supposedly a minor, but they wanted information about the woman who acted as the smuggler. The women feared that they were being forced to confess something they had no knowledge of. Irma related what they had said to the officer:

> But how is it that he wants us to tell him the truth if in fact we are telling the truth, we do not know the woman, we do not know her [. . . .] "Sir: We cannot lie to you and you want us to lie [. . .] that yes, we did know the boy that brought us across the border, but we did not know the 'gringo,' the boy who was driving."

The officer insisted that the women needed to testify because the suspect was a drug addict and criminal. He badgered the women and kept demanding that they confess that they knew the smuggler. They threatened the women by telling them that if they did not speak the truth, they would take away their children.

Betita was inconsolable that her daughter had been taken away. She was so sick with grief that she was taken to a medic while in detention. Irma feared for her, saying that she became unrecognizable with grief. Even as they were transferred to the second detention center, they kept hearing—or imagined that they heard—their children crying.

Biases, Micro-aggressions, and Immigration Enforcement Practices

The practices described in the women's narratives rest on the uncritical view that undocumented immigrants are criminal (Rodriguez and

Paredes 2014) and therefore less deserving than those who are legally present in the United States, and therefore "law-abiding." The perception that such arrestees are criminal, and therefore undeserving, gives rise to their unjust and often overly harsh mistreatment by those in positions of power, who may harbor biases based on one or more social identities, such as ethnicity, race, gender, sexual orientation, or religion (Nadal et al. 2014).

At the heart of this unjust and often overly harsh mistreatment of immigrants are spaces that provide opportunities for enforcement officials to perpetuate "micro-aggressions." Micro-aggressions are hostile, derogatory, and insulting slights that may or may not be intentional (Milovanovic and Russell 2001; Nadal et al. 2014). They target individuals who belong to racialized or minority groups. Although they can take place anywhere, they often happen behind closed doors, outside of the public purview, in interrogation rooms and jail cells where officials have opportunities to abuse their discretionary power during their interactions with arrestees (Milovanovic and Russell 2001). Micro-aggressions are committed by individuals (such as law enforcement officials) who, as members of the larger society, harbor and share biases that work to normalize and even encourage the dehumanization and mistreatment of those they arrest. Micro-aggressions are "everyday instances of harm" that work to maintain differences and inequality (Milovanic and Russell 2001). They have also been shown to have consequences on the mental health of victims (Nadal et al. 2014).

The narratives of the immigrant women I interviewed shed some light on the micro-aggressions that take place where women are under the control of U.S. immigration control agents: the detention cells and the isolated areas of the Arizona desert that are outside of the public eye. Micro-aggressions are reflected in the patterns of mistreatment the women experienced in the hands of immigration enforcement agents:

- Migrants reported on the harsh manner in which they had been transported to the detention center. Migrants regarded incidents of excessive jolting while in transit to detention centers in border patrol vehicles as intentional and mean-spirited.
- Migrants complained about the conditions in the detention center facility, such as not having access to restroom facilities and excessive temperature.

Again, these were regarded by migrants as intentional and designed to make their experience as unpleasant and uncomfortable as possible.

- During arrest and while under custody, migrants regarded their treatment at the hands of U.S. Border Patrol agents as unnecessarily rough and abusive. They also witnessed others being physically abused by U.S. Border Patrol agents.
- Migrants suffered or witnessed unnecessary verbal abuse by U.S. Border Patrol agents. Most considered that this abuse was intended to unnecessarily dehumanize and degrade them.

These mistreatments are not isolated incidents but routine, subtle, and normalized events that denote the biases of the perpetrators—biases that are acted upon freely once the perpetrator is out of the public eye. For example, Milovanic and Russell (2001) argue that law enforcement's targeted surveillance of Blacks who are going about their daily business communicates that Blacks, by virtue of their membership in a racial group, are dishonest and not credible, and therefore undeserving of civility. Racial biases and micro-aggressions are processes that perpetuate the differential treatment of racial minorities under the law. They also explain why racial minorities are more likely to be charged with an offense and to receive harsher sentences compared to Whites.

The intimidation tactics used by Border Patrol agents against Betita and Irma, as well as the acts of abuse the women witnessed while in custody, are examples of micro-aggressions in the context of immigration enforcement. They have become normative behaviors because they take place outside of the public purview and thus "enjoy" impunity. News reports have provided evidence of the daily instances and normalization of harm that occur under the supervision of immigration officials. In June of 2015, an incident involving the shooting and death of nineteen immigrants led to an internal investigation of the U.S. Border Patrol; all but three agents were absolved of any crime (Bennett 2015).[8] Also in June 2015, the American Civil Liberties Union (ACLU) filed a lawsuit on behalf of three immigrants—one man and two women—who claimed they were denied food, adequate clothing, and sleep while in custody. These are not unique circumstances: Reports indicate that immigrant detainees are kept in custody for at least twice the limit of time allowed to process their cases; are locked up for days in overcrowded and unsanitary holding cells, without basic hygiene items such as soap, toilet paper, and sanitary napkins; and are stripped of their outer layers of clothing and forced to suffer in excessive cold temperatures, without beds, bedding, sleep, and medical care (Fischer 2015).

The Impact of Immigration and Justice Practices on Women Migrants' Mental Health

To understand migration-related experiences and their relationship to mental health outcomes, it is imperative to examine the role of the broader social contexts (Kayali and Iqbal 2012). In the case of migrants, immigration control—its measures, enforcement practices, and procedures—provides the context. These would include environments where immigrants contend with a militarized enforcement climate, such as that found in the U.S.-Mexico border region, as well as the micro-agressions that are integral to the experience. The research by Nadal and colleagues (2014) indicates that racial micro-agressions are correlated with negative mental health outcomes, ranging from immediate distress to the manifestation of depressive symptoms. In addition, although little is known about the long-term impact of immigrants' dehumanizing and violent experience with the U.S. legal and immigration systems, a growing number of scholars in the emerging field of immigrant health have expressed concerns about the effects of justice practices on a range of outcomes critical to human development and well-being, including health and education. For example, Sabo and colleagues (2014) and Carvajal and colleagues (2013) identified specific immigration-related stressors linked to the militarization of the border region, such as experiencing or witnessing acts of aggression, use of excessive force by immigration officials, and fear of being separated from family. Mary Romero (2008) has argued that immigration enforcement practices are designed to publicly humiliate and further stigmatize immigrants. These practices also induce shame among nonimmigrant relatives and children, but equally importantly, they routinely occur as family members carry out their routines, such as going to and from otherwise safe places like work, shopping, and schools. This induces fear, restricting the movement of immigrant and nonimmigrant relatives and their employment opportunities (see also Nuñez and Heyman 2007). Such limitations are known to cause stress (Valdez, Abegglen, and Hauser 2013), manifested in feelings of anger, humiliation, and suffering (Sabo et al. 2014). Capps and colleagues (2007) found that families affected by the Postville immigration raid subsequently had to contend with unemployment and the inability to provide for their families. Persistent or perceived threats of immigration enforcement raids also subject children to fear and trauma that disrupt schooling (Capps et al. 2007). Rabin's (2014) study of immigrant women in long-term detention highlighted the extreme stress and anxiety mothers experience as relates to the custody of their children, when facing deportation. Rabin's (2014) report also described the mothers' fear of giving out information about close family members who might be able to take care of their children in the United States but who might also be undocumented, which could lead to the removal of the children and the termination of parental rights of migrant mothers.

Consistent with these findings are results from research by the community organization No More Deaths, based in Tucson, Arizona. This humanitarian group has for many years surveyed recently repatriated migrants in Nogales, Sonora, and documented abuses by the U.S. Border Patrol, issuing a report on the state of health services for deported immigrants (No More Deaths 2011). The report indicated that the migrants experienced high levels of stress: On a scale of one to ten, with ten indicating "most distressed," the respondents had an average score of 8.27 (No More Deaths 2011). In addition, greater distress was correlated with more time living in the United States (No More Deaths 2011). The psychological literature indicates that stressful life events, including poverty, are associated with the onset of mental health disorders, in particular depression (Kayali and Iqbal 2012) and posttraumatic stress disorder (PTSD) (Kaltman et al. 2010). Research on immigrant women shows that they are increasingly exposed to traumatic events, including rape, attempted rape, sexual abuse by police and immigration authorities, physical violence, and other dangerous situations that are part of the migration experience (Falcon 2001; Monteverde García 2004; O'Leary 2009a, 2009b, 2012; Ruiz Marrujo 2009; Steller 2001; Urquijo-Ruiz 2004). These events play a critical role in the development of depressive symptoms, after the migration journey has taken place and after the migrants have settled in the United States (Kaltman et al. 2010). Traumatic experiences may have a lasting effect on the migrants' health and may require long-term health care management and medical treatment over time (Ornelas and Perreira 2011). Kaltman and colleagues (2010) found that 79 percent of immigrant women with depression only and 100 percent of women with both depression and PTSD reported a history of trauma, and that comorbidity is more likely to result from multiple exposures to traumatic events that may have occurred in the country of origin or during the migration process. The psychological impact of the hardships experienced during the migration process is also captured in Ornelas and Perreira's (2011) survey. In this survey, 84 percent of the respondents were women, and two-thirds of these women were undocumented immigrants. This study looked at the traumatic effects of robbery, sexual and physical abuse, and illness—experiences commonly encountered in migration—but the authors did not provide information about the impact of abuses by officials responsible for enforcing immigration laws. Future research is needed to understand the mental health consequences of harsh and even abusive immigration enforcement tactics for immigrant women, especially in light of the research by Nadal and colleagues (2014) that demonstrates that micro-aggressions (both perceived and real) can lead to negative mental health symptoms, such as depression, anxiety, and negative affect.

A few studies have also highlighted the familial and environmental risk factors that are associated with depression among immigrant women (Kayali and Iqbal 2012). Whether in the middle of the migratory journey or in settlement communities, what is at stake for immigrants is their ability to provide for families. The inability to do so carries with it a psychological price: Immigrants may experience a sense of entrapment (Núñez and Heyman 2007; Sabo et al. 2014) and intensified feelings of loneliness and alienation (Salgado et al. 2014). In addition, separation from children and spouses due to migration has been found to contribute to depression after immigrants settle in communities in the United States (Ornelas and Perreira 2011). Betita's story illustrates the importance of familial factors as relates to women's mental health: Her concern over her father's poverty and what that implied for her daughter's safety and well-being could account for her state of mind while in detention.

In tracing the migration of women engaged in the tomato industry, Barndt (2007) has referred to the Marxist concept of "alienation" to advance our understanding of how over time and geography, industrial agriculture, fueled by free trade principles, capitalizes on the displacement of subsistence farmers. As women are dislodged from the land as their means of production, they are led away from collective endeavors that define households and families, including important reproductive activities (Barndt 2007). Leaving family behind sets into motion processes by which social cohesion—and the benefits this provides—is undermined. It has been characterized as a "fracturing experience" whereby the search for better opportunities splinters domestic units (McGuire 2007). In the survey conducted by No More Deaths (2011), family disintegration was an important concern. With important income-earning activities and the ability to provide for the material needs of families impeded by systems of immigration enforcement, women are at risk for hopelessness and depression (Marsiglia et al. 2011).

Recent studies have also shown that when migration is coupled with discrimination and harsh treatment, migrant women are at greater risk of experiencing depressive symptoms than women who have not had a migration experience (Salgado et al. 2014). Although an immigrant who was apprehended by a border patrol official may not have been personally attacked by an official, witnessing the aggression of a loved one (like Elizabeth, quoted previously in this chapter about the border patrol's attack on her husband) is a traumatic event that may result in the development of depressive symptoms.

There have been numerous calls from the mental health professions for studies that take into account the broader social context of psychological disorders. This would include the role of mutually constitutive determinants of discrimination, such as social status, class, race, and stigma, on mental health outcomes. This "intersectional" approach to mental health research not only is attentive to institutional patterns of unequal power relations that contribute to minority health disparities but also promises to lay bare the roles that institutional actors and policies play in racializing immigrant groups, producing hostile and even violent environments that have an adverse impact on migrants' mental health outcomes (Viruell-Fuentes, Miranda, and Abdulrahim 2012; Carvajal et al. 2013).

Towards Proactive Strategies to Mitigate Harm

More and more undocumented immigrant women with long-standing connections in the communities where they have settled are subjected to immigration enforcement (Rocha Romero and Ocegueda Hernández 2013). Immigration enforcement is becoming more common in places far from the border, thus increasing the likelihood that more migrants will come in contact with immigration authorities and the U.S. justice system. In this way, nonborder populations may experience the same legal practices and abuse by authorities that populations in the border region have long experienced,[9] such as being pulled over by a police officer for a minor traffic violation or a broken taillight, being the subject of further inquiry, and subsequently being turned over to an immigration enforcement officer (Rocha Romero and Ocegueda Hernández 2013). Moreover, given the rising number of women migrating to the United States, it is essential to study current justice interventions and to produce empirical knowledge that will help reduce the likelihood that more women will suffer adverse health outcomes as a result of increasing efforts to enforce immigration laws. With this in mind, the literature suggests some strategies to mitigate harm.

Recommendation #1: Conduct multilateral, collaborative research on immigration and mental health outcomes.

Existing research tends to have a unilateral view of immigration wherein borders are defined as spaces that separate nations and their populations from outsiders (O'Leary, Deeds, and Whiteford 2013). A binational or multilateral approach to immigration research is better suited to identifying the factors that affect communities on both sides of the U.S.-Mexico border. It calls for collaboration between government stakeholder agencies, consulate services, community health workers, and nongovernmental social service agencies in the United States and Mexico. It also requires sharing reports on mental health resources and trends; developing metrics for documenting trends and program outcomes; identifying and providing mechanisms for filing grievances; and addressing systemic failures in the justice delivery system (O'Leary, Deeds, and Whiteford 2013).

Recommendation #2: Adopt a holistic approach to mental health assessment.

Mental health service providers should first be aware of the link between micro-aggressions and mental health (Nadal et al. 2014) and use assessment strategies that take into consideration the broader social determinants of psychological disorders related to immigration. For example, they may use instruments that measure the effects of trauma, violence, isolation, humiliation, and degradation by authorities, as well as low self-esteem and feelings of frustration that come from individuals' inability to provide material support to their family. A holistic approach to mental health assessment would capture vital information about individuals' premigration and postmigration contexts that could be used to select interventions to reduce stressors and prevent more debilitating psychological disorders.

Recommendation #3: Evaluate availability of social support networks and community resources for immigrant women.

Border regions are highly dynamic, with highly transited nodes of social interaction in a constant state of flux. This is especially true on the Mexican side of the U.S.-Mexico border, where migrants often find themselves stranded after being removed from the United States. Accordingly, there is a need for ongoing appraisal of the region in terms of available resources to mitigate the potential damaging effect of isolation, alienation, and hopelessness. Women are particularly vulnerable to victimization as a subgroup of the total immigrant population. For women immigrants, building extra-familial networks that can increase access to resources is hampered by cultural norms (O'Leary 2012). Women's isolation, often within the confines of households, means that family members and husbands in particular can exert pressure on wives and daughters to abide by gender-specific norms, thus limiting their mobility and access to resources (Silvey and Elmhirst 2003). Municipalities should thus invest in periodic needs assessments designed to identify and update the resources available in the area, and through the use of social media technology and in collaboration with local stakeholders (using community-based participatory research methods) disseminate this information proactively to immigrant families, with particular attention to female members of households.

Recommendation #4: Create interdisciplinary research partnerships.

With increased migration, highly transited nodes of social interaction introduce different cultural understandings of mental health, including the stigma often associated with mental disorders. Stigma results in the underutilization of mental health services and counseling; it also obfuscates understanding of the debilitating impact mental disorders may have on individuals and families. Because mental illness is a frequent concern of both scientific researchers and various administrative officials, research should include interventions using community outreach and community health workers and cross-disciplinary partnerships between health sciences and social sciences. Such collaborations will allow researchers to better grasp the relationship between psychological conditions and sociocultural environments and structures.

These recommendations are consistent with the American Psychological Association's (2007) Guidelines for Psychological Practice with Women and Girls. In particular, they provide directions for increasing awareness and knowledge of the sociopolitical and geopolitical contexts in which women's and girls' complex life experiences take form and meaning. Transnational and interdisciplinary research on Mexican women's migration experiences will yield valuable insight into the intersection of immigration, race, geography (e.g., rural or urban residence), class, and gendered socialization as it affects these women's mental health needs and outcomes, and may be used to design gender-sensitive programming for immigrant women involved in the justice system.

Conclusion

This chapter has highlighted the harms that undocumented immigrant women experience in the U.S. immigration control and justice systems. As efforts to identify and remove immigrants from the country intensify, undocumented immigrant women increasingly come in contact with law enforcement officials, prosecutors, detention facilities, lawyers, and judges, primarily through those connected with enforcing U.S.

immigration laws. At issue are the ways in which unsubstantiated negative assumptions and social constructs about immigrants as criminals work to influence the practices of those responsible for upholding the rule of law.

This chapter also examined the little research available on immigration and mental health to point out some of the possible long-term psychological outcomes of immigrant women's interaction with the U.S. justice system. The review of the literature available on the U.S. side of the border indicated that long-term mental health disorders may be attributed to postmigration stress, and more particularly, to the traumatic events experienced during migration and settlement in the United States. The dearth of research on the Mexican side of the border makes it difficult to assess the psychological needs of women who have been deported and repatriated to their communities of origin. It also makes it difficult to determine what support services, if any, are available. In sum, more research is needed to advance understanding of the mental health needs of immigrant women and to develop culturally and gender-sensitive interventions on both sides of the U.S.-Mexico border that will mitigate the harms they experience during the migration journey.

NOTES

1 See also chapter 7 in Koulish (2010) for a history of the development of state and local laws and ordinances.

2 According to personal communications between the author and the Secretaria de Relaciones Externales, July 13–Oct. 19, 2010.

3 The term "undocumented," while ambiguous, has real and symbolic consequences for those living in the United States. Immigrants are "undocumented" if they entered the United States without official authorization or may have entered legally but subsequently overstayed the term limit of their visa. For an in-depth analysis of this term, see Plascencia (2009).

4 For more on the range of methodological challenges that border researchers contend with when conducting research among vulnerable undocumented immigrants, see the volume by O'Leary, Deeds, and Whiteford (2013).

5 INEGI is the equivalent of the U.S. Census Bureau in Mexico.

6 The names of the women interviewed have been changed to protect their privacy.

7 The 2005 smuggling law has since been struck down as part of the Obama administration's challenge of the 2010 SB 1070, in part because the law had come under heavy criticism for being used to charge migrants, rather than their smugglers, with conspiring to smuggle themselves across the border (Billeaud 2014).

8 The three cases not absolved were pending as of this writing.

9 In 1975, in *United States v. Brignoni-Ponce*, the U.S. Supreme Court found that the "Mexican appearance" of the driver and passengers was one of several factors that could be used in combination with proximity to the border to warrant stopping and questioning the driver and passengers. The Court relied on a statute of the Immigration and Nationality Act that provides any officer of the (then) INS the power without warrant to interrogate "any alien or person believed to be an alien" (Perez 2011). A year later, in 1976, in another Supreme Court case, *United States v. Martinez-Fuentes*, the tactics of stopping and searching people in efforts to detain all individuals entering the country "illegally" was seen as an extension of the border patrolling. The Court upheld these tactics because of the perceived threat of a growing "problem" of "illegal" immigrants in the border region and in the country as a whole. Later, in 1996, Section 287(g) was added to the Immigration and Nationalization Act by the Illegal Immigration Reform and Immigrant Responsibility Act, which authorized the federal government to enter into agreements with state and local law enforcement agencies, permitting these to perform immigration law enforcement functions.

REFERENCES

Alvarado, Jeanette E. 2004. "The Federal Consequences of Criminal Convictions: Illegal Reentry after Removal." Unpublished manuscript prepared for the State Bar of Arizona.

American Psychological Association. 2007. Guidelines for Psychological Practice with Girls and Women. Accessed December 15, 2015, http://www.apa.org.

Barndt, Deborah. 2007. *Tangled Routes: Women, Work, and Globalization on the Tomato Trail.* Lanham, MD: Rowman and Littlefield.

Beebe, James. 2001. *Rapid Assessment Process: An Introduction.* Walnut Creek, CA: AltaMira.

Bennett, Brian. 2015. "Border Agents Cleared in Shootings." *Arizona Daily Star*, June 16.

Billeaud, Jacques. 2014. "Arizona Immigrant Smuggling Law Struck Down." *Washington Times*, November 8, http://www.washingtontimes.com.

Capps, Randy, Rosa Maria Castañeda, Ajay Chaudry, and Robert Santos. 2007. "Paying the Price: The Impact of Immigration Raids on America's Children," http://www.urban.org.

Carvajal, Scott C., Clara Kibor, Deborah Jean McClelland, Maia Ingram, Jill Guernsey de Zapien, Emma Torres, Floribella Redondo, Kathryn Rodriguez, Raquel Rubio-Goldsmith, and Joel Meister. 2013. "Stress and Sociocultural Factors Related to Health Status among US–Mexico Border Farmworkers." *Journal of Immigrant and Minority Health* 16 (6): 1–7. doi: 10.1007/s10903-013-9853-1.

Castro Luque, Ana Lucía, Jaime Olea Miranda, and Blanca E. Zepeda Bracamonte. 2006. *Cruzando el Desierto: Construcción de una Tipología para el Análisis de la Migración en Sonora.* Hermosillo, Sonora, Mexico: El Colegio de Sonora.

Cerrutti, Marcela, and Douglas S. Massey. 2001. "On the Auspices of Female Migration from Mexico to the United States." *Demography* 38 (2): 187–201.

Cunningham, Hilary, and Josiah Heyman. 2004. "Introduction: Mobilities and Enclosures at Borders." *Identities: Global Studies in Culture and Power* 11 (3): 289–302. doi: 10.1080/10702890490493509.

De Leon, Jason. 2013. "The Efficacy and Impact of the Alien Transfer Exit Programme: Migrant Perspectives from Nogales, Sonora, Mexico." *International Migration* 51 (2): 10–23. doi: 10.1111/imig.12062.

Donato, Katherine M. 1994. "Current Trends and Patterns of Female Migration: Evidence from Mexico." *International Migration Review* 27 (4): 748–72.

Falcon, Sylvanna. 2001. "Rape as a Weapon of War: Advancing Human Rights for Women at the U.S.-Mexico Border." *Social Justice* 28 (2): 31–51.

Fischer, Howard. 2015. "Lawsuit: Many Border Patrol Detainees Mistreated." *Capitol Media Services/Arizona Daily Star*, June 20, http://tucson.com.

Harnett, Helen M. 2008. "State and Local Anti-Immigrant Initiatives: Can They Withstand Legal Scrutiny?" *Widener Law Journal* 17: 365–82.

Hing, Bill Ong. 2014. "Developing a New Mind-Set on Immigration Reform." In *Constructing Immigrant "Illegality": Critiques, Experiences, and Responses.* Edited by Cecilia Menjivar and Dan Kanstroom, 353–79. New York: Cambridge University Press.

Hing, Bill Ong. 2010. *Ethical Borders: NAFTA, Globalization, and Mexican Migration.* Philadelphia: Temple University Press.

Juby, Cindy, and Laura E. Kaplan. 2011. "Postville: The Effects of an Immgration Raid." *Families in Society* 92 (2): 147–53.

Kaltman, Stacey, Mihriye Mete, Nawar Shara, and Jeanne Miranda. 2010. "Trauma, Depression, and Comorbid PTSD/Depression in a Community Sample of Latina Immigrants." *Psychological Trauma* 2 (1): 31–39.

Kayali, Tamara, and Furhan Iqbal. 2012. "Making Sense of Melancholy: Subcategorisation and the Perceived Risk of Future Depression." *Health, Risk, and Society* 14 (1): 171–89.

Koulish, Robert E. 2010. *Immigration and American Democracy: Subverting the Rule of Law.* New York: Routledge.

Lydgate, Joanna. 2010. "Assembly-Line Justice: A Review of Operation Streamline," https://www.law.berkeley.edu.

Marsiglia, Flavio F., Stephen Kulis, Hilda Garcia Perez, and Monica Parsai. 2011. "Hopelessness, Family Stress, and Depression among Mexican-Heritage Mothers in the Southwest." *Health and Social Work* 36 (1): 7–18.

McCarty, Dawn. 2007. "The Impact of the North American Free Trade Agreement (NAFTA) on Rural Children and Families in Mexico: Transnational Policy and Practice Implications." *Journal of Public Child Welfare* 1 (4): 105–23.

McGuire, Sharon. 2007. "Fractured Migrant Families." *Family and Community Health* 30 (3): 178–88.

Menjívar, Cecilia, and Daniel Kanstroom, 2014. "Introduction—Immigrant "Illegality": Constructions and Critiques." In *Constructing Immigrant "Illegality": Critiques, Experiences and Responses.* Edited by Cecilia Menjívar and Dan Kanstroom, 1–36. New York: Cambridge University Press.

Milovanovic, Dragan, and Katheryn K. Russell. 2001. "Introduction: Petit Apartheid." In *Petit Apartheid in the U.S. Criminal Justice System*. Edited by Katherine K. Russell and Dragan Milovanovic, xv–xxiii. Durham, NC: Carolina Academic Press.

Monteverde García, Ana María. 2004. "Propuesta de Campaña Preventiva Contra la Violencia Hacia la Mujer Inmigrante y Operadora de la Industria Maquiladora en la Ciudad de Nogales Sonora." *UDLA Tesis Digitales.*

Nadal, Kevin L., Katie E. Griffin, Yinglee Wong, Sahran Hamit, and Morgan Rasmus. 2014. "The Impact of Racial Microaggressions on Mental Health: Counseling Implications for Clients of Color." *Journal of Counseling and Development* 92 (1): 57–66. doi: 10.1002/j.1556–6676.2014.00130.x.

Nazarian, Edith. 2011. "Crossing Over: Assessing Operation Streamline and the Rights of Immigrant Criminal Defendants at the Border." *Loyola Law Review* 57 (2): 1399–1430.

No More Deaths. 2011. *A Culture of Cruelty: Abuse and Impunity in Short-Term U.S. Border Patrol Custody*, http://nomoredeaths.org.

Núñez, Guillermina Gina, and Josiah Heyman. 2007. "Entrapment Processes and Immigrant Communities in a Time of Heightened Border Vigilance." *Human Organization* 66 (4): 354–65.

O'Leary, Anna Ochoa. 2012. "Of Coyotes, Crossings, and Cooperation: Social Capital and Women's Migration at the Margins of the State." In *Political Economy, Neoliberalism, and the Prehistoric Economies of Latin America*. Vol. 32 of *Research in Economic Anthropology*, edited by Ty Matejowsky and Donald C. Wood, 133–60. Bingley, UK: Emerald Group.

O'Leary, Anna Ochoa. 2009a. "The ABCs of Unauthorized Border Crossing Costs: Assembling, Bajadores, and Coyotes." *Migration Letters* 6 (1): 27–36.

O'Leary, Anna Ochoa. 2009b. "In the Footsteps of Spirits: Migrant Women's Testimonios in a Time of Heightened Border Enforcement." In *Human Rights along the U.S.-Mexico Border*. Edited by Kathleen Staudt, Tony Payan, and Z. Anthony Kruszewski, 85–104. Tucson: University of Arizona Press.

O'Leary, Anna Ochoa. 2009c. "Mujeres en el Cruce: Remapping Border Security through Migrant Mobility." *Journal of the Southwest* 51 (4): 523–42.

O'Leary, Anna Ochoa. 2008. "Close Encounters of the Deadly Kind: Gender, Migration, and Border (In)Security." *Migration Letters* 15 (2): 111–22.

O'Leary, Anna Ochoa, Colin Deeds, and Scott Whiteford. 2013. "Introduction." In *Unchartered Terrain: New Directions in Border Research Method and Ethics*. Edited by Anna Ochoa O'Leary, Colin Deeds, and Scott Whiteford, 1–26. Tucson: University of Arizona Press.

O'Mahony, Joyce M., and Tam T. Donnelly. 2013. "How Does Gender Influence Immigrant and Refugee Women's Postpartum Depression Help-Seeking Experience?" *Journal of Psychiatric and Mental Health Nursing* 20 (8): 714–25. doi: 10.1111/jpm.12005.

Ornelas, India J., and Krista M. Perreira. 2011. "The Role of Migration in the Development of Depressive Symptoms among Latino Immigrant Parents in the USA." *Social Science and Medicine* 73 (8): 1169–77. doi: 10.1016/j.socscimed.2011.07.002.

Orraca Romano, Pedro Paulo, and Francisco DeJesus Corona Villavivencio. 2014. "Risk of Death and Aggressions Encountered while Illegally Crossing the U.S.-Mexico Border." *Migraciones Internacionales* 7 (3): 9–42.

Perez, Javier. 2011. "Reasonably Suspicious of Being Mojado: The Legal Derogation of Latinos in Immigration Enforcement." *Texas Hispanic Journal of Law and Policy* 17 (1): 99–123.

Peterson, Cassie L. 2009. "An Iowa Immigration Raid Leads to Unprecedented Criminal Consequences: Why ICE Should Rethink the Postville Model." *Iowa Law Review* 95 (1): 323–46.

Plascencia, Luis. 2009. "The 'Undocumented' Mexican Migrant Question: Reexamining the Framing of Law and Illegalization in the United States." *Urban Anthropology* 38 (2–4): 378–44.

Rabin, Nina. 2014. "Disappearing Parents: A Report on Immigration Enforcement and the Child Welfare System," http://www.detentionwatchnetwork.org.

Rocha Romero, David, and Marco T. Ocegueda Hernández. 2013. "Después de Tantos Años me Deportaron. Proceso de Identificación y Deportación de Mujeres Inmigrantes No Delincuentes." *Estudios Fronterizos* 14 (28): 9–34.

Rodriguez, Nestor, and Cristian Paredes. 2014. "Coercive Immigration Enforcement and Bureaucratic Ideology." In *Constructing Immigrant "Illegality": Critiques, Experiences, and Responses*. Edited by Cecilia Menjivar and Dan Kanstroom, 63–83. New York: Cambridge University Press.

Romero, Mary. 2008. "The Inclusion of Citizenship Status in Intersectionality: What Immigration Raids Tell Us about Mixed-Status Families, the State, and Assimilation." *International Journal of the Family* 34 (2): 131–52.

Ruiz Marrujo, Olivia T. 2009. "Women, Migration, and Sexual Violence: Lessons from Mexico's Borders." In *Human Rights along the US-Mexican Border*. Ed. Kathleen Staudt, Tony Payan, and Z. Anthony Kruszewski, 31–47. Tucson: University of Arizona Press.

Sabo, Samantha, Susan Shaw, Maia Ingram, Nicolette Teufel-Shone, Scott Carvajal, Jill Guernsey de Zapien, Cecilia Rosales, Flor Redondo, Gina Garcia, and Raquel Rubio-Goldsmith. 2014. "Everyday Violence, Structural Racism, and Mistreatment at the US-Mexico Border." *Social Science and Medicine* 109: 66–74.

Salgado, Hugo, Isa Haviland, Marcella Hernandez, Diana Lozano, Ruby Osoria, David Keyes, Eastern Kang, and María Zúñiga. 2014. "Perceived Discrimination and Religiosity as Potential Mediating Factors between Migration and Depressive Symptoms: A Transnational Study of an Indigenous Mayan Population." *Journal of Immigrant and Minority Health* 16: 340–47.

Santa Ana, Otto. 1999. "'Like an Animal I Was Treated': Anti-immigrant Metaphor in US Public Discourse." *Discourse and Society* 10 (2): 191–224.

Silvey, Rachel, and Rebecca Elmhirst. 2003. "Engendering Social Capital: Women Workers and Rural-Urban Networks in Indonesia's Crisis." *World Development* 31 (5): 865–80.

Slack, Jeremy, Daniel E. Martínez, Scott Whiteford, and Emily Peiffer. 2013. *In the Shadow of the Wall: Family Separation, Immigration Enforcement, and Security.* Tucson: Center for Latin American Studies, University of Arizona. http://las.arizona.edu.

Steller, Tim. 2001. "Border Unit Fights an Enemy Within." *Arizona Daily Star*, June 16.

Urquijo-Ruiz, Rita E. 2004. "Police Brutality against an Undocumented Mexican Woman." *Chicana/Latina Studies* 4 (1): 62–84.

Valdez, Carmen R., Jessica Abegglen, and Claire T. Hauser. 2013. "Fortalezas Familiares Program: Building Sociocultural and Family Strengths in Latina Women with Depression and Their Families." *Family Process* 52 (3): 378–93.

Viruell-Fuentes, Edna A., Patricia Y. Miranda, and Sawsan Abdulrahim. 2012. "More Than Just Culture: Structural Racism, Intersectionality Theory, and Immigrant Health." *Social Science and Medicine* 75: 2099–2106.

Williams, Heather. 2008. "Written Statement (Amended) before the U.S. House of Representatives Subcommittee of Commercial and Administrative Law, Oversight Hearing on the 'Executive Office for United States Attorneys.'" House Judiciary Committee, U.S. House of Representatives.

11

Women and the Criminal Justice System

A Psychology of Men Perspective

JONATHAN SCHWARTZ AND JENNIFER BAHRMAN

Early in my career, I (Jonathan Schwartz) organized and ran men's court-mandated domestic violence groups. This involved not only working with abusive men but also working with the court system as an advocate. During this time, I discovered the literature on the psychology of men. It was an important moment in my career as it assisted me in understanding not only some of the dynamics that led to abuse and the behavior I saw in group therapy but also the insidious patriarchal and misogynistic dynamics I was witnessing in the courts. It also was key in helping me to understand why the men struggled with vulnerable emotions and overall connection with others.

Men's gender role socialization has negative consequences for both men and others: "Rigid, sexist, or restrictive gender roles, learned during socialization, result in personal retraction, devaluation, or violation of others or self" (O'Neil 1990, 25). Men with rigid and traditional gender roles suffer the intrapersonal and interpersonal consequences of conforming and thus limiting their behaviors—as well as the behaviors of others. When gender role expectations are so rigid that men cannot meet them, negative evaluation of self and others, psychological distress, and behavioral problems result.

The purpose of this chapter is to explicate the ways in which hegemonic male gender roles impact the experience of women in the justice system. The percentage of women involved in the criminal justice system has been growing at a higher rate than the percentage of men (Richie, Tsenin, and Widom 2000). The psychology of men and masculinity provides a framework with which to examine how the criminal justice system operates and how men contribute to the increasing rates of women's arrest and incarceration. The psychology of men focuses not only on individuals' experiences but also on the influence of social processes and gender norms in particular. For example, there is minimal yet increasing attention in the psychology of men literature to the ways in which hegemonic masculinity, sexism, and gender stereotypes support gender-based oppression (O'Neil 2015).

Hegemonic masculinity can be described as a pervasive ideology that men's role is to be dominant in society and that subordination of women is required for men to maintain power (Mankoski and Maton 2010). Like feminism, the psychology of men has produced theories that can help us to understand criminal behaviors and justice practices as social rather than individual issues, and that highlight the link among masculinity, power, and male privilege.

In this chapter, we examine the criminal justice system through the lens of the psychology of men and discuss why it is important that this system take into account men's power and role as relates to women's involvement in prostitution and human trafficking in particular.

The Psychology of Men

The psychology of men is an academic field situated in the broader context of gender studies. It was born in the 1970s in the wake of the feminist movement (Goldberg 1977). As with feminism, one of the fundamental tenets of the psychology of men is that an understanding of sexism only comes from deconstructing masculine gender roles (Enns and Williams 2012; O'Neil and Renzulli 2013) and examining their impact on both men and women (Pleck 1995; O'Neil 1981). The psychology of men has produced theories about the socialization of boys and men that explain how individuals internalize culturally specific beliefs about gender roles (Levant 2011, 1996; Pleck 1995; Thompson and Pleck 1995).

Scientific understanding of gender ideology and gender role socialization has evolved over the last thirty years (O'Neil 2008; Smiler 2006). Today, gender roles are viewed as one aspect of identity that is subject to change (O'Neil 2010; Pleck 1995) and that interacts with other dimensions of individual experiences such as race, class, ethnicity, religion, and sexual orientation (O'Neil 2015). A key concept of gender role theory is hegemonic masculinity, or the idea that in patriarchal social contexts, men enact gender roles to promote male dominance through the subordination of women (Malamuth et al. 1991; Mankowski and Maton 2010).

Gender role socialization and gender role strain are two core theories of the psychology of men. Gender-role socialization describes how children and adults learn socially defined notions of what constitutes gender-appropriate (i.e., masculine and feminine) attitudes and behaviors (O'Neil 1981, 2008; Prentice and Carranza 2002). Typical masculine qualities include, but are not limited to, the following: aggression, independence, individualism, decisiveness, self-sufficiency, leadership ability, ambition, forcefulness, and dominance (Prentice and Carranza 2002). The theory of gender role socialization posits that masculine or feminine stereotypes that are rigidly learned and internalized can result in gender role conflict, which refers to the negative outcomes associated with these stereotypes (O'Neil, 1981). The inability to express or understand emotions or the tendency to focus overly much on success, power, and competition are examples of such negative outcomes (O'Neil 1981).

Gender role strain (GRS) occurs as a result of the rigid and restrictive gender roles that develop from individuals' internalization of sexism. The GRS theory attempts to explain the link between men's mental health outcomes and their integration of masculine role norms into a sense of self (Pleck 1981, 1995), in particular the relation between rigid and restrictive gender roles and psychological distress, health problems, and interpersonal difficulties in men (Good and Mintz 1990; Magovecviv and Addis 2005; Sharpe and Heppner 1991; Schwartz et al. 2004). According to the GRS theory, conflict may occur when individuals who internalize and endorse rigid gender roles condemn and devalue those who do not conform to such traditional roles (O'Neil 1981). Underlying gender role conflict in men is a fear of anything feminine that would challenge their masculine identity. Thus, socialized masculinity leads to blatant and subtle sexism toward women (Glick and Fiske 1996) and directly influences how men who are in power respond to women, for example, in legal cases related to prostitution and human sex trafficking.

Gender Ideology and Men's Attitudes and Behaviors toward Women

There has been substantial research supporting the relationship between gender ideology and negative attitudes and behaviors toward women (O'Neil 2015). The internalization of traditional masculine roles rooted in hegemonic sexism has been associated with hostility toward women (Robinson and Schwartz 2004) and heterosexual relationship problems in men (Moore and Stuart 2005). Adherence to traditional gender roles has been linked to anger, abuse, and desire for aggression against women (Eisler et al. 2000; Franchina, Eisler, and Moore 2001; Moore et al. 2010). This suggests that gender socialization directly contributes to men's attitudes and behaviors toward women. Studies also found that male privilege mediated the effect of masculine gender roles on men's negative attitudes and behaviors toward women (Hill and Fischer 2001; Schwartz and Tylka 2008).

Although sexism often is blatant and hostile, it can also be expressed in covert and seemingly positive ways (Glick and Fiske 1996). Hostile sexism corresponds to obvious forms of male dominance, such as aggressive behaviors intended to punish women who challenge male power. This includes hostile heterosexuality such as rape, degradation of female prostitutes, or victim blaming in the case of human sex trafficking. Benevolent sexism, on the other hand, refers to paternalistic attitudes towards women, in particular the belief that women need protection from men because they are frail. Ambivalent sexism refers to a form of sexism that integrates both hostile and benevolent attitudes towards women (Glick and Fiske 2002). It promotes the view that men are more capable, more able-bodied, and more suited for positions of power and status, and that women are men's sexual partners, responsible for satisfying men's sexual needs, and are best suited for domestic roles of low social value (e.g., caring for children, the elderly, and the infirm). Ambivalent sexism carries the message that men need women for the domestic and caregiving services they offer; however, it also suggests that women, and women only, should be in these roles (Glick and Fiske 1996). Recently, ambivalent sexism has been related to bias against female drivers, nonegalitarian beliefs about appropriate dating behaviors, and antichoice attitudes toward abortion (Begun and Walls 2015; Mc-Carty and Kelly 2015; Skinner, Stevenson, and Camillus 2015).

Sexist attitudes are explicit and implicit, that is, conscious and out of awareness (Greenwald and Banaji 1995; Nosek, Greenwald, and Banaji 2007). Attitudes develop from past experiences as well as social and familial beliefs and values that individuals internalize beginning at an early age. Attitudes are implicit when individuals do not recognize they are the basis for individual actions (Nosek et al. 2007). For example, a person may unconsciously believe in the superiority of men and thus may treat women differently; yet, when questioned about their beliefs, they are more likely to deny differential treatment as this is not socially and personally acceptable.

Hostile, benevolent, explicit, and implicit sexism have implications for our understanding of prostitution and human sex trafficking as well as criminal justice responses to men who solicit prostitutes. It explains why women, rather than men, have been the target of criminal prosecution based on the perception that they are violating gender-related social standards and are therefore blameworthy, deserving of punishment, or needing protection, while men who seek prostitutes are seen as abiding by gender role expectations.

Multiculturalism and the Psychology of Men

There is not one but several masculine ideologies that influence men's interactions with others in ways that help them preserve their dominant positions and privileges in society (O'Neil 2015). These masculine ideologies are distinct and context dependent: They emerge from the intersection of gender, race, social class, age, and sexual orientation in diverse cultural settings, and have a unique impact on the mental health of diverse men (Levant, Richmond, et al. 2003; Levant and Majors 1997; Levant, Majors, and Kelly 1998; Levant and Richmond 2007; Levant and Wong 2013; Pleck, Sonenstein, and Ku 1994; Wu, Levant, and Sellers 2001). For example, in some Mexican and Mexican American communities, Arciniega and colleagues (2008) found that traditional machismo, with its emphasis on individual power and hypermasculinity, was associated with aggression, antisocial behaviors, and restricted emotional awareness. An understanding of multiple and context-specific masculinities is needed to evaluate the intrapersonal and interpersonal impact of these beliefs. For example, we need to investigate how context-specific masculinities determine policy and behavior toward women in the legal system. Levant and Wong (2013) studied the moderating influence of race on the relation between alexithymia, a clinically significant inability to identify and describe emotions, and beliefs about masculinity; the results of their investigation suggested that White men who endorsed traditional masculine norms were more likely than racial-minority men who endorsed traditional masculinity to experience and express a limited range of affect. Research has also produced evidence that internalized racism moderated the relationship between gender role conflict and psychological stress for Latino, Asian American, and same-sex populations (Liang et al. 2009; Liang, Salcedo, and Miller 2011; Sánchez et al. 2010; Shek and McEwen 2012; Wester et al. 2006). While limited, the scientific evidence points to the role of race and culture in individuals' endorsement and enactment of their beliefs about how men should be, feel, think, and act.

To increase our understanding of women in the justice system, the psychology of men should further examine the cultural specificity of masculinity as relates to men's attitudes and behaviors and their impact on disadvantaged groups (O'Neil and Renzulli 2013). It should also investigate how oppressed and marginalized groups experience gender role devaluations (O'Neil and Renzulli 2013) and examine how diverse men use the social privileges bestowed upon them by virtue of their race, gender, and class (see Hill and Fischer 2001; McIntosh 2003) in ways that perpetuate the marginalization of disadvantaged others. There is a need to shed light on the multidimensional and interdependent social processes that participate in the reproduction of social disadvantages, and thus provide information that is essential to the development of gender- and culturally responsive interventions designed to change men's behaviors and to reduce their harmful effects on diverse women.

Masculinity, Gender Roles, and the Criminal Justice System

The psychology of men examines the rigid and restrictive masculine gender role norms that lead to gender role conflict and the devaluation, restriction, and violation of women (O'Neil 1981, 2013). The psychology of men also focuses on the patriarchal processes that operate to establish male domination within systems of social relations; these processes include marginalization, domestication, discrimination, subjugation, disproportionate representation, and violence (Barzilai 2004). These are persistent characteristics of the criminal justice system (Barzilai 2004), and according to MacKinnon (1983, 207), "[T]he law sees and treats women the way men see and treat women." In other words, the implementation of the law follows patriarchal principles in ways that perpetuate male domination and produce further harm.

A focus on gender and masculinities is central to understanding victimization and crime, the reproduction of gendered inequalities, and the impact of criminal justice interventions on both men and women. Feminist criminology has paved the way towards greater gender sensitivity in efforts to understand women's criminal behaviors (Chesney-Lind and Morash 2013; Hughes 2005; Richie 2012; Sprague 2005). Feminist legal scholars have described women's pathways to crime and defined women's criminal behaviors as different from men's. In particular, they have highlighted that women often participate in illegal activities under pressure from male partners or out of necessity to provide for their needs and those of their children (Belknap 2007; Farrington 2007; Mallicoat 2007). However, feminist criminologists have not examined how men's endorsement of traditional masculinity contributes to women's involvement, victimization, and marginalization in the criminal justice system.

The tenets of the psychology of men have not been used to study criminal behaviors and legal practices; yet, they have the potential to expand our understanding of the criminal justice system, in particular the individual behaviors and processes that support the devaluation and violation of women involved in prostitution and sex trafficking. For example, there is no known research examining masculine ideologies and sexist attitudes among criminal justice professionals. For the most part, scholars have documented the differential treatment of women offenders, including the restriction of women's autonomy and expectations of obedience based on the perception that they are weaker than men (Belknap 2001; Chesney-Lind and Shelden 2013; Glick and Fiske 1996; Kempf-Leonard and Johansson 2007; Myers and Sangster 2001; Snyder and Sickmund 2006). The psychology of men calls attention to the men who solicit prostitutes and to the fact that they are generally excused for behaviors perceived as congruent with their prescribed gender role. It shifts the focus from women to men, and renders men visible and accountable for their contribution to "female" crimes.

Men's Invisibility in Prostitution and Human Sex Trafficking: Social and Justice Processes

To show how the psychology of men can increase gender sensitivity as relates to criminal justice, we use gender role theory to reveal the normative assumptions that underlie interventions for prostitution and human sex trafficking. Every year, seven hundred thousand people are trafficked across international borders for the purpose of sexual exploitation (Kandathil 2005), and 80 percent of those trafficked are women (United States Department of State 2008). Trafficking is a form of gender violence that is rooted in misogynistic views of women as frail and subservient to men, and in traditional gender role norms that support the objectification and sexualization of women (Mankoski and Maton 2010; Levant and Wong 2013). Together, these views and norms create a context that promotes men's acceptance of sex trafficking and their participation in this illegal trade, and that justifies the classification of women who sell sexual services, willing or coerced, as offenders. This categorization of women prostitutes as offenders intensifies the social stigma they experience as a result of breaking gender-based norms about appropriate sexual behaviors (Almog 2010; Chesney-Lind 1986).

While there is general consensus among criminology scholars that women are treated differently than men in the criminal justice system, there is disagreement with regard to *how* women are treated. According to the chivalry hypothesis, criminal justice systems in male-dominated societies show more leniency towards female offenders because women are perceived as weak and irrational (Grabe et al. 2006; Belknap 2001; Embry and Lyons 2012). However, research findings suggest that selective chivalry is more commonly observed (Embry and Lyons 2012) and that the type of offense, rather than the severity of the offense, determines how women are treated in the criminal justice system (Grabe et al. 2006; Chesney-Lind 1986; Jeffries 2002; Embry and Lyons 2012). Specifically, women who commit offenses that are inconsistent with gender norms receive harsher punishment than women who do not.

This differential treatment occurs not only within the criminal justice system but also in the media. News coverage of female offenders sends subtle messages that justify double standards (Weimann and Fishman 1988; Grabe et al. 2006). Female offenders who commit "unfeminine" crimes are viewed more negatively than women who commit "feminine" crimes, and more negatively than men who engage in the same criminal behaviors (Grabe et al. 2006). The assumption is that women who commit "unfeminine" crimes should be punished twice as much for violating the law and for breaking gender norms. Further, women are judged more harshly for sexual acts that are acceptable for men (Crawford and Popp 2003). This explains women's harsher punishment in the case of prostitution. From a psychology of men perspective, the act of blaming women for prostitution is supported by the belief that men who seek sex by soliciting prostitutes are performing socially acceptable masculine behaviors (O'Neil 2015; Sakaluk and Milhausen 2012).

In male-dominated societies, the assumption is that only women prostitute themselves and exchange sexual labor for compensation. Women who engage in prostitution are disproportionately more likely than the men who pay for their sexual services to be arrested and to face jail time, fines, and/or probation (Jolin 1994). In fact, men's moral standing is never questioned, even though they are buying the sexual services (Overall 1992). In theory, one may argue that the men who are the consumers of prostitution should face the same legal consequences as the women who sell sexual services. However, they are often allowed to take part in restorative justice diversion programs, known as "John Schools," to avoid criminal prosecution (Monto 1999). This practice is supported by the belief that "men will be men" and that they have a need for sex (Dalrymple 2005). The implication is that men who participate in the sex trade are less accountable before the law than women who provide sexual services, because men's sexual desire is socially appropriate while women's sexual desire is not. This double standard has been well researched (Crawford and Popp 2003), and studies have found that for similar sexual behaviors, women are judged more harshly than men (Sakaluk and Milhausen 2012).

This double standard regarding women's and men's sexuality influences the way prostitution is defined, which in turn guides the development of justice and psychological interventions to tackle this social issue. It also determines our ability to understand and address the concerns of women in the sex trade. From a capitalist patriarchal perspective, prostitution constitutes a labor field similar to any other profession (Overall 1992). The framing of prostitution as a line of work suggests that sexual activities are consensual and discounts the possibility that women may experience coercion in their relationships with sex traffickers. These relationships are characterized by traditional gender-based dynamics where men exercise control and dominance over women and where women are psychologically dependent on men.

Prostitution has also been defined as a morality politic (Wagenaar and Altink 2012). Broadly speaking, the concept of morality politic refers to policies in which central, universal principles relating to aspects of personal life (e.g., birth, death, life, and the body) are at stake, and public opinion is heavily divided. A morality politic has six characteristics: "It is ruled by explicit ideology; experts have limited authority as everyone feels they 'own' prostitution policy; it is highly emotionally charged; it is resistant to facts; the symbolism of policy formulation is seen as more important than policy implementation; and it is subject to abrupt changes" (Wagenaar and Altink 2012, 279). A morality politic is based on explicit ideology to the extent that it is used to advocate a moral cause larger than the immediate implications of the social issue in question. Since attitudes towards prostitution— and to an extent laws—are based on a moral reaction to the nature of the sexual acts involved, anyone may believe he or she has the right to offer an opinion on the issue of prostitution policy, as the issue concerns principles relating to aspects of personal life. The highly emotionally charged nature of a morality politic contributes to widespread disregard for precise, reliable facts that may or may not support arguments for and against differing prostitution policy. What matters is the creation of policies rather than their implementation; what the policies represent and support is more important than action and change. In other words, the formulation of policies serves to support the moral standards that guide the categorization of women's sexual behaviors as illegal. When prostitution is viewed as a morality politic, it is not considered as serious as other crimes (e.g., violent or drug-related) (Wagenaar and Altink 2012), although it also involves severe forms of victimization (Overall 1992).

Men's Roles in the Sex Trade: Indirect Impact on Sex Trafficking, Prostitution, and Women

Men occupy at least two positions in the sex trade, as consumers of sexual services and as traffickers who coerce women and girls into prostitution. As consumers, they contribute to the demand for sexual services; as traffickers, they participate in the supply of sex. At both ends, they support the persistence of prostitution as well as the commodification of women's bodies, thus reproducing the gendered organization of social relations.

While no research has examined the typologies of men who are either traffickers or consumers in the sex trade, it is likely that human sex traffickers, who treat women as objects, have extremely rigid and restrictive traditional views of gender roles. In general, violence toward women has been associated with men's belief that they are superior to women and should have sexual access to them (Flood and Pease 2009; Koss and Cleveland 1997). Men traffickers treat women as a commodity and thus dehumanize them. This suggests that men traffickers are limited in their capacity to experience sympathy and empathy. It also raises questions about the relationships among masculine gender role ideology, psychopathology, and sociopathic deviance in particular.

There have been few studies of male consumers in the sex trade, possibly because scholars share the common perception that sex seeking is normal male behaviors (Ben-Israel et al. 2005; Perkins 1999). Existing research on men's motivations has found higher levels of acceptance of rape myths among men who reported projected or actual participation in the sex trade. These men were also more likely to display sexually coercive and aggressive behaviors toward women (Farley at al. 2011; Kinnell 2008; Lowman and Atchison 2006; Pitts et al. 2004; Schmidt 2003; Xantidis and McCabe 2000). Studies of masculine ideology have established a link among masculine gender roles, restrictive emotionality, and men's preferences for impersonal or nonrelational sexuality (Levant, Cuthbert, et al. 2003). In addition, men's domineering and controlling tendencies in heterosexual relationships, acceptance of violence against women, and solicitation of prostitution have been associated with masculine ideology that supports hostility towards women (Farley et al. 2011; Malamuth and Thornhill 1994). Overall, it appears that masculine ideology that emphasizes male dominance and objectification and hostility towards women are key characteristics of men who solicit prostitutes.

Although research is limited as relates to men who solicit prostitutes, existing studies highlight the need to address masculine role socialization and its impact on men's attitude and behaviors in their interactions with women. Consistent with the social justice principles of the psychology of men (Bartky 1990; Fredrickson and Roberts 1997), it is not enough to focus on men's motivation for buying sex. Instead, there is a need for greater consideration, in the literature and research, of the social processes involved in the perpetuation of prostitution and human trafficking.

John Schools: How Men Can Help Reduce the Trafficking of Women

"John Schools" are court-diversion and educational programs for men charged with solicitation of prostitution. John Schools were developed out of a need to reduce demand for prostitution by addressing the men who solicit prostitutes. The John Schools constitute a problem-solving approach to the legal issue of illegal sex trade (Brewer et al. 2006; Shively et al. 2008). Their goal is to reduce recidivism by informing first-time offenders about the negative consequences of prostitution. They are one of the few justice interventions that seek to decrease the demand for illegal sex through prevention strategies focusing on male consumers.

John Schools currently exist in the United States, Canada, South Korea, and the United Kingdom. Within the United States, John Schools have been established in at least six major cities: Washington, D.C., New York, San Francisco, Pittsburgh, West Palm Beach, and Buffalo (Shively et al. 2012). One of the most well-known John Schools in operation, the First Offender Prostitution Program in San Francisco, offers a one-day class to sex-trafficking consumers in an attempt to inform them about the victimization of those who are trafficked as well as the legal and health outcomes associated with commercial sex (Shively et al. 2008). Fees are collected from the participants and used to fund social and therapeutic programs for female survivors of sex trafficking (Shively et al. 2012). The programs are typically run by hired facilitators and often include testimony from former prostitutes and presentations on sexually transmitted diseases and human trafficking laws.

John Schools are innovative justice strategies that address the social problem of prostitution and human trafficking by moving the focus from female prostitutes to the men who solicit them and by attempting to reduce demand rather than supply. There is some evidence that John Schools change attitudes and slightly reduce recidivism (Shively et al. 2008); however, these outcomes are short-term. Although education can be an impactful intervention, it has not been demonstrated to successfully alter gender role norms (O'Neil 2015), which serve to perpetuate the sex trade. The education the John Schools provide is not enough to change the broader social factors that support the objectification of women and men's solicitation of prostitution.

Given the tendency to blame women and minimize men's responsibility in the sex trade (Sidun and Rubin 2013), it is not surprising that John Schools, together with awareness campaigns and neighborhood watch programs, are some of the few prevention programs currently in existence in the nation. For the most part, legal strategies emphasize punishment and deterrence (Adelman 2004) in ways that further harm women who participate in the illegal act of providing sexual services (Spohn and Tellis 2012; see also Bryant-Davis, Adams, and Gray, chapter 3 in this book). It is imperative to develop justice interventions that take into consideration the processes of victimization that women experience in the context of prostitution (Spohn 2014), not only to assist women in finding alternatives to sex work and to address the abuse they have endured but also to promote change in men's gender role ideology and to increase men's knowledge of the health, legal, and social consequences associated with prostitution and sex trafficking.

Unfortunately, the field of psychology has been generally absent in the creation of interventions to combat human trafficking and prostitution. It is critical that psychologists and justice officials work together to develop comprehensive prevention and treatment programs designed to change the normative attitudes and gender roles that support the objectification and oppression of women. Psychologists, in particular those who understand the psychology of men, have the training and knowledge required to develop culturally and gender-sensitive interventions that go beyond education and that have the potential to produce positive behavioral and social change. For example, O'Neil, Egan, Owen, and Murry's (1993) Gender Role Journey is a developmental model of gender role identity that can be used to design preventive programming for men in the criminal justice system. The Gender Role Journey describes how adult men and women move from acceptance of traditional gender roles to positions of gender role transcendence and feminist activism. Comprised of five phases, this model is one of the few that describes the processes involved in transitioning between gender roles. The five phases include Acceptance of Traditional Gender Roles, Ambivalence, Anger, Activism, and Celebration and Integration of Gender Roles. Interactions with gender-nonconforming peers and education about sexism and its impact on personal growth are events that facilitate individuals' transitions from one phase to the next. The Gender Role Journey could be used in justice programming to guide men's assessment of their personal beliefs about gender roles. It would also provide a map for treatment with specific phases of development. Identifying the barriers that prevent men's progress through each stage of the journey would also be an important component of preventive justice programming for men.

Conclusion

This chapter has offered a psychology of men perspective on criminal justice responses to prostitution and human sex trafficking. Double standards that explain why men and women are treated differently in the case of prostitution and human trafficking have been described. The theory of gender role conflict and gender role strain were highlighted to describe men's behaviors as consumers and traffickers in the sex trade.

Many factors account for women's involvement in criminal activities: social, educational and employment problems, personality characteristics, antisocial beliefs and values, history of criminal engagement, criminally involved peers, mental disorders, history of victimization, and substance abuse (Kissin et al. 2014; Andrews, Bonta, and Wormith 2006; Hall et al. 2013). To better assist female offenders and to minimize the unfair treatment of women in the criminal justice system, individual risks must be addressed in conjunction with the gendered processes (i.e., gender socialization and gender role strain) that support men's role in female offending and victimization. It is important that men be the

294 | JONATHAN SCHWARTZ AND JENNIFER BAHRMAN

target of preventive interventions that reduce gender role rigidity and increase social consciousness. Such interventions should aim to change justice practices as well as individual behaviors related to sex trafficking and the solicitation of prostitution.

It is critical that men who solicit prostitutes participate in assessment and diversion programs that address gender role ideology and hostile masculinity in particular (Malamuth and Thornhill 1994). Given that men are socialized in diverse social contexts, it can be a challenge to design programs that address culturally specific attitudes and behaviors and that can be applied to multiple contexts. Research is needed to inform the development of comprehensive preventative assessment and treatment programs that will reduce men's gender role rigidity, foster their social and legal consciousness, and increase their appreciation of women's social value. These are essential treatment outcomes for men that will have an indirect positive impact on the health—physical, psychological, and relational—of women involved in prostitution and sex trafficking. These types of interventions put the onus on men to address social structures that are abusive to women and have the potential to enhance legal responses to prostitution and other "female" crimes by increasing men's knowledge of their role and responsibility in the criminalization of women.

REFERENCES
Adelman, Michelle R. 2004. "International Sex Trafficking: Dismantling the Demand." *Southern. California Review of Law and Women's Studies* 13: 387.
Almog, Shulamit. 2010. "Prostitution as Exploitative: An Israeli Perspective." *Georgetown Journal of Gender and the Law* 711: 132–42.
Andrews, Don A., James Bonta, and J. Stephen Wormith. 2006. "The Recent Past and Near Future of Risk and/or Need Assessment." *Crime and Delinquency* 52 (1): 7–27.
Arciniega, G. Miguel, Thomas C. Anderson, Zoila G. Tovar-Blank, and Terence J. G. Tracey. 2008. "Toward a Fuller Conception of Machismo: Development of a Traditional Machismo and Caballerismo Scale." *Journal of Counseling Psychology* 55 (1): 19–33.
Bartky, Sandra Lee. 1990. *Femininity and Domination: Studies in the Phenomenology of Oppression*. New York: Routledge.
Barzilai, Gad. 2004. "Culture of Patriarchy in Law: Violence from Antiquity to Modernity." *Law and Society Review* 38 (4): 867–83.
Begun, Stephanie, and N. Eugene Walls. 2015. "Pedestal or Gutter: Exploring Ambivalent Sexism's Relationship with Abortion Attitudes." *Affilia: Journal of Women and Social Work* 30 (2): 200–215. doi: 10.1177/0886109914555216.

Belknap, Joanne. 2007. *The Invisible Woman: Gender, Crime, and Justice*, 3rd ed. Belmont, CA: Thompson Wadsworth.

Belknap, Joanne. 2001. *The Invisible Woman: Gender, Crime, and Justice*, 2nd ed. Belmont, CA: Wadsworth.

Ben-Israel, Hanny, No'omi Levenkron, Natalie Mendelsohn, and M. S. L. Zarim. 2005. "The Missing Factor: Clients of Trafficked Women in Israel's Sex Industry." Tel Aviv, Israel: Hotline for Migrant Workers, Hebrew University in Jerusalem, http://lastradainternational.org.

Brewer, Devon D., John J. Potterat, Stephen Q. Muth, and John M. Roberts Jr. 2006. "A Large Specific Deterrent Effect of Arrest for Patronizing a Prostitute." *PloS one* 1 (1): e60.

Chesney-Lind, Meda. 1986. "Women and Crime: The Female Offender." *Signs* 12 (1): 78–96.

Chesney-Lind, Meda, and Merry Morash. 2013. "Transformative Feminist Criminology: A Critical Re-thinking of a Discipline." *Critical Criminology* 21 (3): 287–304.

Chesney-Lind, Meda, and Randall G. Shelden. 2013. *Girls, Delinquency, and Juvenile Justice*, 2nd ed. Pacific Grove, CA: Wiley.

Crawford, Mary, and Danielle Popp. 2003. "Sexual Double Standards: A Review and Methodological Critique of Two Decades of Research." *Journal of Sex Research* 40 (1): 13–26.

Dalrymple, Joyce Koo. 2005. "Human Trafficking: Protecting Human Rights in the Trafficking Victims Protection Act." *Boston College Third World Law Journal* 25 (2): 451–73.

Eisler, Richard M., Joseph J. Franchina, Todd M. Moore, Hunter G. Honeycutt, and Deborah L. Rhatigan. 2000. "Masculine Gender Role Stress and Intimate Abuse: Effects of Gender Relevance of Conflict Situations on Men's Attributions and Affective Responses." *Psychology of Men and Masculinity* 1 (1): 30–36.

Embry, Randa, and Phillip M. Lyons. 2012. "Sex-Based Sentencing Discrepancies between Male and Female Sex Offenders." *Feminist Criminology* 7 (2): 146–62.

Enns, Carolyn Zerbe, and Elizabeth Nutt Williams. 2012. *The Oxford Handbook of Feminist Multicultural Counseling Psychology*. New York: Oxford University Press.

Farley, Melissa, Jan Macleod, Lynn Anderson, and Jacqueline M. Golding. 2011. "Attitudes and Social Characteristics of Men Who Buy Sex in Scotland." *Psychological Trauma: Theory, Research, Practice, and Policy* 3 (4): 369–83.

Farrington, David P. 2007. "Advancing Knowledge about Desistance." *Journal of Contemporary Criminal Justice* 23 (1): 125–34.

Flood, Michael, and Bob Pease. 2009. "Factors Influencing Attitudes to Violence against Women." *Trauma, Violence, and Abuse* 10 (2): 125–42.

Franchina, Joseph J., Richard M. Eisler, and Todd M. Moore. 2001. "Masculine Gender Role Stress and Intimate Abuse: Effects of Masculine Gender Relevance of Dating Situations and Female Threat on Men's Attributions and Affective Responses." *Psychology of Men and Masculinity* 2 (1): 34–41.

Fredrickson, Barbara L., and Tomi⊠Ann Roberts. 1997. "Objectification Theory: Toward Understanding Women's Lived Experiences and Mental Health Risks." *Psychology of Women Quarterly* 21 (2): 173–206.

Glick, Peter, and Susan T. Fiske. 2002. "Ambivalent Sexism." *Advances in Experimental Social Psychology* 33: 115–88. doi: 10.1016/S0065-2601(01)80005-8.

Glick, Peter, and Susan T. Fiske. 1996. "The Ambivalent Sexism Inventory: Differentiating Hostile and Benevolent Sexism." *Journal of Personality and Social Psychology* 70 (3): 491–512.

Goldberg, Herb. 1977. *The Hazards of Being Male.* New York: New American Library.

Good, Glenn E., and Laurie B. Mintz. 1990. "Gender Role Conflict and Depression in College Men: Evidence for Compounded Risk." *Journal of Counseling and Development* 69 (1): 17–20.

Grabe, Maria Elizabeth, K. D. Trager, Melissa Lear, and Jennifer Rauch. 2006. "Gender in Crime News: A Case Study Test of the Chivalry Hypothesis." *Mass Communication and Society* 9 (2): 137–63.

Greenwald, Anthony G., and Mahzarin R. Banaji. 1995. "Implicit Social Cognition: Attitudes, Self-Esteem, and Stereotypes." *Psychological Review* 102 (1): 4–27.

Hall, Martin T., Seana Golder, Cynthia L. Conley, and Susan Sawning. 2013. "Designing Programming and Interventions for Women in the Criminal Justice System." *American Journal of Criminal Justice* 38 (1): 27–50.

Hill, Melanie S., and Ann R. Fischer. 2001. "Does Entitlement Mediate the Link between Masculinity and Rape-Related Variables?" *Journal of Counseling Psychology* 48 (1): 39–50.

Hughes, Lorine A. 2005. "The Representation of Females in Criminological Research." *Women and Criminal Justice* 16 (1–2): 1–28.

Jeffries, Samantha. 2002. "Does Gender Really Matter? Criminal Court Decision Making in New Zealand." *New Zealand Sociology* 17 (1): 135–49.

Jolin, Annette. 1994. "On the Backs of Working Prostitutes: Feminist Theory and Prostitution Policy." *Crime and Delinquency* 40 (1): 69–83.

Kandathil, Rosy. 2005. "Global Sex Trafficking and the Trafficking Victims Protection Act of 2000: Legislative Responses to the Problem of Modern Slavery." *Michigan Journal of Gender and Law* 12: 87.

Kempf-Leonard, Kimberly, and Pernilla Johansson. 2007. "Gender and Runaways Risk Factors, Delinquency, and Juvenile Justice Experiences." *Youth Violence and Juvenile Justice* 5 (3): 308–27.

Kinnell, Hilary. 2008. *Violence and Sex Work in Britain.* Cullompton, UK: Willan.

Kissin, Wendy B., Zhiqun Tang, Kevin M. Campbell, Ronald E. Claus, and Robert G. Orwin. 2014. "Gender-Sensitive Substance Abuse Treatment and Arrest Outcomes for Women." *Journal of Substance Abuse Treatment* 46 (3): 332–39.

Koss, Mary P., and Hobart H. Cleveland. 1997. "Stepping on Toes: Social Roots of Date Rape Lead to Intractability and Politicization." In *Researching Sexual Violence against Women: Methodological and Personal Perspectives.* Edited by Martin D. Schwartz, 4–21. London: Sage.

Levant, Ronald F. 2011. "Research in the Psychology of Men and Masculinity Using the Gender Role Strain Paradigm as a Framework." *American Psychologist* 66 (8): 762–76.

Levant, Ronald F. 1996. "The New Psychology of Men." *Professional Psychology: Research and Practice* 27 (3): 259–65.

Levant, Ronald F., Adele Cuthbert, Katherine Richmond, Alfred Sellers, Alexander Matveev, Olga Mitina, Matvey Sokolovsky, and Martin Heesacker. 2003. "Masculinity Ideology among Russian and U.S. Young Men and Women and Its Relationships to Unhealthy Lifestyles Habits among Young Russian Men." *Psychology of Men and Masculinity* 4 (1): 26–36.

Levant, Ronald F., and Richard G. Majors. 1997. "An Investigation into Variations in the Construction of the Male Gender Role among Young African American and European American Women and Men." *Journal of Gender, Culture, and Health* 2 (1): 33–43.

Levant, Ronald F., Richard G. Majors, and Michelle L. Kelley. 1998. "Masculinity Ideology among Young African American and European American Women and Men in Different Regions of the United States." *Cultural Diversity and Mental Health* 4 (3): 227–36.

Levant, Ronald F., and Kate Richmond. 2007. "A Review of Research on Masculinity Ideologies Using the Male Role Norms Inventory." *Journal of Men's Studies* 15 (2): 130–46.

Levant, Ronald F., Katherine Richmond, Richard G. Majors, Jaime E. Inclan, Jeannette M. Rossello, Martin Heesacker, George T. Rowan, and Alfred Sellers. 2003. "A Multicultural Investigation of Masculinity Ideology and Alexithymia." *Psychology of Men and Masculinity* 4 (2): 91–99.

Levant, Ronald F., and Joel Y. Wong. 2013. "Race and Gender as Moderators of the Relationship between the Endorsement of Traditional Masculinity Ideology and Alexithymia: An Intersectional Perspective." *Psychology of Men and Masculinity* 14 (3): 329–33.

Liang, Christopher T. H., Alvin N. Alvarez, Linda P. Juang, and Mandy X. Liang. 2009. "The Role of Coping in the Relationship between Perceived Racism and Racism-Related Stress for Asian Americans: Gender Differences." *Asian American Journal of Psychology*, no. 1: 56–69.

Liang, Christopher T. H., Jime Salcedo, and Holly A. Miller. 2011. "Perceived Racism, Masculinity Ideologies, and Gender Role Conflict among Latino Men." *Psychology of Men and Masculinity* 12 (3): 201–15.

Lowman, John, and Chris Atchison. 2006. "Men Who Buy Sex: A Survey in the Greater Vancouver Regional District." *Canadian Review of Sociology/Revue Canadienne de Sociologie* 43 (3): 281–96.

MacKinnon, Catharine A. 1983. "Feminism, Marxism, Method, and the State: Toward Feminist Jurisprudence." In *Violence Against Women: The Bloody Footprints*. Ed. Pauline B. Bart and Eileen Geil Moran, 201–28. Newbury Park, CA: Sage.

Magovcevic, Mariola, and Michael E. Addis. 2005. "Linking Gender-Role Conflict to Nonnormative and Self-Stigmatizing Perceptions of Alcohol Abuse and Depression." *Psychology of Men and Masculinity* 6 (2): 127–36.

Malamuth, Neil M., Robert J. Sockloskie, Mary P. Koss, and J. S. Tanaka. 1991. "Characteristics of Aggressors against Women: Testing a Model Using a National Sample of College Students." *Journal of Consulting and Clinical Psychology* 59 (5): 670–81.

Malamuth, Neil M., and Nancy Wilmsen Thornhill. 1994. "Hostile Masculinity, Sexual Aggression, and Gender-Biased Domineeringness in Conversations." *Aggressive Behavior* 20 (3): 185–93.

Mallicoat, Stacy L. 2007. "Gendered Justice Attributional Differences between Males and Females in the Juvenile Courts." *Feminist Criminology* 2 (1): 4–30.

Mankowski, Eric S., and Kenneth I. Maton. 2010. "A Community Psychology of Men and Masculinity: Historical and Conceptual Review." *American Journal of Community Psychology* 45 (1–2): 73–86.

McCarty, Megan, and Janice Kelly. 2015. "Perceptions of Dating Behavior: The Role of Ambivalent Sexism." *Sex Roles* 72 (5–6): 237–51. doi: 10.1007/s11199-015-0460-6.

McIntosh, Peggy. 2003. "White Privilege: Unpacking the Invisible Knapsack." In *Understanding Prejudice and Discrimination*. Edited by Scott Plous, 191–96. New York: McGraw-Hill.

Monto, Martin A. 1999. "Focusing on the Clients of Street Prostitutes: A Creative Approach to Reducing Violence against Women (Final Report)," https://www.ncjrs.gov.

Moore, Todd M., and Gregory L. Stuart. 2005. "A Review of the Literature on Masculinity and Partner Violence." *Psychology of Men and Masculinity* 6 (1): 46–61.

Moore, Todd M., Gregory L. Stuart, James K. McNulty, Michael E. Addis, James V. Cordova, and Jeff R. Temple. 2010. "Domains of Masculine Gender Role Stress and Intimate Partner Violence in a Clinical Sample of Violent Men." *Psychology of Violence* 1 (S): 68–75.

Myers, Tamara, and Joan Sangster. 2001. "Retorts, Runaways, and Riots: Patterns of Resistance in Canadian Reform Schools for Girls, 1930–60." *Journal of Social History* 34 (3): 669–97.

Nosek, Brian A., Anthony G. Greenwald, and Mahzarin R. Banaji. 2007. "The Implicit Association Test at Age 7: A Methodological and Conceptual Review." In *Social Psychology and the Unconscious: The Automaticity of Higher Mental Processes*. Edited by John A. Bargh, 265–92. New York: Psychology Press, 2007.

O'Neil, James M. 2015. *Men's Gender Role Conflict: Psychological Costs, Consequences, and an Agenda for Change*. Washington, DC: American Psychological Association.

O'Neil, James M. 2013. "Gender Role Conflict Research 30 Years Later: An Evidence☐ Based Diagnostic Schema to Assess Boys and Men in Counseling." *Journal of Counseling and Development* 91 (4): 490–98.

O'Neil, James M. 2010. "Is Criticism of Generic Masculinity, Essentialism, and Positive-Healthy-Masculinity a Problem for the Psychology of Men?" *Psychology of Men and Masculinity* 11 (2): 98–106.

O'Neil, James M. 2008. "Special Issue: Summarizing Twenty-five Years of Research on Men's Gender Role Conflict Using the Gender Role Conflict Scale: New Research Paradigms and Clinical Implications." *Counseling Psychologist* 36 (3): 358–445.

O'Neil, James M. 1990. "Assessing Men's Gender Role Conflict." In *Problem-Solving Strategies and Interventions for Men in Conflict*. Edited by Dwight Moore and Fred Leafgren, 23–38. Alexandria, VA: American Counseling Association.

O'Neil, James M. 1981. "Patterns of Gender Role Conflict and Strain: Sexism and Fear of Femininity in Men's Lives." *Personnel and Guidance Journal* 60 (4): 203–10.

O'Neil, James M., Jean Egan, Steven V. Owen, and Velma McBride Murry. 1993. "The Gender Role Journey Measure: Scale Development and Psychometric Evaluation." *Sex Roles* 28 (3–4): 167–85.

O'Neil, James M., and Sara Renzulli. 2013. "Introduction to the Special Section: Teaching the Psychology of Men—A Call to Action." *Psychology of Men and Masculinity* 14 (3): 221–99.

Overall, Christine. 1992. "What's Wrong with Prostitution? Evaluating Sex Work." *Signs* 17 (4): 705–24.

Perkins, Roberta. 1999. "'How Much Are You, Love?': The Customer in the Australian Sex Industry." *Social Alternatives* 18 (3): 38–47.

Pitts, Marian K., Anthony M. A. Smith, Jeffrey Grierson, Mary O'Brien, and Sebastian Misson. 2004. "Who Pays for Sex and Why? An Analysis of Social and Motivational Factors Associated with Male Clients of Sex Workers." *Archives of Sexual Behavior* 33 (4): 353–58.

Pleck, Joseph H. 1995. "The Gender Role Strain Paradigm: An Update." In *A New Psychology of Men*. Edited by Ronald F. Levant and William S. Pollack, 11–32. New York: Basic Books.

Pleck, Joseph H. 1981. *The Myth of Masculinity*. Cambridge, MA: MIT Press.

Pleck, Joseph H., Freya L. Sonenstein, and Leighton C. Ku. 1994. "Attitudes toward Male Roles among Adolescent Males: A Discriminant Validity Analysis." *Sex Roles* 30 (7–8): 481–501.

Prentice, Deborah A., and Erica Carranza. 2002. "What Women and Men Should Be, Shouldn't Be, Are Allowed to Be, and Don't Have to Be: The Contents of Prescriptive Gender Stereotypes." *Psychology of Women Quarterly* 26 (4): 269–81.

Richie, Beth E. 2012. *Arrested Justice: Black Women, Violence, and America's Prison Nation*. New York: NYU Press.

Richie, Beth E., Kay Tsenin, and Cathy Widom. 2000. "Research on Women and Girls: Plenary Papers of the 1999 Conference on Criminal Justice Research and Evaluation—Enhancing Policy and Practice through Research." Washington, DC: U.S. Department of Justice, Office of Justice Program, National Institute of Justice, https://www.ncjrs.gov.

Robinson, Dianne T., and Jonathan P. Schwartz. 2004. "Relationship between Gender Role Conflict and Attitudes toward Women and African Americans." *Psychology of Men and Masculinity* 5 (1): 65–71.

Sakaluk, John K., and Robin R. Milhausen. 2012. "Factors Influencing University Students' Explicit and Implicit Sexual Double Standards." *Journal of Sex Research* 49 (5): 464–76.

Sánchez, Francisco J., John S. Westefeld, William Ming Liu, and Eric Vilain. 2010. "Masculine Gender Role Conflict and Negative Feelings about Being Gay." *Professional Psychology: Research and Practice* 41 (2): 104–11.

Schmidt, Megan A. 2003. "Attitudes toward Prostitution and Self-Reported Sexual Violence in College Men." *Journal of Applied Social Psychology* 32 (9): 1790–96.

Schwartz, Jonathan P., Walter C. Buboltz, Eric Seemann, and Anita Flye. 2004. "Personality Styles: Predictors of Masculine Gender Role Conflict in Male Prison Inmates." *Psychology of Men and Masculinity* 5 (1): 59–64.

Schwartz, Jonathan P., and Tracy L. Tylka. 2008. "Exploring Entitlement as a Moderator and Mediator of the Relationship between Masculine Gender Role Conflict and Men's Body Esteem." *Psychology of Men and Masculinity* 9 (2): 67–81.

Sharpe, Mark J., and Puncky Paul Heppner. 1991. "Gender Role, Gender-Role Conflict, and Psychological Well-Being in Men." *Journal of Counseling Psychology* 38 (3): 323–30.

Shek, Yen Ling, and Marylu K. McEwen. 2012. "The Relationships of Racial Identity and Gender Role Conflict to Self-Esteem of Asian American Undergraduate Men." *Journal of College Student Development* 53 (5): 703–18.

Shively, Michael, Sarah Kuck Jalbert, William Rhodes, Peter Finn, Chris Flyage, Laura Tierney, Dana Hunt, David Squires, Christina Dyous, and Kristin Wheeler. 2008. "Final Report on the Evaluation of the First Offender Prostitution Program," https://www.ncjrs.gov.

Shively, Michael, Kristina Kliorys, Kristin Wheeler, Dana Hunt. 2012. "An Overview of John Schools in the United States," http://www.demandforum.net.

Sidun, Nancy M., and Deborah A. Rubin. 2013. "Sex Trafficking of Women." In *Violence Against Women and Girls: International Perspectives*. Vol. 2, *In Adulthood, Midlife, and Older Age*. Edited by Janet A. Sigal and Florence Denmark, 159–82. Santa Barbara, CA: Praeger.

Skinner, Allison L., Margaret C. Stevenson, and John C. Camillus. 2015. "Ambivalent Sexism in Context: Hostile and Benevolent Sexism Moderate Bias against Female Drivers." *Basic and Applied Social Psychology* 37 (1): 56–67. doi: 10.1080/01973533.2014.996224.

Smiler, Andrew P. 2006. "Conforming to Masculine Norms: Evidence for Validity among Adult Men and Women." *Sex Roles* 54 (11–12): 767–75.

Snyder, Howard N., and Melissa Sickmund. 2006. "Juvenile Offenders and Victims: 2006 National Report," http://www.ojjdp.gov.

Spohn, Cassia. 2014. "The Non-Prosecution of Human Trafficking Cases: An Illustration of the Challenges of Implementing Legal Reforms." *Crime, Law, and Social Change* 61 (2): 169–78.

Spohn, Cassia, and Katharine Tellis. 2012. "The Criminal Justice System's Response to Sexual Violence." *Violence Against Women* 18 (2): 169–92.

Sprague, Joey. 2005. *Feminist Methods for Critical Researchers: Bridging Differences*. Walnut Creek, CA: Altamira.

Thompson, Edward H., and Joseph H. Pleck. 1995. "Masculinity Ideology: A Review of Research Instrumentation on Men and Masculinities." In *A New Psychology of Men*. Edited by Ronald F. Levant and William S. Pollack, 129–63. New York: Basic Books.

United States Department of State. 2008. "Trafficking in Persons Report," http://www.state.gov.

Wagenaar, Hendrik, and Sietske Altink. 2012. "Prostitution as Morality Politics; or, Why It Is Exceedingly Difficult to Design and Sustain Effective Prostitution Policy." *Sexuality Research and Social Policy* 9 (3): 279–92.

Weimann, Gabriel, and Gideon Fishman. 1988. "Attribution of Responsibility: Sex-Based Bias in Press Reports on Crime." *European Journal of Communication* 3 (4): 415–30.

Wester, Stephen R., David L. Vogel, Meifen Wei, and Rodney McLain. 2006. "African American Men, Gender Role Conflict, and Psychological Distress: The Role of Racial Identity." *Journal of Counseling and Development* 84 (4): 419–29.

Wu, Rongxian, Ronald F. Levant, and Alfred Sellers. 2001. "The Influences of Sex and Social Development on the Masculinity Ideology of Chinese Undergraduate Students." *Psychological Science-Shangai* 24 (3): 365–66.

Xantidis, Luke, and Marita P. McCabe. 2000. "Personality Characteristics of Male Clients of Female Commercial Sex Workers in Australia." *Archives of Sexual Behavior* 29 (2): 165–76.

Conclusion

Gender, Psychology, and Justice

The Case for Systemic Change

JULIE R. ANCIS AND CORINNE C. DATCHI

The authors of this volume have answered critical questions about the experiences of diverse women and girls in the U.S. justice system and highlighted the complex interactions of gender, race, and class and their impact on legal decisions and interventions in family court, drug court, law enforcement, community corrections, and detention facilities. The chapters of this book have drawn attention to a number of themes that are specific to justice-involved women and girls and relate to their distinct social and psychological experiences and concerns.

The Relationship between Systemic Processes and Women's and Girls' Entanglement with the Justice System

First, women's and girls' presence in various justice arenas is a multi-systemic issue: Micro- and macro-level social processes are linked to individual behaviors that bring women and girls into contact with justice officials. These processes occur both outside and inside a justice system that is generally oblivious to or not equipped to take into consideration human differences and contextual factors that influence individual actions. In particular, the lack of awareness about gender, race, and class produces adverse consequences for women and girls: Social biases and disadvantages go unchallenged and complicate women's and girls' ability to resume independent living outside the purview of the legal system; they also contribute to women's and girls' further victimization while in the hands of the law.

The chapters have identified several contextual factors that influence girls' and women's contact with the justice system. *Gender violence* is a pervasive theme and a primary risk for women's and girls' involvement in various legal arenas. Specifically, family and intimate partner violence, parent-child conflict, as well as neglect and abuse, sexual and physical, increase the likelihood that women and girls will engage in "survival crimes." For example, running away from abusive homes increases girls' vulnerability to homelessness and the likelihood that they will engage in criminal activities—theft and prostitution—to provide for their basic needs. Similarly, women who have experienced intimate partner violence may reach out to the justice system for assistance and protection. Unfortunately, women often come face to face with legal officials' social biases and victim-blaming practices that further traumatize them and put them and their children at risk for continued exposure to family violence. Blaming is also apparent in the social discourses that describe justice-involved women as individuals who prefer to depend on public resources and as "bad mothers" who make poor choices. Blaming is a mechanism that deflects attention from the socio-structural inequities that contribute to women's entanglement with the justice system.

Economic deprivation is an additional contextual factor that accounts for women's participation in crime and their subsequent contact with the justice system. In particular, *poverty* has a significant influence on women's and girls' experiences in the justice system: It limits their access to strong legal counsel, their ability to seek health- and mental health–care, and their ability to avoid incarceration.

Recent *legal policies and guidelines* have also played a critical role in women's justice involvement: They have redefined women's and girls' attempts to cope with violence and social disadvantage as delinquent or criminal behaviors worthy of legal punishment. School-based fights, parent-child conflict, breaking curfew, sex trafficking, and addictions have become the target of law enforcement and offender rehabilitation, and have increased women's and girls' vulnerability to arrest, prosecution, and sentencing regardless of the circumstances that have led to their participation in illegal activities.

Since the 1980s, federal initiatives to address the problem of drug abuse have resulted in record-high incarceration rates, with Hispanic and African American women being the most impacted by the far-reaching and get-tough approach of the United States' war on drugs. Upon returning home, these women face additional legal challenges— state laws that bar individuals with a felony conviction from housing and financial assistance, and thus perpetuate their economic disadvantage and diminish their chance of success in the community. In sum, laws, justice policies, and guidelines have largely contributed to the social disenfranchisement and legal entanglement of diverse women and girls, and contributed to the reproduction of institutionalized discrimination.

Institutionalized discrimination operates through gender, class, and racial biases that influence legal decisions and interventions. In the criminal justice system, these biases shape the perception that non-gender-conforming behaviors are suspicious and unlawful, and lead to the profiling and arrest of law-abiding citizens. They also explain why girls and women who do not conform to gender role expectations receive longer jail and prison sentences; in this case, incarceration represents an attempt to punish and control behaviors that deviate from gender norms. The intersections of racial, ethnic, and class biases with gender stereotypes determines justice officials' assessment of female offenders and the level of monitoring and intervention aimed at diverse women and girls under correctional supervision. For example, Black girls are frequently perceived as more aggressive and crime prone than White girls, particularly when they act in ways that are not gender conforming, and are thus subject to harsher punishment.

Social prejudices and myths pervade the *unsubstantiated theories and assumptions* that often guide the behaviors and decisions of justice officials and mental health professionals. These include age-old notions that women are hysterical, emotionally unstable, manipulative, and somehow deserving of abuse. Many of these myths perpetuate victim blaming and give rise to harmful decisions such as reversing custody and sending children to live with an abusive parent, as well as arresting minor-aged girls for prostitution and women domestic violence victims. These stereotypes, biases, and myths justify legal practices that further expose women and girls to violence and victimization while they are under legal supervision. They also restrict justice officials' ability to consider contextual variables and integrate information about gender, race, class, and culture into justice decisions and interventions.

Institutionalized Discrimination Exacerbates the Concerns of Justice-Involved Women and Girls.

In addition to gender-based myths and stereotypes, the authors of this book have described how the justice system often involves a "one size fits all" approach to law enforcement and criminal offending and have shown that gender "blindness," or the expectation that treatment for men can be generalized to women, remains a challenge. In particular, women involved in the criminal justice system are offered services originally designed for men with violent offenses. These services do not match the nature and severity of women's and girls' criminal behaviors (e.g., nonviolent, property, and drug-related crimes); they marginalize women's and girls' unique social, medical, and psychological concerns. For example, women's primary caregiving role and its implications for rehabilitation in the community as well as in prison have yet to receive full consideration. Correctional institutions provide limited opportunities for ongoing and health-promoting parent-child contact, and imprisonment creates significant distress and difficulties for mothers behind bars, including psychological pain associated with prolonged separation from children and the termination of their parental rights based on the Adoption and Safe Families Act enacted by Congress in 1997. In turn, this distress exacerbates their mental health problems and diminishes their ability to comply with the rules and policies of correctional settings, hence resulting in technical violations that prolong their involvement with the justice system.

When legal practices do not take into account the interconnected systemic factors that constitute women's pathways into the justice system, they often reproduce the abuse dynamics that many girls and women experience in their families and communities. Instead of finding protection and restitution in the legal system, girls and women are often punished and held accountable for the consequences of actions that are not fully under their control. For example, women in contested custody disputes with violent ex-partners find the same abuse dynamics perpetuated in family court where the behaviors and decisions of justice officials and mental health professionals are influenced by dual relationships, economic gain, and limited expertise in intimate partner violence. Likewise, incarcerated girls in juvenile detention facilities are often subject to the same violence they experienced at home: Being yelled at, demeaned, threatened, and physically restrained by staff further exacerbates the trauma-related impairment of girls and women exposed to interpersonal violence outside the justice system.

Lastly, the authors of this book note that justice involvement is associated with social stigma and that this stigma is particularly significant for girls and women whose contact with justice officials is perceived as evidence of "bad" and "un-ladylike" behavior or as a violation of gender norms. Shame intensifies psychological distress and increases social marginalization in ways that reduce girls' and women's chance of success in the community. Together with legal punishment and marginalization, it is a social mechanism that serves to enforce gender conformity.

There Is a Dire Need for Psychological Research, Interdisciplinary Partnerships, and Evidence-Based, Gender- and Culturally Responsive Legal Interventions.

The authors of this volume have drawn attention to the lack of research on gender- and culturally responsive programming for diverse women and girls in various arenas of the justice system. A number of obstacles to conducting such research must be acknowledged. A primary obstacle concerns the fact that gender- and culturally responsive interventions are not necessarily standard practice. Moreover, such research requires consideration of context, including the micro- and macro-level dynamics described in the chapters (Ancis 2004). Such variables are not always measured due to methodological challenges or lack of consideration on the part of the researchers. Careful attention to the process and outcome of interventions as relates to multiple aspects of psychosocial functioning is also indicated, requiring careful and time-intensive longitudinal observations.

The paucity of empirical knowledge as it applies to legal policies, procedures, and treatment interventions perpetuates mythology, stereotyping, and discriminatory practices that harm girls and women. This book's authors have outlined a number of areas requiring further investigation. For example, there is a critical need for data on the concerns and needs of lesbian, bisexual, queer, gender-nonconforming, and transgender girls, who, for the most part, have remained invisible in the juvenile justice system. Transnational research on both sides of the U.S./Mexico border is also necessary to document mental health trends and resources for immigrant Mexican women and their children. Such research will require the development of interdisciplinary partnerships to gain a deeper understanding of women's and girls' involvement in and interactions with the legal system, using an ecological, social justice approach to the study of legal practices and their outcomes for female populations.

In addition to the need for research, it is important that existing empirical evidence be accessible and applicable to various justice settings. The authors' analyses of girls' and women's experiences in various justice settings highlight the need for attention to guidelines that promote sensitivity and responsiveness to gender and cultural diversity. Guidelines, such as those developed by various APA task forces, include recommendations for further research as well as principles for best practice with diverse women and girls. For example, there is now a substantial body of scientific knowledge detailing domestic abuse and its impact, including the ways in which abuse dynamics manifest in family court. Yet, mental health practitioners, attorneys, and judges continue to rely on discredited theories such as parental alienation. The tendency to blame women and girls or hold them accountable for conditions for which they have no or limited control makes attention to their experiences of victimization and, relatedly, gender-responsive practice less likely. Increased awareness and application of guidelines is warranted.

Ensuring that clinicians remain informed of the current literature and translate it into evidence-based recommendations for justice officials is essential to promoting gender and cultural responsivity, equity, and fairness for diverse justice-involved women and girls. It is also imperative that mental health professionals work with judges, attorneys, correctional personnel, and other legal officials to implement an intersectional approach to the treatment of justice-involved girls and women. At a minimum, they should be prepared to educate justice staff about existing guidelines for the treatment of diverse populations, including the American Psychological Association's (APA) guidelines for psychological practice with girls and women (2007); the APA guidelines for multicultural education, training, research, practice, and organizational change (2003); the APA guidelines for psychological practice with lesbian, gay, and bisexual clients (2012); the APA guidelines for psychological practice with older adults (2014); and the APA guidelines for psychological practice with transgender and gender-nonconforming people (2015). These guidelines may serve to create gender- and culturally affirming environments in various justice systems, with a focus on empowering diverse girls and women and enabling them to participate in treatment decisions, rather than defining them as the object of mental health and legal interventions.

Translating evidence-based psychological guidelines into recommendations for legal practice is a critical next step: This will involve promoting a relational approach to justice interventions that interrupts the dynamics of abuse in girls' and women's family and social history; advancing a comprehensive approach to treatment that combines psychological and support services in order to address girls' and women's various social and mental health concerns; and using culturally sensitive assessment strategies to identify and target the contextual factors that influence girls' and women's mental health and legal outcomes. Strategies that harness girls' and women's strengths rather than stress punishment and self-reformation are needed.

When psychological evidence serves as a foundation for legal policies, practices, and interventions, it is possible to shift attention from girls' and women's intrapersonal variables to the conditions of their involvement in the justice system, including the structural inequities and pervasive trauma that shape their lives, from their criminal behaviors to men's role in female offending, and from retribution to prevention at individual, family, community, and social levels. Systemic change through advocacy and prevention is necessary to improve the psychological and social outcomes of justice-involved women and girls. This may involve, for example, the development and implementation of antidiscrimination policies that promote the rights of diverse girls and women—the right to safety, equal opportunities in employment, education, health care, and housing.

It is equally important that psychologists and other mental health clinicians be better prepared to work with justice-involved women and girls during and after their graduate training. APA-accredited programs in psychology are required to provide evidence that their curriculum addresses issues related to individual and cultural diversity in ways that promote the development of multicultural competencies. However, these

programs often adopt a single-course approach to multicultural education that has limited capacity to increase gender and cultural responsiveness in clinical practice (Petierse et al. 2009). The lack of a unifying
framework for multicultural training is also a concern and an obstacle
to advanced multicultural competencies (Ancis and Rasheed Ali 2005).
The chapters of this book provide specific recommendations for training that support the development of the knowledge and skills necessary
to work with diverse women and girls in the U.S. justice system, including knowledge of the pathways that lead to women's involvement in the
justice system, their diverse experiences of legal interventions, as well
as awareness of the gender, sexual, racial, and class biases that permeate
legal decisions and interventions.

Conclusion

The authors and editors of this book propose a contextualized and
evidence-based approach to the treatment of women and girls in the
justice system. This approach takes into consideration the ecological
processes that influence justice policies and practices and that have a
primary impact on girls' and women's legal, social, and psychological
outcomes. Gender- and culturally responsive justice depends on the
translation of sound psychological research into new and revised legal
and therapeutic frameworks for working with women and girls in various arenas of the justice system.

REFERENCES
American Psychological Association. 2015. "Guidelines for Psychological Practice with
    Transgender and Gender-Nonconforming People." *American Psychologist* 70 (9):
    832–64. doi: 10.1037/a0039906.
American Psychological Association. 2014. "Guidelines for Psychological Practice with
    Older Adults." *American Psychologist* 69 (1): 34–65. doi: 10.1037/a0035063.
American Psychological Association. 2012. "Guidelines for Psychological Practice
    with Lesbian, Gay, and Bisexual Clients." *American Psychologist* 67 (1): 10–42. doi:
    10.1037/a0024659.
American Psychological Association. 2007. "Guidelines for Psychological Practice with
    Girls and Women." *American Psychologist* 62 (9): 949–75.
American Psychological Association. 2003. "Guidelines on Multicultural Education,
    Training, Research, Practice, and Organizational Change for Psychologists." *Ameri-
    can Psychologist* 58 (5): 377.

Ancis, Julie, ed. 2004. *Culturally Responsive Interventions: Innovative Approaches to Working with Diverse Populations*. New York: Brunner-Routledge.

Ancis, Julie R., and Saba Rasheed Ali. 2005. "Multicultural Counseling Training Approaches: Implications for Pedagogy." In *Teaching and Social Justice: Integrating Multicultural and Feminist Theories in the Classroom*. Edited by Carolyne Z. Enns and Ada L. Sinacore, 85–97. Washington, DC: American Psychological Association.

Pieterse, Alex L., Sarah A. Evans, Amelia Risner-Butner, Noah M. Collins, and Laura Beth Mason. 2009. "Multicultural Competence and Social Justice Training in Counseling Psychology and Counselor Education." *Counseling Psychologist* 37 (1): 93–115. doi: 10.1177/0011000008319986.

Tyonna Adams currently attends Pepperdine University, where she is pursuing her PsyD in Clinical Psychology. She serves as Research Associate of Pepperdine's Oasis–Culture and Trauma Lab.

Julie R. Ancis is Associate Vice President for Institute Diversity at the Georgia Institute of Technology. She is a Fellow of the American Psychological Association.

Jennifer Bahrman graduated from New Mexico State University with a master's in counseling and guidance and a master's in criminal justice. She is currently completing her PhD in counseling psychology at the University of Houston.

Kendra R. Brewster is Assistant Professor in the Public and Community Service Studies Program at Providence College. In 2014, she was honored with the Dissertation Research Award from the International Association for Service Learning and Community Engagement.

Thema Bryant-Davis is Associate Professor of Psychology at Pepperdine University. She is a former representative to the United Nations and Past President of the Society of the Psychology of Women. Her books include *Thriving in the Wake of Trauma* and *Surviving Sexual Violence*.

Aisha Canfield received her master's in Public Policy from Mills College and focuses primarily on juvenile justice reform, especially on preventing system involvement for lesbian, gay, bisexual, transgender, and gender-nonconforming youth of color while improving outcomes for those already system involved.

Carlye B. Conte is a graduate student pursuing her PhD in Clinical Psychology at Nova Southeastern University.

Kathleen M. Cumiskey is an interfaith minister and Associate Professor in the Psychology Department and Women, Gender, and Sexuality Program at the College of Staten Island–City University of New York. She has coedited a volume with Larissa Hjorth entitled *Mobile Media Practices, Presence, and Politics*.

Corinne C. Datchi is Assistant Professor in the Department of Professional Psychology and Family Therapy at Seton Hall University.

Alexis Forbes is Associate Trial Consultant and Research Coordinator with Bonora Rountree, LLC. She has a PhD in Psychology and Law from John Jay College and the Graduate Center at CUNY, New York.

Anthea Gray currently attends Pepperdine University, where she is earning her PsyD in Clinical Psychology.

Amy E. Green is Assistant Project Scientist in the Department of Psychiatry at the University of California–San Diego and Investigator at the Child and Adolescent Services Research Center.

Angela Irvine is Research Director at the National Council on Crime and Delinquency (NCCD).

Nicole C. Kellett is Assistant Professor of Anthropology at the University of Maine–Farmington.

Elizabeth A. Lilliott is Program Evaluator and Associate Research Scientist for the Behavioral Health Research Center of the Southwest.

Kevin L. Nadal is Associate Professor of Psychology at CUNY and is also the Executive Director of CLAGS: Center for LGBTQ Studies at the CUNY Graduate Center, as well as the President of the Asian American Psychological Association.

Anna Ochoa O'Leary is Associate Professor in the Department of Mexican American Studies at the University of Arizona and Codirector of the Binational Migration Institute at the same institution. She received a Fullbright scholarship in 2006 to conduct research on migrant women's encounters with immigration enforcement agents. She edited a two-volume reference work, *Undocumented Immigrants in the United States Today: An Encyclopedia of Their Experiences.*

Jessica Roa was the project manager of a two-year national study of LGBT youth involved with the juvenile justice system. She is currently evaluating a juvenile probation youth program that is being implemented by a community-based organization in three California counties.

Erica G. Rojas is an advanced doctoral candidate in the Counseling Psychology Program at Teachers College, Columbia University.

Jonathan Schwartz is Associate Dean for Graduate Studies in the College of Education at the University of Houston. He is the past president of Division 51, Psychology of Men and Masculinity, of the American Psychological Association. Dr. Schwartz received the 2011 Fritz and Linn Kuder Early Career Scientist/Practitioner Award from the American Psychologist Association Division of Counseling Psychology. Dr. Schwartz was recently named a Fellow of Division 17, Society of Counseling Psychology, of the American Psychological Association.

Randolph M. Scott-McLaughlin II is a doctoral student in counseling psychology at Teachers College, Columbia University.

Laura Smith is Associate Professor in the Department of Counseling and Clinical Psychology at Teachers College, Columbia University.

Elise M. Trott is a Research Assistant at the Pacific Institute of Research and Evaluation, and a PhD candidate in the Department of Anthropology at the University of New Mexico.

Lenore E. A. Walker is Professor of Psychology at Nova Southeastern University and is the coordinator of the Clinical Forensic Psychology Concentration.

Cathleen E. Willging is Senior Research Scientist II at the Pacific Institute for Research and Evaluation.

INDEX

abstinence, 112, 113

abuse, 3, 5, 49; and child custody cases, 23, 26;during detention, 13;dynamics, 25;emotional, 24, 37; myths about, 28;and justice-involved girls, 13;prevalence of, 50; physical, 112, 131, 204, 238; psychological, 53; sexual, 37, 38, 112, 131, 153, 204, 238, 268

acculturation, 56

addiction, 12, 102, 105, 108, 114; and incarcerated women, 236;medication, 117, 133; and trauma, 112

Addiction and Trauma Recovery Integration Model, 145

Adoption and Safe Families Act, 239, 305

administrative segregation, 188, 190

advocacy, 14, 64, 90, 91, 92, 195

agency, 110, 111, 117, 119, 151, 159, 160

alexithymia, 285

Alien Transfer Exit Program, 258

AMICUS Girls, 165

Anger Replacement Therapy, 166

antidiscrimination policies, 195, 213, 217, 308

anxiety, 33, 34, 80, 108, 136; and immigration, 268; symptoms of, 52–53

arrest, 2; of girls, 203, 204; of transgender women, 186–87

art therapy, 90

bail, 231, 233

battered woman's syndrome, 53

Battered Women Syndrome Questionnaire, 51

batterer intervention program, 61

battering, 51. *See also* abuse; domestic violence; intimate partner violence

bipolar disorder, 238

Border Patrol, 15, 256; mistreatment of migrants, 259–61, 266

"Broken Windows" theory, 153

burnout, 93

cisgender, 178, 182

child custody, 4; and the best interests of the child, 24, 27, 36; disputes, 3, 10, 33; evaluations, 23, 28; financial consequences, 35; psychological reactions, 34–35; shared, 3, 28; chivalry, 3, 287; and double standards, 287–288; classism, 108, 156, 225, 229–30, 238, 246; and incarceration, 142; institutional classism, 231; interpersonal classism, 231; and mental health, 166; and stereotypes, 82. *See also* socioeconomic status

cognitive behavioral therapy, 86, 145; and recidivism, 166

colonialism, 130, 142;.and incarceration, 142

commercial sex industry, 77. *See also* sex trade

compassion fatigue, 93

conditioning, 105

confirmatory bias, 39

coping, 8, 68, 111, 115, 205; criminalization of, 10

prevalence of, 77; and recruitment, 79–80; risks for, 78; sex work, 179, 194. *See also* sex trade

sexual orientation, 14, 210; of transwomen, 182; and assessment of youth, 206

sexuality, 4

shame, 55, 61, 83, 110–111

socioeconomic status, 89, 114. *See also* poverty

solitary confinement, 13, 188, 189, 190, 206

Southern Oaks Girls School, 165

spirituality, 55; and treatment, 89, 90, 244

stigma, 75, 77, 82, 87, 111, 139, 195, 306; and justice-involved youth, 215; and service utilization, 273

"stop and frisk" policy, 186

substance dependence, 5, 131

Survivor Therapy Empowerment Program, 64–66

Surveillance techniques, 105, 107

Tates v. Blanas, 189

therapeutic jurisprudence, 4, 5, 62, 102, 104

Thinking for a Change, 166

tough-on-crime policies, 14, 233

transgender, 8, 9, 14, 177, 179; and homelessness, 182, 193; identity, 182

transphobia, 179, 183, 192, 210

transwomen, 9, 13, 177; and detention, 187

trauma, 10, 52, 58; and delinquent behaviors, 204; and family court, 30, 37;

and girls, 152; and immigration, 15, 269; and incarcerated women, 238–39; -informed care, 63–64, 67; lifetime exposure to, 37, 239; secondary and tertiary, 23, 26; and sex trafficking, 11, 83, 85

Trauma Recovery and Empowerment Model, 145

T-SISTA protocol, 192

victim blaming, 62, 75, 83, 92, 303

victimization, 15, 75, 81, 302; of girls, 152; report of, 83; and substance-using women, 115; of transwomen, 185–86, 187, 189

violence: and border crossing, 15; and gender, 50, 59, 303; physical, 2, 15; and sex trafficking, 84; sexual, 2, 15, 37. *See also* abuse

Violence Against Women Act, 49, 56, 60

war on drugs, 2, 127, 131, 229, 234

Welfare Reform Bill of 1996, 241–42; and justice-involved women, 242

Working to Insure and Nurture Girls Success, 165

World Professional Association for Transgender Health, 192

zone of social abandonment, 152–153; and incarceration, 156

CPSIA information can be obtained
at www.ICGtesting.com
Printed in the USA
FSHW011253101219
64937FS

9 781479 885848